A HISTORY OF
CAPITALISM

A HISTORY OF

CAPITALISM

1500–2000

MICHEL BEAUD

*Translated by Tom Dickman
& Anny Lefebvre*

Monthly Review Press
New York

Library of Congress Cataloging-in-Publication Data
Beaud, Michel.
    [Histoire du capitalisme de 1500 à 2000. English]
    A history of capitalism, 1500–2000 / Michel Beaud ; translated by Tom
Dickman & Anny Lefebvre.
        p.   cm.
    Includes bibliographical references and index.
    ISBN 1–58367–041–6 (pbk.) — ISBN 1–58367–040–8 (cloth.)
    1. Economic history.   2. Capitalism—History.   I. Title.
    HC51.B383132001
    330.12'2—dc21   2001—045221

ISBN 1–58367–041–6 (paper)
ISBN 1–58367–040–8 (cloth)

Monthly Review Press
122 West 27th Street
New York, NY 10001

Designed and typeset by Illuminati, Grosmont
Manufactured in Canada

10   9   8   7   6   5   4   3   2

CONTENTS

LIST OF TABLES
AND DIAGRAMS

ACKNOWLEDGMENTS

I thank the teachers and students of the college of political economy at the University of Paris VIII who, through their own research, questions, and criticism, have moved me to broaden and deepen my thinking.

Marguerite Leblanc, director of the study center for economics and statistics, and Madeleine Julien, director of the library at the University of Paris VIII, as well as their assistants, have helped me in gathering necessary documentation. I thank Patrick Allard, Denise Barbeyer, Jerome Brassens, and Bernadette Duvernay, who have read all or part of this book and whose comments have been helpful.

I thank again Editions du Seuil, and especially Edmond Blanc, who, by accepting the project of this *History of Capitalism* and that of *Socialism, Social-Democracy and State Collectivism.* have encouraged me to write the two books. Finally, I thank the English translators, Tom Dickman and Anny Lefebvre, and all those at Monthly Review Press who have helped in the production of the first English edition.

Quotations from English-language works have for the most part been traced to the original and cited accordingly. In those cases where only the French edition is cited, the English translations have been done by the translators.

PREFACE TO THE
ENGLISH EDITION

Events overtake each other with dazzling speed in the contemporary world. A new type of society, a world profoundly transformed, is in the process of being born. We should, of course, choose, impose our collective destiny. But how difficult it is to sort out all the elements, all the factors at play. And that myopia which afflicts all historical actors prevents us from grasping, in their historic movement, all the transformations now underway.

The history of capitalism can shed light on this movement. The essential elements of this system are already discernible in the thirteenth through fifteenth centuries; during the sixteenth century, the system in all its facets begins to crystallize. In successive waves, it enriches and secures the preeminence of first Holland then England and France and, finally, the United States, Germany, and Japan. Technology is mastered, the working classes dominated, and ever larger regions of the globe are taken in tow by this new system. But then new technologies appear on the scene, the organized working class scores important victories, and the colonies win independence as the countries of the third world assert themselves.

Five centuries: an ephemeral moment in the infinite becoming of the world. But also an incandescent flash which strikes humanity at its very root. Even that essential grain of sand—the planet Earth—is not spared.

This book may be compared to a flashback: who has not experienced that moment of intense reflection when his or her life has arrived at a crossroads? For it shows that capitalism, once having spanned every corner of the globe, entered on a new phase in its history. In the course of three great crises—at the end of the nineteenth century, during the 1930s, and the present impasse—the system was transformed, reoriented, and restructured. Each great crisis has been a period of mutations, of profound transformations. This is especially true of the crisis which since 1973 has buffeted us about—or, in the case of the least favored, swallowed us up.

But isn't this crisis too often simply regarded as an inexorable calamity which, like floods and droughts, will in time pass if we are only patient? Isn't it necessary, on the contrary, to view it as an opportunity? Isn't it vital at some point to grasp the possibilities inherent in the crisis? For if the new technology can indeed underpin new systems of unfettered domination and control, it can also serve as a powerful stimulus to new forms of democratic life, decentralization and, finally, liberty. And the dominant reality of the new relations which have been established between nations is certainly one of hostility, rivalry, and confrontation; but these relations are also potentially bonds of solidarity and cooperation.

New forms of work and production have materialized; new products have seen the light of day. New ways to feed and house ourselves, to care for and educate ourselves, to move ourselves about—in short, a new way of living—is now within our grasp. We, the youth of this epoch, aren't we all perhaps on the eve of a prodigious adventure? For in the course of the present crisis, new ways of working, producing, and living may be invented, selected, and set in motion.

The socialists, the humanists, of the nineteenth century dared to dream a moral, just, free, and unified society. Much has already been accomplished to that end. Let us seize the opportunity that the present crisis affords to advance a little bit further.

Paris, July 1983

PREFACE TO THE
FRENCH EDITION

I am completing this book at the time of the destruction, by government order, of the premises of Vincennes, University of Paris VIII, where I have taught since 1968.

This book owes a great deal to the discussions and the work carried on for twelve years at Vincennes: first of all at the college of political economy, with teachers and students too numerous to name here individually; then with those working in other disciplines—historians, sociologists, geographers, specialists in political science or geopolitical zones, and philosophers; and finally with so many others who came to discuss and contribute to the collective thinking, especially at the time of the symposia on the Crisis (1975), France and the Third World (1978), and the New Domestic Order (1979).

Mentioning University of Paris VIII at Vincennes, I will mention also two persons who are deceased: Nikos Poulantzas, whose work has helped us to analyze more closely social classes, the state, fascism, dictatorship, and democracy; and Jaimes Baire, student in the college of political economy, tortured to death by the National Guard of El Salvador, and whose master's degree was upheld *in absentia*. May the name of each one remind us of the price of freedom.

University of Paris VIII,
Saint-Denis, October 1980

INTRODUCTION
TO THE FIRST EDITION
(1980)

This book is born from the solid conviction that one cannot understand the contemporary period without analyzing the profound upheavals which the development of capitalism has brought about in societies throughout the world.

It is born also from a desire to understand the various aspects of this development: simultaneously economic and political and ideological; simultaneously national and multinational; simultaneously liberating and oppressive, destructive and creative.

The book is born finally from the ambition to put into perspective a group of questions which are inseparable and which are nevertheless too often studied in isolation: the formation of political economy in its relation to "the long journey toward capitalism"; the affirmation of the democratic ideal against the aristocratic Old Regimes and the rise of new ruling classes who made use of the new democratic institutions; the link between the development of national capitalisms, the strengthening and achievements of workers' movements, and accomplishments within the working world; the increasingly complete and complex capitalist domination of the world; the connection between class domination and domination by nations; and crises as indicators of blockages and as moments of renewal, particularly the present "Great Crisis."

We will follow the blind forward movement which leads, over four centuries, from the *conquistadores* to the *Pax Britannica*; from bankers and merchants in Genoa, Antwerp, and Amsterdam to England, workshop and banker for the world; from the spinning wheel to the power loom; from the windmill to the steam engine; from trade and banking activity to industrial capitalism; from Machiavelli to Marx, from *The Prince* to *Capital*.

In one century we have been caught up in a fascinating spiral: from British hegemony to the affirmation of American power and its subsequent questioning; from the progress and victories of the workers' movement to the breaking out into the open of its own contradictions, in the presence of new national and worldwide situations; from coal to gasoline, electricity, and new forms of energy; from mechanization and Taylorism to computerization and robotics; from the first forms of finance capital to the establishment of a hierarchical and diversified imperialist system; and finally, through periods bound together by sequences of prosperity, crisis, and war, from the Great Crisis of 1885–93 to the Great Crisis of 1970-80.

A book which is parallel to this one and in some ways its companion considers how, in the context of changes brought about by the industrial revolution and the French revolution, the idea of socialism was founded, how the many-sided workers' movement of the nineteenth century seized hold of this idea, but also how the ordeal of reality has led the October revolution to state collectivism. This is an occasion to reflect on the nature of social formations which today call themselves socialist—as much in the East as in the West and in the third world—and to consider what can still be, at this close of the twentieth century, a socialist project which takes into account the lessons of the past century and the great challenges of the century to come.

INTRODUCTION
TO THE FIFTH EDITION
(1999)

Following the events of 1968, there appeared a huge number of analyses, interpretations, and debates about capitalism. Many of these analyses questioned the simplistic certitudes of Marxist dogma, and at the same time went beyond the confines of their various initial historical, institutional, and structuralist frameworks.

So far as I was concerned, capitalism had been "taught" to me at the Sorbonne's school of law, through courses in "systems and structures" (specifically those of André Marchal) as well as through courses in the "history of thought" (especially those of Henri Denis and Alain Barrère). My reading at this time, when I was a student and novice teacher, included writers such as Marx, Weber, Schumpeter, Perroux, and Galbraith.

Overall, the analyses of this period depended on the opposition between "capitalism" and "socialism."

For Marx, as for many of the reformers, communists, and socialists of the nineteenth century, the promise of socialism was tightly connected to the critique and denunciation of industrial capitalism. Similarly, the struggles of the workers' movement were strongly tied to the hope for another society which would be fraternal, equitable, and respectful toward humanity. Such a society was summed up by the word "socialism."

From the 1920s onward the reality of a "socialism being built" functioned as counterpoint to the hope for socialism, buoying the simple hope by showing that "it is possible," but at the same time weakening it by forcing its removal from the realm of the abstract.

How could an impressionable mind during the postwar period fail to be struck then by the two major assertions which served as organizing principles in Joseph Schumpeter's book:[1] "Can capitalism survive? No, I don't believe it can." And "Can socialism work? Without a doubt, it can."[2]

The postwar period was distinguished, however, by three major developments:

1. The expansion, supported actively by its government, of American capitalism.
2. The proliferation, in many different countries of Europe, Asia, and other parts of the third world, of "actually existing socialism," which arose, in fact, upon statist foundations.[3]
3. The new direction of national capitalisms in which one form or another of social compromise took hold. Such compromises ranged from the Japanese system to the European social democratic compromise. Within Europe there existed differences between the French model based on legal and legislative agreements and the German social market economy.

Though the opposition capitalism/socialism remained a major ideological battleground within the political debates of many countries, the successes of the various national compromises produced, on the one hand, confusion—many countries were described as socialist whose productive structure remained quite capitalist—while on the other hand the credibility of a "third way" was strengthened.

Bearing the marks of a complex history—of banks and of industry, of working conditions and of the working world, of worker and union struggles, of repression, of studies by historians and social scientists, of ideological and political debates—the word "capitalism" carries multiple meanings. Using the word at all is hardly a neutral undertaking, since for some people "capitalism" has been a symbol to rally round, while for others it has represented a system to be destroyed.

Some liberal[4] authors such as Friedrich Hayek, along with many among the employing classes, refuse to use the word or even to hear it: they prefer broader labels such as "market economy." For others, it is a frequently used term which describes a wide range of modern economies. And for some authors within certain theoretical traditions "capitalism" is a complexly defined concept within economic and social analysis.

For my part I was far from having a clear view of all this when I began to use the word. I have always tried to understand the world and the developments now taking place—including what is not working and why—and how things may be made better. The word "capitalism" very quickly appeared to me to describe some of the important realities of our time. Understanding these realities allows us to shed light on some essential processes, to identify problems, and to reflect on solutions. The word is irreplaceable in that it is the only one which clearly describes these realities. If one refuses the word, one refuses to take into account many important aspects of today's world.

Having said this, using the word "capitalism" remains fraught with difficulty, so heavy are the ideological and political connotations—both positive and negative—which it carries. And of course all this makes it exceedingly difficult to predict how the word will be understood when it is used.

I was taught that capitalism is an economic system. I understood quickly enough that one could not reduce it to the economic dimension alone,[5] and that it is necessary to take into account the social, ideological, political, and ethical dimensions as well. Fundamentally, what we call "capitalism" is inseparable from the societies and states with which it develops. This insight led me very early on to be suspicious of analysis in terms of a mode of production: capitalism can never be reduced to a mode of production alone.

Capitalism, whether it be Dutch, British, American, or Japanese, has most often been understood as a national phenomenon. Such an approach is able only partially to grasp the world transformations capitalism has brought about. From another direction, some contemporary authors, such as Immanuel Wallerstein, have considered capitalism as a world reality from the start, even though, at its origins, the outlines of this reality were not uniformly clear.[6] I understood, from the first edition of this book onward, that capitalism as a reality has always had a national basis, though the powerful and dynamic capitalisms have tended to overflow their national boundaries and have helped redraw the political map of the world.[7]

Capitalism has evolved through history, from merchant capitalism to manufacturing capitalism to industrial capitalism, and now to the emerging postindustrial capitalism.[8] It has evolved by stratification, in which each stratum develops by partially destroying the preexisting strata, by transforming whatever remains of the earlier layers, and by transforming itself as part of an endless process.

One difficulty in analyzing this process is that our readings of capitalism are dominated by analyses begun in the nineteenth century and developed more fully in the first two-thirds of the twentieth century. These analyses are thus strongly colored by the characteristics of industrial capitalism, a coloring which may prevent us from correctly understanding current developments. Another difficulty is that the word hides certain traps: some people speak of capitalism as an actor, which it is in fact not. The actors are the financiers, the bankers, the executives of the huge corporations, as well as the small and middle-level entrepreneurs, the wage-laborers, the dependent producers, the savers, and the consumers. Other people speak of capitalism as a system. Now the idea that there might exist a panoply of systems among which one could choose appears to me as wrong. Beyond that, I doubt increasingly whether we may speak of a capitalist system in general. Yet such systematization, taking industrial capitalism as "the" capitalist system, is just what has been practiced for too long.

I have come to believe now that capitalism is above all a complex social logic,[9] able to transform the world around it at the same time as it is able to transform itself. Capitalism emerged, at the time invisibly, in the fifteenth and sixteenth centuries, forcibly asserted itself through industrialization in the nineteenth century, and today dominates the world.

Within the very slow evolution of humanity and the world, a change of rhythm, power, and range of influence is increasingly visible from 1500 onward. Among the important moments of this great historical change, we note the following:

—The great "discoveries" and the first colonies.
—The first energy and industrial revolution.
—The development of world trade and the dividing-up of the world among a limited number of European nations.
—Successive changes in transport, communication, and access to information, including, most recently, new energy, industrial, and information revolutions.
—The establishment of huge corporations increasingly operating on a planetary scale.
—The establishment of monetary and financial networks, also operating on a planetary scale.
—A profound and unceasing transformation of productive techniques and lifestyles.

We could extend this list. The importance of interactions between these various domains of change is obvious, for the interactions themselves have deepened, widened, and accelerated the overall historical change. One may debate whether these interactions took place on their own within each domain, or whether an entirely new reality formed itself within the same movement that brought forth and intensified the interactions. We have chosen the second interpretation.

Among the many aspects of the newly developing reality, the following were central:

—The extension of money and exchange relations.
—The generalization of market relations, which gradually became essential elements of the social fabric.
—The business company, which, by relying on forecasts of future conditions, as well as on monetary accounting procedures, chose what to produce based on expectations of future profits. Realized profits were then poured back into the business as part of new productive expansion.
—Banks, credit, finance, and speculation, all of which acted as powerful motors, weaving together and stimulating both production and distribution.
—New relationships between all these forces and the modern state.
—An increasingly rationalized and systematic mobilization of potential techniques and scientific knowledge toward the goal of creating new commodities.
—The expectation that the rich, and those who become rich, will develop new needs.
—The whole collection of forces which broke from the past and which threw themselves into the future at an accelerating rate.

Some aspects of this powerful movement had been glimpsed in the analysis by Turgot and the physiocrats of the "advances" made in this period. Adam Smith contributed his analysis of the market, while Ricardo and Marx more clearly analyzed capital, Weber described capital-based business, and Schumpeter focused on the innovating entrepreneur and on creative destruction. All these aspects are part of what is meant by the word "capitalism." The word has been used now since the end of the nineteenth century by countless authors of all tendencies around the world. From start to finish in this book, we have tried to make more precise the various meanings of the reality this word names.

There remains one last question: after the collapse of "communism," or, more precisely, of Soviet statism, is this "new reality" that we call "capitalism" the unique, the necessary, and the unavoidable path toward the human future?[10] Does capitalism itself bear the values of Modernity, Progress, Democracy, and the Great Society? In a word, is capitalism The Human Path?

We do not believe so; if we did believe such a statement were true, we would call it The Human Path. We don't believe this is so, first, because we do not believe human history contains an *a priori* meaning or purpose. History is what men make, through a vast number of decisions of unequal importance and significance. We do not believe this is so, in the second place, because capitalism maintains contradictory relations with democracy, and can prosper very well under authoritarian regimes. Capitalism maintains ambivalent relations with the market, which it makes use of by relying on, and sometimes abusing, unequal power relations: the most competitive businesses are always trying to escape the constraints of the market by rising to monopoly position. Finally, we believe it is not The Human Path because capitalism skews progress by developing only products likely to make money.

Beside these considerations, human history is composed of advances and retreats, action, resistance, and confrontation, forward movements and jumps backward. Now, facing the problems, perils, and threats—either identified or latent—of our time, to which the dynamics of capitalism contribute a large share, it would be absurd to exclude, *a priori*, that in the near or distant future, another path or other paths might become open.

This history of capitalism begins in 1500, a key date which opens a century that can be considered a "great turning point in world history."[11]

This beginning point is well suited to the subject of the present book, for what we today call "capitalism" essentially assumes clear and definite form by that date.

Yet it is clear that this new reality did not arise *ex nihilo*. Its origins extend far into the human past; the complex social logic of capitalism is deeply rooted in the ancient logics of possession and power, of enrichment and exchange.

Having said this, I believe this historic turning point forms the leading edge of a accelerating process which is in the current period launching the world into a new stage of history.[12] An immense problem remains, however: if we explain the emergence and the vitality of the new social logic of capitalism in order to understand this historical turning point, how, without falling into Eurocentrism, can we speak of the origins of a reality which, historically, was first formed in Europe? We wish to give adequate weight to the historical situations in which all the components of capitalism—accumulated wealth, enterprising power, technical means— were present, and yet where capitalism did not emerge. If we stress the advances made by different world civilizations, do we not risk establishing a background which appears as the cradle of capitalism at its birth in Europe in the fifteenth and sixteenth centuries?

These questions remain for me today extremely difficult, and to deal with them properly would call for another book.

A last word of introduction. At Vincennes, where I was teaching economics, Jean Bouvier, a remarkable historian who had published material on the history of capitalism and especially on the history of banking in France, was teaching history. In the course of our discussions I told him that we needed a history of capitalism, which would be both succinct and aimed at a wide audience. The short book by Henri Sée appeared to me both out of date and inadequate. I thought Bouvier alone capable of successfully carrying out the project. He gave me a sly smile, shook his head "no," and then, after a lengthy pause, said: "A historian could never risk such a project."

I was forty-three. I was not worried about the scientific authority-figures of my discipline, nor the reactions of my colleagues, nor my own abilities. I took on this project. I recognize and admit the temerity which possessed me back then; now, twenty and more years later, I am no longer sure I would attempt it again.

Part I

FROM GOLD TO CAPITAL

...the secret of obliging all the rich to make all the poor work.
—Voltaire

Capitalism was formed within the merchant and monetary societies of Western Europe. Many merchant and monetary societies have existed in the world, however, without developing into this new form of capitalism, endowed with such great creative and destructive capabilities.

We will follow the developments through the sixteenth, seventeenth, and eighteenth centuries, which lead to the British industrial capitalism of the nineteenth century; the changes in social classes and in forms of government; the first wave of world conquest by the European powers; as well as the thinking and the controversies which accompany these developments and the progressive awareness which they express.

Chapter 1

THE LONG JOURNEY
TOWARD CAPITALISM

Feudal society had been established by the eleventh century: within the framework of the estate, the organization of production (bondage, forced labor, corvée) and the extortion of surplus labor (in the form of rent in labor) were carried out for the benefit of the seigneur, an exalted landlord and possessor of political and jurisdictional prerogatives.

Hardly had feudal society been established, however, when the process of its decomposition began. Rent in labor changed into rent in kind or in money, with the development of free labor and forms of peasant property. Simultaneously there was a renewal of commerce through commercial fairs, reactivation of the artisan class (in the framework of the guilds), a renaissance of urban life, and the formation of a commercial bourgeoisie. It is in this decomposition of the feudal order that the formation of mercantile captialism took root.

Over a period of several centuries the "long journey" toward capitalism extended in this direction: a complex and interlocking process which involved the formation of merchant and banking bourgeoisies, the appearance of nations and the establishment of modern states, the expansion of trade and domination on a world scale, the development of techniques of transportation and production, the introduction of new modes of production and the emergence of new attitudes and ideas.

The first stage of this long journey was marked by the conquest and pillage of America (sixteenth century), the second stage by the rise and affirmation of the bourgeoisies (seventeenth century).

COLONIAL PILLAGE AND WEALTH
OF THE PRINCE (SIXTEENTH CENTURY)

The Crusades were the opportunity for the formation of considerable fortunes, notably the legendary one of the Templars. Commerce, banking, and finance flourished first in the Italian republics of the thirteenth and fourteenth centuries, and then in Holland and England. With the invention of the printing press, progress in metallurgy, the employment of water power, and the use of carts in the mines, the second half of the fifteenth century was distinguished by a clear advance in the production of metals and textiles. During this time the first cannons and other firearms began to be produced, while improvements in the construction of caravels and in navigational techniques allowed for the opening up of new maritime routes.[1]

Capital, more abundant merchandise, sailing ships, and weapons: these were the means of expansion for commerce, discoveries, and conquests.

In the same movement and upon the same base of the decomposition of the feudal order, great monarchs joined forces together through marriages, and carved out empires and kingdoms from the conquests of war. Well before national unity was achieved, the strengthened states worked to enlarge their autonomy in relation to the papacy. The clamor for the reform of the Church opened the way for the Reform, which became a war machine against the Pope. While the morality of the Middle Ages extolled the just price and prohibited lending at interest,[2] this morality had already been seriously unsettled by the time Calvin justified commerce and lending at interest, before he went on "to make of commercial success a sign of divine election."[3]

Monarchs greedy for greatness and wealth, states battling for supremacy, merchants and bankers encouraged to enrich themselves: these are the forces which inspired trade, conquests, and wars; systematized pillage; organized the traffic in slaves; and locked up the vagabonds so as to force them to work.

What Western history calls the "great discoveries" enter at the junction of this twofold dynamic: in 1487 Bartholomeu Díaz rounded the Cape of Good Hope; in 1492 Christopher Columbus discovered America; in 1498 Vasco da Gama, having skirted Africa, arrived in India. A great hunt after wealth—trade and pillage—began.

THE GOLD OF AMERICA

Following the return of Columbus with reports of the New World, the Council of Castile resolved to take possession of a land whose inhabitants were unable to defend themselves. "The pious purpose of converting them to Christianity sanctified the injustice of the project. But the hope of finding treasures of gold there, was the sole motive which prompted them to undertake it.... All the other enterprises of the Spaniards in the new world, subsequent to those of Columbus, seem to have been prompted by the same motive. It was the sacred thirst of gold...."[4] Hernán Cortés, conqueror of Mexico, confessed: "We Spanish suffer from a sickness of the heart for which gold is the only cure."

In 1503 the first shipment of precious metals arrived from the Antilles; in 1519 the pillage of the treasure of the Aztecs in Mexico began; in 1534 the pillage of the Incas in Peru. In Peru,

> the conquistadores carried away 1,300,000 ounces of gold in a single load. They found four large statues of llamas and a dozen life-sized statues of women made of refined gold. The king offered as ransom a room full of gold; his subjects had in their gardens, their houses and their temples, trees, flowers, birds and animals of gold; their utensils were of gold; sheets of silver twenty feet long by two feet wide and two fingers thick served as tables.[5]

According to official figures, 18,000 tons of silver and 200 tons of gold were transferred from America to Spain between 1521 and 1660; according to other estimates, double this amount.

"One who has gold," observed Christopher Columbus, "does as he wills in the world, and it even sends souls to Paradise."[6] In a little more than a century the Indian population was reduced by 90 percent in Mexico (where the population fell from 25 million to 1.5 million), and by 95 percent in Peru. Las Casas estimated that between 1495 and 1503 more than 3 million people disappeared from the islands of the New World. They were slain in war, sent to Castile as slaves, or consumed in the mines and other labors: "Who of those born in future generations will believe this? I myself who am writing this and saw it and know most about it can hardly believe that such was possible."[7]

The production of sugarcane, for rum, molasses, and sugar, the trade in black slaves, and the extraction of precious metals established considerable sources of wealth for Spain throughout the sixteenth century. The king paid back his enormous foreign loans (to lighten this burden, he issued a decree in 1557 that reduced the interest he owed by two-thirds), and financed his wars. Like the adventurers, the nobles, and the merchants who had become rich, he bought from the markets of Italy, France, Holland, and England.[8] The abundance of precious metals was dispersed in wider and wider waves.

WEALTH OF THE PRINCE AND PARADOXES OF MONEY

In the same period that precious metals became more abundant, prices rose. In Western Europe the average price of wheat, which had risen very little between the beginning and the middle of the century, quadrupled between the middle and the end of the century. In Spain itself prices tripled or quadrupled between the beginning of the sixteenth century and the beginning of the seventeenth century; in Italy the price of wheat rose by a factor of 3.3 between 1520 and 1599; between the first and the last quarter of the sixteenth century, prices rose by a factor of 2.6 in England and by 2.2 in France. In being diluted, the flow of precious metals reduced its effect on prices. Money wages rose less quickly; it has been estimated that real wages went down by 50 percent during the sixteenth century. Popular discontent worsened and revolts of the poor broke out.

Faced with this great confusion of money and prices, the rulers issued edicts: in France the edict of Villers-Cotterêts (1539) forbade workers' alliances; while the poor laws in England prohibited vagabondage and begging from the end of the fifteenth century.[9] To these were added, in the second half of the sixteenth century, the creation of workhouses for forced labor. Governments sought also to halt the rise in prices: in Spain, the Crown fixed maximum legal prices, without success; in France, wages and prices were fixed by edicts in 1554, 1567, and 1577; in England, the system for the regulation of prices and wages proved to be equally ineffective, and after 1560 wages were reviewed each year at Easter by the county judge.

Discussion and thinking about money and prices developed as parallel aspects of this process. In Gresham's *Information Touching the Fall of Exchange* (1558) we note the "law" according to which bad money chases out good, an observation expressed many times since the sixteenth century. A confused debate began in which a variety of factors were accused at random of causing high prices: farmers, middlemen, exporters, foreigners, merchants, and usurers as well as "monetary revaluations" that reduced the content of precious metals in money. In this debate the analysis of J. Bodin, jurist from Anjou, stands out today. Bodin wrote that "the principal and virtually sole cause" of the rise in prices was "the abundance of gold and silver which is greater today than it has been during the four previous centuries.... The principal cause of a rise in prices is always an abundance of that with which the price of goods is measured."[10]

This explanation had the great advantage of corresponding in large part to reality, while it avoided putting into question other sources of inflation:

the luxury of kings and nobles, the cost of wars, and the burden of indebtedness which made succeeding "revaluations" necessary. Prefiguring the future quantitative theory of money, this explanation was gradually accepted and coexisted with the other leading idea of the sixteenth century, with which it was largely incompatible: that it is the abundance of precious metals which creates the wealth of the kingdom.

Machiavelli formulated this second idea somewhat provokingly early in the century when he stated in *The Prince* (1514): "In a well-organized government, the state should be rich and the citizens poor." While everyone did not adopt this formulation, and while others would emphasize later the link between the wealth of the state and the wealth of the merchants, Machiavelli had put his finger on a central question of the sixteenth century: how to increase and maintain the wealth of the prince— wealth which for everyone was embodied in reserves of gold and silver.

At first, governments took measures following common sense; they tried to prevent gold and silver from leaving the kingdom. In Spain, from the beginning of the sixteenth century, the export of gold or silver was punished by death; in France, exporting coined money was prohibited in 1506, and again in 1540, 1548, and 1574; in England, two attempts, in 1546 and 1576, to place money dealings, and even the trade of bills of exchange, under the control of government agents were unsuccessful.[11]

Then, toward the middle of the century, writings circulated which called for other measures:

> By halting the importation of goods produced abroad, and which could be made in our own country; by restricting the exportation in raw form of our wool, animal hides, and other products; by bringing under the control of the towns, craftsmen currently living outside the towns who are producing goods suitable for export; by investigating these goods ..., I think our towns could quickly recover their former wealth.[12]

Bodin advocated the same policy in *The Republic* (1576): create numerous mills and forbid the export of raw textile materials. The kings of Spain, France, and England took steps in this direction: creation of mills; monopolies or privileges granted to new products; prohibition of, or tariffs against, the entry of foreign goods; interdiction of the export of raw materials. The formation of national unity saw the beginnings of a national market.

Thus the dominant ideas of this period regarding economic questions followed closely the preoccupations of the prince: the wealth of the prince had to be guaranteed—not only for himself, but also to finance the never-

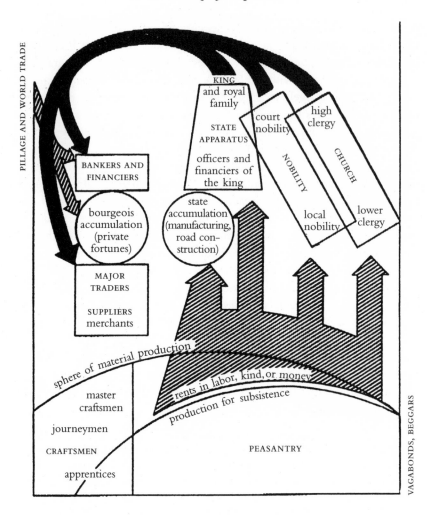

PILLAGE AND WORLD TRADE

KING and royal family

STATE APPARATUS

court nobility

high clergy

officers and financiers of the king

BANKERS AND FINANCIERS

NOBILITY

CHURCH

bourgeois accumulation (private fortunes)

state accumulation (manufacturing, road con- struction)

local nobility

lower clergy

MAJOR TRADERS

SUPPLIERS merchants

sphere of material production

rents in labor, kind, or money

production for subsistence

master craftsmen

journeymen

CRAFTSMEN

apprentices

PEASANTRY

VAGABONDS, BEGGARS

DIAGRAM I　SOCIAL CLASSES AND THE CIRCULATION OF VALUE AND WEALTH IN SIXTEENTH-CENTURY FRANCE

ending wars. The prescription for doing this was simple: prevent precious metals from leaving, by prohibiting their departure and limiting imports; make the entry of precious metals easy, by encouraging the export of what was not necessary to the kingdom. Both of these measures encouraged national production. Protected by this first idea, the related idea of public enrichment developed itself: "Each individual is a member of the commonweal," wrote Hales in his *Discourse*, "and any trade lucrative for the individual can also be lucrative for whomever else wishes to practise it as well; what is profitable for one will also be profitable for his neighbor and consequently for everyone." The way was opened to the idea that the wealth of the kingdom depended on the wealth of the merchants and manufacturers.

With the flow of precious metals from America and the development of production, commerce improved in Europe; with forced labor in America (particularly in the production of sugar) and the lowering of real wages linked to European inflation, an additional surplus was released; with the debut of enclosures in England, a labor force of vagabonds and defenseless beggars was set loose. The merchant and banking bourgeoisies gathered strength. After Venice and Florence, Antwerp, London, Lyons, and Paris developed, with populations surpassing 50,000—even 100,000.

These bourgeoisies took their bearings in part from the ideas of the Reform, in part from the affirmation of the rights of the individual in the face of the sovereign, and most of all from the various expressions of humanist thought such as are found in the works of Erasmus, Rabelais, and Montaigne. The art and universal spirit of Michelangelo bears witness to this epoch during which the Polish astronomer Copernicus brought forth the idea that the earth turns and is not the unmoving center of the universe.

But let us not exaggerate: anyone could see that the sun and the stars revolve around the earth in an unchanging order fixed by God, and the Church saw to it that no one doubted this truth. The peasant continued to till the land and to be crushed by taxes and corvée labor, the nobleman continued to hunt and to feast, the king continued to reign and to make war. Who could have conceived at that time that a new god, capital, was preparing to dominate the world? Perhaps Thomas More felt it coming in 1516 when he wrote his *Utopia*, in which the Portuguese navigator Hythloday declares: "But, Master More, to speak plainly what is in my mind, as long as there is private property and while money is the standard of all things, I do not think that a nation can be governed either justly or happily...."[13]

THE OLD AND THE NEW

Considering only the social formations out of which capitalism began to emerge, older formations continued to be predominant: an essentially rural population; primarily agricultural production; and relatively little exchange, with a large part of the population engaged in subsistence production. Rent (in labor, in kind, or in money) was levied on the great

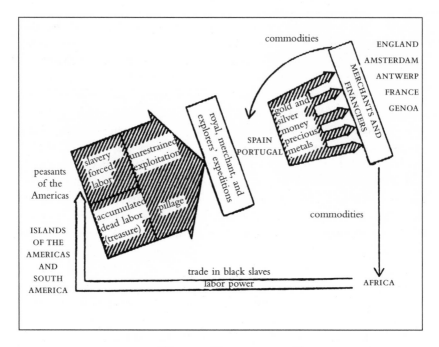

DIAGRAM 2   WORLD TRADE AND PILLAGE OF
THE AMERICAS IN THE SIXTEENTH CENTURY

peasant masses, for the profit of the clergy, the nobility, and the royal state:
through their spending, this rent allowed for the accumulation of private
fortunes by the great traders and bankers.

Market exchange mainly involved craft production, which took place
within the framework arranged by the guilds; only a small percentage of
agricultural production was sold on the market. This slight amount of
production for the market may be summarized by the formula $(C \rightarrow M$
$\rightarrow Ci)$: the merchant-producer, in selling the goods a he produced,
received a sum of money M which allowed him to buy other goods i.
Dealers intervened as intermediaries, buying the goods i in order to resell
them, realizing a profit ΔM: $(M \rightarrow Ci \rightarrow M'$, where $M' = M + \Delta M)$.
This ΔM came either from the surplus labor imposed on the small artisans
or journeymen and apprentices, or from a part of the rent extorted from
the peasantry.

Capitalist forms of production did exist, in certain cases even involving
wages, although this was not widespread.

The two principal forms of accumulation were (a) accumulation by the state (royal manufactures, king's highways, ports); and (b) bourgeois accumulation (private fortunes, money, precious metals, real estate). The principal source of this accumulation was the surplus labor of the peasant, as in preceding centuries and other social formations, although the pillage of the Americas must of course be added in.

For if we consider the international dimension, the new factor at this time was not trade with distant countries, which is present in all social formations dominated by a tributary mode of production.[14] In 1500 trade with Venice affected directly all of the Mediterranean and the whole of Western Europe and extended, by relay, beyond the Levant to the Indian Ocean, into the interior of Europe, and, in the north, to the Baltic and Norway.[15] What was new was the incredible pillage of the Americas, which was composed of two related aspects: (a) the pillage of existing treasures (dead labor accumulated in the extraction of precious metals and the fabrication of works of art); and (b) the production of new value (forced labor or slavery) either in the gold and silver mines or in cultivation (sugar cane, etc.).

Conquest, pillage, extermination: this is the reality out of which came the flow of precious metals to Europe in the sixteenth century. But the ocean is immense, and passing by way of the royal treasuries of Spain and Portugal, the money boxes of the merchants, and the accounts of the bankers, this gold was totally "laundered" by the time it got into the coffers of the financiers of Genoa, Antwerp, and Amsterdam.

This gold, gold of the prince, gold of the state (these "purses" were at that time hardly distinct one from another)—how to keep it once one had it? How to siphon it off from somewhere else when it was lacking? The formula of the hoarders, corresponding to a static view of the world—forbidding precious metals from leaving the kingdom—didn't work. Another formula was proposed by the mercantilists: buy little from, and sell more to, other countries; and in order to do that, produce more goods of better quality. Wasn't this in the interests of both the prince and the merchants?

Thus in the sixteenth century the conditions for the future development of capitalism were put into place: banking and merchant bourgeoisies having at their disposal both immense fortunes and banking and financial networks; national states having available the means for conquest and domination; and a conception of the world which valued wealth and enrichment. It is in this sense only that one can date the capitalist era as beginning in the sixteenth century.[16] But it requires hindsight, illuminated by an understanding of the later development of industrial capitalism, in order to perceive and name as "mercantile capitalism" what was in the sixteenth century only the embryo of the development that later on could be called capitalism.

THE RISE OF THE BOURGEOISIES IN THE SEVENTEENTH CENTURY

In the same way, one would have had to be exceptionally acute to see the beginning of a new mode of production in the development of manufacture in the seventeenth century. Nine-tenths of the population still lived off agriculture: superficial tillage, seedlings packed together, a lack of fertilizer; grain yields were poor (four or five, sometimes three or two, to one); fallow ground caused half of the workable land in the south and one-third of that in the north to be barren; harvesting was done with a sickle; the few farm animals which did exist were not well nourished. Food consisted of soup and bread, and famine was rife after bad harvests.

The nobility was attached to its rank and privileges: at the Estates-General in 1614 the civil lieutenant Henri de Mesme declared that "the three orders were brothers: children of the same mother, France," to which the nobles replied that they "didn't want the children of cobblers and shoemakers to call them brothers and that there was as much difference between us and them as there is between a lord and a valet."[17]

The Church maintained order within the domain of ideas. Erasmus was put on the Index in 1559. Giordano Bruno, another great humanist, was burned as a heretic in 1600. Campanella spent twenty-seven years in prison between 1599 and 1626. Galileo, who in 1632 had published his *Dialogues on the Principal Systems of the World*, the following year was forced by the Inquisition to abjure his "errors and heresies."

Only the Low Countries stand out clearly against this general background: commerce there was developed and active, agriculture modern, the nobility almost nonexistent and the bourgeoisie powerful. Its tolerance was renowned: it was in Holland that Descartes settled (1625) and wrote and published his *Discourse on Method* (1637) and *Meditations* (1641). The Low Countries, which received their political independence from Spain in 1609, seemed to depend on Spain very little at this time.

By 1580 the Spanish Hapsburgs had put under their authority the whole of the Iberian peninsula, all of Latin America, Central America, the Philippines, the region of Milan, the kingdom of Naples, Sardinia, and

Sicily, in addition to the remains of the former state of Burgundy; they had a powerful ally in their cousins, the Austrian Hapsburgs, who added the kingdoms of Bohemia and Hungary to their patrimonial states. But this territorial might was in a way illusory. The defeat of the "Invincible Armada" in 1588 symbolized the beginning of a decline: the quantities of gold and silver extracted from Latin America diminished from 1590 on (these were half as much in 1650 as in 1550). Seville's trade went down (from fifty-five ships totaling 20,000 tons in 1600–04, to eight ships totaling 2,500 tons in 1701–10).[18] The costs of war grew heavier, supplementary taxes were not sufficient, the budget was unbalanced, domestic production was insufficiently developed, and the king of Spain could find no new sources from which to borrow money. Money was devalued, economic activity slowed down, and the population fell to 6 million at the end of the sixteenth century. Spain sunk into an inexorable decline.[19]

Spain's ally, the empire of Austria, occupied by the successive waves of the Thirty Years War, was able to get out of the war only by means of considerable concessions at the Peace of Westphalia (1648). Thus it was neither in Spain nor in Austria, but principally in Holland, England, and France, that the long journey toward capitalism continued in the seventeenth century.

COLONIAL EXPANSION AND CAPITALISM IN HOLLAND

Given impetus by an active merchant and banking bourgeoisie, open to new ideas and hospitable to those of initiative, merchant and manufacturing capitalism developed considerably in Holland. Its strength rested on three pillars: the Dutch East India Company, the Bank of Amsterdam, and the merchant fleet.

Six chambers of merchants gathered together in 1602 to form the Dutch East India Company. This included seventy-three directors, all of whom were administrators of trading companies. Direction of common affairs was carried out by a College of Seventeen, named by the chambers, eight of which were named by the Chamber of Amsterdam, which paid for half of the joint expenses. Each chamber decided on the business of its members: the purchases to be made in India, the amount of gold to be sent, and the sale of merchandise received. The College of Seventeen decided the organization of the fleets, their destination, and the price of the goods. The company enjoyed a monopoly on trade with India, where it practiced the *mare clausum* (closed sea), forbidding India to the English, the Portuguese, and the French. In fact, it exercised regal rights: war, peace, treaties with the pagans, nomination of governors and councils with the power to carry out civil and criminal justice in the company trading posts. In the end the company had a land-based army in India of 10,000–12,000 troops, and a sea navy of forty to sixty ships, bringing into Europe each year 10–12 million florins' worth of goods, and giving dividends of 25 to 30 percent, such that its stock value had gone from 3,000 to 18,000 florins by 1670.[20]

The Bank of Amsterdam was created in 1609. The money-changers having been accused of being responsible for monetary disorder, the city of Amsterdam suppressed them, created a bank, and granted it a monopoly of exchange.[21] This bank received all deposits in money or ingots greater than 300 florins. The security it offered caused deposits to flow in, even from foreign countries. Thus it was able to furnish to merchants the money of any country, which permitted the purchase of merchandise of any origin, and attracted foreign traders. The bank also acted as a bank of payments: it carried out without charge all the merchants' payments, within the limits of their deposits, by simply transferring written notes without manipulating precious metals. For this it used a currency with a stable value, the bank florin, which reassured the clients. It gradually became a credit bank. It began by giving credit to the city of Amsterdam in times of war and to the East India Company, though by the end of the century the bank was making loans to private companies. Private banks, however, subsisted on loans and the accounting of bills of exchange.

Finally, there was the merchant fleet. Like the English, the Dutch had heavy, solidly built, and well-armed ships for the route to the Levant and India. But for the maritime routes of Western and Northern Europe they built the *fluitschip*, light and slender, yet nonetheless able to carry heavy, cumbersome cargo (on the order of 100 to 900 tons). By paying quickly they obtained planks and masts from Norway, at a better price than the Norwegian shipbuilders could buy them; they standardized production and used machines in construction (wind-powered sawmills, cranes). The Dutch employed foreigners (often English or French) on these ships at lower wages, for at this time sailors were the bottom layer among workers. "The crews had to submit to very harsh discipline, were compelled to cleanliness and were fed frugally."[22] The Dutch fleet alone in 1614 employed more sailors than the combined fleets of Spain, France, England, and Scotland.

Dutch ships arrived in Japan in 1600, and in China in 1601. In 1621 the Dutch West Indies Company was created, though the Dutch had trouble implanting themselves solidly on the coasts of America: if they took hold of Pernambuco, Surinam, Caracas (1830), and Curaçao (1832), the dream of a Dutch empire in Brazil fell apart in 1653, and New Amsterdam, founded in 1626, was purchased by the English in 1664 to become New York. On the other hand, from 1619 to 1663 the Dutch dominated the routes of the Far East: they settled in Batavia (1619), massacred the English in Amboina, Indonesia (1624), opened up the island of Deshima near Nagasaki (1638); they set up in Malacca (1641), took the Cape from the Portuguese (1652), and established themselves in Aden, Muscat, Cochin (1663), Singapore, and Tasmania (1642).

Holland imported from the Far East pepper and spices (66 percent of all purchases in 1648–50, 23 percent in 1698–1700) and textiles (respectively 14 percent and 55 percent of the purchases at the same dates); supplied Spain with food even during the war (half of the gold and silver acquired by Spain ended up in Amsterdam); developed sugarcane cultivation in Java; and traded with Africa and Northern Europe, reaping substantial profits from this worldwide trade. One can understand very well why Holland ardently defended the principle of the *mare liberum* ("open sea") except in its own colonies, where it imposed the *mare clausum*.

As a commercial power Holland developed processing industries: wool in Leyden, linen in Haarlem; the cutting of diamonds and dyeing, weaving, and spinning of silk in Amsterdam; sugar refining, finishing of English fabrics, brewing, distilling, salt, tobacco, and cocoa refining, and lead working in Rotterdam; polishing of optical lenses, construction of microscopes, clocks, and navigational instruments, terrestrial and maritime mapmaking, book printing in all languages, and so on. Half of the Dutch population of the time (2.5 million) lived in cities.

A rich bourgeoisie stimulated these activities and dominated the country. The trader Louis Trip possessed wealth of a million florins in 1674; the silk merchant Jean de Neufville, who arrived with nothing in 1647, died at the end of the century with nearly 800,000 florins; in 1674, 54 members of the bourgeoisie held between 200,000 and 400,000 florins; 140 between 100,000 and 200,000 florins. This bourgeoisie carried out trade, developed industry, organized "Chambers of Commerce," controlled colonial companies, watched over the University of Leyden, endowed the Bank of Amsterdam, and made Amsterdam the financial center of the time; indeed, it was tempted to impose the hegemony of Holland onto the Low Countries as a whole.

From this attempt at hegemony came conflict and compromises with the family of Orange, which relied on the traditional strength of the other provinces and which succeeded in asserting itself, especially during times of war and international tension: Maurice de Nassau, Prince of Orange, against the Great Pensioner Oldenbarnvelt in 1619, and William III of Orange against Jean de Witt, in 1672.

With the rise of English capitalism and French protectionism, with the three wars against England (that of 1652–54 and especially those of 1665–67 and 1672–74), with the war against France in 1672 and especially by participating in the War of Spanish Succession (1702–14), with the economic depression and the fall in prices of the second half of the seventeenth century, Dutch capitalism became indebted, weakened, and finally lost its dominant position. This did not prevent Holland from being "the capitalist nation *par excellence*," according to Marx, and more precisely, "the symbol of commercial and financial capitalism," in the words of Henri Sée.

Rembrandt's paintings testify to the past might of this bourgeoisie: the syndicate of merchants (1661), the shipbuilder and his wife (1643), the weigher of gold (1639), Jean Six, City Master of Amsterdam (around 1650)—as do his drawings of poor peasants, beggars, and blacks.

FROM MERCANTILISM TO LIBERALISM IN ENGLAND

Allied with the monarch because of their common interest in colonial expansion and mercantilism, the English bourgeoisie knew how to use popular discontent in its fight against absolutism, which was at the same time a fight for the strengthening of its own power.

Colonial expansion and mercantilism

England asserted itself as a maritime and colonial power by opposing Spain at the end of the sixteenth century, Holland in the seventeenth century, and France in the eighteenth century.

From the beginning of the seventeenth century, England was engaged in colonial expansion. The English East India Company was created in 1600, with a charter from Queen Elizabeth; fifteen years later the company had trading posts numbering in the twenties, in India, the islands in the Indian Ocean, Indonesia, and in Hiratsuka, Japan. England was in Persia in 1628 and in Bombay in 1668. The English settled in Barbados in 1625, took Quebec (1629) and Jamaica (1655), before taking New Amsterdam (1664); after the pilgrims of the *Mayflower* (1620) other refugees founded the colonies of North America.

England's foreign trade increased tenfold between 1610 and 1640. Production developed; by 1640 some coalfields were producing 10,000–25,000 tons of coal per year, compared to a few hundred tons a century earlier. Blast furnaces, forges with large water-powered hammers, paper and alum works employed several hundred workers; merchants and textile makers put several hundred, sometimes several thousand, sewers and weavers to work at home. The bourgeoisie, which inspired this commercial and manufacturing expansion, needed both encouragement and protection.

In 1621, in his *Discourse on English Trade with the East Indies*, Thomas Mun emphasized the importance of foreign trade: it was not so much a question of accumulating precious metals as of making them circulate in order to produce a positive balance. The mercantilist spirit was reflected in the *Report to the Private Council on Textiles* (1662):

> The remedies which we humbly propose are the following: in order to prevent foreign fabrication, it should be forbidden under severe penalties to export from England, Ireland or Scotland, fleece, fuller's earth, or charcoal; ... in order to bar products of poor quality, clear rules should be proclaimed, ... in each country a corporation should be established of those persons who are well-off and competent to control the proper fabrication, dyeing and finishing of woolen and other cloth; ... in order to lighten the taxes on our exported cloth, His Majesty is humbly asked to negotiate with the Archduke of the Low Countries and the Estates General; ... because of the scarcity of currency in the kingdom, care should be taken to prevent the removal of our money, and offenders should be severely punished.... It is especially important that the deficit in our foreign trade be remedied, for if there are more imports of vanity and luxury goods than there are exports of our products, then the reserves of this kingdom will be squandered, as it will be necessary to export our currency to reestablish equilibrium.[23]

Effectively, James I and then Charles I distributed privileges and monopolies, regulated and organized the control of manufactures, prohibited the export of wool, and raised taxes on imported French and Dutch fabrics; Acts of Parliament went so far as to make obligatory the use of woolen cloth for mourning clothes. "The state arbitrarily governed the economy, multiplied monopolies, and thwarted agricultural innovations even when technically justified."[24]

In *England's Treasure by Foreign Trade*, written between 1622 and 1650 and published in 1664, Thomas Mun widened the perspective, calling foreign trade: "The great Revenue of the King, The honour of the Kingdom, The Nobel profession of the Merchant, The School of our Arts, The supply of our wants, The employment of our poor, The improvement of our Lands, the Nurcery of our Mariners, The walls of the Kingdoms, The means of our Treasure, The Sinnews of our Wars, the terror of our Enemies." In the same work he noted: "If we duly consider Englands Largeness, Beauty, Fertility, Strength, both by Sea and Land ... we shall find this Kingdome capable to sit as master of a Monarchy. For what greater glory and advantage can any powerful Nation have, than to be thus richly and naturally possessed of all things needful for Food, Rayment, War, and Peace, not onely for its own plentiful use, but also to supply the wants of other nations, in such a measure, that much money may be thereby gotten yearly, to make the happiness compleat."[25]

National greatness, enrichment of the state and of the merchants, mastery of the universe: here was the basis for a compromise between the bourgeoisie and the sovereign. A difficult compromise: for not having respected the prerogative of Parliament to vote taxes, which the rich classes clung to, Charles I had his head cut off in a great movement of popular discontent. An attempt at an oligarchic republic with Cromwell turned to dictatorship, which did not outlive the "Lord protector of England, Scotland, and Ireland."

Cromwell carried out aggressive mercantilist policies. In 1651, faced with a crisis, he issued the first navigation act: European goods could be transported only on English ships or on ships belonging to their country of origin; products from Africa, Asia, or America could be imported only on ships of England or the colonies. The second navigation act, in 1660, specified that the captain and at least three-fourths of the crew had to be English. The wars with Holland in the second half of the century show how the rivalry sharpened between these two national capitalisms in this depression phase.

The affirmation of the bourgeoisie

In his 1688 estimate of the population and the wealth of England and Wales, the English mercantilist Gregory King gave an interesting picture of English society in the seventeenth century. Table 1.1 shows social layers arranged according to decreasing annual family income. We see that the rural world remained predominant: high, middle, and low landed nobility owing their wealth mainly to the working peasantry who were their subjects, a peasantry that was clearly stratified and produced most of the wealth from which the dominating classes and the state benefited.

The poorest layers of this peasantry—small peasants, plowmen, poor who managed to live thanks to the commons—were hurt badly by the new wave of enclosures. By the middle of the sixteenth century, John Hales was writing:

> these inclosures doe undoe vs all, for they make vs paye dearer for our land that we occupie, and causes that we can have no land in maner for oure monye to but to tillage; all is taken vp for pastures, either for shepe or for grasinge of

TABLE 1.1   Social Classes and Income in England in the Seventeenth Century

	Number of families	Family annual income (£)	Total class income (£)
Lords	186	2,590	481,800
Baronets	800	880	704,000
Knights	600	650	390,000
Squires	3,000	450	1,350,000
Traders (maritime)	2,000	400	800,000
Gentry	12,000	280	3,360,000
State officials	5,000	240	1,200,000
Traders (land)	8,000	200	1,600,000
Jurists and lawyers	10,000	140	1,400,000
State clerks	5,000	120	600,000
Rich farmers	40,000	84	3,360,000
Navy officers	5,000	80	400,000
Army officers	4,000	60	240,000
High clergy	2,000	60	120,000
Professionals	16,000	60	960,000
Middle-level peasants	140,000	50	7,000,000
Low clergy	8,000	45	360,000
Merchants and shopkeepers	40,000	45	1,800,000
Farmers	150,000	44	6,600,000
Artisans	60,000	40	2,400,000
Sailors	50,000	20	1,000,000
Laborers	364,000	15	5,460,000
Soldiers	35,000	14	490,000
Poor and landless peasants	400,000	6.10s	2,600,000
Vagabonds	30,000 persons	2	60,000

Source: Compiled from data in Peter Mathias, *The First Industrial Nation* (New York: Scribners, 1970), p. 24.

cattell, so that I have knowen of late a docen plowes with in lesse compasse than 6 myles aboute me laide downe within theise yeares; and whereas xl persons had theire lyvinges, nowe one man and his shepard hathe all. Which thinge is not the least course of theise vprors, for by theise inclosures men doe lacke livinges and be idle; and therefore for verie necessitie they are desirous of a chaunge, being in hope to come therby to somewhat; and well assured, howe soeur it befall with theim, it can not be no harder with theim then it was before. Moreover all things are so deare that by theire daily labour they are not able to live.[26]

Lupton wrote in 1622: "Enclosures make the herds fat and poor people thin." The enclosures provoked new peasant uprisings at the beginning of the seventeenth century. At this time the terms Levellers and Diggers began to be used, so called because they "dug and planted the commons."[27]

In the wave of profound discontent out of which arose the first over-throw of the king, peasant grievances started again and created diverse forms of agitation. Restrained aspirations were expressed in the program of the Levellers (1648):

> That you would have made good the supreme [authority] of the people, in this Honourable House, from all pretences of Negative Voices, either in King or Lords.
>
> That you would have made lawes for election of representatives yearly...
>
> That you would have made both Kings, Queens, Princes, Dukes, Earls, Lords, and all Persons, alike liable to every Law of the Land, made or to be made...
>
> That you would have freed all Commoners from the jurisdiction of the Lords in all cases...
>
> That you would have freed all Trade and Merchandising from all Monopolizing and Engrossing, by Companies or otherwise.
>
> That you would have abolished Excise, and all kinds of taxes, except subsidies...
>
> That you would have laid open all late Inclosures of Fens, and other Commons, or have enclosed them onely or chiefly to the benefit of the poor...
>
> That you would have removed the tedious burthen of Tythes...
>
> That you would have bound yourselves and all future Parliaments from abolishing propriety, levelling mens Estats, or making all things common.[28]

In short: parliamentary democracy, freedom, property: these were the as-pirations of the middle and well-off peasants, the dealers, the artisans, and the men important locally.

The discourse of the Diggers appeared more in the popular idiom: "Cry then, howl, you rich. God will come to you to punish you for your oppressions; you live from the work of other men, but you give them only bran to eat, extorting enormous rents and taxes from your brothers. But what will you do from here on? For the people will submit no longer to your slavery, as the understanding of the Lord enlightens them."[29] One imagines the overtaxed farmer, the exhausted plowman, the occasion of a revolt, in such outcries.

At the same time a new mode of value extortion developed, resulting from the indirect domination which the traders exercised over the artisans. These passages from *The Delights of the Master Draper* at the end of the seventeenth century give an indication of this domination:

> We heapeth up richest treasure great store
> Which we get by griping and grinding the poor.

And this is a way for to fill up our purse
Although we do get it with many a curse.

And first for the combers, we will bring them down,
From eight groats a score until half a crown;
If at all they murmur and say 'tis too small
We bid them choose whether they will work at all.
We'll make them believe that trading is bad
We care not a pin, though they are n'er so sad.

We'll make the poor weavers work at a low rate,
We'll find fault where there is none, and so we will bate;
If trading grows dead, we will presently show it,
But if it grows good, they shall never know it;
We'll tell them that cloth beyond sea will not go,
We care not whether we keep clothing or no.

Then next for the spinners we shall ensue;
We'll make them spin three pounds instead of two;
When they bring home their work unto us, they complain
And say that their wages will not them maintain;
But that if an ounce of weight they do lack,
Then for to bate threepence we will not be slack.

And thus, we do gain our wealth and estate
By many poor men that work early and late;
If it were not for those that labour full hard,
We might go and hang ourselves without regard;
The combers, the weavers, the tuckers also,
With the spinners that work for wages full low,
By these people's labour we fill up our purse,
Although we do get it with many a curse.[30]

These poor artisans, these men who worked for merchant-producers—it wasn't freedom, it wasn't democracy that they called for—it was protection by regulation, always with the same objectives: an increase in prices or in wages; a reduction of the working day; and protection from foreign competition.

Democracy, liberty—these were demanded by the banking and trading bourgeoisies, the jurists and the men of the law, the liberal professions, the important men in the rural areas, the merchants and wealthy farmers, as well as by a part of the gentry.

In these groups lay an important new social force, underestimated by the monarchy that had been reestablished after the death of Cromwell. This monarchy increased discontent by its tendencies toward absolutism, its alliance with France, and its penchant for Catholicism. Growing opposition to Charles II became open confrontation against his heir James II,

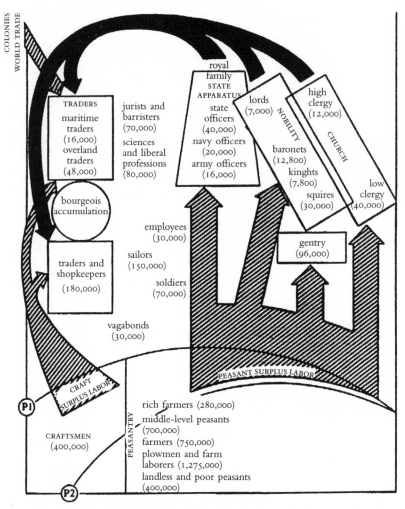

COLONIES
WORLD TRADE

TRADERS
maritime traders (16,000)
overland traders (48,000)

bourgeois accumulation

traders and shopkeepers (180,000)

jurists and barristers (70,000)
sciences and liberal professions (80,000)

royal family
STATE APPARATUS
state officers (40,000)
navy officers (20,000)
army officers (16,000)

lords (7,000)
NOBILITY
baronets (12,800)
kinghts (7,800)
squires (30,000)

high clergy (12,000)
CHURCH
low clergy (40,000)

gentry (96,000)

employees (30,000)
sailors (150,000)
soldiers (70,000)

vagabonds (30,000)

PEASANT SURPLUS LABOR

CRAFT SURPLUS LABOR

P1

CRAFTSMEN (400,000)

PEASANTRY

rich farmers (280,000)
middle-level peasants (700,000)
farmers (750,000)
plowmen and farm laborers (1,275,000)
landless and poor peasants (400,000)

P2

From a drawing made by Gregory King in 1688 for the King of England and Wales. The figures in parentheses indicate the total numbers within each class or social stratum. The two circles at the bottom indicate the spheres of material production (P1) and subsaistence production (P2). The arrows indicate the major flows of the circulation of value.

DIAGRAM 3   SOCIAL CLASSES AND EXTRACTION OF VALUE
IN SEVENTEENTH-CENTURY ENGLAND

who was forced into exile. Parliament then offered the crown to William, who had to promise to respect a "Declaration of Rights": the king could not "suspend the application of the laws, collect taxes, or raise and maintain an army in times of peace without the consent of Parliament." This was in 1689.

A reverse absolutism, this was not a question of establishing a democratic regime based on universal suffrage. Only a small number of those in the propertied classes (about 50,000) were allowed to appoint representatives in Parliament. Having benefited for a long time from the mercantilist policies of the monarchy, the bourgeoisie knew how to use the popular movements against absolutism as a lever; in the presence of the common people, the bourgeoisie made a careful compromise with the nobility, the earlier and still powerful dominating class.

Freedom and liberalism

Freedom, free consent, the right of insurrection; the English bourgeoisie found in John Locke the theoretician to refute the ideas developed by Hobbes in the middle of the era of the absolute state. Locke justified the overthrow of the sovereign.

Like Hobbes, Locke began with the first social contract, though he arrived at a position opposed to that of Hobbes:

> The reason why Men enter into Society, is the preservation of their Property; and the end why they choose and authorize a Legislative is, that there may be Laws made and Rules set as Guards and Fences to the Properties of all the Members of the Society, to limit the Power, and moderate the Dominion of every Part and Member of the Society. For since it can never be supposed to be the Will of the Society, that the Legislative should have a power to destroy that, which every one designs to secure, by entering into Society, and for which the People submitted themselves to the Legislators of their own making; whenever the *Legislators endeavor to take away, and destroy the Property of the People*, or to reduce them to Slavery under Arbitrary Power, they put themselves into a state of War with the People.[31]

Thus for Locke, what establishes society and government is the free consent of the citizens:

> That which begins and actually *constitutes any Political Society*, is nothing but the consent of any number of Freemen capable of a majority to unite and incorporate into such a Society. And this is that, and that only, which did, or could give *beginning* to any *lawful Government* in the world ... governments were *made by the consent of the People*; there can be little room for doubt, either where the Right is, or what has been the Opinion, or Practice of Mankind, about the *first erecting of governments*.[32]

And this foundation even justifies the right of insurrection:

> Whenever *the Legislators endeavor to take away, and destroy the Property* of the People, or to reduce them to Slavery under Arbitrary Power, they put themselves into a state of War with the People, who are there upon absolved from any further Obedience, and are left to common Refuge, which God bath provided for all Men, against Force and Violence. Whensoever therefore the *Legislative* shall transgress this fundamental Rule of Society; and either by Ambition, Fear, Folly or Corruption, *endeavor to grasp* themselves, *or put into the hands of any other an Absolute Power* over the Lives, Liberties and Estates of the People; By this breach of Trust they *forfeit the power*, the People had put into their hands.... *The People generally ill treated*, and contrary to right, will be ready upon any occasion to ease themselves of a burden which sits heavy upon them.[33]

Thus Locke conceived of civil government as the "true remedy for the drawbacks in the state of nature"; he rejected absolutism, which placed the sovereign above the law and thus beyond civil society.

But let us make no mistake: Locke was born into a family of merchants and men of the law, physician to Lord Ashley in 1666, secretary of the Board of Trade from 1672 to 1675; he had traveled in France and sojurned in Holland; he did not believe the working classes were capable of governing. To cope with the poor, he recommended force, as the journals of 1679 as well as the report to the Commission on Trade in 1699 indicate: "Able-bodied vagabonds from fourteen to fifty years of age in the maritime counties, who have taken to begging, should be comdemned to serve three years in the Navy. Those from other counties should be made to work for three years in the workhouses. Young beggars less than fourteen years of age should be whipped and put in a work school." For Locke, free men, those who enter into the social contract, are the members of the nobility, the clergy, the gentry, the commercial and financial bourgeoisie, and particularly the enlightened landowners, the bourgeois who have shown the ability to manage their own affairs; these are the ones who should be responsible for questions of government.

The ideas of Locke are those of an enlightened bourgeois, which explains their success among the ruling classes of England and Holland, and in the following century, among the jurists and philosophers in France.

One year after the publication of the *Essay on Civil Government*, in 1691, an English gentleman and admirer of Descartes, who had been a merchant in Turkey, a high government functionary, and mayor of London, expressed positions which were clearly different from the principles of mercantilism. Sir Dudley North wrote in his *Discourse on Trade*:

That the whole World as to Trade, is but as one Nation or People, and therein Nations are as Persons....

That all favour to one Trade or Interest against another, is an Abuse, and cuts so much of Profit from the Publick.

That no Laws can set Prices in Trade, the Rates of which, must and will make themselves.

When a Nation is grown rich, Gold Silver, Jewels, and everything useful, or desirable ... will be plentiful.

No People ever yet grew rich by Policies, but it is Peace, Industry, and Freedom that brings Trade and Wealth and nothing else.[34]

The coincidence is striking: the principles of political freedom were expressed at practically the same time as was the necessity for economic liberalism. The bourgeoisie, having become strong enough to defy absolutism, needed to legitimate the newly established form of government. And in the same movement, certain members of the bourgeoisie saw that they would find in free trade the stimulus for a new expansion of commerce and production.

The freedom to export grains, a means to encourage agriculture, was obtained in 1670. In 1703 the Treaty of Methuen opened up Brazil; in 1713 the Peace of Utrecht opened to the English the huge market represented by the Spanish empire. In 1694, the Bank of England was created.

MERCANTILISM AND ABSOLUTISM IN FRANCE

It was in France that absolutism and mercantilism appeared most clearly as a couple, one which corresponded to an alliance between a still-weak bourgeoisie and a monarchy whose absolutism reached fulfillment with Louis XIV. This alliance opposed both the still-powerful nobility and, when necessary, the uprisings of the poor: the Fronde of the nobility (1648–53), which deeply impressed the young king Louis XIV; peasant wars (particularly between 1636 and 1639) and urban revolts (frequent between 1623 and 1652) which called into question the royal Treasury in the most direct way possible—tax collectors and their assistants were often killed, quartered, and perforated with nails...

Through poor harvests or low prices, the various levies and deductions—taxes, rents in money or in kind, ecclesiastical tithes—quickly became beyond the means of the peasants; and in the cities, the poverty of the vagabonds, the beggars, and those without work merged with the discontent of the wage earners; for the guilds were closed and the employers required work days of from twelve to sixteen hours and exerted pressure to reduce the number of holidays. Secret unions were formed; resistance began to take many forms.

The French bourgeoisie remained enthralled by the royal state and the nobility. Offices of finance, justice, and the police were the most sought after; the king created new offices in order to sell and tax them. Traders and manufacturers grew wealthy:

> Sainctot, Nicolas Le Camus, who had a fortune of 9 million and who carried away at one time 200,000 *écus* worth of goods from the fair in Frankfurt, the cloth dealer Claude Parfaict, the muslin dealer Edouard Colbert, uncle of the future minister, and many others in the large cities, financed the manufacture of cannons, arms, saltpeter, silks, tapestries, textile mills, and metallurgical businesses. They acquired lands and promoted their families into the offices of the state, the city and the Church.[35]

Such people were determined to "live nobly" and hoped one day to be ennobled. Where the nobility rejected them, they gave their abilities to the king, knowing that in one way or another they would be paid for what they had contributed.

The mercantilist ideal

French mercantilism was well expressed by Montchrétien at the beginning of the century. Born in 1576, the son of an apothecary, he corresponded with and frequented the nobility; in 1605, he killed his adversary in a duel and fled to England; after a stay in Holland, he married a rich and noble widow, then created a utensil and tool mill. Persuaded that the wealth of the state required the wealth of the bourgeois, and that public prosperity (economic) and prosperity of the Treasury (political) were indivisible, he presented his *Treatise on Political Economy* to the Lord Chancellor in 1616; the work was approved and earned him the title of baron.[36] "It is not at all an abundance of gold and silver, of pearls and diamonds, which makes states wealthy," he wrote. "Rather it is the provision of things necessary for living and for clothing." But at the same time: "It is impossible to wage war without men, to maintain the men without paying them, to supply their pay without taxes, to levy taxes without trade." Which led to this conclusion: "The merchants are more than useful to the state, and their concern for profit which manifests itself in work and industry is what creates a good part of the public good. For this reason they should be allowed their love and quest for profit." On the condition, of course, that these are merchants of *this* nation: "Foreign merchants are like drains which extract from the kingdom … the pure substance of our people …; they are like bloodsuckers which attach themselves to the great body of France, drawing away the best blood and gorging themselves on it."

Montchrétien summed up mercantilist thought in one phrase: "We must have money, and if we have none from our own productions, then we must have some from foreigners." In order to do this, he recommended encouraging national trade by preventing foreign merchants from exporting the gold and silver of the kingdom, regulating the professions, creating in the various provinces trade workshops, "whose superintendence and direction, with useful and honorable privileges, would be given to those having capable minds, of the necessary intelligence." He advocated colonial conquest, of course, in order to "make known the name of God, our creator, to so many barbarous peoples lacking civilization, who call to us, who open up their arms to us, who are ready to subject themselves to us, so that by holy teachings and good examples, we may lead them onto the road to salvation." "As God himself promises to those who seek out his kingdom, that he will add to it the utmost degree of all that is good, we must not at all doubt that besides the benediction of God, which would come to this great and powerful state for such pious, just, and charitable undertakings … , he would open up in this way, as much here as there, great and inexhaustible sources of wealth."

Richelieu and then Colbert worked to carry out these policies.

Mercantilist policies

After the assassination of Henri IV, with the regency of Marie de Medici, royal power went through a period of decline. In 1624 Cardinal Richelieu was called to handle royal finances and remained director of the council until 1642, compromising with Parliament, breaking the pride and the conspiracies of the powerful, bringing the Protestants to ask for mercy in the siege of La Rochelle (1627–28), organizing the state—in short, establishing absolutism. At the same time, he encouraged conflicts which weakened the Hapsburgs, involving France in these conflicts when necessary. He watched over the restoration of the means of producing wealth: agriculture, highways, canals and ports, some manufacturing productions, and particularly trading companies. He wrote in his *Memoirs*:

> This great knowledge which the cardinal had of the sea made him introduce into the assembly of notables of that time, several necessary, useful, and glorious propositions, not so much to recall the previous dignity of the French navy, as to restore France, by means of the navy, to its former splendour. He showed them that there was no kingdom so well situated as France and so rich in all the resources necessary for making her master of the seas. In order to arrive at this goal, it was necessary to see how our neighbors managed to do it—by creating large companies and obliging merchants to make use of them through the bestowal of valuable privileges. Without these companies, each small trader

trades alone and for himself, using for the most part small and ill-equipped ships which are easy prey for the corsairs and the princes of our allies, because they do not have the means to resist, as would a large company, and to pursue justice to the end. These large companies would nonetheless not be sufficient by themselves unless the King for his part were armed with a good number of ships to uphold with force the company ships in case they were openly attacked. Besides this, the King would reap the further advantage that in case of war it would not be necessary for him to go begging to his neighbors for help.[37]

Although certain attempts failed—Morbihan (founded in 1625), Nacelle Saint-Pierre (founded in 1627, whose monopoly was to have covered the entire world)—others succeeded: the 100 Associates Company developed its activities in Canada, the Cape Verde Company in Senegal, the Islands of America Company in the Antilles (1635), and the East Indies Company in Madagascar. In 1628 a French trading post was established in Algiers, and in 1631 the first French consuls settled in Morocco.

Protectionist measures followed Richelieu, particularly in 1644, with the protective tariff on textiles, and in 1659, with the tax of 50 sous per ton on foreign ships. But it was with Louis XIV and Colbert that the union of absolutism and mercantilism triumphed: the alliance of the Sun King and the bourgeoisie. The court remained for the nobility. But the bourgeoisie increasingly took over the responsibilities of the state. The king chose his ministers, his councillors, his attendants: Le Tellier, Colbert, Louvois, Barbezieux; he ennobled them and admitted them to the court, creating a new kind of bourgeois nobility. The old aristocracy disapproved: "It was a reign of the low bourgeoisie," grumbled Saint-Simon.[38]

Mercantilism in France reached its highest point from 1663 to 1685, under Louix XIV and Colbert, for whom "the trading companies are the armies of the king and the manufactures of France are his reserves." Noting that "it is only an abundance of money in a state which makes a difference in its greatness and its power," and that "one cannot increase the money of a kingdom without at the same time taking away the same quantity of money from neighboring states," Colbert perceived the benefits of lessening French dependence on Holland for foreign trade.

Besides the advantages which would be produced by the entry of a greater quantity of cash into the kingdom, it is certain that through manufacturing, a vast number of people now languishing in idleness will be able to earn their living. An equal number will be able to earn their living in navigation and at the ports; the nearly infinite multiplication of ships will multiply in the same way the greatness and power of the state. In my view, these are the ends to which the King's attention, goodness, and love for his people should be directed.[39]

At first the state took defensive measures: the effective imposition of a tax on foreign ships, the protective tariffs of 1664 and 1667. It then adopted a policy of developing production. Beginning in 1663, Colbert undertook

> a wide-ranging inquiry into the resources of France, about the possibilities in each region for agriculture, trade, industry, the methods employed, and the attitudes of the people. Once this information was gathered, Colbert prepared a plan listing what needed to be produced and the places where these productions could be carried out. Things needed for production would be imported from abroad: machines, in particular those not yet used in France, for example one which made stockings "ten times more quickly than with a needle"; and technical workers: Germans and Swedes for iron-working, Dutch for cloth, Venetians for embroidery and glass, and Milanese for silk—all of them recruited by the French consuls. The most celebrated case was that of Zeelander Josse Van Robais de Middlebourg, who settled in Abbeville with all of his own workers, to produce woolen cloth there, with a license of 20 years.[40]

In this way, Colbert watched over the establishment of more than 400 manufactures. There were "collective" works which brought together several artisan centers which benefited as a group from conferred privileges: woolens of Sedan or Elbeuf, knitwear of Troyes, arms manufacture of Saint-Etienne. There were "private" works, individual enterprises (Van Robais in Abbeville), or large companies with branches in several provinces, especially in mining and metallurgy (Dallier de la Tour made forges, cannons, anchors, arms) and woolen goods. Finally there were royal manufactures, which were the property of the sovereign: Gobelins, Sèvres, Aubusson, Saint-Gobain—as well as arsenals and cannon foundries. The counterpart to the privileges (monopolies of production or of sale, exemptions and financing) was strict controls (standards, quantity, quality). These policies developed luxury and export production (tapestries, porcelain, glassware, luxury fabrics) as well as basic production (iron working, paper making, armaments) and products for common consumption (woolen and linen fabrics, etc.).

The state ensured that these new manufactures had a labor force. Beggars, closed up in hospitals, had to learn a trade; the unemployed, celibate women, and those in convents, were forced to work in manufactures; children had to enter an apprenticeship. For the workers, there was Mass at the beginning of the day, and silence or canticles during work; fines, whippings, or the punishment of an iron collar in case of errors; a working day of from twelve to sixteen hours; low wages; and the threat of prison in case of rebellion.

State policy extended to commerce as well as production.[41] The French East Indies Company (1664) received a fifty-year monopoly on trade and navigation in the Indian Ocean and the Pacific Ocean; its success was mediocre, and it did not reach prosperity until the following century. The Levant Company (1670) benefited from subsidies and agreements with the manufacturers of woolens and sugar; after a brief period of prosperity, it suffered from attacks by traders from Marseilles and competition from Holland, and became inactive around 1680. The presence of the French in the world became more widespread: Santo Domingo (1665), the Mississippi Valley (1673), Pondicherry (1674).

Thus in a general context of economic depression, a manufacturing and colonial capitalism was established in France to confront the powerful merchant capitalisms of Holland and England. Its base was limited yet solid. The royal state, the absolute state, solidly maintained the effort of developing manufacturing production and worldwide trade. The French bourgeoisie was formed under the protection of this state, and would carry for a long time the imprint of this development.

Mercantilism called into question

But mercantilism aroused criticism. Investors were up in arms as soon as their interests were threatened: small producers upset by manufacturers; dealers in Nantes, Rouen, and Marseilles annoyed by trading companies or by Dutch or English retaliation. Thus in the *Memoir to be of Use to History* we read:

> Monsieur Colbert is not aware that by wanting to put the French in a position of surpassing all other peoples he will instill in these other peoples the desire to do the same thing for themselves. For it is certain that they will take another route to go seek out elsewhere most of the things that they used to get for themselves in our provinces. One of the principal causes of the shortage of money which is apparent in France, in the middle of such a great abundance of grains and wines, is that the Dutch no longer come to take these goods away, as they used to. They see clearly from our conduct with them, so far as trade is concerned, that we want to take nothing from them in exchange.... So that after having wiped out these tiresome obstacles, we will necessarily be back in the same state we were in previously, or else we will have no more contact with anyone, which is impossible....[42]

Boisguilbert, observing the poverty of the peasants and the lowering of income in the countryside at the end of the century, called into question taxes, "the uncertainty of the *taille*," and customs laws—"the assistance and the customs-taxes on passages through and exits from the kingdom" (*Le Détail de la France*, 1695). In *Le Factum de la France* (1707), he considered the interdependence of activities in a generalized market system:

We must agree on one principle, that all professions, whatever they may be in a given country, work for each other and maintain each other reciprocally, to provide not only for their needs, but for their own existence as well. A person will buy the produce of his neighbor or the fruits of his labor only on the condition, however tacit and unexpressed, that the seller will do the same with the produce of his buyer. This occurs either immediately or, as happens sometimes, by circulating through several hands or intermediaries, which amounts to the same thing.... Nature then, or Providence alone can ensure that justice is observed, so long as no one else meddles with it. It establishes first an equal necessity to sell and buy in all sorts of dealings, so that the desire for profit becomes the aim of all these dealings, in the seller as well as in the buyer. With the help of this equilibrium and balance, both are forced equally to listen to the voice of reason and submit themselves to it.... Disobedience of this law, which should be sacred, is the first and main cause of public misery. It is further a law most often ignored.[43]

In the *Political Will of M. de Vauban* (1712), Boisguilbert demanded freedom in pricing and freedom for foreign trade.

SUMMARY

At the end of this "long journey" of several centuries toward capitalism, capital, considered as a social relation of domination for the extortion of surplus value, had nowhere emerged in its mature form. And it is only in the light of its later full development that we can speak of "interest capital" [*capital usuraire*], "commercial capital," "merchant capitalism," or even "manufacturing capitalism."

In the European social formations where capitalism developed, the principal means for the extortion of surplus labor remained "tributary": rents of different kinds taking various forms poured out from the peasantry to the nobility, the Church, and the royal state.

To this was added the influx of wealth resulting from the pillage of treasures in America, the extortion of surplus labor based upon the slave trade of Africa, and the development in America of mineral and agricultural productions depending upon forced labor or slavery—a brutal exploitation of Africans and Americans.

It was from these two sources of value that the enrichment of the bourgeoisies of Europe was drawn: either through the trade of merchandise $(M \rightarrow C \rightarrow M')$, or through the exchange of money $(M \rightarrow M')$.

The creation of manufactures, the submission of craft work to trader-producers who imposed their rules upon the artisans, the first mills, are all the beginning of a new mode of production which organizes all production

(P) toward the goal of creating a supplementary value (transformation of C into C′), by means of which a profit ($\Delta M = M' - M$) may be realized. This process may be summarized by the formula $M \rightarrow C \rightarrow P \rightarrow C' \rightarrow M'$. But this remained still tentative and embryonic, strictly localized as to sector and geography.

These different sources of value, and principally the first two, made possible two main forms of accumulation: (a) state accumulation (roads, canals, ports, navies, as well as royal manufactures) and (b) bourgeois accumulation (monies, precious metals, diamonds, merchandise, ships, as well as production tools and manufactures).

Opposed by the dominant class of feudal and post-feudal society—the nobility—the rising class of the commercial and banking bourgeoisie most often allied with the sovereign, in what could be called the "mercantilist compromise," advancing first the "wealth of the prince," then the common interest between the prosperity of the state and the prosperity of the merchants in order to encourage defense against foreign competition, and promote commercial and colonial expansion and the development of production.

When the bourgeoisie felt itself strong enough to dominate the world market, it abandoned mercantilist theses in favor of the virtues of free trade. When it felt strong enough to confront absolutism, it both armed itself with the new ideas of freedom and free consent (thereby gaining petty bourgeois and popular support) and allied itself with the enlightened layers of the nobility (which wanted to quiet rumblings of peasant uprisings and popular discontent).[44] In each case its presence was felt at the highest levels of the state apparatus (high assistants, intendants, officials of the state, as well as in Parliament and the judiciary)—thereby sowing the seeds of a state "techno-bourgeoisie," which drew real power from its knowledge of the practical affairs of the state.

What one in any case should remember is the importance of the state in the birth, the first beginnings, of capitalism; this is linked, too, to the national character of the formation of capitalism: there is no capitalism without the bourgeoisie, which developed within the framework of the nation-state at the same time as the rise of *nations* occurred. Within these boundaries the labor power necessary for the development of capitalism was progressively created, shaped, and adapted. Finally, for dominating capitalism, for the triumphant bourgeoisie, the geographical horizon of activity is the entire world: it is on a world scale that capitalism procures the labor power and the raw materials which it buys, sells, and plunders.

From its beginnings, capitalism has been national *and* global, competitive *and* monopolistic, liberal *and* state-connected.

As a transforming power, capitalism at this stage is not yet highly visible. The main Eurasian civilizations have hardly been influenced by the changes going on in western Europe. However, the former civilizations of the Americas were violently attacked by the conquerors who had traversed the Atlantic. And during this period African societies were subjected to an intensification of the slave trade. Within these developments, however, it is difficult to distinguish the dawning spirit of capitalism from the desire for gain and profit, the thirst after wealth, and the appetite for conquest.

Within Europe itself, the primary transforming factor is the state. National unity, currency standardization, juridical coherence, military strength, and the beginnings of a national economy: all these were created and developed by the state, or with the state as organizing principle. Scientific and technical advances play a part here as well—for navigation and weaponry, and, in a more progressive direction, for manufacturing production and agriculture.

No one during this period perceives that a new and complex social logic is being formed out of the preexisting logics, which, of course, have not vanished: mercantilist exchange and logic; small-scale market production and concern for efficiency; and the search for gain and profit, and for personal or family enrichment.... Yet the two structuring motivations of society remain, on the one hand, assuring one's own subsistence and the payment of tributes to the powerful; and, on the other hand, acquiring and increasing power and wealth. Seeking out a monetary profit primarily in order to reinject such profit into one's lucrative activities (banking, trade, manufacturing) represents the central motive for only a restricted number of bankers and merchants. And such a motive was not yet clearly distinguished from the already existing and widely accepted motive of increasing one's own family wealth.

During this period, however, the two organizing structures which have given coherence to the modern world—the state and mercantilism—are beginning to take shape. The state coalesced as the power and instigator of projects in the name or interest of a national group. Mercantilism, and the rise in importance of money-based relationships, were described at the turn of the seventeenth into the eighteenth century by North and Boisguilbert, each in his own way. Yet this was also the period which produced Thomas More, and we cannot, today, read More's dire warning as anything other than premonitory: "Where money is the measure of all things ... justice and prosperity will be nearly impossible."

Chapter 2

THE CENTURY OF THE
THREE REVOLUTIONS
(EIGHTEENTH CENTURY)

The century of enlightenment, of French *esprit*, of enlightened despotism, this is how the eighteenth century is usually presented—a century of expanding trade, especially world trade, and of increasing market, agricultural, and manufacturing production, accompanied by rising prices and population growth.[1] All of this was most evident in the second half of the century, accompanied by vastly increased wealth and worsening poverty.[2]

This was also the century of the strengthening of English capitalism, at the same time as it weakened in Holland, stagnated in largely rural France, which was dominated by the court and the "salons," and hardly emerged at all in countries such as Prussia, where the "enlightened despots" adopted the old mercantilist formulas. Capitalism was still mainly colonial, merchant, and manufacturing, though it was able to adapt to the new situation brought about by the independence of the American colonies. From the new wave of enclosures and the proletarianization of the rural masses, along with the cumulative movement of accumulation and technical progress, it was also able to create the conditions for the great industrial revolution of the nineteenth century.

This was, then, the century in which the contradictions linked to the development of market relations and of capitalism were accentuated. These were contradictions of colonial domination, with wars between France and England and the independence of the North American colonies; contradictions between the nobility and the bourgeoisie in France, which exploded in the revolution of 1789; and contradictions between the development of market exchange and the limits of manufacturing production, from which came the first spark of the industrial revolution in England.

44

COLONIAL DOMINATION, RIVALRIES BETWEEN THE GREAT POWERS, AND THE AMERICAN REVOLUTION

The treaties of 1703 and 1713 opened the markets of Brazil and those of the Spanish colonies to England, which also enjoyed a clear maritime advantage; the wars fought by Louis XIV had drained the energies of France.

The pillage and the exploitation of the colonies intensified in the eighteenth century. From 1720 to 1780 production of gold in Spanish America and Brazil averaged twenty tons per year, whereas during the previous century it had been at most ten tons per year. Sugar produced by black slaves was another important source of wealth for the English (in Barbados and Jamaica), the French (in Santo Domingo, Martinique, and Guadeloupe), and the Portuguese (in Brazil).[3] The slave trade also expanded, averaging 55,000 per year for the century as a whole (compared to roughly 2,000 per year during the sixteenth century), and reaching 100,000 per year in some periods.[4] One of the ship owners who participated in the slave trade believed in the advanced ideas of his century and christened his ships with the names *Voltaire*, *Rousseau*, and *The Social Contract*.

Millions of Africans were torn away from their countries and their lands through violence and barter. And millions of unpaid workers were used up, exhausted and consumed within a couple years. We should never forget that this was an essential basis (though largely erased and ignored in Western thought) for the bourgeois enrichment of the sixteenth, seventeenth, and eighteenth centuries.

Dominated Latin America "played a decisive role in the accumulation of wealth by the bourgeoisie of Western Europe," while black Africa functioned as "the periphery of the periphery" and "was reduced to the role of furnishing slave labor for the plantations."[5] In effect, the forced labor of black slaves and of the populations of South America permitted the release of a huge mass of surplus value, which was appropriated in monetary form mainly by the traders, manufacturers, bankers, and financiers of England. But surplus value was also appropriated by the North American colonies and by Europe, either directly or indirectly by the sale of manufactured products (fabrics, arms) or by the provision of transport.[6]

This forced labor gave rise on the one hand to the development of private enrichment in Europe and on the other hand to an increase in purchasing power in the rest of the world, especially in Asia.[7] The process

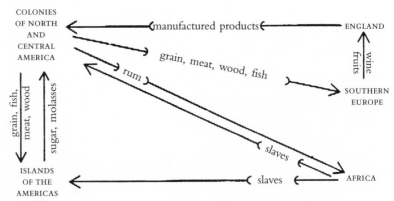

Adapted from P. Mauro, *L'Expansion européenne (1600–1870)*.

DIAGRAM 4   ENGLISH TRADE WITH ITS AMERICAN
COLONIES IN THE EIGHTEENTH CENTURY

trading companies extended their activities, making huge profits (the profit rate often reached 100 percent, and sometimes exceeded 200 percent).

New companies also were created, among them the United Company (a new English company in India, 1709), the English Company of the South Seas (1710), the French Occidental Company (1717), the Company of Ostend (1722), and the reestablished French Company of India (1723). English colonies were created in North America: Carolina in 1729, Georgia in 1732, New Orleans in 1718, and little by little the French went up the Mississippi Valley. Dupleix was the governor of Chandernagore in 1730, and in 1742 became governor-general of French India, where the French Company of India carried out an active commercial policy and increased its trading posts. French cloth and fabrics at this time competed with English fabrics, while French merchants became increasingly obstructive to British trade. The island of Malta became an essential relay point for French trade in the Mediterranean.

English merchants and manufacturers began to think that it was time to halt French expansion in the world.

But it was Spain which England attacked first in 1739, because the Spanish royal power tried to limit the activities of English traders in its empire. And the War of Austrian Succession (1740–48), in which France and Spain, with the sporadic support of Prussia, opposed England and Austria, ended at Aix-la-Chapelle in a peace treaty which did not settle

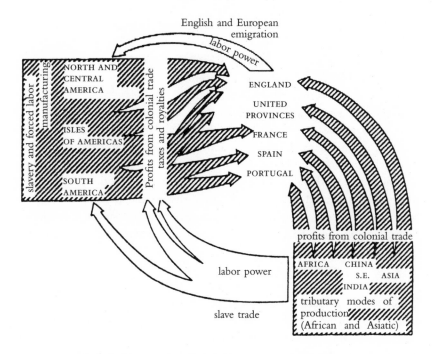

English and European
emigration

labor power

NORTH AND
CENTRAL
AMERICA

slavery and forced labor
manufacturing

ISLES
OF AMERICAS

SOUTH
AMERICA

Profits from colonial trade
taxes and royalties

ENGLAND

UNITED
PROVINCES

FRANCE

SPAIN

PORTUGAL

profits from colonial trade

labor power

AFRICA   CHINA
                 S.E.   ASIA
            INDIA

slave trade

tributary modes of
production
(African and Asiatic)

DIAGRAM 5   EXTRACTION OF VALUE
ON A WORLD SCALE IN THE EIGHTEENTH CENTURY

the main issues. Even after taking account of what had been won in the war, French opinion considered that France had fought "for the king of Prussia." For the English colonists of North America, the vast domain acquired by the small French colony had not been reduced, and English traders found that French competition remained a threat.

These traders found in William Pitt, British prime minister in 1756, a firm supporter: "When trade is threatened," he declared, "retreat is no longer possible." In 1754 French and English colonists opposed one another in skirmishes in the Ohio Valley. In 1755 the English fleet attacked a convoy transporting French reinforcements to Canada, and then went on to seize 300 French ships. During the Seven Years' War the English scored victories in colonies which France neglected to defend: they took over Calcutta and Chandernagore (1757), Louisbourg and Fort-Duquesne (1758), Quebec (1759), Montreal (1760), Pondicherry and Mahé (1761). With the Treaty of Paris (1763) England considerably expanded its empire: from France it obtained all of Canada and that part of Louisiana to the east of the Mississippi; from Spain it received Florida. Besides these, it obtained several Antillean islands (Dominica, Saint Vincent, Tobago, Grenada, and the Grenadines) as well as Saint Louis and the French outposts in Senegal. Finally, England's hands were free to carry out a policy of territorial annexation in the Indies.

Thus a period of worldwide supremacy opened up for England; and it was on an enlarged territorial basis that English capitalism developed its markets, extended its domination, and organized accumulation. This was surely the purpose of the colonies: what could be more natural?

Malachi Postlethwayt, a staunch mercantilist, asserted that the colonies must never forget they owe their prosperity to the mother country. In return, they owed gratitude and "all indispensable duty—to be immediately dependent on their original parent and to make their interest subservient thereunto."[8]

While the exploitation of the southern part of North America was mainly agricultural and slave dependent, that of the Northeast was already three-sided: agricultural, commercial (participation in the "triangular trade"), and manufacturing (transformation of agricultural products, iron, and wood). Naval construction benefited a great deal from the navigation acts of the previous country; A. Harper estimated that by 1776 one-third of the English fleet had been constructed in the colonies.[9] Western territorial expansion, at first blocked by the French and Spanish presence, as well as the Indians, proceeded once the first two obstacles were lifted in 1763; constant skirmishes against the third expanded into full-scale wars between 1759 and 1761, as for example against the Cherokees in Georgia and the Carolinas. Thus in the "melting-pot" of North American immigration, a rural aristocracy of slave owners established itself in the South, while variously throughout the colonies emerged a colonizing peasantry, a market and manufacturing bourgeoisie, an urban petty bourgeoisie, and a stratified working class with a high rate of turnover in the ports and cities.

The colonies of North America, like all English colonies, were subject to an exclusionary policy: the mother country had a monopoly on buying and selling. After 1763 the British government, in order to rebuild its finances, decided to impose taxes on sugar (1764) and stamps (1765). Faithful to the tradition of the English bourgeoisie, the new bourgeois of North America responded that they reserved the fundamental right to consent to taxation, and that since they were not represented in the English Parliament, they were not required to pay the taxes which Parliament had voted. These demands were for the most part satisfied in 1766, but the second Pitt government imposed new taxes on imported paper, glass, lead, and tea. North American merchants reacted with boycotts and smuggling. These taxes were lifted in 1770 by Lord North, all except for tea. But it was the direct sale of tea, by the East India Company and with the accord of the English government, which inflamed matters and resulted in the Boston Tea Party of 1773. In 1774 Boston and all of Massachusetts were put under military rule by the English, who annexed the Northwest Territories through Ohio to Quebec.

In 1774 the First Continental Congress brought together the representatives of the thirteen colonies. The Second Congress met in 1775–76, but lacking support from the Canadians and anxious to obtain backing from France, they adopted the Declaration of Independence on July 4, 1776, which was deeply influenced by European philosophers.

> We hold these truths to be self-evident: that all men are created equal and are endowed by their Creator with certain inalienable rights; that among these rights are life, liberty and the pursuit of happiness. Governments are established among men to guarantee these rights and their just power comes from the consent of the governed. Any time a government becomes destructive of this end, the people have the right to change or abolish it, and to establish a new government.

The War of Independence lasted six years. The North Americans benefited from an alliance with France (1778) and from the entry into the war of Spain (1779) and Holland (1780). These alliances were in effect more an opportunity for these countries to weaken England, the principal power in Europe, than to help the English colonies win their independence. Once independence was assured, Louis XVI, who had obtained only the return of the islands of Tobago and Santa Lucia and France's posts in Senegal, at the Treaty of Paris, gave the United States £12 million outright and a loan of £6 million for economic reconstruction.

Thus the first colonization gave rise to the first war of independence. Other movements, however, failed: the revolt of Tupac Amaru in Peru (1780–81), the uprising led by Toussaint L'Ouverture in Santo Domingo during the great upheaval of the French revolution (1791–95). The Napoleonic Wars, the occupation, then the weakening of Spain, and the general insurrection of the colonies of the Americas opened the way for a new wave of independence movements: Argentina (1816), Colombia (1819), Peru, Mexico, Venezuela (1821).

Thus the European expansion on a world scale, which took place through colonial domination and the development of commercial trade, led to large-scale extraction of wealth from the dominated countries. In developing, however, the European expansion created forces which rose up in resistance. The first movement toward decolonization occurred in North America, against the premier European power, Great Britain. Out of this decolonization there will appear, in a later epoch, a new and powerful expansion of capitalism, followed by imperialism.

BOURGEOISIE AGAINST NOBILITY IN FRANCE: FROM IDEOLOGICAL STRUGGLE TO REVOLUTION

During the several Years that I have made it my Business to enquire into that Matter, by all I can observe and find, in these late Times, near a tenth Part of the People are actually reduc'd to Beggary; that of the other nine Parts, not five of them are in a Condition to give Alms to that Tenth, by reason of the mizerable Condition they are reduc'd to, and the small Pittance that is left them. That of the four other Parts of the People, three are in hard Circumstances, by reason of their great Debts, and the inextricable Law-Suits they are intangled in, and that of the other tenth Part, in which I comprehend the Gentlemen of the Sword (as they're call'd) those of the Robe, both Clergy and Laity, the Nobility of all Sorts, all those who bear Civil or Military Offices, the rich Merchants and Burghers who have Estates, and others who are pretty well to pass, I say, of all these there cannot be reckon'd above a Hundred thousand Families. And I should not be much out of the way if I averr'd, that, great and small together, there are not Ten thousand of them whose Circumstances are easie.[10]

BOURGEOISIE AGAINST NOBILITY

Ten thousand families very well off. These included the high nobility—the 3,000 or 4,000 families introduced at the court, who benefited from the greatest privileges, offices, and lucrative pensions—approximated more and more closely, in the eighteenth century, by the great families of the state nobility (intendants, and state and parliamentary councillors).[11]

They also included the high bourgeoisie: bankers, great maritime traders, manufacturers, and businessmen, who were not yet highly important within French society but had active and imaginative allies among the lawyers, jurists, lovers of literature holding salons, and finance officers.

After the death of Louis XIV, the nobility, long kept away from affairs of state, wanted to return to them. Philippe d'Orléans created seven councils of nobles to look after different branches of government in place of ministers; but intrigues and a lack of conscientiousness and work caused this effort to fail. There was then a return to absolute monarchy, though it was mainly from among the nobles that the monarch chose his councillors.

Parliamentary seats, high administrative and judicial posts, high clergy, and any officerships—these were all closed to commoners. Between nobles and commoners there was scorn and mutual harassment; the rift between these two groups deepened. And yet a good many of the commoners developed their businesses and grew wealthy. The efforts of John Law, who founded the first bank in France, though it ultimately collapsed due to the issue of paper currency, gave impetus to this movement. The Paris Stock Exchange was created in 1724 and the liberal policies of Cardinal Fleury (1726 to 1743) facilitated trading activity. The royal corvée permitted an improvement of roads; the school of bridges and roads was created in 1743 and the corps of engineers during the 1750s. With colonial trade and the traffic in slaves, Bordeaux, Nantes, and Le Havre expanded and saw the development of trading, shipbuilding, sugar refining, and textile manufacturing. Marseilles continued to trade with the Levant and participated more actively in colonial trade. Manufacturing production remained strictly localized: in Reims, for example, more than half of the wool looms were concentrated in a few mills. Indeed, it was in the interest of the merchants to gather the workers under one roof to supervise their work and to avoid the costs of transportation. The same was true also of many mills in the south of France.

Craft work and production-in-the-home organized by the dealer-merchant still predominated. For example:

> In Brittany the linen industry was exclusively rural and domestic. Those who were employed in it were small landlords, farmers (who often had their servants working), and day-laborers who made linen during months of unemployment. The wages of the weavers were very low and profits went mainly to the manufacturers, that is, to the merchants who collected the finished products and who often supplied the raw materials. In the regions where agriculture was more prosperous, as in eastern Normandy, Picardy, and Flanders, the peasants who practiced rural industry were the ones who didn't own enough land to be able to live off of their own cultivation. In eastern Normandy, the Parliament of Rouen, from 1722 on, gave examples of peasants abandoning cultivation of the land in order to spin or card cotton, and the Parliament complained about the resulting damage this caused agriculture. There was not a village in Normandy without its spinners and its weavers; 180,000 were kept busy in this kind of work by the "manufacture" of Rouen.[12]

Sometimes group production and home production were combined: the twelve "royal manufactures" of wool had the finishing done in group workshops, but the spinning and weaving were done at home by the peasants. In Abbeville, the Van Robais had 1,800 workers in their

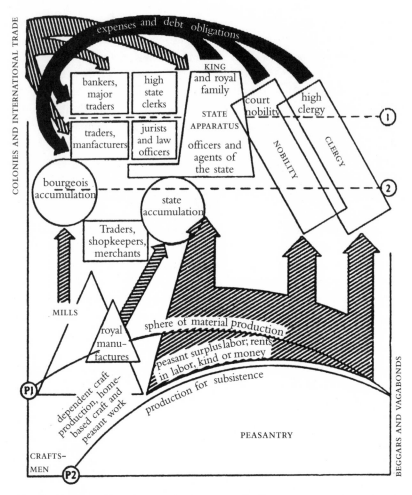

Above line (1) are the "ten thousand families very well off," according to Vauban. Above line (2) are the "hundred thousand well off families" (one-tenth of the population). According to Vauban, vagabonds and beggars accounted for one-tenth of the population. (P1) is the sphere of material production; (P2) is the sphere of subsistence production.

DIAGRAM 6   SOCIAL CLASSES AND THE EXTRACTION OF
VALUE IN EIGHTEENTH-CENTURY FRANCE

workshops and about 10,000 at home. The same was true with iron: nails, stoves, and cauldrons were often made by peasants in their homes.

How many were there? Five hundred thousand, a million? Estimates are difficult, and figures vary according to the season and the situation.

Competition sharpened among workers available in the cities, craft workers prepared to work for dealers, and peasants available for seasonal work. Businessmen were in a good position to harden their conditions: the working day was lengthened. Father Berthelon remarked: "The manufacturing worker always starts before dawn and is still working late in the night, in order to compensate, by the length of time, for the low and insufficient wages."[13]

In the countryside, vagabonds, beggars, and men and women without work or means made up an unstable mass of available labor power: "isolated day laborers who, belonging to no one anymore, having neither masters nor, consequently, guardians interested in their defence and succor, were left impoverished and at the mercy of the very greed they helped to enrich." These were poor peasants taken to the limits of misery following a bad harvest. Thus, during the winter of 1710, "men and women, children big and small, could be seen with their muddy hands and faces, scratching the earth with their nails, searching for certain small roots which they devoured whenever they found any. Others, less industrious, browsed the grass with the animals, while still others, completely despondent and beaten, lay along the high roads waiting for death."[14] And in 1739 the Marquis of Argenson noted in his memoirs: "For a year now misery has been progressing in the kingdom at an incredible rate; men die like flies, poverty stricken and browsing grass.... The Duke of Orleans brought recently to the Council a piece of bread made from a fern ..., saying 'Sire, this is the kind of bread your subjects are eating nowadays'."[15]

Sometimes discontent came to a head. Revolts broke out and were quickly crushed.

Thus on the one hand, the nobility closed ranks around the king and the court, reserving access to offices and jealously watching over its privileges and prerogatives. On the other hand, the bourgeoisie grew richer and stronger from trade with the colonies and the expansion of manufacturing production, yet they continued to suffer by being kept from affairs of state.

In the salons, in the luxury of velvet, lace, and gold, the discoveries of scientists and the ideas of philosophers germinated and circulated, and it was here that the various currents of opposition developed.

THE IDEOLOGICAL TUMULT

Knowing, observing, explaining, understanding, doubting, debating, discovering—so long as it was done in the right manner, everything could be said, or almost everything.

> This was a period of great and exaggerated admiration for the observation of matter and nature. Collections of animals, plants, rocks, and "cabinets" of physics every day became more numerous: dukes, magistrates, abbots, physicians, ladies, and religious congregations had them. Louis XV had his own and beyond this, Buffon developed the King's Cabinet and the King's Garden, which had been founded by Louis XIII: he doubled the gardens, and added greenhouses and an amphitheater.... Public lectures spread the taste for science. In the King's Garden, the chemist Rouelle would begin his public lecture in a wig and lace cuffs. But he would get warmed up, and would remove first his cuffs and wig, then his coat, and ended up tearing off his waistcoat, finishing his lecture in shirtsleeves, and his passion communicated itself to his audience. Books popularizing science multiplied, some of them of great value, such as the *Spectacle of Nature* by Abbé Pluche, the *Lessons in Experimental Physics* by Abbé Nollet (1748), the *Natural History* by Buffon and the *History of Electricity* by Priestley (1775). A multitude of digests, dictionaries, and manuals also appeared constantly kept up to date and revised.[16]

Scientific research and discoveries also abounded: d'Alembert systematized the principles of mechanics (1743); Lavoisier analyzed first the composition of air (1770–71), then of water (1783); Berthollet studied chlorine (1772); Lagrange established the principles of analytical mechanics (1787).

In this context the ideas of philosophers flourished: evidence, clarity, conformity to reason; a wonderful universe, mechanics following eternal laws established by a supreme being, God, at once "all powerful and all knowing"; a world based upon natural laws, natural right, and natural morality, that were to be rediscovered; happiness, pleasure, egoism, utilitarianism, but also indulgence, tolerance, and a certain humanity.[17] And then, becoming more and more prevalent, the idea of progress: human progress winding its way through the intellectual progress of individuals, the development of the mind, of knowledge and of enlightenment.[18] These ideas were cultivated within the milieu of the state nobility—financiers and jurists—and, since all of the European aristocracy spoke and thought in French, they were diffused into the courts of enlightened despots.

The Encyclopedia (1751–64) was the philosophical and scientific summation of these ideas, destined to replace the *Summa Theologica* of Thomas Aquinas: "the work of 130 collaborators, lawyers, physicians, professors, priests, academicians, industrialists, and manufacturers, most of them well off and bearing titles. Because of its price, it was directed to the enlightened bourgeoisie: it was a bourgeois work."[19]

The Catholic church condemned the Encyclopedia for the first time in 1752 and again in 1759, though this condemnation did not impede its success among the restricted public who did read it.

Democracy, freedom, general will

Enlightened by the English revolutions and the writings of Hobbes and Locke, encouraged by the aspirations of the nobility to be the support of the kingdom, and by the claims of the high bourgeoisie who wanted to be consulted by the monarch and to influence affairs of state, reflective thinking continued on, dealing with questions of power, political regimes, laws and rights, the general interest, the social contract, and the general will.

In *L'Esprit des lois* (1748), Montesquieu, polishing formulas, had examined the "kinds of governments": "republican, monarchist, and despotic." In the democratic republic, "the will of the sovereign is itself sovereign." But Montesquieu called attention immediately to the limits of what is today called direct democracy: "The people, in a democracy, are, in some respects, the monarch; in other respects, the subject.... The people who have the sovereign power should do themselves what they can do well; what they cannot do well, they must have done by their ministers.... The people are admirable for choosing those to whom they must entrust some part of their authority.... But will the people be able to conduct an affair, know the places, the opportunities and the moments to profit from it? No, they will not."[20]

A monarchist, fascinated, as were so many enlightened minds of his time, by the English parliamentary monarchy, Montesquieu extolled both the balance of powers—the people, the nobility, and the monarch—and the separation of powers—the legislative, the executive, and the judiciary. He was not at all a utopian:"The true spirit of equality is as far away from the spirit of extreme equality as the sky is from the earth." Neither was he a cynic:"A man is not poor because he has nothing, but because he does not work.... In a good democracy, where nothing is spent but for the necessary, everyone must have the necessary, since from whom would one receive it?" And in cases where it has been impossible to prevent misery, "the state needs to provide prompt assistance, either to stop the people's suffering, or to prevent their revolting."[21]

Democracy, freedom, the social contract: these new ideas found in Jean-Jacques Rousseau an ardent propagandist. The first chapter of *The*

Social Contract opens: "Man was/is born free, and everywhere he is in chains." "To renounce one's freedom is to renounce one's status as a man, the rights of humanity and even its duties.... Such a renunciation is incompatible with the nature of man, and taking away all his freedom of will is taking away all morality from his actions." How to find a form of association which defends and protects, with the strength of the whole group, the person and the goods of each member, and by which each person, in uniting with the whole, obeys, however, only himself or herself, and remains as free as before: this is the fundamental problem to which *The Social Contract* gives the solution: "What man loses by the social contract is his natural freedom and an unlimited right to everything that tempts him and that he can get; what he gains is civil freedom and the proprietorship of everything he possesses."[22]

Rousseau presents the sovereignty of the people, the general will, as unalterable, indivisible, infallible if it is well informed, absolute so long as it does not go "beyond the limits of general conventions," and thus "sacred" and "inviolable." He distinguishes the sovereign from the government: "The government receives from the sovereign the orders that it gives to the people; and in order for the state to be in good equilibrium, all things considered, the product or power of the government, taken by itself, must be equal to the product or *the power of the citizens, who are sovereigns on the one hand and subjects on the other*."[23] Following Montesquieu, he studied the forms of government: the simple ones (democracy, aristocracy, monarchy) and the mixed ones; the diversity of conditions gives the result that "all forms of government are not suitable for all countries."

Democracy fascinated him: "If there were a people of Gods, it would govern itself democratically. Such a perfect government is not suited to men." Furthermore: "In the strict sense of the term, a true democracy has never existed and never will exist. It is contrary to the natural order that the majority govern and the minority be governed. It is unimaginable that the people remain constantly assembled to attend to public affairs, and it is obvious that it could not establish commissions to manage these affairs, without changing the form of administration."[24]

Hostile to absolutism, Rousseau gives the impression of reserving democracy (for us, direct democracy) for small states, and preferring instead the lesser evil of an elective aristocracy (in some ways, our representative democracy).[25] In fact, he never did decide. In a 1767 letter to the Marquis de Mirabeau, he is no longer sure that it will be possible to find a "form of government which places the law above men"; if this is not possible, "we must go to the other extreme, and all at once, place men as far above the law as is possible, and consequently, establish arbitrary despotism, the most arbitrary which is possible: I would like the despot to be God. In a word, I cannot see a bearable medium between the most austere democracy and the most perfect Hobbes-ism, for the conflict between men and laws which puts the state into continual civil war is the worst of all political situations."[26]

Sovereignty of the people, the general will, freedom: the great themes of the bourgeois revolution were in place. Sovereignty of the people, direct democracy, freedom: the great themes of the popular movements were there too. Other debates developed: about wealth, equality, and property.

Equality and property

In the face of the reality—not yet defined explicitly or named, but growing larger—of merchant capitalism, and especially considering the spectacle of poverty and misery in the countryside and in the cities, and the spectacular acquisition of wealth by a few, social indignation grew: some writers prolonged and renewed the fascinating Utopian tradition, while others took pity and recommended charity.[27]

Commissioned to write the article on "Political Economy" for the Encyclopedia (1755), Rousseau harshly summarized the social pact which the rich man proposes to the poor: "You need me, for I am rich and you are poor; let us then make an agreement between ourselves; I will grant you the honor of serving me, on the condition that you give me the little you have left for the trouble I will take to order you about."[28]

Throughout his writing and throughout his life, Rousseau berated wealth and the wealthy: "It is the state of the wealthy," he wrote to Mme. Franceuil in the letter which explained why he had placed his children in an orphanage (1751): "it is your state which steals from mine my children's bread." The rich being inhuman, it is from among them that he chooses Emile in order to educate him: "We will be sure at least to have one more man than before; whereas a poor person can become a man by himself."

The rich man "does not find it strange that profit is in inverse relation to work and that an idler, hard and voluptuous, gets fat from the sweat of a million wretches, exhausted from fatigue and need." Rousseau continues his denunciation: "In our societies, accumulated wealth always facilitates the means to accumulate greater wealth, and … it is impossible for those who have nothing to acquire anything."[29] The "Discourse on the Origin of Inequality Among Men" (1754) ends with these words: "It is manifestly against the law of nature, in whatever manner it is defined, … that a handful of men be glutted with superfluities, while the starving multitude lacks necessities."[30]

Rousseau here explicitly links the problem of inequality and the question of property:

> The first man who having enclosed a piece of land dared to say: "This is mine," and found people foolish enough to believe it, was the true founder of civil society. How many crimes, wars and murders, how many miseries and horrors the human race would have been spared by the man who, tearing out the fence-stakes or filling in the ditch, shouted to his fellow creatures: "Beware of listening to this imposter; you are lost if you forget that all the fruits of the earth are yours and that the earth itself is no one's!" Though it is likely that by then things had already come to the point where they could not continue on any longer as they were.[31]

Rousseau did not advocate the abolition of private property, however. In the article on "Political Economy" for the Encyclopedia he wrote: "the right of property is the most sacred of all the rights of the citizens," although he foresaw limiting this right through taxation and by changing the rights of inheritance.

> It is precisely because the force of circumstances tends always to destroy equality that the power of legislation must always tend to maintaining equality…. It is therefore one of the main functions of government to prevent an extreme inequality of wealth, not by taking fortunes away from their owners, but by depriving everyone of the means for accumulating fortunes; not by building hospitals for the poor, but by assuring that the citizens will not become poor.[32]

The brother of the French philosopher Etienne Condillac, Father Mably, took up again the critique of private property: "What is the principal source of the misfortunes which afflict humanity? It is the property of goods."[33] He armed himself against the physiocrats:

> Even if landed property were much more favorable than it actually is to the reproduction of wealth, it would still be necessary to prefer the community of goods. What use is this greater affluence, it if encourages men to be unjust and to arm themselves with force and fraud in order to get rich? Can one seriously doubt that in a society where greed, vanity and ambition were unknown, the lowest citizen would be happier than our richest landlords are today?[34]

Mably opposed to the physiocrats the Spartans and the Indians of Paraguay: "The state, owning everything, distributes to individuals the things which they need. Here, I must say, is a political economy that I like."[35]

But Diderot, although he deplored the fact that "between men, indigence condemns some to work while others get fat from the sweat and toil of those who work," saw in private property a protection of the individual.[36]

Helvétius, preoccupied with the happiness of humanity, resumed the critique of inequality: "In most nations there are only two classes of citizens: one who lack what is necessary, the other who are overflowing with excess. The first can provide for their needs only by excessive work." He appealed to the government to reduce the wealth of the few, and to increase the wealth of the others. "Do all the citizens have some property? Are all of them fairly well off and can they with a work day of seven to eight hours provide abundantly for their own and their families' needs? They are as happy as can be."[37] D'Holbach, another enlightened mind intent on replacing religion with natural morality, asked the government to tax luxury, to give to the poor the possibility of living by their work, and to prevent the accumulation of wealth in a few hands. Besides workshops for the needy, he proposed that "all uncultivated lands should be returned to the commons, in order to be given to those who can make use of it for themselves and for society."[38]

Father Raynal, a man of the salons and a friend of Diderot, famous for his *Philosophical History of the Two Indes* (1770), also denounced inequality and wealth: "Fear the affluence of gold which brings, along with luxury, the corruption of morals and the contempt for law; fear a greatly unequal division of wealth, which gives rise to the appearance of a small number of opulent citizens and a multitude of citizens in misery, from which is born the insolence of the former and the degradation of the latter." He had this formula: "Everywhere the rich exploit the poor," and foresaw the suppression of inheritance, going so far as to write: "Hang them, if need be, these treacherous rich, and recover your dignity!"[39]

With Linguet, a lawyer and publicist, denunciation became more precise: he published in 1767 the *Theory of Civil Laws, or Fundamental Principles of Society* and, from 1777 to 1792, the *Political, Civil and Literary Annals*, which was outlawed several times.

Society and property have the same basis: violence. "Greed and violence have seized hold of the earth … so that possession today rests upon the most shocking usurpation." And the spirit of property, once it has "begun to take hold of souls …, shrinks them, materializes them so to speak. It closes them to almost any motive other than self-interest." Linguet examined the situation of the laborers of his time—successors to slaves and serfs, their fate appeared to him to be infinitely more miserable than that of their fathers:

They whine under the disgusting rags which are the uniform of the destitute. They have no share in the abundance whose source is their labor. Wealth seems to pardon them, when it consents to receive the presents they make to it ..., at the same time it lavishes on them the most insulting scorn.... These are the servants who have actually taken the place of the serfs among us; they are indisputably very numerous and are the largest portion of each nation. We must consider what is the effective gain for them which has been brought about by the abolition of slavery. I say with as much sorrow as frankness: all that they have won is to be at every moment tormented by the fear of dying of hunger, an unhappiness from which their predecessors in this lowest rank of humanity were at least exempt. Misery reduces them to kneeling before the rich man in order to obtain from him the permission to make him richer still.[40]

It is to this that "freedom" condemns the laborers: thus, "the declamations [of the rich] against servitude are like the cries uttered by a bird of prey while ripping apart the dove grasped in its talons."

Linguet was nothing of a Utopian: "To want to make everyone happy, in a state, is a project as false in politics as is searching for the philosopher's stone in chemistry."[41] Economists deceive us by promising to expand wealth, for "the secret of increasing the wealth of a people is only that of increasing the number of its unfortunates." In fact, it is not wealth that is the source of life for the "hired man"; it is the life of the "hired man" that creates the opulence of the rich: "You have reasoned precisely like a man who would like a river to feed the brooks which have formed it, instead of the brooks feeding the river."[42] The day laborer is caught in the trap of the "free" market: "He has nothing to sell but the rent of his arms, which [the 'renter' of his arms] can do without for two days, three days, while he is sold bread that he cannot do without for twenty-four hours."[43] "It is then a sad irony to say that workers are free and have no master. They do have one, the most terrible, the most imperious of masters.... The poor man is not at all free and he serves in all countries. The poor are not under the orders of one man in particular, but under the orders of everyone in general."

It is understandable that on the eve of the Estates-General, Linguet could call himself the interpreter of the wishes of the fourth estate: "At this moment when there is in France an assembly designed to bring about general reform, there must be at least one spokesman for the protests of the class most numerous, most mistreated, and most deprived of the means for making itself heard."[44]

While Linguet analyzed and denounced the situation of the proletarian (day laborer, unskilled laborer, hired hand) who has nothing to sell but the strength of his arms, Turgot and the physiocrats in France and Adam

Smith in England saw the necessity for "advances," that is to say, of part of the "net product" used for the accumulation of capital. Thus each one illuminated one aspect of capitalism.

The ideas of the economists

Voltaire asked the central question: "Since you have established yourselves as a people, have you not yet discovered the secret of forcing all the rich to make all the poor work?"[45] Undoubtedly there is here a possible definition of capitalism: the system which obliges the rich to make the poor continually work longer and harder.

Rousseau opposes to this logic the rights of workers, which will uphold socialist thought:

> It is impossible to conceive of the idea of property arising from anything except manual labor; because one cannot see what man can add, other than his own labor, in order to appropriate things he has not made. It is labor alone, which giving the cultivator a right to the product of the land he has tilled, gives him a right to the soil as a consequence, at least until the harvest, and thus from year to year; which, creating continuous possession, is easily transformed into property.[46]

In the second half of the century a wide debate developed around the question of production. How to produce better? How to produce more in order to clear a "net product"? Who is productive? How to withdraw a surplus necessary for accumulation? Among the philosophers, the "economists" in particular examined these questions.

Quesnay was the undisputed leader of the physiocratic school. Born in 1694 near Versailles into a family of well-off farmers, he obstinately acquired an education, established himself as a surgeon in Nantes, and published several medical works. He entered into the service of Mme. de Pompadour (1748), became the general physician to the king, and was knighted in 1752. In 1754 he bought a property in the Nivernais.

France was at this time principally rural and agricultural (over three-fourths of the population was engaged in agriculture); while Holland and England had already largely adopted the new methods of cultivation, French agriculture remained very traditional: lands remained rocky, plowing superficial, sowings late, and yields poor. The practice of leaving lands fallow made one-half, two-thirds, and sometimes more of the arable land barren. "Carelessness of the big landlords; inertia of the peasants, discouraged by the taxes and obligations which weighed them down; insufficient routes for transport and especially the bad state of cross-country

TABLE 2.1   Actual versus Good Cultivation Yields (1757)

	Actual	Good	Difference	
For the landlord	76,500,000	400,000,000	323,500,000	(more than 4/5)
For the land tax	27,000,000	165,000,000	138,000,000	(more than 5/6)
For the farmers	27,000,000	165,000,000	137,500,000	(more than 5/6)
For the tithe	60,000,000	155,000,000	105,000,000	(more than 2/3)
For expenses	415,000,000	930,000,000	515,000,000	(more than 5/9)
Product less expenses	178,000,000	885,000,000	707,000,000	(more than 4/5)
Total product	595,000,000	1,815,000,000	1,220,000,000	(more than 2/3)

Source: François Quesnay, "Grains," in *François Quesnay et la Physiocratie*, vol. II (Paris: INED, 1958), p. 478.

roads; impediments to the trading of agricultural produce and the free choice of cultivation: all these are reasons which explain the poor development of agriculture."[47]

In an article entitled "Farmers" in the Encyclopedia (1757), Quesnay showed the superiority of tenant farming over the *métayage* system, and the advantages of the horse over the ox for plowing. In an article entitled "Grains" (1757), he depicted the conditions of large and small grain cultivation at that time, showed what the proper cultivation could produce, and summarized the difference in a table (see Table 2.1).

He wrote: "Revenues are the product of lands and of men," before stating his "maxims of economic government," in which his central ideas already come through: productivity exclusively from the earth, the sterility of industry, and the rejection of the policy of increasing wealth through balance of trade.[48]

Quesnay wrote the article on "Man" in 1757, but it was not published in the Encyclopedia, which had lost the support of the government. Quesnay preferred to retain the manuscript, in which his idea that wealth comes from agriculture became more precise:

Let us not be distracted, we who are so rich in estate holdings, by a small trade in luxuries which gives back only the costs of labor-power; fertilize our lands, sell grains, wines, hemp, and woolen cloth—as much as is possible. The product will in reality multiply the wealth, and these riches always being reborn annually will assure us manufactures and works of industry of all kinds.

For affluence is the mother of the arts and of luxury."[49] This idea was made increasingly explicit in the different editions of the *Economic Tableau* (1758–59), in the *Rural Philosophy* (1763), coauthored with Mirabeau, and in the *Analysis of the Arithmetic Formula of the Economic Tableau* (1766), which begins with these lines:

> The nation is reduced to three classes of citizen: the productive class, the possessing class, and the unproductive class.
>
> The productive class is the class which reproduces the annual wealth of the nation by cultivation of the earth. This class gives the advances on the costs of agricultural works, and pays each year for the income of the landowners. We include in the dependency of this class all the work projects and all the expenses which these incur until the sale of the first-hand productions; it is by this sale that one knows the value of the annual reproduction of wealth of a nation.
>
> The possessing class includes the sovereign, the landowners, and the tax collectors. This class subsists on the income or net product of cultivation, which is paid to them annually by the productive class. The productive class deducts, from the reproduction of wealth which it creates each year, what is necessary to reimburse itself for its annual advances, and to support the wealth of exploitation.
>
> The unproductive class includes all citizens occupied in services and work other than agriculture, and whose expenses are paid by the productive class and the possessing class, who themselves draw their income from the productive class.[50]

Analysis of the circulation of wealth; analysis linked to classes and the production-utilization of this wealth; the development of a net product, that is, an available surplus; the emphasized role of "advances," that is to say, of the utilization of a part of this surplus to expand the investment with a view toward renewed or enlarged production—Quesnay was the theoretician of an agrarian capitalism which was not at all absurd at the time. This was a period when (a) agriculture in France was fairly unproductive, having not taken advantage of techniques already proven in England and Holland; and (b) capitalism remained for the most part at a merchant and colonial stage, and in France had hardly reached the manufacturing stage.

Turgot was an employee of the royal state (an intendant before becoming general controller) commissioned to write the articles on "Trade Fair" and "Establishment" for the Encyclopedia, knew Voltaire, Du Pont de Nemours, and Adam Smith, and published *Reflections on the Formation and Distribution of Wealth* in 1766. He was greatly influenced by physiocratic thought: "The earth was ever the first and only source of all riches."[51]

But, lacking the doctrinaire mind of Quesnay and having a sufficient knowledge of economic reality, he questioned himself:

> What is the wealth of a state? What gives value to the lands, if not the number of inhabitants? ... If labour is the true wealth, if money is only the indication of this wealth, the richest country, is it not the one in which there is the most work? Is it not the one in which the greatest number of inhabitants obtain for themselves employment from others?[52]

But he does not consider the ones who employ to be on the same plane with those who are employed:

> Whoever has seen the workhouse of a tanner, cannot help feeling the absolute impossibility of one, or even several indigent persons providing themselves with leather, lime, tan, utensils, &c. and causing the requisite buildings to be erected to put the tan/house to work, and of their living during a certain space of time, till their leather can be sold.... Who shall now collect the materials for the manufactory, the ingredients, the requisite utensils for their preparation? Who is to construct canals, markets, and buildings of every denomination? How shall that multitude of workmen subsist till the time of their leather being sold, and of whom none individually would be able to prepare a single skin; and where the emolument of the sale of a single skin could not afford subsistence to any one of them? Who shall defray the expences for the instruction of the pupils and apprentices? Who shall maintain them until they are sufficiently instructed, guiding them gradually from an easy labour proportionate to their age, to works that demand more vigour and ability? It must then be one of those proprietors of capitals, or moveable accumulated property that must employ them, supplying them with advances in part for the construction and purchase of materials, and partly for the daily salaries of the workmen that are preparing them. It is he that must expect the sale of the leather, which is to return him not only his advances, but also an emolument sufficient to indemnify him for what his money would have procured him, had he turned it to the acquisition of lands, and moreover of the salary due to his troubles and care, to his risk, and even to his skill; for surely, upon equal profits he would have preferred living without solicitude, on the revenue of land, which he could have purchased with the same capital. In proportion as this capital returns to him by the sale of his works, he employs it in new purchases for supporting his family and maintaining his manufactory; by this continual circulation, he lives on his profits, and lays by in store what he can spare to increase his stock, and to advance his enterprize by augmenting the mass of his capital, in order proportionately to augment his profits.[53]

Thus, as early as 1766, Turgot clearly saw the prospect of the development of a manufacturing capitalism at the same time as he kept sight of the development of capitalism in agriculture. From this basis, he furthered the analysis of classes: the industrious class is "subdivided into two classes. The one, of the undertakers, manufacturers and masters, all proprietors of large capitals, which they avail themselves of, by furnishing work to the other class, composed of artificers, destitute of any property but their hands, who advance only their daily labour, and receive no profits but their salaries."[54] "The class of cultivators may be divided, like that of manufacturers, into two branches, the one of undertakers or capitalists, who make the advances, the other of simple stipendiary workmen."[55] Despite the form of the expressions, we are closer here to Marx than to Quesnay. Finally, "the profession of a trader, or what is properly called commerce, divides into an infinity of branches, and it may be said of degrees."[56]

Turgot was not only a witness to the development of manufacturing capitalism. He justified it and argued in its favor. He praised low interest rates: "It is the abundance of capitals that animates enterprise; and a low interest of money is at the same time the effect and a proof of the abundance of capitals."[57] He was opposed to a planned economy and to protectionism: if it is a question of providing for and educating men, of assuring good morals, "should we accustom men to demand everything, to receive everything, and to owe nothing to themselves?" he asked. "Are men so strongly interested in the good you wish to obtain for them? *Let them be*, this is the great and sole principle."[58] He extolled economic freedom, for "a man knows his own interest better than another man who is entirely indifferent to this interest.... But it is impossible, in commerce left to itself, that the particular interest wouldn't contribute equally to the general interest."[59]

These ideas spread during the second half of the century.[60] Turgot attempted to put them into practice when he held a government position, from 1774 to 1776. He decreed free trade for grains in 1774, as had been done in 1763 and 1770, but this was once more suspended. The edict of 1776, which suppressed masterships and wardenships of the guilds, and which gave freedom to any person to carry out such kinds of commerce and trades (as the guilds controlled), encountered strong opposition, was not enforced, and led to Turgot's downfall. Later, trade agreements were signed with England in 1786 and with Russia in 1787.

Quesnay's diagram portrays well enough the production and circulation of wealth such as it could be observed in agricultural France of the eighteenth century, and opens the prospect of the development of a capitalist agriculture. Turgot's diagram takes up this prospect of the development of capitalism in agriculture, but presents it alongside a reality of the period which Quesnay neglected: the development of a manufacturing capitalism.

Thus, in the tumult of ideas in eighteenth-century France, an ideological arsenal of extreme diversity was developed: weapons for contesting the

66

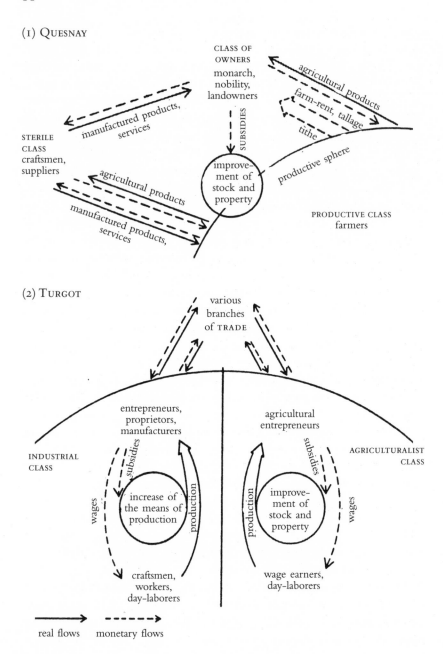

(1) QUESNAY

CLASS OF
OWNERS
monarch,
nobility,
landowners

agricultural products

farm-rent, tallage

tithe

manufactured products,
services

STERILE
CLASS
craftsmen,
suppliers

SUBSIDIES

improve-
ment of
stock and
property

productive sphere

agricultural products

manufactured products,
services

PRODUCTIVE CLASS
farmers

(2) TURGOT

various
branches
of TRADE

entrepreneurs,
proprietors,
manufacturers

agricultural
entrepreneurs

INDUSTRIAL
CLASS

AGRICULTURALIST
CLASS

subsidies

wages

increase of
the means of
production

production

production

improve-
ment of
stock and
property

subsidies

wages

craftsmen,
workers,
day-laborers

wage earners,
day-laborers

real flows   monetary flows

DIAGRAM 7   SOCIAL CLASSES AND NET PRODUCTION
ACCORDING TO QUESNAY AND TURGOT

monarchy (social contract, general will, democracy), for questioning the privileges of the nobility (freedom, equality), for rallying the peasants and urban artisans (freedom, equality, property), and for responding to the aspirations of the manufacturers and traders (freedom, once more, but to produce and to trade).

The long stand-off of the nobility and the bourgeoisie reached a denouement in the crises at the end of the century, the bourgeoisie knowing how, initially, to gain support from peasant discontent and the movement of the people. They found additional allies among certain layers of the nobility and clergy.

The main aspirations of the rising bourgeoisie were attained in the revolution of 1789: the abolishment of privileges, the dismantling of the corporative order of guild wardenships, the abolishment of the privileges of trading companies, and the suppression of mining company monopolies. The king was swept away in the great whirlwind of revolution.

During the Estates-General of 1789, some workers, not admitted into the main assemblies which drew up the records of grievances, put forward a "record of the poor," demanding "that wages no longer be so coldly calculated following the murderous maxims of unbridled luxury or of insatiable cupidity; that the preservation of a working and useful man be for the Constitution an object no less sacred than the property of the rich, and that no working man be uncertain of his subsistence...."[61] The law of Le Chapelier (1791) suppressed workers' associations and prohibited masters as well as workers from organizing themselves or acting together, and from "decision-making and deliberating ... about their supposed common interests.... All crowds composed of artisans or workers ... or incited by them will be considered to be riots."[62] Its victory against the nobility appearing to be assured, the bourgeoisie was already protecting itself against the working classes.

AT THE DAWN OF THE INDUSTRIAL REVOLUTION IN ENGLAND

An anonymous text of 1791, entitled *Considerations upon the East India Trade*, showed remarkable perspicacity:

> Let this not be taken as a paradox: the trade with India may have as a consequence the manufacturing of goods with less labor, and while wages remain the same there may be a general lowering of prices. For if goods can be manufactured with less work, their prices, naturally, will be lower.... The India trade

will very likely provide the opportunity to introduce more order and regularity into our English industries. It will, in effect, cause the disappearance of those industries which are the least useful and the least profitable. The people who were employed there will look for other occupations, the simplest and the easiest they can find, or else they will apply themselves to partial and specialized tasks in more complicated industries. For the simplest work is the most quickly learned, and is the work carried out with the greatest degree of perfection and diligence. Thus the India trade will have the following result: the different operations that make up the most difficult tasks will be entrusted to several qualified workers, instead of being left to the skill of one overburdened worker alone.... Finally the East India trade, by bringing us manufactured goods at prices lower than ours, will very probably have the effect of obliging us to invent processes and machines which will enable us to produce with less man-power and fewer expenditures. This will lead to a reduction in the prices of manufactured goods.[63]

In fact, production in England at the beginning of the eighteenth century was still predominantly agricultural and at the craft level. Wood was used not only as fuel, but also for the tanning of hides, and furnished the potash used in textile and glass manufacturing and the tar used in ship construction: as soon as it began to become scarce, these activities suffered for lack of it. Large numbers of artisans who owned their own tools yet continued to farm produced fabrics, knives (Sheffield), arms, ironmongery, trinkets (Birmingham), and pins (Bristol). Increasingly, merchant-manufacturers had the processing of raw materials done for them. Within this framework the catalyst for change became worldwide trade, which was largely based upon colonial exploitation.

COLONIAL EXPLOITATION AND THE WORLD MARKET

At the end of the seventeenth century the India Company became the object of sharp attacks by traders lacking privileges, interlopers who made every effort after the revolution of 1688 to do away with the India Company's monopoly. In 1698 they formed a competing company. Then in 1702 an accord was reached which led in 1708 to a merger of the two companies into one, called the United Company (1709).

It was at this time that tea, introduced in England since the beginning of the Restoration, became an article of regular importation; that Chinese porcelains, long valued by the Dutch and made fashionable by Queen Mary, became the rage at the court and among upper-class English society; and that fabrics of printed cotton, chintz, calico and muslin whose names even exposed their oriental origin became so widespread as to alarm the manufacturers of woolen cloth.

The trade with the Indies extended to a great diversity of products, assumed many forms and increasingly became one of the indispensable elements in the wealth of England.[64]

During this same time the Bank of England was created (1694). It was started by a group of financiers who promised to lend the Crown £1,500,000 at 8 percent, necessary to cover the expenses of the war against Flanders; in return they received "the title of corporation, with the right to receive deposits, to discount commercial bills—in short, to carry out all the operations of a bank."[65] In 1708 the bank obtained a monopoly on the issuance of bank notes for England and Wales; though, faithful to the tradition of the London financiers, the bank was especially interested in worldwide exchanges: it borrowed in order to lend (particularly to trading companies and states), accepted or guaranteed bills of exchange, and insured payments throughout the world. It was the provincial banks, often created by manufacturers—among them Lloyds and Barclays—which filled the more "modest" needs of industrialists and dealer-fabricators.[66] In the city of London there were 24 banks in 1725, 42 in 1770, and 52 in 1786; the number of National Banks, however, rose from 12 in 1755 to 150 in 1776 and 400 in 1793.

The commercial expansion was tremendous. The value of commercial exchange increased by a factor of 5.5 during the century, while the national income quadrupled. English commerce was foremost in the world and included the export trade (manufactured products, coal, and, less and less, wheat); the transportation of goods for traders of other countries; and warehousing, at the heart of the tightly knit network of exchanges which crossed between the Americas, the Indies, Mediterranean Europe and the Europe of the Baltic. This many-sided commerce transformed the whole of England.

The development of triangular trade and of shipping and shipbuilding led to the growth of the great seaport towns.... It was the slave and sugar trades which made Bristol the second city of England for the first three-quarters of the eighteenth century.... When Bristol was outstripped in the slave trade by Liverpool, it turned its attention from the triangular trade to the direct sugar trade.... Not until the Act of Union of 1707 was Scotland allowed to participate in colonial trade. That permission put Glasgow on the map. Sugar and tobacco underlay the prosperity of the town in the eighteenth century.... The growth of Manchester was intimately associated with the growth of Liverpool, its outlet to the sea and the world market. The capital accumulated by Liverpool from the slave trade poured into the hinterland to fertilize the energies of Manchester; Manchester goods for Africa were taken to the coast in the Liverpool slave vessels.[67] Guns formed a regular part of every African cargo. Birmingham became a center of the gun trade as Manchester was of the cotton trade.[68]

The development of exchange necessitated an improvement in the means of transport, and work on the highway network was undertaken from the middle of the century onward. This work was based not upon the corvée, as in France and several other countries on the continent, but upon the initiative of local associations (large landowners, traders, shepherds, farmers) who financed the roads and collected the tolls. Carts for hauling goods replaced packhorses; commercial travelers carried samples and took orders, eventually competing with the merchants at the market fairs. But even more than roads, this period was the opening of the epoch of canals: at the request of the textile manufacturers of Leeds, Wakefield, and Halifax, the Aire and the Calder were made navigable; work performed along the Trent and the Derwent encouraged the industrial development of Derby and Nottingham; the dredging of the Mersey, and construction of the canal, around 1720, facilitated exchange between Liverpool and Manchester. Other work on rivers and the digging of canals simplified the transport of coal, above all to Liverpool and Manchester, and led to a halving in the cost of coal. Toward the end of the century a regular network of canals promoted the circulation of goods between the different centers of English commercial activity.

To produce more in order to sell more: this was one step in the spiral which had definitely begun in England, with the many changes this involved for agriculture, mining, and processing activity.

The Emergence of Capitalist Production: The Mill

The enclosures movement continued vigorously during the eighteenth century, particularly after 1760; increasingly it took the form of laws voted by Parliament (enclosure acts). Squatters living on the commons were driven off; impoverished peasants who owned tiny patches of land could not bear the costs of enclosure and were unable to live on the poor lands they received; they left, as did others, which rendered useless the expansion of animal breeding. Still others left after being induced to sell their farms to the large landowner nearby. One saw "the rich man's joys increase, the poor's decay."[69] Spurred on by the landed aristocracy, Lord Townshend at their head, and by the large landowners, modern methods of cultivation and animal breeding were instigated, including draining the swamps, plows made of iron, selection and cross-breeding of stock, and crop rotation.

These changes in property and agricultural usage made available a considerable labor force, deprived though it often was of the essentials for living. This labor force made possible an increase in mining and manufacturing production.

Stimulated by the scarcity of wood and encouraged by the reduction in the costs of transportation, the production of coal doubled once during the first half of the century (from 2.5 to 5 million tons) and again during the second half of the century (reaching 10 million tons in 1800: two-thirds of European production as a whole). The system of wage payments to workers expanded, though in Scotland workers in the coal and salt mines were serfs—by law until 1775, with some holdouts until the end of the century. They were bound to the mine, were sold with it, and wore a collar engraved with the name of their owner.[70]

Work at a craft level remained important for processing activity, though other forms of production competed. Work at home for a merchant-manufacturer extended to formerly independent artisans and to peasant families, and constituted the principal form of British manufacturing capitalism: the dealer sent his agents "to distribute the supplies, either directly to the dispersed spinners and weavers, or else to the manufacturers in the countryside who in their turn divided up the supplies."[71] Manufacturing which brought together in a single building various workers producing with traditional methods was never highly developed in England, and in any case never became dominant there. What, on the other hand, did develop during the second half of the century was the system of mills in a movement which at first was slow but which then accelerated.

Throughout this period of improvements, technical inventions responded to the desire for increasing production. At the beginning of the century John Lombe learned in Livorno, Italy, the secrets of the Italian machines for spinning silk; with his brother he constructed a mill (1717) which received a license for fourteen years. During this same time the Darbys, ironmasters at Coalbrookdale, improved the production of cast iron with mixtures of coke, peat, and coal dust, making use of powerful blowers. Steam-powered atmospheric pumps were used in the mines to drain them of water. In 1733 the weaver John Kay invented the "flying shuttle," which permitted textile production in greater quantity, and in larger single pieces. Though his house was destroyed by angry workers and artisans, the flying shuttle became widespread twenty-five years later. In 1735 the Darbys carried out the smelting of iron with coke, a practice which was applied generally in England by 1760. In 1749 Huntsmann, a clockmaker from the Sheffield region, made cast steel, though in small quantities.

From 1730 to 1760 the use of iron rose by 50 percent (tools and instruments for agriculture and processing, especially). From 1740 to 1770 the consumption of cotton rose by 117 percent, but the development of weaving created a scarcity of thread. Then in 1764 the weaver James Hargreaves perfected the spinning jenny, a hand-operated spinning wheel which permitted several threads to be spun at one time. In 1767 the wool-comber Thomas Highs, and in 1768–70 the barber Arkwright, devised the water-frame to harness the energy of running water to activate the spinning wheels. Use of the spinning jenny spread among workers in the home, despite angry protests and destruction of machines by out-of-work artisans (for example, in 1777–79). Combining these two inventions, Compton, a spinner and weaver, put into working order in 1779 the mule jenny, and spinning mills were set up along waterways.

In a parallel development, Watt, a scientist who was not averse to technique, invented the single-effect steam engine, which was being used in industry by 1775. The production of iron advanced: in 1776 the first iron rails were produced (the use of which became widespread in the mines), in 1779 the first iron bridge was made, and in 1787, despite the derision of the incredulous, the first iron boat was floated. The puddling of iron, by means of the decarburation of cast iron, was carried out by Henry Cort, a master smith, and Peter Onions, a foreman, in 1783.

In 1783 Watt produced the double-effect steam engine, and in 1785 the first spinning mill run by steam engines was constructed at Nottingham. It was then the development of weaving which lagged behind, in the face of an abundant production of thread: in 1785 the pastor Cartwright made a mechanical loom which was gradually perfected and which was put into general use by the end of the century. At the same time, technical advances took place in other aspects of textile production (machines for threshing, carding, rough spinning, bleaching, dyeing) and in other industries (paper mills, saw mills, woodworking).

It was in this movement that a new form of production, the mill, had its beginning. The mill used an energy source (coal for heat, water power to run the apparatuses) and machines. It was only at the end of the century that the steam engines conceived of and worked on by Watt between 1765 and 1775 were used to power machines (there were about 500 in service around 1800). With this energy a system of machines was set into operation which necessarily resulted in an organization of production and of work rhythms, and which involved a new discipline for the laborers who served the machines. Spinning mills were built and installed in brick buildings four or five stories high, employing several hundred workers; iron and cast iron mills gathered together several blast furnaces and forges.

Those who had been artisans or who had worked at home loathed going to work in these mills, where they were "subjected to inflexible regulations, and driven like gear-wheels by the pitiless movement of a mechanism without a soul. Entering a mill was like entering barracks or a prison."[72] It was, then, from among the wretched proletariat driven from the open countryside that the first industrialists found their laborers:

> The personnel in the mills was at the beginning composed of the most disparate elements: peasants chased away from their villages by the expansion of large properties, laid-off soldiers, indigents in the care of the parish, outcasts of every class and every trade. The manufacturer had to instruct, train, and above all, discipline these inexperienced workers, who had little preparation in working together: he had to transform them so to speak into a human mechanism, as regular in its workings, as precise in its movements, and as exactly combined for the purpose of producing a single product as the wood and metal mechanism of which these workers became the auxiliary. Instead of the unconstrained atmosphere of the small workshops, there arose the most inflexible rules: the arrival of the workers, their meals, and their leaving were timed by a bell. Inside the mill, everyone had his assigned place and his strictly delimited task, always the same; each person had to work with regularity and without stopping, under the eye of the foreman who forced obedience with the threat of fines or of dismissal, and sometimes with even more brutal compulsions.[73]

In textile manufacturing the workforce was mainly composed of women and children, especially children receiving aid who were supplied by the parishes: in 1789, for example, in the three Arkwright mills in Derbyshire, out of a labor force of 1,150 persons, two-thirds were children.

Thus began in England the capitalist transformation of production, one aspect of which will later be stressed under the name of the industrial revolution: colonial domination, worldwide trade, and merchant capitalism, with the development of exchange, an increasing supply of primary products (tea, sugar, cotton) and an increase in market outlets (textiles, manufactured products); enclosures and the first modernization of agriculture supplied an uprooted and available proletariat; the scientific spirit and techniques applied to production led to a series of inventions which grew one upon the other; available capital, especially from commerce and agriculture, allowed for the construction of mills. Production increased tremendously, the system of wage payments for workers was extended, and workers' struggles multiplied and became organized.[74]

The state played a large role in this, with protectionist measures and the licenses and monopolies of mercantilist policies; with political and military support for commercial and colonial expansion; with the police against the poor and the suppression of workers' revolts: the law of 1769 classified as a felony the voluntary destruction of machines and the buildings which contained them, and instituted the death penalty for those found guilty of this crime. Troops were sent to break up riots in 1779 in Lancaster and in 1796 in Yorkshire; the law of 1799 prohibited workers' associations formed for the purpose of obtaining wage increases, reduction in the working day, or any other improvement in the conditions of employment or work.[75]

At the heart of this diverse and active movement was the first outline of the fusion of the future bourgeoisie: members of the aristocracy giving life to commercial enterprises, farms, and mines; great merchants and financiers displaying their success by the purchase of estates; merchants becoming manufacturers and then establishing mills; manufacturers and dealers becoming bankers: they handled the whole of the country's business. Among the men of the law, the local notables, the well-off farmers, the men of the Church and of the university, there were at this time 450,000 who had the right to vote: it was their interests which were reflected in the voting of Parliament (enclosure acts, poor laws, laws against workers, etc.). Their influence was that much greater because the politics of the country were not well understood by the two "German kings," George I (1714–27) and George II (1727–60). Under this constitutional monarchy, the traditional aristocracy and the rising bourgeoisie were in possession of the real power. William Pitt recognized this in the famous aphorism: "British policy is British trade."

PROGRESS OF POLITICAL ECONOMY AND OF LIBERALISM

The progression of liberal ideas and awareness of the new economic reality: these two aspects of a double movement were linked.

Already the English banker Richard Cantillon, in his *Essay on the Nature of Trade in General* (written in 1734 and published in 1755), widened the break with mercantilist thinking, pointing out particularly that "an overabundance of money, while it lasts, forms the strength of states, but by degrees it rejects them and pushes them naturally into indigence"; he prepared the way for physiocracy by exalting the economic role of property owners. David Hume, in his *Economic Essays* (1752), emphasized in his turn that wealth does not reside in an abundance of precious metals, since these metals, by bringing a rise in prices, lead to a disequilibrium in the balance of trade. He carried his analysis further into the reasons for "the advantage of foreign trade, from the point of view of increasing State power, as well as of the wealth and happiness of the subjects":

> the advantage of foreign commerce, in augmenting the power of the state, as well as the riches and happiness of the subject. It increases the stock of labour in the nation, and the sovereign may convert what share of it he finds necessary to the service of the public. Foreign trade, by its imports, furnishes material for new manufactures; and by its exports, it produces labour in particular commodities, which could not be consumed at home. In short, a kingdom, that has a large import and export, must abound more with industry, and that employed upon delicacies and luxuries, than a kingdom which rests contented with its native commodities. It is, therefore, more powerful, as well as richer and happier.[76]

He stressed to the point of caricature the liberal logic according to which people have to be governed not by regulations and controls, but rather by their own interests: "Their greed must be made insatiable, their ambition beyond measure, and all their vices profitable for the public good" (*The Independence of Parliament*, 1741). Situated within the Newtonian perspective of universal attraction, the idea was being elaborated that from the attraction of multiple interests and multiple individual egoisms, a new social harmony can arise.

Adam Smith was more explicit. A disciple of Hume, he pursued the thinking that Hume had developed in his *Treatise on Human Nature* (1738). In his *Theory of Moral Feelings* (1759), Adam Smith tried to justify the social order based upon the quest after individual interests; he emphasized and deepened the notion of sympathy; he justified the enjoyment of nobleness and of wealth, which was the privilege of the few:

> It is well that nature imposes upon us in this manner. It is this deception which rouses and keeps in continual motion the industry of mankind. It is this which first prompted them to cultivate the ground, to build houses, to found cities and commonwealths, and to invent and improve all the sciences and arts.[77]

He advances the idea of the "invisible hand":

> An invisible hand ... make[s] the same distribution of the necessaries of life which would have been made had the earth been divided into equal portions among its inhabitants; and thus, without intending it, without knowing it, advance the interest of the society, and afford means to the multiplication of the species. When providence divided the earth among a few lordly masters, it neither forgot nor abandoned those who seemed to have been left out in the partition. These last, too, enjoy their share of all that it produces.[78]

Closing his eyes to the wretchedness surrounding him, he goes so far as to write about the poor: "In what constitutes the real happiness of human life, they are in no respect inferior to those who seem so much above them. In ease of body and peace of mind, all the different ranks of life are nearly upon a level, and the beggar, who suns himself by the side of the highway, possesses that security which kings are fighting for."[79]

Chosen as preceptor for a young gentleman, Smith traveled in Europe (1765–66). He met Voltaire, Quesnay, Turgot, d'Alembert, and Helvétius; he frequented the salons. Ten years later he published his *Enquiry into the Nature and Causes of the Wealth of Nations* (1776).

In the name of the interests of the consumers, Smith rejected the mercantilist system. He lampooned Quesnay, "a very speculative physician," and while he acknowledged the physiocrats' contribution to economic science, he thought their chief error to be that of considering "the class of craftsmen, manufacturers and merchants as totally sterile and unproductive." He extolled the obvious and simple system of natural liberty, where:

> Every man, as long as he does not violate the laws of justice, is left perfectly free to pursue his own interest his own way, and to bring both his industry and capital into competition with those of any other man, or order of men. The sovereign is completely discharged from a duty, in the attempting to perform which he must always be exposed to innumerable delusions, and for the proper performance of which no human wisdom or knowledge could ever be sufficient; the duty of superintending the industry of private people, and of directing it towards the employments most suitable to the interest of the society.[80]

In this system:

> the sovereign has only three duties to attend to; three duties of great importance, indeed, but plain and intelligible to common understandings: first, the duty of protecting the society from the violence and invasion of other independent societies; secondly, the duty of protecting, as far as possible, every member of the society from the injustice or oppression of every other member of it, or the duty of establishing an exact administration of justice; and, thirdly, the duty of erecting and maintaining certain public works and certain public institutions....[81]

This is certainly very far from mercantilism.

Smith also observed and analyzed the reality of his own time. He minutely described the division of labor in a mill manufacturing pins; he saw the link between division of labor and mechanization and extension of the market: "The invention of all these machines by which labour is so much facilitated and abridged, seems to have been originally owing to the division of labour." But let us not mistake the perspective: his world is not the world of large industry, nor even that of steam power.

The world of Smith is that of manufacturing capitalism; his "mills" (nails, pins) gather together workers with manual skill; the trades to which he refers remain at the craft level (fuller, spinner, weaver, dyer, master tailor, shoemaker, mason, carpenter, furniture maker, cabinetmaker, cutler, locksmith, etc.); he sees the shopkeepers (grocer, apothecary, butcher, baker, jeweler, goldsmith, barber), the transporters (carter, porter, chair-carrier, sailor), the farmers, the shepherds, the woodcutters.

From the very beginning of his book, Smith emphasized the importance of labor: "The annual labour of every nation is the fund which originally supplies it with all the necessaries and conveniences of life which it annually consumes, and which consist always either in the immediate produce of that labour, or in what is purchased with that produce from other nations." Labor is "the real measure of the exchangeable value of all commodities"; and the labor of the husband and wife should be able to bring them something more than just what is indispensable for their subsistence if they are expected to be able to raise a family.

Smith strictly tied this thinking about productive labor ("which adds value to the object on which it is applied") to his analysis of capital accumulation. For, at heart, what interests him is capital. Smith saw this capital functioning before his eyes, as though on a human scale:

> A capital may be employed in four different ways: either, first, in procuring the rude produce annually required for the use and consumption of the society; or, secondly, in manufacturing and preparing that rude produce for immediate use and consumption; or, thirdly, in transporting either the rude or manufactured produce from the places where they abound to those where they are wanted; or lastly, in dividing particular portions of either into such small parcels as suit the occasional demands of those who want them. In the first way are employed the capitals of all those who undertake the improvement or cultivation of lands, mines, or fisheries; in the second, those of all master manufacturers; in the third, those of all the wholesale merchants; and in the fourth, those of all retailers.[82]

He observed the ways in which this capital functioned: thus, for the master manufacturer, one portion "is employed as a fixed capital in the instruments of his trade.... Part of his circulating capital is employed in purchasing materials.... But a great part of it is always, either annually, or in a much shorter period, distributed among the different workmen whom he employs."[83]

But at the same time, Smith understood the global logic of this capital, the logic of accumulation. Rejecting the criterion, at that time dominant, of the balance of trade, he stressed the importance of "another balance" which "according as it happens to be either favourable or unfavourable, necessarily occasions the prosperity or the decay of every nation":

> This is the balance of the annual produce and consumption. If the exchange-able value of the annual produce, it has already been observed, exceeds that of the annual consumption, the capital of the society must annually increase in proportion to this excess. The society in this case lives within its revenue, and what is annually saved out of its revenue, is naturally added to its capital, and employed so as to increase still further the annual produce.[84]

Then he classified activities according to this criterion: "After agriculture, the capital employed in manufactures puts into motion the greatest quantity of productive labour, and adds the greatest value to the annual produce. That which is employed in the trade of exportation, has the least effect of any of the three."[85] And: "According to the natural course of things, therefore, the greater part of the capital of every growing society is, first, directed to agriculture, afterwards to manufactures, and last of all to foreign commerce."[86]

Thus during the period in which manufacturing capitalism was drawing to a close and industrial capitalism, with its mills, was beginning, Smith analyzed the capital whose accumulation, based upon productive labor, permitted "both the people and the sovereign at the same time to be enriched." Influenced by the ideology of the Enlightenment, of natural laws and universal harmony, Smith put his trust in "the system of natural freedom" which manifests itself by means of the market. He was against agreements between dealers and manufacturers: "People of the same trade seldom meet together, even for merriment and diversion, but the conversation ends in a conspiracy against the public, or in some contrivance to raise prices."[87] He was against anything which might restrain the "freedom to work": "The patrimony of a poor man lies in the strength and dexterity of his hands; and to hinder him from employing this strength and dexterity in what manner he thinks proper without injury to his neighbour, is a plain violation of this most sacred property. It is a manifest encroachment upon the just liberty both of the workman, and of those who might be disposed to employ him."[88] This implied accepting inequality and defending, if need be, the existing social order: "Civil government, so far as it is instituted for the security of property, is in reality instituted for the defence of the rich against the poor."[89]

Thomas Paine carried further the expression of the liberal utopia. In 1776, in *Common Sense*, he registered the distinction between society and government: "Society is produced by our wants, and government by our wickedness.... Society in every state is a blessing, but government even in its best state is but a necessary evil."[90] And if governments approaching the form of a republic have an advantage, it is that in these governments, the sovereign has less to do. In 1791, in *The Rights of Man,* Paine went so far as to see the dissolution of the necessity for government in the formation of a generalized market society.

> The mutual dependence and reciprocal interest which man has upon man, and all the parts of a civilized community upon each other, create that great chain of connection which holds it together. The landholder, the farmer, the manufacturer, the merchant, the tradesman, and every occupation, prospers by the aid which each received from the other, and from the whole. Common interest regulates their concern, and forms their law.... In fine, society performs for itself almost everything which is ascribed to government.... It is to the unceasing circulation of interest, which, passing through its million channels, invigorates the whole mass of civilized man ... infinitely more than to anything which the best instituted government can perform that the safety and prosperity of the individual and of the whole depends.[91]

Without going so far as to foresee or to call for the withering away of the state, the ruling class, the capitalist bourgeoisie, will find in this thinking inexhaustible ideological material.

SUMMARY

The creation of the mill in the eighteenth century established capitalism as a distinctive mode of production. Its development at this time was based upon an accumulation of wealth which continued to come from two principal sources: (a) the traditional extortion of peasant surplus labor; and (b) extreme colonial exploitation taking diverse forms: pillage, forced labor, slavery, unequal exchange, colonial taxes, and so on.

The development of markets (domestic and worldwide) and the expansion of exchange made an increase in production necessary, first in the traditional forms of production (manufacture, work in the home) and then with new techniques and within the framework of the energy-powered mill. In this there lay a third source of value, still limited but in full expansion.

Thus besides the circulation of money ($M \rightarrow M'$), small merchant production ($C \rightarrow M \rightarrow C'$), and commercial exchange ($M \rightarrow C \rightarrow M'$), there developed production organized to make the most of capital:

$$M \rightarrow C \rightarrow \begin{cases} mp \\ lp \end{cases} \rightarrow P \rightarrow C' \rightarrow M'$$

A manufacturer having at his disposal a sum of money M buys goods C (means of production mp and labor power lp), combines them in the production P of goods which carry a value C′, greater than C. The sale of these goods permits him to receive a sum of money M′ = M + ΔM.

Manufacture began this evolution and the mill completed it. This process was made easier by the labor force which had become available through the growth of population and the modernization of agricultural production.

From this time on, though state accumulation continued in the same domains as in preceding centuries (roads, waterways, harbors, fleets, administrative machinery), bourgeois accumulation began a decisive change: while proceeding, of course, through an increase in private fortunes and stocks of merchandise, more and more this accumulation took the form of productive capital (raw materials, machines, mills).

Observant minds (Quesnay, Turgot, Smith) saw the new logic: from productive labor, a "net product" was extracted which allowed particularly for the setting up of "advances" owing to which the bases of production could be enlarged or improved. Marx will later analyze this as "the formal submission of labor to capital," where techniques remain at the craft and mill-work stage, and where the principal means for extracting surplus value are the extension of working time and the intensification of labor.[92]

The principal agent of this movement was the bourgeoisie which was formed from the banking and commercial bourgeoisies, from dealers and manufacturers who had become rich, and, in England, from a portion of the nobility. This new ruling class everywhere cultivated a key word: *freedom*.

In England, where this class was involved with the affairs of state, the freedom in question was above all economic freedom: freedom of trade and of production, as well as freedom to pay for labor power at the lowest possible price, and so to defend itself against workers' alliances and revolts.

In France, where the working class was excluded from the affairs of state, the freedom which was called for was above all political freedom: the suppression of privileges, a constitution, equality. Aspirations for economic liberalism were present in France as well, however.

With the French and American revolutions, and with the development of the "industrial revolution," a new period opened up, characterized by the irresistible rise of capitalism. At the same time the transforming capacity of capitalism increased, due to several developments: the expansion of the terrain open to the market, including the market on a world scale; new techniques and new ways to organize production; transformations of society then beginning, especially in England.

Though each of these aspects is visible, the movement as a whole remains for the most part opaque to the men and women who lived through it: hadn't there already been market expansions, technical progress, and social changes during other historical periods? Nothing allowed them to foresee that in the changes going on around them lay the beginning of a spiraling development whose intensification would represent a break relative to all previous history.

Among the transforming forces at work within European societies, the state remains the most powerful. Its role is to establish the conditions necessary for a national market, to encourage and protect production renewal, and to organize conquest and domination in the world.

Many aspects of science amaze and fascinate the enlightened minds of the time, though science is praised more for the promises it carries and the progress it indicates than for its immediate, concrete effects.

As for capital and the capitalists, a few economists sense and perceive their importance, though none of the economists imagines capital's enormous potential for overturning production, the market, society, and the world.

Chapter 3

THE IRRESISTIBLE RISE OF
INDUSTRIAL CAPITALISM
(1800–70)

Can the path covered in three centuries be seen clearly enough? At the beginning of the sixteenth century, in the name of God and the king, armed expeditions conquered large areas in the Americas, massacring, pillaging, and bringing back fabulous treasures. At the end of the eighteenth century, in the name of nature and freedom, economists, anxious to discover the source of wealth, described the conditions of capital accumulation.

What was at stake at first was the wealth of the prince; then it became a question of healthy royal finances and of enriching the nation, especially by means of exports; following this, in the same perspective, the manufacturing and labor of the nation were stressed. The next factor to be considered closely was productive labor: the labor which permits a surplus to be extracted by means of which production can be carried out on an enlarged scale.

National unity was established around the person of the king, against feudalism, but also against other kings, in a terrible succession of wars. The rising class took shelter in royal authority against the nobility; this class used mercantilist ideas to promote its own interests, in the time before its most advanced and strongest elements adopted liberal ideas. At the end of the eighteenth century, the idea of the nation was asserted against the king.

God and the nobility, religion and the order which grew out of feudalism, ensured social cohesion. God was torn apart in the Reformation and disintegrated or became abstract at the hands of the philosophers; the nobility, between the king and the bourgeoisie, were losing their power and their privileges. Thinking about the social contract, about political regimes, and about democracy gave the bourgeoisie the institutional forms and the justifications for the types of government it was able to control: it could, from this time on, do without a king.

82

Colonial domination, pillage, and exploitation of imported or native slaves throughout this period constituted a fundamental source of enrichment for the colonizing countries. In the sixteenth century the greatest portion of the wealth passed first of all through royal treasuries; in the eighteenth century this wealth was first handled by colonial companies and financiers. But already conflicts of interest were arising which opposed the bourgeoisies of Europe against the descendants of colonists who had come from Europe. These colonial descendants fought in the name of the European bourgeoisies' own ideas of democracy and freedom, even as in their own countries they used slave labor and massacred the Indians.

Monopoly *and* competition; state intervention *and* private initiative; the world market *and* the national interest were, under different forms, present together throughout the formation of capitalism. This formation was given life by the national bourgeoisies; was upheld and defended by national states; and was supported by the workers of these countries and by the subjugated or dominated peoples throughout the world.

During the years 1790–1815, the attention of all eyes was drawn by the French revolution and the wars which rent Europe. Less spectacular, another revolution began in England, through which the capitalist logic of production was established and enlarged: the exploitation of a growing number of workers *and* the production of an ever greater mass of goods. At one pole a vertiginous accumulation of wealth; at the other an increase and aggravation of misery. Through the industrialization movement of the nineteenth century, this logic imposed itself with greater and greater force among widening sectors of society.

At the turn of the century, harsh ideological conflicts expressed the sharpening of contradictions which this evolution developed.

THE CONFLICT OF IDEAS

At the beginning of the nineteenth century, the capitalist development of industry, which had been set in motion in England, was still far from being dominant. A new generation of manufacturers and industrialists asserted themselves (with Jean-Baptiste Say in France and David Ricardo in England as their spokesmen), but the industrial bourgeoisie did not yet constitute a distinct social layer. The mill workers, a great many of whom were women and children, were subjected to the pitiless discipline of mechanical production and the terrible menace of unadorned wretchedness: uprooted and without culture or stability, they did not at this time form a class.

On the other hand, the classes of the former society were still very much present: nobility and landowners; farmers, artisans, shopkeepers. They felt the change which was beginning to affect them, and it was often from among these classes that voices were raised to criticize the transformations which were occurring, either in the name of the values of the past (Burke in England; Bonald and Maistre in France), or in the name of an alternative society conceived according to the norms of reason and equity (Godwin and Owen in England; Saint-Simon and Fourier in France).

In the debates which took place at this time, the chief ideas were affirmed which would be taken up again and again during the first half of the century, and in the case of certain of these ideas, throughout the century and even to our own time.

OF POOR AND RICH

Writing at the end of the century, William Godwin denounced inequality born of accumulation. He appreciated that what was fundamental to inequality was the exploitation of labor:

> There is scarcely any species of wealth, expenditure or splendour, existing in any civilized country, that is not, in some way, produced by the express manual labour, and corporeal industry, of the inhabitants of that country. The spontaneous productions of the earth are few, and contribute little to wealth, expenditure or splendour. Every man may calculate, in every glass of wine he drinks, and every ornament he annexes to his person, how many individuals have been condemned to slavery and sweat, incessant drudgery, unwholesome food, continual hardships, deplorable ignorance, and brutal insensibility, that he may be supplied with these luxuries. It is a gross imposition that men are accustomed to put upon themselves when they talk of the property bequeathed to them by their ancestors. The property is produced by the daily labour of men who are now in existence. All that their ancestors bequeathed to them was a mouldy patent which they show as a title to extort from their neighbours what the labour of those neighbours has produced.[1]

It is the social logic of this exploitation which Godwin lays bare:

> If, inequality being thus introduced, the poorer member of the community shall be so depraved as to be willing, or so unfortunately circumstanced as to be driven, to make himself the hired servant or labourer of his richer neighbour, this probably is not an evil to be corrected by the interposition of government. But, when we have gained this step, it will be difficult to set bounds to the extent of accumulation in one man, or of poverty and wretchedness in another.[2]

This exploitation invades the domain of ideas and of values: "The spirit of oppression, the spirit of servility, and the spirit of fraud: these are the immediate growth of the established administration of property."[3]

The Reverend Thomas Robert Malthus observed the same inequality, the same misery, the same crushing of those having the least means, but it was these poor themselves whom Malthus accused. He began with two postulates:

> First, That food is necessary to the existence of man.
>
> Secondly, That the passion between the sexes is necessary and will remain nearly in its present state ...
>
> Assuming then, my postulate as granted, I say, that the power of population is indefinitely greater than the power in the earth to produce subsistence for man.
>
> Population, when unchecked, increases in a geometrical ratio. A slight acquaintance with numbers will shew the immensity of the first power in comparison of the second.
>
> By that law of our nature which makes food necessary to the life of man, the effects of these two unequal powers must be kept equal.
>
> This implies a strong and constantly operating check on population from the difficulty of subsistence. This difficulty must fall somewhere and must necessarily be severely felt by a large portion of mankind.[4]

The philanthropist, the legislator, are powerless: "It is not in the power of the rich to supply the poor with an occupation and with bread, and consequently the poor, by the very nature of things have no right to demand these things from the rich." "No possible contributions of sacrifices of the rich, particularly in money, could for any time prevent the recurrence of distress among the lower members of society." For Malthus, this is fundamentally a problem of individual morality: "Everyone must delay the establishment of his own happiness until, through his labour and savings, he has put himself in a situation where he can provide for the needs of his family." From this time on, the poor man, the wretch, is guilty for not having respected the law of nature:

> To the punishment therefore of nature he should be left, the punishment of want. He has erred in the face of a most clear and precise warning, and can have no just reason to complain of any person but himself when he feels the consequences of his error. All parish assistance should be denied him; and he should be left to the uncertain support of private charity. He should be taught to know that the laws of nature, which are the laws of God, had doomed him and his family to suffer for disobeying their repeated admonitions.... It may appear to be hard that a mother and her children, who have been guilty of no particular crime themselves, should suffer for the ill conduct of the father; but this is one of the invariable laws of nature.[5]

Malthus goes on to elaborate these ideas in a celebrated passage, which, however, is not included in later editions:

> A man who is born into a world already possessed, if he cannot get subsistence from his parents on whom he has a just demand, and if the society do not want his labour, has no claim of right to the smallest portion of food and, in fact, has no business to be where he is. At nature's mighty feast there is no vacant cover for him. She tells him to be gone, and will quickly execute her orders, if he do not work upon the compassion of some of her guests. If these guests get up and make room for him, other intruders immediately appear demanding the same favor. The report of a provision for all that come, fills the hall with numerous claimants. The order and harmony of the feast is disturbed, the plenty that before reigned is changed to scarcity; and the happiness of the guests is destroyed by the spectacle of misery and dependence in every part of the hall, and by the clamorous importunity of those, who are justly enraged at not finding the provision which they had been taught to expect. The guests learn too late their error, in counteracting those strict orders to all intruders, issued by the great mistress of the feast, who, wishing all her guests should have plenty, and knowing that she could not provide for unlimited numbers, humanely refused to admit fresh comers when her table was already full.[6]

Here, for the pious souls, was enough to render perfectly bearable the terrible misery of the workers and people of the time. For the rational minds, the economists showed the "scientific necessity" of this misery: was it not a result of the "iron law of wages"? Jean-Baptiste Say described in these terms how wages are determined: "When ... demand lags behind the number of people available for work, their earnings decline below the rate necessary for the class [of workers] to maintain their numbers. The families most burdened with children and infirmities perish; from then on the labor supply declines, and since labor is in lower supply, its price goes up."[7] Ricardo, having described the same movement, judged it to be necessary: "Like all other contracts, wages should be left to the fair and free competition of the market, and should never be controlled by the intervention of the legislature." This led him to denounce the English poor laws: "Instead of making the poor rich, they are calculated to make the rich poor."[8]

THE TWO UTOPIAS

Two utopian visions of a world to come were formulated on a wide scale at the beginning of the century; each one guaranteed the happiness of all: on one side the liberal vision, and on the other side the vision based upon an organization of society that in the second third of the century came to be called "socialist."

"Laissez-faire," Turgot and Smith had said, regarding corporate organization, mercantilist policies, the monopolies of the large companies, and the mills benefiting from licenses. "Laissez-faire" without restriction, said the "economists" of the nineteenth century.

For Say, Property, Freedom, and Prosperity are indissociable: property of the productive capital and of the profits which can be drawn from it; freedom to use this capital: "Any restriction which is not necessary to protect the rights of another person is an attack against property";[9] prosperity for all—for the poor and for the rich—because "their interests are exactly the same." Certainly, "it is a great unhappiness to be poor, but it is an even greater unhappiness to be surrounded by people as poor as oneself. Lacking wealth oneself, one must wish wealth for others: an indigent has infinitely greater possibilities for earning his living and becoming well off if he lives among a rich population, than if he is surrounded by poor people like himself. And note that here the hope of the poor is not founded upon the charity of the rich, but upon the interest of the rich. It is in his own interest that the rich man supplies the poor man with land to cultivate, tools, fertilizer, and seeds, and with food on which to live until the harvest."[10]

For Ricardo, the free play of the market, that is to say, the law of supply and demand, assures equilibrium: not only economic equilibrium but also equilibrium among the three classes of society (landowners, owners of capital, and laborers), even if their interests appear to be contradictory. This same process also assures equilibrium between nations, the play of comparative costs and of specialization guaranteeing the reciprocal interest of all nations.

In this spirit, what could be called the "liberal utopia" developed and became more definite: property, free enterprise, and the free play of the market should ensure the best of all possible worlds. This implies reducing as much as possible what comes from the state: "Governmental action is essentially restricted to ensuring order, security, and justice," wrote Bastiat. "Beyond this limit, it is a usurpation of conscience, intelligence, and of labor—in a word, of human freedom."[11] And for the rest? Laissez-faire! Except, of course, "to *prevent* dishonest things." But "as for things which are innocent in themselves, such as work, exchange, teaching, association, banking, etc., one must still choose. The state must either let things be (*laisse faire*), or impose restrictions (*empêche de faire*). If the state lets things be, we will be free and economically administered, for nothing costs less than letting things be. If the state imposes restrictions, this is a calamity for our freedoms and our purse."[12]

This "liberal utopia" from its beginnings possessed the capacity of presenting itself as "scientifically founded": "The economists" (read, Liberals), Bastiat continues on, "observe man, the laws of his organization, and the social relations resulting from these laws." Bastiat opposed this to the approach of the socialists: "The socialists imagine a fantasy society and then a human heart matching that society."[13]

Opposed to the liberal utopia were egalitarian, social, and associationist utopias, which during the 1830s came to be described with one word: socialist. At the time of the French revolution, the writings of l'Ange and Babeuf, and the conjuration of the Equals, bear witness to this. A few sentences from the *Manifesto of the Equals*, drawn up by Sylvain Maréchal, give an idea of the tone:

> People of France!
> For fifteen centuries you have lived as slaves, and consequently, unhappily. For the last six years you have barely breathed, waiting for independence, happiness, and equality.
> Equality! first wish of nature, first need of man, and principal bond of any legitimate association.... Well! we mean from now on to live and die as equals, as we were born: we want real equality or death; this is what we must have.....
> The French revolution is only the forerunner of another much larger and much more solemn revolution, which will be the final revolution....
> The time has come to found the Republic of the Equals, this great home open to all men. The days of the general restitution have arrived. Lamenting families, come sit at the common table set by nature for all her children....
> On the day after this true revolution, they will wonder in amazement: What! General happiness depended on so little? We had only to want it. Ah, why didn't we want it sooner?[14]

Saint-Simon and Fourier also give evidence of utopian socialist thinking. They were admirers of Newton and were fascinated by the harmony originating in universal attraction. In his dream of 1803, Saint-Simon saw the administration of the earth entrusted to a "council of Newton" composed of scientists and artists.[15] In his *Theory of the Four Movements* (1808), Fourier outlined the single, constant, and general law of "passionate attraction"; "phalansteries," complete and autonomous societies of 1,800 persons, were to be the base units of a new "universal harmony." Utopia is here in force: the living certainty of another world, another society, at arm's reach. Saint-Simon paid more attention to "industry," that is to say, to the various forms of productive activity; he emphasized the role of industrialists. He directed his writing toward the workers and was occupied with improving the living conditions "of the most numerous and poorest class."[16]

Fourier criticized the incoherence of the society which he called a "self-contradictory world" and bondage to "repulsive labor"; he extolled the "common sense world," the realization of the state of fellowship founded on "natural, appealing, and truthful industry," of which the phalanstery would be the base unit.[17]

Robert Owen was more pragmatic; at the end of a brilliant career—he was production manager of a spinning mill at age nineteen and boss of a big mill at age twenty-eight—he was one of the first "social employers" of capitalist industry: during the whole first quarter of the nineteenth century, his factory at New Lanark was a model which people came to visit from near and far. Then Owen proposed reforming the whole of society; he questioned religion and the family, and lost the support of the liberal bourgeoisie. With the creation of New Harmony in the United States, he endeavored to realize the utopia he envisioned, a combination of co-operation and communism. It was a failure (1829–29). Owen then became the moving spirit of the British workers' movement and a tireless propa-gandist for his convictions and beliefs.

Thus, faced with the liberal utopia (human happiness assured by the free play of supply and demand in all domains), socialist utopias (human happiness assured by the proper organization of society) were deployed. The former very quickly took the appearance of science ("the law of supply and demand," "the iron law of wages"), while the latter had the tendency to degenerate into mysticism and sectarianism. The liberal utopian vision was taken up and utilized by the merchant flank of the bourgeoisie each time it had need of free rein—against regulations and the corpora-tions, against monopolies and licenses, against laws concerning the poor, and against protectionism. The socialist utopian vision found an echo among the technicians (Saint-Simon, common people (tradespeople and workers), and especially the petty bourgeoisie (artisans and shopkeepers).

Marx provided a scientific version of the socialist utopia by demon-strating, by means of a historical and economic analysis of capitalism, that communism must "necessarily" follow capitalism. The many associationist and cooperative achievements, the struggles by the common people and by the workers, the formation and maturation of the working classes—all these anchored the socialist project and gave it concreteness.[18]

WHAT IS THE SOURCE OF WEALTH?

The economists took up this fundamental question from the book by Adam Smith; along with others, the Englishman David Ricardo and the

Frenchman Jean-Baptiste Say opposed each other over the question of the origin of wealth.

Born in 1772, the son of a Jewish banker who emigrated to Holland, a stockbroker at twenty-two years of age, Ricardo became rich enough through successful speculations to retire from business at forty-two and buy an estate. He became a Member of Parliament in 1819, two years after publishing his principal work, *On the Principles of Political Economy and Taxation*.

Jean-Baptiste Say was born in 1767, the son of a Protestant trader who returned to Lyons from Geneva, where his family had been exiled after the Edict of Nantes. Say worked as a clerk in a bank, traveled in England, and enlisted as a volunteer in the French Revolutionary Wars (1792). Following this, he frequented the "ideological" circles of his time, collaborated on "The Decade," and wrote *Treatise on Political Economy, or a Simple Exposition of the Way in Which Wealth Is Formed, Distributed and Consumed* (1803). He disapproved of the authoritarian measures of the empire and refused the positions which were offered him. During the years 1806–14, he built and ran a cotton spinning mill. Under the Restoration, political economy—at that time tainted with anticlericalism and liberalism—being judged subversive, he was able to teach only at the Athénée, a private institution of higher education (1816–17 and 1818–19) and at the conservatory of arts and trades (from 1820 on); he had to wait until 1830, only a short time before his death, for a chair at the Collège de France.[19]

Say summarized his fundamental ideas in his *Catechism of Political Economy* (1817):

—Is it possible to create wealth?
—Yes, to create wealth, all that is necessary is to create value, or to add to the value which is already found in the things one possesses.
—How can value be added to an object?
—By giving it a use that it did not formerly have.
—How can the value that things already have be increased?
—By increasing the degree of usefulness which existed in them when they were acquired....
—To produce is to give value to things by giving them a use; and the action which results in a product is called Production....
—To whom do the products created each day in a nation belong?
—They belong to the industrious, the capitalists, and the landowners, who, either by themselves or by means of their tools, are the creators of these products, and are consequently what we call producers.[20]

One of the ideological bases of economic thought in the nineteenth and twentieth centuries was hereby presented: to produce is to increase usefulness; three "factors of production"—labor, capital, and land—contribute to production, and are paid for in proportion to their contribution.

Ricardo disagreed with Say on these two points: "Utility," he wrote to Say regarding Say's *Catechism*, "is certainly the foundation of value, but the degree of utility can never be the measure by which to estimate value. A commodity difficult of production will always be more valuable than one which is easily produced.... A commodity must be useful to have value but the difficulty of its production is the true measure of its value. For this reason, Iron though more useful is of less value than gold."[21] In *On the Principles of Political Economy and Taxation*, also published in 1817, Ricardo made his analysis more explicit: he devoted an important first chapter to value. The long section titles of this chapter give the essential in a few sentences: "The value of a commodity, or the quantity of any other commodity for which it will exchange, depends on the relative quantity of labour which is necessary for its production, and not on the greater or less compensation which is paid for that labour." "Not only the labour applied immediately to commodities affect their value but the labour also which is bestowed on the implements, tools and buildings, with which such labour is assisted."

Having thus defined value, of which the price is the monetary expression, the distribution of produced wealth will be based upon wages. Now, "the natural price of labour is that price which is necessary to enable the labourers, one with another, to subsist and to perpetuate their race, without either increase or diminution." From then on, "supposing corn and manufactured goods always to sell at the same price, profits would be high or low in proportion as wages were low or high."[22]

With Say, the interests of the workers, the capitalists, and the landowners are in agreement; with Ricardo, they are in opposition. It is from Ricardo's theses and from the critique of their weak points that Marx will begin to develop his analysis of capital.

The positions of Say and of Ricardo regarding the question of machines are similar: "The use of machines," Say writes in his *Catechism*, is harmful to the working class "only at the time when a new machine is beginning to be used; for experience teaches us that the countries where machines are the most in use are the countries where there is the most employment for workers."[23] Ricardo, discussing the theses of MacCulloch, wrote in 1820: "The employment of machinery I think never diminishes the demand for labour—it is never a cause of a fall in the price of labour, but the effect of its rise."[24] He abandoned this position in 1821, when he added a chapter to the third edition of his *Principles*: "I am convinced, that the substitution of machinery for human labour, is often very injurious to the interests of the class of labourers."[25] However: "The employment of machinery could never be safely discouraged in a State, for if a capital is not allowed to get the greatest net revenue that the use of machinery will afford here, it will be carried abroad, and this must be a much more serious discouragement to the demand for labour, than the most extensive employment of machinery."[26]

These debates were not carried out in thin air, but were rooted in the daily concerns and the confrontations of interest which accompanied the development of mechanical industry.

THE CAPITALIST DEVELOPMENT OF INDUSTRY

During the nineteenth century it was chiefly through the establishment of mechanized industry that the capitalist mode of production was extended. The "mills" which had begun to be built in England at the end of the eighteenth century became more widespread, not only in England itself, but in Belgium, France, Switzerland, Germany, and the United States. The development of these mills was particularly striking in the "driving" sectors of the time: textiles and metallurgy. Men who had previously been traders or merchants, as well as foremen and the sons of artisans, became manufacturers and availed themselves of a labor force that had become available through the transformation of the countryside or through immigration. These laborers were employed with the intention of extracting the maximum, and it was in conditions of misery and unbearable oppression that the original core of the modern working class was formed. This movement was an extension of what had begun in England during the previous century, but with a definite acceleration, which the increase in the annual rate of growth of world industry helps us to understand (see Table 3.1).

THE ADVANCE OF BRITISH CAPITALISM

Capitalist industrialization on a world scale occurred in three major successive flows; 1780–1880 and 1880–1950, with the third still in progress today. Each flux is characterized by a definite extension, both sectorial (by type of industry) and geographic (regional and national).

For the period 1780–1880, three industries had an impact and a rate of growth such that they can be described as driving or propelling industries:

TABLE 3.1   World Industry and Trade, Average Annual Rates of Growth

	World industry	World trade
18th century	1.5*	1.1†
1780–1830	2.6	1.4
1820–40	2.9	2.8
1840–60	3.5	4.8
1860–70	2.9	2.8

* 1705–85   † 1720–80

Source: W. W. Rostow, The World Economy (Austin: University of Texas Press, 1978), p. 67.

cotton, iron, and railroad rails. It was in Great Britain that these industries underwent their earliest and most remarkable development.

With water power and steam engines, which allowed mechanization to reach its full potential for productive output, and employment of a plentiful, cheap, and totally disarmed labor force, levels of production increased dramatically. The British advantage was overwhelming during the whole first half of the century, and remained important after 1850, though it was reduced in certain sectors. The figures indicating quantities of goods produced are eloquent (see Table 3.2).

In England and, with some delay, in France and Germany, this evolution continued, intensified, and accelerated the movement begun in the eighteenth century. In North America a new era was opened by the independence of the United States, and its budding industries were able to benefit from the difficulties which the producers and traders of Europe encountered during the period of wars at the beginning of the century.

These four countries—Great Britain, France, Germany, and the United States—accounted at this time for between two-thirds and three-fifths of the world's industrial production, with the share of Great Britain receding from less than one-quarter to more than one-fifth.

This industrial development inaugurated and then accentuated the end of millennia of primarily agricultural production in overwhelmingly rural societies. A city, with its manufacturing and commercial activities, certainly might have been able to predominate in a small country. But the development of manufacturing activity in this case was occurring for the first time throughout a large country—Great Britain—before spreading to others, France and Germany in particular.

TABLE 3.2   Leading First-generation Industries, Four Principal Capitalist Countries

	Cotton	Cast iron	Railroad rails
GREAT BRITAIN			
Maximum expansion	1780–89	1790–99	1830–39
Leading industry	1780–1869	1780–1889	1830–79
FRANCE			
Maximum expansion	1815–	1850–59	1840–49
Leading industry		1830–59	1840–89
GERMANY			
Maximum expansion	1830–39	1850–59	1840–49
Leading industry		1850–59	1840–89
UNITED STATES			
Maximum expansion	1805–15	1840–49	1830–39
Leading industry	1820–79	1840–1920	1830–99

Source: Compiled from Rostow, *The World Economy*, tables 2, 7, 10, 13, 19.

If material production is divided into two main sectors, agriculture and industry, this evolution appears most noticeably in Great Britain: the share of industry grew from 42 percent to 60 percent in 1831, and reached 73 percent in 1871. In France, industrial production as a percentage of total material production rose from 43 percent in 1781–90 to 55 percent in 1835–44, though it stagnated at this level until 1865–74.[27]

The transformation was felt more deeply in Britain than in France during the first third of the century, and during the second third it continued even more strongly in the land of Queen Victoria, whereas in France the relative backward movement of agriculture was very much slower. To this it must be added that the importance of craft work and of traditional manufacturing activity remained greater in France—while mechanization, and therefore the mill and the factory, were more developed in England. And finally, British industrial development affected more rapidly, and more extensively, the means of production, whose share of total development steadily increased, while in France the production of consumption goods continued to predominate.

Thus in Great Britain the relative importance of production of the means of production within the whole of industrial production, which did not greatly change between 1783 (when it was 29 percent of industrial

TABLE 3.3　First-generation Industrial Production, Four Principal Capitalist Countries

Product	Great Britain	France	Germany	United States
Spun cotton (million lb.)				
1830	250	68	16	77
1850	588	140	46	288
1870	1,101	220	147	400
Coal (million tons)				
1800	10	1	1	—
1830	16	2	1.7	—
1850	49	5	6.7	7
1870	110	13	26.0	30
Cast iron (thousand tons)				
1800	200	60	40	—
1820	400	140	90	20
1840	1,400	350	170	180
1860	3,800	900	500	900
Mechanical power (thousand hp)				
1840	350	34	20	—
1870	900	336	900	—
Railroads (thousand km)				
1850	10.5	3	6	—
1870	24.5	17.5	19.5	52

Source: J. P. Rioux, *La révolution industrielle, 1780–1880* (Paris: Editions du Seuil, 1971), pp. 67, 80, 93, 95, 96.

production as a whole) and 1812 (when it was 31 percent), rose to 40 percent in 1851 and 47 percent in 1881. In France, this part of production remained small throughout the century: 18 percent in 1781–90, 21 percent in 1803–12, and 22 percent in 1875–84.[28] During the same period, the nature of "occupations" and their relative importance changed: a new structure of classes was established.

A NEW CLASS STRUCTURE

Aggregate figures allow us to understand the underlying movements—development of industrial employment, urbanization, and the system of wage payments. In all of these areas, it is in Great Britain that the transformation is most clear.

TABLE 3.4 World Industrial Production (percent)

	Great Britain	France	Germany	Rest of Europe	United States
1820	24	20	15	37	4
1840	21	18	17	38	5
1860	21	16	15	34	14

Source: Rostow, *The World Economy*, pp. 52–53.

The quantitative predominance of the agricultural and rural world remained obvious in France and in the United States; in Great Britain, on the contrary, the world of industry, trade, services, and offices, which at the beginning of the century already accounted for two-thirds of all employment, by 1871 represented more than four-fifths (see Table 3.5).

However, during this period the active population employed in agriculture did not decrease in Great Britain (1.7 million in 1801 and still 1.8 million in 1871); though the manpower employed in industry rose rapidly: 1.4 million in 1801, 3.3 million in 1841, and 5.3 million in 1871. In France the active agricultural population grew (5.5 million in 1781–90 and 7.2 million in 1865–74), and even though the numbers doubled, the manpower employed in industry remained clearly less significant: 1.6 million in 1781–90, 3.5 million in 1835–44, and 3.8 million in 1865–74.

Although the number of workers employed in agriculture and the British countryside remained stable, these regions were an important source of manpower for industry: the exodus from agriculture went from around 25,000 per decade between 1751 and 1780 to 78,000 for the decade of 1781–90, 138,000 between 1801 and 1810, 214,000 between 1811 and 1820, and 267,000 between 1821 and 1830, after which time this movement slowed down considerably.[29]

With the agricultural exodus, to which must be added the flight of ruined artisans, demographic growth gave rise to the formation of a miserable and available labor force which contributed both to the making of the British working class and to British emigration (2.6 million between 1821 and 1850; 4.6 million between 1851 and 1880).[30] Famines were especially deadly in Ireland, as this observation by Fourier shows: "The newspapers of Dublin in 1826 say: 'An epidemic rages here among the people: the sick people who are brought to the hospital get well as soon as they

TABLE 3.5 Active Population (percent)

ENGLAND	Agriculture	Industry and trade	Others
1811	35	45	20
1841	20	43	37
1817	14	55	31

FRANCE	Agriculture, forestry, fishing	Industry, transport, trade, and banking*	Others
1851	64.5	27.5	8
1866	50	37	13

UNITED STATES	Primary†	Secondary	Tertiary
1820	73	12	15
1850	65	17.5	17.5
1870	54	22.5	23.5

* Includes construction and mining.   † Includes mining.

Sources: England and France—P. Bairoch, *Révolution industrielle et sous-développement* (Paris: SEDES, 1964), pp. 267, 342; United States—J. Fourastié, *La Civilisation en 1960* (Paris: PUF, 1965), p. 260.

are fed.' Their sickness then is hunger: one need not be a wizard to guess that this is the case, since they are cured upon eating."[31]

This available population accumulated in the towns, where industrial activity was developing and where industrial workers crowded together: "Since commerce and manufacture attain their most complete development in these great towns, their influence upon the proletariat is also most clearly observable here."[32] "What is true of London, is true of Manchester, Birmingham, Leeds, is true of all great towns. Everywhere barbarous indifference, hard egotism on one hand, and nameless misery on the other, everywhere social warfare ... so openly avowed that one shrinks before the consequences of our social state as they manifest themselves here undisguised...."[33]

Accompanying capitalist industrialization, the process of urbanization occurred particularly early in Great Britain. In 1851 ten cities in Great Britain had more than 100,000 inhabitants, compared to five in France. London reached a population of 2.3 million, while Paris just passed 1 million. Manchester surpassed 400,000 inhabitants, Glasgow 300,000, Birmingham 200,000.

TABLE 3.6   Nineteenth-century Urban and Rural Population

	Total population (million)	Rural (%)	Urban (%)
Great Britain (1851)	18	48	52
France (1851)	36	75	25
Russia (1851)	59	93	7
United States (1850)	23	87	31
Germany (1871)	41	64	36

Sources: Rioux, *La révolution industrielle*, p. 148; Harold Faulkner, *American Economic History* (New York: Harper & Row, 1960).

Manchester was the foremost city of the cotton industry:

> In 1835 the sphere of activity of Manchester—including West Riding, and the neighboring counties of Chester and Derby—brought together 80 percent of the factory workers [of this industry], and 85 percent in 1846. Its geographic situation was excellent. It was close to Liverpool, where cotton importation took place. In addition, it was surrounded on all sides, except the south, by rich coal fields which extended from Ormskirk to Bury and Ashton. The level of production from these fields is difficult to calculate, but it must in any case have been far greater than the 700,000 to 900,000 tons that Manchester alone consumed.
>
> This was enough for two distinct groups of factories to coexist within a relatively small area. The first, and oldest, was almost entirely situated on the plain, south of Preston. It had been established in the 18th century around Bolton, the principal center for light fabrics. Its capital then became Manchester, which in 1820 accounted for a quarter of British-produced brocade. The increasing number of factories—at least 30 were built between 1820 and 1830—created certain difficulties however, due to the increasing number of workers and lack of space: factories of four to eight stories, and sometimes twice this, had to be built, and industry began to invade the residential outskirts. A second group of factories began to be built then, after 1821.[34]

The system of wage payments was also more advanced in Great Britain: the proportion of wage earners within the active population there reached three-fourths during the last third of the century. In France the proportion of wage earners was 55 percent in 1851, 57.5 percent in 1866, and 57 percent in 1882; in the United States it was 63 percent in 1880, and in Germany it was 64 percent in 1882.[35] The system of wage payments affected workers in other sectors besides industry, however, and the productive workers of industry were not all wage earners.

HETEROGENEITY OF THE WORKING CLASS

In studying the situation of the working class in Great Britain at the beginning of the 1840s, Friedrich Engels begins with "factory-workers, i.e., those who are comprised under the Factory Act." This law regulates those who work in the factories where "wool, silk, cotton and flax are spun or woven by means of water or steam-power." He then dealt with "remaining branches of industry" (knitwear, lace, printed fabric, bleachers, dyes, metalwares, pottery, and glass manufacture), and with the agricultural and mining proletariat. Along with many studies of this time, Engels brought to light the harshness of working and living conditions, and the meagerness of wages. He emphasized the slavery in which the bourgeoisie has chained the proletariat through the industrial system:

> The worker is, in law and in fact, the slave of the property-holding class, so effectually a slave that he is sold like a piece of goods, rises and falls in value like a commodity.... The bourgeoisie, on the other hand, is far better off under the present arrangement than under the old slave system; it can dismiss its employees at discretion without sacrificing invested capital, and gets its work done much more cheaply than is possible with slave labour....[36]

By the middle of the century the British industrial system was highly diversified. The previous system continued to exist with craft work, work in the home, manufactory, and workhouses, as well as with the mill, which had appeared at the end of the eighteenth century.[37] In this way, handlooms remained dominant for cotton weaving until 1829–31.

What developed was chiefly the factory system, with mills of increasing size; in addition, the putting out system, a new form of work in the home, became more prevalent. Utilizing a driving force—water power or steam engines—the mill grouped together a system of machines which a labor force composed in large part of women and children "served": "The grand object ... of the modern manufacturer is, through the union of capital and science, to reduce the task of his work-people to the exercise of vigilance and dexterity—faculties, when concentrated to one process, speedily brought to the young."[38]

In 1834 children younger than thirteen represented 13 percent of the labor power in the English cotton industry; this figure fell to 5 percent around 1850, but rose again with the crises to 14 percent in 1874.[39] Extremely severe mill regulations; repression by fines, wage reductions, or dismissal; unwholesomeness of the workplaces; harshness of the labor; length of the working day; sicknesses; accidents: all these attest to the

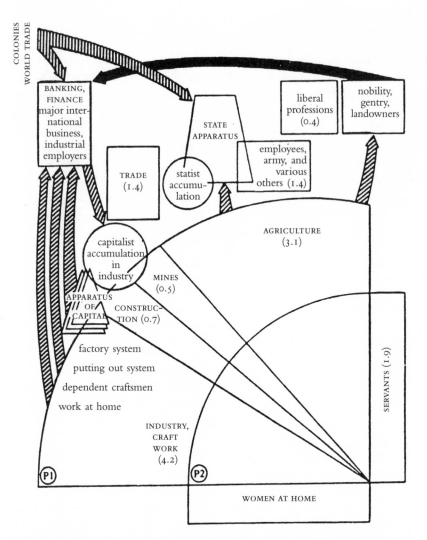

(P1) sphere of material production; (P2) sphere of subsistence production. The figures in parentheses represent the number of people (in millions) involved in each activity or category in 1861. Adapted from M. G. Mulhall, *A Dictionary of Statistics* (1898), cited in P. Bairoch, *Révolution industrielle et sous-développement*.

DIAGRAM 8   SOCIAL CLASSES AND EXTRACTION OF
VALUE IN NINETEENTH-CENTURY BRITAIN

inhuman exploitation which was the basis for the development of British industry in the nineteenth century.

The putting out system was a manifestation of work in the home, in which an entrepreneur gave tasks to poor families to carry out, though it developed into an extension of mill work, especially in the ready-made garment trade and the shoemaking business: the materials being first prepared in the factory, the workers of the putting out system received them (for instance, every week) and were to accomplish a certain type of operation (assembling, sewing, finishing). Payment was by the piece, at low rates, which forced these workers to work very long days. The diffusion of the pedal-operated sewing machine encouraged the extension of this kind of production: in London in 1830 one-third of the production of garments was carried on using this system.[40]

In France the world of craft and industrial production was also abundantly diversified: it encompassed traditional artisanship, peasant families working at home, journeymen of the Tour de France, construction workers, specialized workers (book makers, iron, bronze, and foundry workers), and those not qualified for work in the mechanized mills. The old manufacturing system continued to exist, as Balzac noted in *The Deputy of Arcis*:

> Almost all the knitwear of France, a considerable trade, is made around Troyes. The countryside for ten leagues in all directions is covered with workers whose looms can be seen through the open doors, when passing through the villages. These workers corresponded to middlemen, which led to a speculator called a manufacturer.

In the silk-making business of Lyons, a thousand "dealers" or "merchant-manufacturers" bought the raw material and gave it to the "shop masters" to be worked. These men were master workers who themselves owned the looms set up in the homes. There were 30,000 journeymen working these looms; they were paid by the piece and received generally half the price paid by the dealer to the shop master.[41]

Finally, true mills developed, usually small or medium sized. A few, however, were very large: Dollfus-Mieg and Co. by 1834 employed 4,200 workers on 26,000 spindles, 3,000 mechanized looms, and 120 printing tables; Schneider, in Le Creusot, had 230 workers in 1812, 3,250 in 1850, and 12,500 in 1870; Wendel, in Lorraine, had 9,000 wage earning workers in 1870.[42]

Thus in France under the Second Empire, employment in craft work was more than twice as important as industrial employment. Industrial enterprises remained generally small in size, with an average of fourteen workers per employer.

Long working days, poor health, undernourishment, child labor, sicknesses, accidents: analogous to what was observed in Great Britain, the
misery of the workers in France during the nineteenth century has been
described many times. The subordination of the workers was solidly
assured: the prohibition of strikes and coalitions in the law of Le Chapelier
was taken up again and made more strict by the Penal Code in 1811;
workers' record books were reestablished in 1803; and in case of a dispute,
the Civil Code established in advance on whose side the truth lay: "The
master is believed on his word as to the share and payment of wages, etc."
A physician from Nantes in 1825 wrote this about the worker:

> To live, for him, is to not die. Beyond the piece of bread which is supposed to
> nourish his family and himself, beyond the bottle of wine which is supposed to
> relieve him for an instant from the awareness of his sorrows, he asks for noth-
> ing, he hopes for nothing.... The proletarian returns home to his miserable
> room where the wind whistles through the cracks; and after having sweated
> through a working day of 14 hours, he does not change his clothes when he
> returns, because he has none to change into.[43]

Thus in France as in Great Britain, the capitalist industrialization of the
nineteenth century developed on the basis of a severe exploitation of the
working masses in the leading industries of the time: textiles, metallurgy,
coalmining. This was the case, with a greater or lesser time lag, in all the
countries of Europe and America where the capitalist development of
industry took place.

AFFIRMATION OF THE BOURGEOISIE

The formation of a national capitalism was simultaneously the establishment of a working class and the rise of a new ruling class. Great families
of high finance and international trade, businessmen, manufacturers, ship-
owners, bankers, parliamentarians, jurists, men of law, families of the aristocracy and the gentry (some of whom devoted themselves to business):
among these groups, many connections were formed. There were bonds
of marriage and kinship, of common education and enterprises carried
out together, and of converging interests. Though these groups remained
distinct, they tended, by the adoption of a relatively uniform conception
of life and of society, by their attitude at the time of great social conflicts,
and by their impact on the various aspects of national life, to impose
themselves as the ruling class of capitalist society: the bourgeoisie.

In Great Britain during the second third of the nineteenth century, a
decisive change occurred in the composition of national capital: the various

TABLE 3.7   National Capital of Great Britain (percent)

	1798	1812	1832	1885
LANDED INHERITANCE	63.7	63.5	63.3	23.3
Land	55.0	54.2	54.1	18.1
Farms	8.7	9.3	9.2	5.2
BUILDINGS	13.8	14.9	14.1	22.1
CAPITAL (linked to capitalist development)	20.8	19.8	20.9	48.9
Overseas securities	n.s.	n.s.	4.7	8.2
Railroads and domestic capital (industrial, commercial, and financial)	20.8	19.8	16.2	30.2
PUBLIC PROPERTY	1.7	1.8	1.7	5.7

n.s. = not significant.

Source: Phyllis Deane and William Cole, *British Economic Growth, 1688–1952* (New York: Cambridge University Press, 1969), p. 271.

components of this capital that were linked to the development of capitalism (overseas securities, domestic railroads, industrial capital, commercial and finance capital, including buildings) became dominant in relation to the traditional landed inheritance (estates and farms) (see Table 3.7).

This evolution shows the relative economic decline of the former dominating class (the nobility and gentry) in relation to the rising class of the bourgeoisie. And while it would be tempting to present the great reforms of the British nineteenth century as the successive victories of the rising liberal bourgeoisie over the declining conservative aristocracy, this view, without being entirely false—since the landed aristocracy lost in the course of the century its quasi-monopoly over political power and local administration—would be at the least simplistic.

In fact, on the one hand the overthrow of royal absolutism in the seventeenth century sealed a sort of unwritten pact between the landed aristocracy and the high families of finance, banking, and international trade. On the other hand, between these two poles there was never an insurmountable barrier: members of the first group invested in commercial and financial businesses, and even in mining and manufacturing, while for the bankers, manufacturers, and traders who had grown wealthy, the purchase of an estate, before becoming a social symbol, was a means of entering Parliament. And finally, the aristocracy and the bourgeoisie reacted

with a common reflex of "solidarity" when faced with radical movements
and popular uprisings which threatened property.

Besides this, the peasantry, which in other European countries constituted a large conservative mass, in Great Britain had been subjected for
three centuries to the logic of the enclosures and of profitability. It was
divided and weak in political impact. The heterogeneous working class
competed among themselves and were still searching for their political
expression. From then on, although conservatism was opposed to liberalism, this opposition did not correspond to a confrontation between two
classes whose interests were irreducibly antagonistic.

It was the Tory reformer Peel who in 1829 abolished the Bill of Test
and allowed Catholics to enter public office. In the same way, the electoral reforms of 1832 were acceptable to a large part of the aristocracy,
since these reforms only increased the number of voters from 500,000 to
813,000, which chiefly benefited traders and industrialists. Even the repeal
of the Corn Laws in 1846, despite the harsh confrontations this provoked,
was not a disaster for the landed property owners, who were incited
toward a new effort of "good management" and mechanization. And these
landed property owners, when they gave a reply of sorts to the industrialists through the adoption of the factory laws, found support not only
from the popular movement but also from among the "enlightened"
portion of the employers.[44]

Nevertheless, although the rise of the British bourgeoisie was not carried
out against the aristocracy, and although it occurred in part from the
aristocracy and in liaison with it, this rise characterizes the nineteenth
century, especially the reign of Queen Victoria. In a parallel movement,
the rise of the French bourgeoisie was less clear; this is because it occurred
in quite different conditions, and had to follow a more "eventful" course.

If the revolution of 1789 marked the defeat of the privileged—nobility
and clergy—it operated to the advantage of the growing young capitalist
bourgeoisie, the middle "bureoisie" (jurists, administrators, and local
notables), and the peasantry.[45] The petty bourgeoisie of artisans and traders
must also be considered here. But after the fall of the empire, the bourgeoisie of bankers, manufacturers, and traders could no longer ally themselves with the landed aristocracy, as in Great Britain; they had therefore
to depend on the peasants and the petty bourgeoisie of artisans and traders.

The alliance with the nobility was indeed out of the question:

> There were, after the Hundred Days, two peoples separated by different memo-
> ries, ideas, and habits, and who were no longer able to understand one another.
> They were two armies which had fought one against the other: what one

celebrated as victories the other deplored as defeats. Finally, two owners for the same house, for the same domain.[46]

The landed aristocracy had lived too long in the hope of the return of the legitimate king, Louis XVIII; disappointed by certain of his attitudes, the aristocracy placed their hopes in his successor, Charles X. They reserved their places by excluding the high bourgeoisie: rivals whose economic and financial power was expanding, while the aristocracy's was declining. And when Charles X was overthrown in 1830, a large part of the landed aristocracy resigned themselves—by retiring to their estates or by closing themselves up in their salons—to their own decline.[47]

From then on the capitalist bourgeoisie had to rely upon the petty and middle bourgeoisie, either against the aristocracy, as in 1830, or later against the industrial proletariat. The binding elements of this alliance against the privileged were the ideas of freedom and democracy; property functioned in this role against the "sharers." The condition of the alliance was the protection of precisely those classes which would have been destroyed by a rapid development of capitalism: foreign protectionism, a slow utilization of new techniques, and survival of widespread agriculture and craft work were the price of the alliance. This is surely the principal cause of the slow development of industrial capitalism in France during the nineteenth century.

The merchant wing of the industrial and banking bourgeoisie had to find under Louis-Philippe, and then under Napoleon III, the support, the spur even, of the state, for attempts at development to be made. Sometimes these attempts succeeded, in certain cases spectacularly: for example, the creation of banks during the 1830s and from 1850 to 1860; the development of railroads under the Second Empire; the digging of the Suez Canal; and the great urbanization projects.

But French society remained profoundly provincial, rural, and agricultural, with much of the work still carried on at a craft level. French society at this time was slow and prudent. A part even of industrial and banking capitalism remained as though enclosed within its cocoon: cotton of Alsace or the North, silk production of Lyons, metallurgy of Le Creusot or of Lorraine. Within each branch, the industrialists consulted with one another, made agreements, and organized themselves: "meeting of the silk manufacturers," in 1825; "committee of native sugar processors," created by beet sugar producers against the "colonial" sugar, in 1832; committees of the linen industry, in 1837, and of the cotton industry, in 1839; "committee of metallurgical interests," in 1840; committee of machine manufacturers, and so on.

As for Germany, and more precisely, Prussia, the bourgeois revolution did not take place:

> The 1848 movement and the issuing of a constitution by the king did not mark an important turning-point in the process of the transformation of relations of production; and they did nothing to alter the state's superstructure or the occupier of political power. Despite the customs-union (*Zollverein*) which had already been accomplished by the time of this movement, the landed nobility still retained political power and the Prussian state was to remain for a long time dominated by feudal structures. It was in fact this state which under Bismarck undertook to bring the bourgeoisie to political domination, a process characterized by Marx and Engels as "revolution from above." Under Bismarck, this state transformed itself from within, as it were, in the direction of the capitalist state.[48]

It was with the support of the state that capitalist industrialization, until then moderate, intensified from the 1860s on. The bourgeoisie then found itself facing a working class which very quickly became organized; even when allied with the petty bourgeoisie, the capitalist bourgeoisie was not able to cope on two fronts: it therefore accepted the political domination of the coalition formed by the landed nobility with the high "bureoisie" of the state. As a new ruling class, the bourgeoisie in Germany had to accept second place.

The United States had no old feudal or agrarian society to destroy. Three societies coexisted: a rural society based on plantation slavery and cotton in the South; an industrial capitalism expanding in the Northeast; and a society of farming families extending into the West. The landed aristocracy had dominated the federal state apparatus since the formation of the United States. The creation of the Republican Party in 1854, and its success in 1860, questioned this domination to the advantage of the new ruling class of the Northeast; the Civil War and the defeat of the South prevented the secession of the southern states and abolished slavery, the economic base of the landed aristocracy. The Civil War encouraged industrialization (armaments, railroads), reorganization of the banking sector, protective tariffs, and immigration: in short, the conditions for a new and considerable industrial expansion. A new generation of capitalists was formed and asserted itself during the war: J. P. Morgan, who resold a stock of defective rifles to the U.S. Army and then speculated in gold; Jay Gould, another speculator; Jim Fisk, who sold blankets to the U.S. Army; Cornelius Vanderbilt, who rented boats to the federal government at high rates; and John D. Rockefeller, who already had begun to sell oil.[49]

Thus during the 1860s, the bourgeoisie imposed itself as a dominating class only in Great Britain. In France the bourgeoisie still had to take into account burdensome alliances with the petty bourgeoisie and the peasantry, and was only set loose, for brief favorable periods, with the support of the state. In Germany the bourgeoisie had to be both accepted by the landed nobility and supported by the state. In the United States, it was only after the Civil War that the bourgeoisie found the way open for its rise.

COLONIAL DOMINATION AND WORLD MARKET

England opens all of its ports; it has broken down all the barriers which separated it from other nations; England had 50 colonies, and now has only one, the universe....[50]

England, mistress of the seas at the end of the Napoleonic Wars; England, extending over the entire world its empire and its trade; England, workshop for the world: England in the nineteenth century was clearly the premier merchant power (see Tables 3.8–3.10).

Not only was the British economy the most developed, but its process of development from the outset had been linked to colonial expansion and maritime trade. And already Britain was involved in the logic of specialization and international division of labor. This is evident in the structure of its exports, and increasingly apparent in the structure of its imports.

In addition, the British economy's "effort to export," which was already considerable during the 1820s and 1830s (when one-fifth of production was exported), grew decade by decade to reach one-quarter of all physical production in 1851, one-third in 1861, and two-fifths in 1871.

TABLE 3.8   International Division of Trade (percent)

	Great Britain	France	Germany	Rest of Europe	United States	Rest of world
1780	12	12	11	39	2	24
1800	33	9	10	25	6	17
1820	27	9	11	29	6	19
1840	25	11	8	30	7	20
1860	25	11	9	24	9	21

Source: Rostow, *The World Economy*, pp. 70–71.

TABLE 3.9   Structure of Foreign Trade, Britain and France (percent)

	STRUCTURE OF EXPORTS		
	Raw materials	Food products	Manufacturing products
Great Britain			
1814–16	4	17	79
1824–26	4	11	85
1854–56	8	7	85
France			
1817–20	11	31	58
1827–30	30		70
1850–54	33		67

	STRUCTURE OF IMPORTS		
	Raw materials	Food products	Manufacturing products
Great Britain			
1814–16	54	35	11
1824–26	64	27	9
1854–56	61	33	6
France			
1817–20	56	35	9
1827–30	63	29	8
1850–54	72	23	5

SHARE OF EXPORTS			
Great Britain		France	
1801	31.3	1781–90	8.8
1821	21.7	1815–24	6.2
1831	18.9	1825–34	5.4
1861	34.5	1855–64	13.1
1871	46.5	1865–74	17.3

Sources: Bairoch, *Révolution industrielle*, pp. 261, 335; J. Marczewski, *Cahiers de l'ISEA*, no. 163 (July 1965), p. lvi.

TABLE 3.10   British Balance of Payments (£million annually)

	Commercial balance	Emigrants, tourists, government	Maritime transport	Profits, interest, dividends	Fees and commissions	Net total
1816–20	−11	−3	+10	+8	+3	+7
1826–30	−14	−3	+8.5	+9.5	+2	+3
1836–40	−23	−4	+11	+15	+4	+3
1846–50	−25	−6	+14	+18	+4	+5
1856–60	−33.5	−8	+26	+33.5	+8	+26
1866–70	−65	−9	+45	+57	+13	+41
1876–80	−124	−9	+54	+88	+16	+25
1806–1900	−159	−11	+62	+132	+16	+40
1911–13	−140	−22	+100	+241	+27	+206

	Commodity trading	Foreign investment income	Other operations	Gold and foreign currencies	Net total
1920–24	−279	+199	+221	+21	+162
1925–29	−395	+250	+213	+1	+68
1930–34	−324	+174	+127	−66	−68
1935–38	−360	+199	+133	−77	−105

Sources: A. H. Imlah, *Economic Elements in the Pax Britannica*, cited in Deane and Cole, *British Economic Growth*, p. 36; Mathias, *The First Industrial Nation*, p. 469.

These figures give a measure of how important the conquest of foreign markets was for British industry in the Victorian period. They also give a measure of what was at stake in the debate between supporters of protectionism and partisans of free trade. Was Great Britain going to be able to supply itself with even more agricultural products and raw materials at low prices—and chance sacrificing its own agriculture and animal breeding even further—in order that its industry might be able to produce more cheaply and sell still more?

British trade showed a deficit throughout this period: Great Britain bought from the rest of the world more than it sold. And it was mainly the trade in services, revenue from maritime transport, profits, interest, and dividends received from abroad, and gains from insurance and brokerage activities, that allowed the British balance of payments to be positive—moderately so in the first half of the century, considerably so in the second.

Whether it was a question of exports or investments, Britain's principal partners during the first half of the century were first in Europe and then in America. British industrialists continued to sell fabrics and other consumption products, while they also benefited from the industrialization of these countries and the new markets this industrialization represented: they sold engines, machines, and other equipment goods. Britain was able to buy at the best prices "the wheat and corn of America and eastern Europe, the meats of Australia and Argentina, the dairy products of Denmark, the tropical products of the Empire and central America, tin from Malaysia, iron from South America, wood from Scandinavia, etc."[51]

French exports during the period were more and more oriented toward the surrounding European countries (one-third of exports in 1827–36; more than half in 1869), to the detriment of the United States (13 percent and 5 percent respectively) and the rest of the world (more than half in 1827–36, two-fifths in 1869).[52] As for French investments abroad, at the middle of the century they were almost totally made in Europe: 60 percent in Mediterranean Europe (Italy, Spain, Portugal), 24 percent in Northwest Europe (Belgium, Luxembourg, Holland, Great Britain, and the Scandinavian countries), 12 percent in central Europe (Germany, Switzerland, Austria, Hungary), with the remaining 4 percent in the Americas.[53]

Mistress of the seas and dominating commercial power, Great Britain in the nineteenth century obtained the first colonial empire in the world. The Spanish and Portuguese empires were declining; the Dutch empire had stabilized; Russia, though continuing its expansion, did so toward Asia, by way of the continent. Restoration France took possession again of its colonies which had been neglected during the Revolution and the Empire; it started new ventures in Senegal, Madagascar, Guyana, and Algeria, which the July monarchy pursued further. With the Second Empire, France intervened in Lebanon and Syria, had a presence in Egypt and Tunisia, penetrated into the Sahara, established outposts in New Caledonia and Cochin China, and instituted a protectorate in Cambodia. Everywhere this presence was chiefly military, except in Algeria, where emigrants settled, and in Egypt, where French capital was invested.

At the beginning of the nineteenth century, after the independence of the North American colonies, the British colonial empire appeared to be seriously reduced; the old system of the navigation acts, colonial trade relations, and the slave trade disintegrated; to many Englishmen, the colonies appeared to be without economic interest, a burden even: "The Cape was only a strategic outpost, and Australia a penitentiary establishment. As for Canada, it furnished wood, furs, and fish rather than grains."[54]

TABLE 3.11   British Exports and Foreign Investments (percent)

DESTINATION OF BRITISH EXPORTS

	Europe	America	Asia	Africa	
1816–22	59.6	33.3	6.1	1.0	

	Europe	United States	Latin America	British Empire	Others
1865	48	11	8	24	9

DIVISION OF FOREIGN INVESTMENTS

	Europe	United States	Latin America	British Empire		
1830	66	9	23	2		
1854	55	25	15	5		

	Europe	United States	Latin America	India	Dominions	Others
1870	25	27	11	22	12	3

Sources: Exports—W. G. Hoffmann, *The Growth of Industrial Economies* (Dobbs Ferry, N.Y.: Oceana, 1958); *Statistical Abstract for the United Kingdom, 1867*; investments— A. G. Kenwood and A. L. Lougheed, *The Growth of the International Economy, 1820– 1960* (Albany: State University of New York Press, 1971).

In the very movement of capitalist industrialization and commercial growth, Great Britain followed a policy of territorial expansion: it increased its influence in West Africa and South Africa, where it occupied the Natal (1843). Tasmania was declared an autonomous colony in 1825, as were western Australia in 1829, southern Australia in 1836, New Zealand in 1839, and Victoria in 1850. Singapore was established in 1819, Aden was occupied in 1839, and Hong Kong in 1842. Territorial expansion spread to India and all of Canada.

During this same period, Great Britain diversified, softening when necessary its methods of administration. The union of High Canada

(Anglo-Saxon) with Low Canada (French) occurred in 1840: French-speaking people were a minority, and a federal system was established in 1867. New Zealand was also provided with a federal system. In South Africa, the colonies of the Cape and the Natal were separated, and each one received a representative government. In India, after the revolt of the Sepoys in 1857, the East India Company was suppressed and India was given the status of a crown colony.

Even though it was limited in relation to the economic changes in Great Britain as a whole, the economic aspect of colonization was strengthened: there were increasing purchases of indigo, jute, and cotton in India, where English industry also sold its cotton fabrics (ruining the local artisans), as well as material for railroads and telegraphs; gold mining in Australia (after 1851); and diamond and gold mining in South Africa (after 1867). British emigration grew in waves, to Canada, South Africa, Australia, and New Zealand. By 1870, capital invested in the Empire represented one-third of all foreign-invested British capital.

Besides being his own dream, it was the dream of the British ruling class that Cecil Rhodes, creator of British South Africa, expressed: "Bringing the majority of the world under our laws will mean the end of all war...."[55]

RESISTANCE AND THE COMING OF AWARENESS

As it developed, nineteenth-century capitalism engendered a brutal confrontation: between bourgeois wealth and workers' misery; between cultivated comfort and unrefined anguish; between power and absolute dependence.

These were two estranged universes, implacable enemies, and yet inseparable one from the other. An industrialist from the Nord, Mimerel, wrote in a matter-of-fact way: "The fate of the workers is not bad: their labor is not excessive since it does not go beyond 13 hours.... The manufacturer whose profits are poor is the one to be pitied."[56] As for Thiers (president of the French Republic, 1871–73), he emphasized the merit of the philanthropist: "The rich man is sometimes charitable, and he leaves his palace to visit the cottage of the poor man, braving the hideous filth and the contagious disease, and when he has discovered this new enjoyment, he develops a passion for it, he delights in it, and cannot do without it." This was simply one more reason why the ideas of reform should not be applied: "Suppose all fortunes were equal, suppose the suppression of all wealth and all misery; then no one would have the means to give … you would have suppressed the sweetest, most charming, and most gracious action of humanity. Sad reformer, you would have spoiled the work of God by wanting to retouch it."[57]

Two universes in the same mill, in the same city: here, the neighborhoods where order, calm, and "good taste" reign; there, the unhealthy neighborhoods: filth, promiscuity, vulgarity, insecurity. Often the mansion of the industrialist was near the mill, in the middle of a park, and then further on, there were the workers' homes, crowded together or lined up in a row. Already, the first paternalistic activities were developing. Already, enlightened minds were preoccupied with this explosive situation; among them Louis-Napoleon Bonaparte:

> The working class, who own nothing, must become owners. Their arms are their only wealth; these arms must be given an employment useful to all.... They must be given a place in society, and their interests must be attached to the interests of the soil. Finally, the working class is without organization and without ties, without rights and without a future—they must be given rights and a future; they must be lifted up, in their own eyes, by association, education, and discipline.[58]

But after 1848 hatred burst out in France. Maréchal Bugeaud wrote to Thiers on April 7, 1849: "What brutal and ferocious beasts! How does God permit mothers to make them like that! Ah! These are the real enemies, and not the Russians or the Austrians." And Charles Morny, half-brother of Louis-Napoleon Bonaparte, wrote to the latter:

> Socialism has made frightening progress.... The only thing left to do will be to pack your bags, organize the civil war, and pray for the Cossacks to come help us. I laugh while writing this sentence, and I think that your national pride will be outraged, but, believe me, if you saw a socialist up close, you would not hesitate in preferring a Cossack to him. My patriotism stops there.[59]

MATURATION OF THE WORKERS' MOVEMENT

When Morny talks of the (frightening) progress of socialism, he summarizes in one sentence what was a slow and many-sided movement. There were, first of all, workers' struggles, which in the nineteenth century were often the acts of men and women driven by misery and hunger, pushed to risking prison, deportation, or their lives in order to survive. There were the harsh reactions of artisan workers, who had been ruined and deprived of work by the expansion of mechanical production, and who broke machines and burned mills. There were despairing and threatening processions of those without jobs, those who were starving; and brutal explosions of rage at the aggravation of exploitation: the reduction of wages, the lengthening of the working day, the hardening of workshop regulations; sometimes a spark was enough, a single injustice, one arbitrary decision.

There was also, more or less in clandestinity, the untiring effort of organization, of forming into one group, of solidarity: the effort to maintain or revive the old trade structures, workers' associations, secret societies; gatherings in taverns; groups forming around a newspaper; the particular influence, in a city or neighborhood, of a worker, a printer, or a shopkeeper, who had read and who spoke with others. Relief societies, mutual benefit societies, and cooperatives were created: the ideas of Owen, Fourier, and Proudhon were taken up, discussed, distorted, and applied.

For there was also socialist thought which was ripening and gaining strength, with such giants as the nineteenth century was able to produce: Blanqui, Proudhon, Bakunin, Engels, Marx; Saint-Simonists who went into the midst of workers' surroundings; women such as Flora Tristan, who denounced the oppression of women and the oppression of the proletariat; workers who read and who wrote their observations or their memoirs; dreamers, rebels, idealists, the passionate reformers. Innumerable pamphlets advocated, with disarming conviction, *the* solution to pauperism. Social ideas were not the monopoly of "socialists": the great classical economist John Stuart Mill was a reformer, a path which had been opened, in certain ways, by Sismondi.

These different forces at work, arising within or around the working class, interfered or combined with one another, and sometimes clashed. Just as the working class, because of its very diversity, remained linked at numerous points to other layers of the common people, these forces within the working class made contact with other forces—from the petty and middle bourgeoisie—which were leading the struggle for democracy and the republic. These struggles, often separate, sometimes met. Thus the path by which the workers' movement matured was marked by infinite diversity and great richness.

After a dazzling rise and success as a "social employer," Owen did not let himself become disheartened by the failure of the community he had created in the United States; at the time of the first organizational phase of the trade union movement in Great Britain, he became one of the principal figures in the workers' movement: the Grand National Consolidated Trade Unions reached 500,000 members in 1833 before being dismantled. A large part of British workers' energies were invested in a great popular movement, the Chartist Movement, inspired by William Lovett and Feargus O'Connor: its principal objective was to establish a true political democracy, including universal male suffrage and parliamentary compensation, so that candidates without fortunes could be elected. Adopted in 1839, by 1842 the chart had 2–3 million signatures, and in 1848, 5–6 million. But the movement divided (Lovett was hostile to the month-long general strike and the violence which O'Connor advocated), encountered parliamentary evasion, was threatened and repressed, and ended in confusion.

Emigration functioned as an outlet throughout this period. After the middle of the century, a part of the working class saw their real wages increase and the conditions of exploitation become milder. Universal male suffrage was granted in 1867. A new and decisive phase of union organization was then in progress, which led to the foundation of the Trades Union Congress in 1868. Universal suffrage and trade union organization: the workers' movement was from this time on considered by the British bourgeoisie as a force to be taken into account.

In 1830 French workers were active among the popular and republican forces which drove out Charles X. But they had not manned the barricades for a Louis-Philippe; besides, nothing diminished their oppression and the precariousness of their existence. Although quit-rents were lowered, this concerned only a few tens of thousands of owners.[60] In strikes, riots, and street actions, popular and workers' discontent continued to be expressed. The silk workers of Lyons rose in rebellion: "We are fighting for bread and for work"; troops reconquered the city, killing or wounding one thousand people. As agitation continued, the ruling class was ready for anything: "There must be no quarter," said Thiers. "All of them must be killed. No quarter at all. Be pitiless.... We must make arms and legs out of 3,000 troublemakers," ordered Bugeaud. This was the massacre of the rue Transnonain.

In July 1830, all classes were united against the landed aristocracy. In February 1848 they were united against the high bourgeoisie, Louis-Philippe and Guizot; but the republican and workers' forces did not want to give up this victory. The Republic was indeed declared, as were universal suffrage and the right to work, although the decision for national workshops was made only under pressure, and workers' unrest continued: "It was," wrote de Tocqueville, "an extraordinary and painful thing to see the whole immense city, full of so many riches, in the hands of those who owned nothing." Anxiety and fear united all the property owners, from the largest to the smallest: the working people of Paris were isolated at the time when they were given over to the repression of General Cavaignac, who was "charged with crushing the enemy." There were thousands of deaths, more than 11,000 arrests, a few who were sentenced to death or to lifelong forced labor, and many who were deported, most often to Algeria.

The right to work was transformed into the "freedom to work." A president was to be elected by universal suffrage: the first one to be elected was Louis-Napoleon Bonaparte. Once emperor, he who had advocated the "extinction of pauperism" through "a combination of socialism and militarism," and by the creation of an intermediate class of "arbitrators" between employers and workers, officers in the industrial army—he who had stood for all these now promoted mainly industrial and banking capitalism. It was, however, under the "liberal" empire that the right to strike was recognized (1864), and that French trade unionism experienced its first real expansion.

In Germany, too, the workers' movement was born from harsh conflicts and bloody struggles, as in the case of the uprising by the Silesian weavers in 1844. In 1862 Lasalle founded the General Association of German Workers, and the trade union movement grew. The constitution of 1867 established universal suffrage, and in 1869 Bebel and Liebknecht founded the social-democratic workers' party. In other countries of Europe, as well as in the United States, the workers' movement grew and trade union organization developed, sometimes in a context of brutal repression. The first large centralized U.S. trade union, the National Labor Union, was founded by W. H. Sylvis in 1866.

In 1864 English trade unionists, militant French workers, and émigrés from Germany (including Karl Marx), Italy, Switzerland, and Poland created the International Workingman's Association in London, which simultaneously opened a new dimension within the workers' movement and made it concrete, though in a limited way: internationalism.

Thus hardly had the British bourgeoisie begun to impose itself as a dominating class on the basis of a flamboyant and conquering capitalism, and while the bourgeoisies of France, Germany, and the United States still had to rely on alliances which impeded their growth, the working classes compelled their own recognition as political and social forces. They who had been for so long crushed, disarmed, and subjected to daily oppression and brutal repression now organized, formed parties, trade unions, newspapers, and other autonomous means for their development. Neither oppression nor repression ceased, but from this time on the dominating class faced a class which was capable of imposing a balance of forces. And this balance of forces deeply influenced the future transformations of capitalism.

CAPITAL, AS ANALYSIS OF CAPITALISM

Marx owed a great deal to the thought of classical economists, to the observations of those who witnessed a conquering capitalism, and to the critique of socialists, even though in order to distinguish himself from them, or to advance his thinking, he criticized them, often excessively. His strength lay in systematizing, at the price of a colossal and exhausting theoretical effort, his profound intuitions, which had been essentially formed by the middle of the century. The provisional evaluation he himself made in 1852 is enlightening:

> And now as to myself, no credit is due to me for discovering the existence of classes in modern society or the struggle between them. Long before me bourgeois historians had described the historical development of this class struggle and bourgeois economists the economic anatomy of the classes. What I did that was new was to prove: 1) that the *existence of classes* is only bound up with particular historical phases in the development of production, 2) that the class struggle necessarily leads to *the dictatorship of the proletariat*, 3) that this dictatorship itself only constitutes the transition to the *abolition of all classes* and to a classless society....[61]

He considered class struggle at length:

> The history of all hitherto existing society is the history of class struggles. Freeman and slave, patrician and plebeian, lord and serf, guild-master and journeyman, in a word, oppressor and oppressed, stood in constant opposition to one another, carried on an uninterrupted, now hidden, now open fight, a fight that each time ended either in a revolutionary reconstruction of society at large, or in the common ruin of the contending classes.[62]

He demonstrated the basis of the class struggle: "Men are the producers of their conceptions, ideas, etc., but these are real, active men, as they are conditioned by a definite development of their productive forces and of the relationships corresponding to these up to their highest forms."[63] And he described its evolution: "In broad outlines, we can designate the Asiatic, the ancient, the feudal, and the modern bourgeois methods of production as so many epochs in the progress of the economic formation of society."[64] For Marx, the class struggle reaches a paroxysm in capitalistic society:

Our epoch, the epoch of the bourgeoisie, possesses, however, this distinctive feature; it has simplified the class antagonisms. Society as a whole is more and more splitting up into two great hostile camps, into two great classes directly facing each other: Bourgeoisie and Proletariat.[65]

Masses of labourers, crowded into the factory, are organized like soldiers. As privates of the industrial army, they are placed under the command of a perfect hierarchy of officers and sergeants. Not only are they the slaves of the bourgeois class, and of the bourgeois State, they are daily and hourly enslaved by the machine, by the overlooker, and, above all, by the individual bourgeois manufacturer himself. The more openly this despotism proclaims gain to be its end and aim, the more petty, the more hateful and the more embittering it is.[66]

The contradictions deepen, which can only lead to the collapse of capitalism:

For many a decade past the history of industry and commerce is but the history of the revolt of modern productive forces against modern conditions of production, against the property relations that are the conditions for the existence of the bourgeoisie and of its rule. It is enough to mention the commercial crises that by their periodical return put on its trial, each time more threateningly, the existence of the entire bourgeois society.... In these crises there breaks out an epidemic that, in all earlier epochs, would have seemed an absurdity, the epidemic of overproduction. Society suddenly finds itself put back into a state of momentary barbarism; it appears as if a famine, a universal war of devastation has cut off the supply of every means of subsistence; industry and commerce seem to be destroyed; and why? Because there is too much civilization, too much means of subsistence, too much industry, too much commerce. The productive forces at the disposal of society no longer tend to further the development of the conditions of bourgeois property; on the contrary, they have become too powerful for these conditions, by which they are fettered, and so soon as they overcome these fetters, they bring disorder into the whole of bourgeois society, endanger the existence of bourgeois property. The conditions of bourgeois society are too narrow to comprise the wealth created by them.[67]

This is a matter of more than a simple overthrow of capitalism, for what is at stake is the end of class society. By 1844 Marx "sees" for the proletariat, multiplied and strengthened by capitalist development, a historic "mission":

So where is the *positive* possibility of German emancipation?
    This is our answer. In the formation of a class with *radical chains*, a class of civil society which is not a class of civil society, a class which is the dissolution of all classes, a sphere which has a universal character because of its universal suffering and which lays claim to no *particular right* because the wrong it suffers is not a *particular wrong* but *wrong in general*; a sphere of society which can no longer lay claim to a *historical* title, but merely to a *human* one, which does not stand in one-sided opposition to the consequences but in all-sided opposition

to the premises of the German political system; and finally a sphere which cannot emancipate itself without emancipating itself from—and thereby emancipating—all the other spheres of society, which is in a word, the *total loss* of humanity and which can therefore redeem itself only through the *total redemption of humanity*. This dissolution of society as a particular class is the *proletariat*.[68]

If the *revolution of a people* and the *emancipation of a particular class* [*Klasse*] of civil society are to coincide, if *one* class is to stand for the whole of society, then all the deficiencies of society must be concentrated in another class [*Stand*], one particular class must be the class which gives universal offence, the embodiment of a general limitation: one particular sphere of society must appear as the *notorious crime* of the whole of society, so that the liberation of this sphere appears as universal self-liberation. If one class [*Stand*] is to be the class of liberation *par excellence*, then another class must be the class of overt oppression.[69]

A "Messiah" of modern times, this proletariat? Not at all, responds Marx:

When socialist writers attribute this historic role to the proletariat, it is not, as Critical Criticism pretends to think, because they regard proletarians as *gods*. On the contrary. Because the abstraction of all humanity and even the *semblance* of humanity is practically complete in the fully developed proletariat, because the conditions of life of the proletariat bring all the conditions of present society into a most inhuman focus, because man is lost in the proletariat but at the same time has won a theoretical awareness of that loss and is driven to revolt against this inhumanity by urgent, patent, and absolutely compelling *need* (the practical expression of *necessity*)—therefore the proletariat can and must emancipate itself. But it cannot emancipate itself without transcending all the inhuman conditions of present society which are summed up in its own situation.[70]

Thus:

All the preceding classes that got the upper hand sought to fortify their already acquired status by subjecting society at large to their conditions of appropriation. The proletarians cannot become masters of the productive forces of society, except by abolishing their own previous mode of appropriation, and thereby also every other previous mode of appropriation. They have nothing of their own to secure and to fortify; their mission is to destroy all previous securities for, and insurances of, individual property.[71]

Marx and Engels state this clearly in *The Communist Manifesto*:

The history of all past society has consisted in the development of class antagonisms, antagonisms that assumed different forms at different epochs.

But whatever form they may have taken, one fact is common to all past ages, viz., the exploitation of one part of society by the other. No wonder, then, that the social consciousness of past ages, despite all the multiplicity and variety it displays, moves within certain common forms, or general ideas, which cannot completely vanish except with the total disappearance of class antagonisms.

... The first step in the revolution by the working class, is to raise the proletariat to the position of ruling class, to win the battle of democracy.[72]

This is a powerful certitude:

If the proletariat during its contest with the bourgeoisie is compelled, by the force of circumstances, to organize itself as a class, if, by means of a revolution, it makes itself the ruling class, and, as such, sweeps away by force the old conditions of production, then it will, along with these conditions, have swept away the conditions for the existence of class antagonisms, and of classes generally....[73]

An admirable conviction, which underlay his entire life, and which Marx for decades sought to support scientifically through the study and critique of political economy.

In his *Contribution to the Critique of Political Economy*, Marx summarized his conception of historical movement:

In the social production which men carry on they enter into definite relations that are indispensable and independent of their will; these relations of production correspond to a definite stage of development of their material powers of production. The sum total of these relations of production constitutes the economic structure of society—the real foundation, on which rise legal and political superstructures and to which correspond definite forms of social consciousness.... At a certain stage of their development, the material forces of production in society come in conflict with the existing relations of production, or—what is but a legal expression for the same thing—with the property relations within which they had been at work before. From forms of development of the forces of production these relations turn into their fetters. Then comes the period of social revolution.[74]

With pen in hand, and a critically alert mind, he read the essentials of the economic literature then available. He worked on his economic notebooks and wrote out chapters on the real subordination of labor to capital, on productive and unproductive labor, on crises, and on the immediate process of production. In this last he gave himself the objective of studying:

1. Commodities as products of capital, of capitalist production;
2. Capitalist production as production of surplus-value;
3. Capitalist production as production and reproduction of the entire relation; it is this which confers on the immediate process of production its "specifically capitalist" character.

It was, then, from an enormous amount of work and discussion, particularly with Engels, and from an active observation of history in the process of being made, that *Capital* was born. Volume 1, published in

1867, opens with a flourish: "The wealth of those societies in which the capitalist mode of production prevails, presents itself as 'an immense accumulation of commodities,' its unit being a single commodity. Our investigation must therefore begin with the analysis of a commodity."[75] Commodity use-value, value, surplus value:

> The product appropriated by the capitalist is a use-value, as yarn, for example, or boots. But, although boots are, in one sense, the basis of all social progress, and our capitalist is a decided "progressist," yet he does not manufacture boots for their own sake. Use-value is, by no means, the thing "qu'on aime pour lui-même" in the production of commodities. Use-values are only produced by capitalists, because, and in so far as, they are the material substratum, the depositaries of exchange-value. Our capitalist has two objects in view: in the first place, he wants to produce a use-value that has a value in exchange, that is to say, an article destined to be sold, a commodity; and secondly, he desires to produce a commodity whose value shall be greater than the sum of the values of the commodities used in its production, that is, of the means of production and the labour-power, that he purchased with his good money in the open market. His aim is to produce not only a use-value, but a commodity also; not only use-value, but value; not only value, but at the same time surplus-value.[76]

Thus: "Capital is dead labour, that, vampire-like, only lives by sucking living labour, and lives the more, the more labour it sucks. The time during which the labourer works, is the time during which the capitalist consumes the labour-power he has purchased of him."[77]

After having hesitated for a long time, Marx did in fact clarify this point: it is not labor, but labor power, that the proletarian sells to the capitalist.[78] The value of this labor power is determined by the costs of maintaining the laborer and his family; and it is by being constrained to produce more than the value of his own labor power that the worker produces surplus value. "The degree of exploitation of labour, the appropriation of surplus-labour and surplus-value, is raised notably by lengthening the working-day and intensifying labour."[79]

Marx clarified the basis of capitalist accumulation, of expanded reproduction, of the tendency toward a falling rate of profit, of crises and proletarianization, and finally, of the necessary collapse of capitalism. Though it is not possible to take up every point in Marx's analysis here, we note a few of the major steps:

> Capitalist production, therefore, under its aspect of a continuous connected process, of a process of reproduction, produces not only commodities, not only surplus-value, but it also produces and reproduces the capitalist relation; on the one side the capitalist, on the other the wage-labourer.[80]

But if a surplus labouring population is a necessary product of accumulation or of the development of wealth on a capitalist basis, this surplus-population becomes, conversely, the lever of capitalist accumulation, nay, a condition of existence of the capitalist mode of production. It forms a disposable industrial reserve army, that belongs to capital quite as absolutely as if the latter had bred it at its own cost. Independently of the limits of the actual increase of population, it creates, for the changing needs of the self-expansion of capital, a mass of human material always ready for exploitation.[81]

The law, finally, that always equilibrates the relative surplus-population, or industrial reserve army, to the extent and energy of accumulation, this law rivets the labourer to capital more firmly than the wedges of Vulcan did Prometheus to the rock. It establishes an accumulation of misery, corresponding with accumulation of capital. Accumulation of wealth at one pole is, therefore, at the same time accumulation of misery, agony of toil, slavery, ignorance, brutality, mental degradation, at the opposite pole, *i.e.*, on the side of the class the produces its own product in the form of capital.[82]

But:

Along with the constantly diminishing number of the magnates of capital, who usurp and monopolise all advantages of this process of transformation, grows the mass of misery, oppression, slavery, degradation, exploitation; but with this too grows the revolt of the working-class, a class always increasing in numbers, and disciplined, united, organised by the very mechanism of the process of capitalist production itself. The monopoly of capital becomes a fetter upon the mode of production, which has sprung up and flourished along with, and under it. Centralisation of the means of production and socialisation of labour at last reach a point where they become incompatible with their capitalist integument. This integument is burst asunder. The knell of capitalist private property sounds. The expropriators are expropriated.[83]

Here, "demonstrated," is the profound and fundamental intuition which Marx had carried within him since the 1840s. He would come back to it untiringly, obstinately, with the will to elucidate the irreducible character of the contradiction which is at the heart of capitalism, and therefore the necessity of its overthrow. Thus in Volume III of *Capital*:

The *real barrier* of capitalist production is *capital itself*. It is that capital and its self-expansion appear as the starting and the closing point, the motive and the purpose of production; that production is only production for *capital* and not vice versa, the means of production are not mere means for a constant expansion of the living process of the *society* of producers.... The means—unconditional development of the productive forces of society—comes continually into conflict with the limited purpose, the self-expansion of the existing capital. The capitalist mode of production is, for this reason, a historical means of developing the material forces of production and creating an appropriate world-market and is, at the same time, a continual conflict between this its historical task and its own corresponding relations of social production.[84]

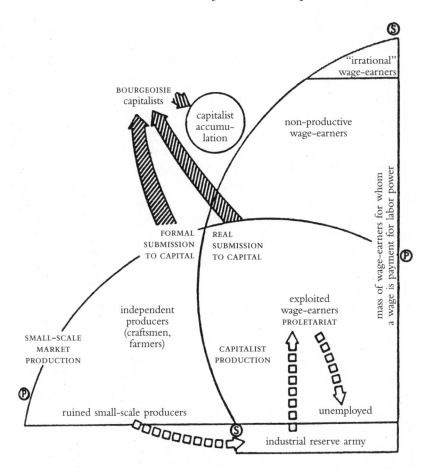

Shaded arrows = flows of value; broken arrows = flow of workers; (P) = sphere of production; (S) = sphere of wage-earning. The wages of "irrational wage-earners" is not the price of their labor power, but is the counterpart of their unquantifiable "abilities" or "talents."

DIAGRAM 9   SOCIAL CLASSES AND EXTRACTION
OF SURPLUS VALUE ACCORDING TO MARX

What has had the most effect: the few dozen pages of the *Communist Manifesto*, or the thousands of pages of study and critique of political economy? The flashing denunciation, or the powerful apparatus for the analysis of capitalist economy? The profound conviction, or the guarantee that the exposé of the "historical law" provides to support the conviction?

Everything, the best and the worst, has been able to flow from the thought of Marx, or to refer to it: generations of militants have found in it a weapon, but it has also nourished its share of catechisms and dogmatisms; the yeast of so many revolts, it has been able also to be changed into the heavy cloak of state ideology; fruitful for philosophy and the whole of the social sciences, it can also dry up into economism and flat mechanism; a force always at work in the battles against capitalism and imperialism, damned by the possessing and ruling classes, it also has been used as the justification for the power of new dominating classes.

At the end of the nineteenth century, the thought of Marx, not yet widely dispersed and only partially known, found in Engels its first propagandist. In Engels' view, the "two great discoveries" which "we owe" to Marx are "the materialist conception of history and the revelation of the secret of capitalist production through surplus value." It is thanks to these that "socialism became a science."[85] From then on, "utopian socialism" was opposed by "scientific socialism."

SUMMARY

The first two-thirds of the nineteenth century were marked by the irresistible rise of capitalism, first of all in Great Britain.

The old extortion of peasant surplus labor continued, to the profit of the landed property owners and the state. But what became dominant was the capitalist exploitation of labor in industry. This entailed what Marx called the "formal submission" of labor (of traditional artisans, for example) to capital (dealers or manufacturers) and also the "real submission" of labor, that is, of wage earners, within the framework of manufactures and increasingly of mills. The development of textile and metallurgical industries, and then of matériel for railroads, were the principal supports for this exploitation of labor. Finally, the extortion of value on a world scale—colonial exploitation and unequal exchange—remained an important source of accumulation, especially for Great Britain, the first colonial and commercial power, first supplier of equipment goods, a true "workshop to the world."

With the mill, the logic of capitalist production became generalized:

$$M \to C \to \begin{cases} mp \\ lp \end{cases} \to P \to C' \to M'$$

A manufacturer uses a sum of money M in order to buy commodities C necessary for the production P which he wants to set in motion: means of production (or constant capital: mp = c) and labor power (or variable capital: lp = v); he obtains a new commodity C′ whose value is greater than that of C; from which comes the profit $\Delta M = M' - M$. He may be brought to share this surplus value with the banker who lent him money (interest) and with the dealer who sells his merchandise (commercial profit). More generally, the sharing of the socially produced surplus value is at stake in a lively intercapitalist battle, a battle in which competition and monopoly, free trade and protectionism, are only different modalities.

On this basis the bourgeoisie asserted itself: a bougeoisie which, because of world domination and the weakening of the peasantry and of the *modus vivendi* found among the old ruling class, bloomed in all its splendor in Great Britain. In France, it was still in conflict with the old ruling class (and had therefore to depend on burdensome allies); while in Germany the bourgeoisie developed thanks to the spur and support of the state, and in the United States, the bourgeoisie had to confront the plantation owners of the South.

The wealth and the power of the bourgeoisie developed on the basis of the dreadful misery of the workers of the nineteenth century: working days lengthened and wages were reduced, because of the competition between different types of workers. The conditions of life were often judged to be harder than the serfs of former times had endured. Charity and paternalism sometimes softened the most complete destitution, emigration was an outlet, and there were revolts, but the repression was pitiless. Solidarity, cooperatives, mutuals, unions, trade unions: after many attempts, the organization of the working world attained considerable progress during the 1860s.

Throughout this period capitalism was shaken by crises during which the grip of misery and hunger became even firmer. Economists considered the crises in order to propose remedies; socialists denounced them, and along with them, the incoherence of the system which produces crises. Marx produced the analysis of this system in order to illuminate the logic of capitalism and its necessary downfall.

Respect for the established order and especially for property; respect for wealth, religion, and the state; superiority of the white race and of Western culture—ideological norms shaped the whole of society. And if necessary, there were the police, the judge, the army, imprisonment, or deportation to intervene.

For the intellectuals and those who read them, all audacities and dreams of romanticism were allowed, as well as all of the certitudes of positivism and scientism. Refusing a harrowing reality, two utopias faced each other during the first half of the century: the liberal utopia and the socialist utopia, each one promising the happiness of everyone in a harmonious world. With the "laws of supply and demand in pure and perfect competition," and later on with marginalist theories, the liberal utopia will take on the appearance of a "scientific theory." The socialist utopia, which Marx criticized at the same time that he drew from it his youthful convictions, will be transformed by Marx into "historical necessity" following from analyses of "scientific socialism." These two utopias will remain vital until at least the end of the twentieth century.

Marx announced the inevitable collapse of capitalism and the arrival of a classless society: communism. Writing in the same year, J. S. Mill was persuaded that a durable "stationary state," which would finally allow men to enjoy the benefits of a more productive society, would soon be established.[86]

Turgot, Smith, Goodwin, Say, Ricardo: each in his own way had observed the emergence of a new reality. Marx's magisterial analysis of this reality made him the first "reader" of capitalism and the initiator of a new theoretical approach and vision of the world. His influence has been immense—in part because of the importance of his analyses themselves, but also in part because the reality he dedicated himself to analyzing has continued to expand its scope, weighing more and more heavily on the destiny of man and human society.

In Marx's footsteps have followed disciples, exegetes, continuators, catechists, orthodox followers, bearers of official Marxist truth, schism furrowers, reformers, renovators, commentators in both good and bad faith, critics of all kinds, broad-minded and narrow-minded adversaries, and every conceivable kind of enemy. In one way or another, every analysis of capitalism has been affected by Marx's analysis. This fact leads us to make the following specific comments.

Marx's works, and especially *Capital*, have given rise to a huge literature on the political economy of capitalism. Some of this literature has helped explain the cycles of expansion and crisis, the twofold advance of wealth and poverty, and the development of monopolies and domination on a world level. But at the same time we have also witnessed an outpouring of stock phrases and discourse which have served only to deaden and dull thought, and which have in fact interfered with our understanding of unfolding trends. By reducing all phenomena to economics alone, and by neglecting actual history, many Marxists have failed to recognize the complexity of social relations, as well as the reality of politics and the state.

Once again, this has impeded our understanding of the whole, and has led to the progressive impoverishment of an entire section of Marxist thought

Above all, *Capital*'s interpretive framework for understanding capitalism grew from observation of nineteenth-century industrial capitalism, which for Marx was the "true capitalist mode of production." This framework was less useful for understanding other forms of capitalism—mercantile, banking, and manufacturing[87]—and it became less and less adequate for analyzing the industrial capitalism of the twentieth century. Today, this interpretive framework hinders our ability to understand current mutations of capitalism and to analyze the new forms of capitalism that are based on control of technoscience.

We must therefore continue our analysis of capitalism "in general." The essential elements remain the quest for profit, accumulation, enlarged reproduction of production and circulation, and thus an ever wider market. What appears absolutely fundamental and central, however, is the transformative potential of capitalism: its tendency, as Marx put it, to "revolutionize" both production and society, or, in Schumpeter's phrase, its capacity for "creative destruction."

Through the industrial revolution and the process of industrialization, capitalism acquired an unprecedented transformative power. Great Britain was the first nation to experience this upheaval, which affected all aspects of society: productive systems, producing classes, mentalities and values, transportation and communication, and ways of living and consuming. Other European countries followed the same path, at various rates of transformation. Whole regions of the world, India in particular, were affected by these changes, while some of the newer nations, including the United States, followed the path toward capitalist modernization.

British predominance in the world during this period was uncontested at many levels, ranging from industry and trade to banking. The appearance of steamships, railroads, and the telegraph deepened the global dimension of trade and interdependence, and thus of capitalism. From this point on, the revolutionizing of all social relations as well as the process of creative destruction—in a single phrase, the transformative potential of capitalism—were carried out on a world scale.

Part II

THE ERA OF IMPERIALISM

Capitalism rules the world and makes our statesmen dance like puppets on a string.

—W. Sombart

Capitalism is neither a person nor an institution. It neither wills nor chooses. It is a logic at work through a mode of production: a blind, obstinate logic of accumulation.

This is a logic which depends on the production of goods, in which use-value is the support for the surplus value which must return to capital. Still, the value must be realized, the commodity must be sold; otherwise, accumulation is blocked and crisis may follow.

This logic was extended, during the last third of the eighteenth century and the first third of the nineteenth century, at the time of the "first industrialization," to clothing and textiles, machines, tools and metal domestic utensils, railroads and armaments.

It first developed in Great Britain and then, with some time lag, in the other countries of Europe and in the United States.

From the time that one speaks of capitalism as it has been historically realized, one must go beyond the single formula of a mode of production and its logic. There are the nations in which capitalism has developed, and the rivalries between nations, though encouraged and characterized by the oppositions between national capitalisms, cannot be reduced to these oppositions. There are the classes which dissolve and re-form in liaison with the large movement of capitalist development, with the struggles and alliances—all of these being specifically determined within each social formation. There is the state, an apparatus of domination and strategic ground of class alliances and relations of force. There are ideas, beliefs, religions, the unstable duo of knowledge and ignorance, ideologies; there is racism, nationalism, militarism, the spirit of domination, and the spirit of profit.

Expanding capitalism encountered these social realities: it conflicted with them or made use of them, it overturned or transformed them, it restrained or exacerbated them. All these factors must, then, be considered if one wishes to understand capitalism in its historical movement. But how can this be done without falling into reductionism and simplistic thinking?

Consider the family: with capitalism it became the base unit for the reproduction and maintenance of labor power, without ceasing to be the complex ground for the reproduction of the society as a whole. It was through the family that the old and declining classes perpetuated themselves; it was also through the family that new classes formed out of the old classes: uprooted peasants or artisans who had become workers, as well as noble families allying themselves with bankers or traders in order to found a "bourgeois dynasty" linked to industry, trade, or banking. It is true that many of the fundamental norms of society (hierarchy, discipline, savings, consumption) have been transmitted by the family, but it is also true that without the family many of the struggles of the workers' movement could not have developed, and many strikes would not have succeeded.

Consider the school: it is fashionable among those on the Left after 1968 to denounce the capitalist school, and certainly the school has served to diffuse the values, ideas, and norms of capitalist society. But the school has also diffused the principles and ideals of legitimate government, of democracy, and often of socialism; reading, writing, and knowledge are the bases of freedom and democratic life, even if these have allowed the development of writing which debilitates and new forms of propaganda.

By the decade of the 1870s, capitalism had as yet revolutionized only a part of Great Britain, and had established firm ground only in strictly bounded zones of continental Europe and North America. In one century it spread, became concentrated, and asserted itself with incredible strength: through the rise of new techniques and new industries, on the basis of ever larger and more powerful concentrations of capital whose field of action expanded to include the entire world; with the decline of the first imperialisms and the rise of new ones; with the affirmation and acknowledgment of the workers' movement, and the establishment of new means of domination over the workers.

An extraordinary tidal wave which from a first great depression led to imperialism, to the dividing up of the world and to the "Great War"; and then from a first reconstruction, with brief prosperity here and the rise of fascism there, to a fall into the depression of the 1930s followed by World War II; and finally, after a new reconstruction, decolonization, growth, and prosperity, until the bursting out of a new worldwide "great crisis." And there are those who think this latest crisis may give rise to World War III.

A century of exploiting and sacking the planet; a century of accelerated industrialization, modernization, and the "development of underdevelopment"; a century of imperialism.

In the first edition of this book, the preceding text was the beginning of Part II. There is no doubt I would write it differently today (1999), but instead I have changed not a word. I have chosen, rather, to add the following reflections, for two reasons. The first is that in the last twenty years of the twentieth century the capitalist transformation of the world deepened and widened. The second reason is simply that, during these twenty years, my own thinking has evolved.

One result of the broadened perspective offered by these twenty years is the necessity to stress the significance of the rupture, within human history, represented by the emergence of mercantile and manufacturing capitalism, the transition from manufacturing capitalism to industrial capitalism (usually called the "industrial revolution") and the capitalist industrialization of the nineteenth century.

The effects of this historical break were evident in every area of life, from production to consumption, from transportation to communication. While the changes were relatively localized from the sixteenth through the eighteenth centuries, they expanded during the nineteenth and twentieth centuries, and by the closing decades of the twentieth century had accelerated even further and become worldwide. In production per inhabitant of the planet, and to a greater extent when examining production per inhabitant of the rich countries (Diagram 10), the rates of increase are startling. From the beginning of the nineteenth century to the end of the twentieth, worldwide per capita production was multiplied by a factor of six; since world population during this time span rose from one billion to six billion, we may estimate that total world production was multiplied by a factor of thirty-six. These are huge figures, which have never been equaled or even approached during such a brief period within human history.

Per capita production for the years 1500, 1820 and 1990, where the civilizations of antiquity have the index value 1. On the same scale as the previous 170 years, the year 2000 would be located on the horizontal axis 20 cm to the left of the vertical axis.

DIAGRAM 10   GLOBAL PER CAPITA PRODUCTION
AS A MULTIPLE OF THE ERA OF ANTIQUITY

In a similar movement, as is evident in Diagram 11, from the beginning of the nineteenth century to the end of the twentieth, man's speed of movement over land increased by a factor of 14; the ability to make use of concentrated energy grew more than 300 million times over; the destructive capacity of the most powerful weapons increased by a factor of more than a billion; and the capacity (measured in both speed and quantity) to transmit information grew several trillion times over. These were changes which vastly increased the power of the already powerful, and opened up new possibilities for the various social strata who possessed adequate purchasing power.

If one considers only the last twenty years of the twentieth century, many important changes have taken place. Many of the new centers of industrialization and capitalist modernization, which had appeared in the

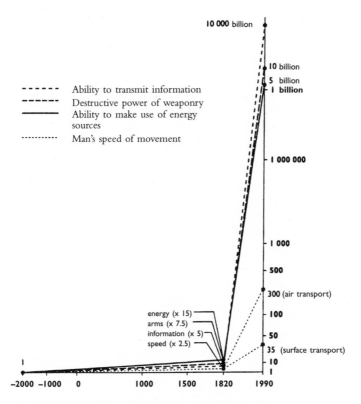

Base index: antiquity = 1. In comparison with 2000 BC, man's speed of movement on the earth's surface was 2.5 times greater in 1820, and 35 times greater (on land) in 1990.

Source: Michel Beaud, *Le basculement du monde* (Paris: La Decouverte, 1997), p. 101.

DIAGRAM 11 SELECTED HUMAN CAPABILITIES:
A COMPARISON BETWEEN THE TIME OF THE INDUSTRIAL
REVOLUTION AND THE PRESENT

third world following World War II, were caught up in the crisis of the 1980s. Several of the new "dragons" in East Asia and Southeast Asia were shaken by the crisis at the end of the 1990s. The USSR, the Soviet empire, and the statist economic system, have collapsed, leaving capitalism in an uncontested position as worldwide transformative force. American leaders and economists, along with the International Monetary Fund and the World Bank, all speak of a "market economy," but what they are in fact urging is that capitalism be given free rein everywhere.

During this same period, capitalism within the nations of the Triad has vastly increased its transformative strength by putting to work the results of scientific research. Increasingly this research is given direction and is even controlled by corporate capitalism. Beyond the industrial capitalism of the twentieth century, a new, technoscientistic capitalism is emerging. Exchanges and interdependences are growing, as are inequalities and disparities. The idea of globalization, while it describes certain undeniable realities (global finance, planetary environmental problems, products available around the world, the Internet...), also fulfills an ideological function. Globalization justifies the unjustifiable decisions (or non-decisions) of corporate directors and political leaders, and thus conceals, under the cover of a seductive and soothing allegory, the harmful and debilitating effects of liberal capitalism's unfettered resurgence.

The first part of this book led us from the pillage of gold in the Americas to the accumulation of capital, and from mercantile to industrial capitalism. The second part will lead from industrial capitalism to technoscientistic capitalism, and from imperialism to "globalization," behind which lie huge corporations, the dominant capitalisms, and the great state powers.

Chapter 4

FROM THE GREAT DEPRESSION
TO THE GREAT WAR
(1873–1914)

Before capitalism became dominant, economic life was shaken, more or less regularly, by changes in weather conditions, good and bad harvests, demographic changes, and wars. The whole phase of capitalist industrialization was accomplished through cyclical movements having a certain regularity: periods of prosperity and euphoria checked by a recession or broken by a crisis.

The crisis of the nineteenth century had multiple origins: the loss of outlets or supplies due to a war or reconversion following a war; the tightening of the market among rural populations because of one or several poor harvests, or, increasingly, because of the excessive development of production capacities; the sharpening of competition; and the fall in profits, linked both to the difficulty of realizing the produced value and to the fall in prices.[1]

The "great depression," which began with the crisis of 1873 and extended until 1895, opened what could be called the second period of capitalism: the period of imperialism. This involved particularly:

—the development of a second generation of industrial techniques and industries;
—the affirmation of the workers' movement, which gained considerable concessions in the industrialized countries;
—the concentration of capital and the emergence of finance capital;
—a new wave of colonization and expansion on a worldwide scale, leading to the "dividing up of the world" and the Great War.

THE GREAT DEPRESSION (1873-95)

At first glance, each of the crises which made up this great depression of the nineteenth century seems to have occurred as a continuation of the crises of the nineteenth century.

1873: the stock exchange crash in Vienna was followed by bank failures in Austria and then in Germany; heavy German industry, which had just undergone a strong expansion with the war effort and the construction of railroads and ships, contracted in the face of price rises and a drop in profitability; the production of cast iron fell 21 percent in 1874 and its price dropped 37 percent; unemployment caused some workers to return to the countryside, and in October 1875 the Baron von Oppenheim wrote that there had not been such a prolonged crisis in fifty-six years.[2]

In the United States the length of completed railroad lines increased by 50 percent between 1869 and 1873; when speculation, scarcity of labor power, and a rise in prices combined, profitability fell, railroad companies went bankrupt, banks failed, and there was a frantic stock exchange panic. Since railroad construction was an essential outlet for the production of cast iron, the price of cast iron fell by 27 percent between 1873 and 1875. Unemployment rose, wages fell, and the crisis reached textiles and the building trades. In England exports fell by 25 percent between 1872 and 1875; the number of bankruptcies increased (7,490 in 1873, 13,130 in 1879); unemployment extended and prices fell. Surplus production capacities were enormous: while forge owners in 1873 were able to produce 2.5 million tons of rails, consumption fell to 500,000 tons and their price dropped by 60 percent between 1872 and 1881.

1882: the stock exchange crash of Lyons was followed by the failure of the banks of Lyons and the Loire, and then by the failure of the General Union Bank and several others. Industries were affected as well: mines and metallurgy, construction, textiles, and porcelain. Unemployment spread further and wages dropped. "Never have I seen such a catastrophe," declared a director of Crédit Lyonnais.[3] Coming after the expansion linked to the establishment of the "Freycinet plan" for public works, the slackening of public employment projects, and particularly railroad construction, helped cause this depressive whirlpool.

1884: The construction of railroads in the United States, which had in fact started up again (4,300 km in 1878, but 18,600 km in 1882), gave way to the "railroad panic": only 6,300 km of railroad lines were constructed in 1884. The railroad companies were caught between rising construction costs and the competition they engaged in among themselves. The price of Union Pacific stock collapsed, and this was followed by the collapse of several other railroad securities. Banks failed and there was a slowdown in industrial activity, with bankruptcies, more unemployment, and wage reductions (from 15 to 22 percent in metallurgy, from 25 to 30 percent in textiles). During this crisis the Carnegie group grew stronger, particularly through purchasing competing factories at low prices.

Germany, which had just experienced a long period of depression, entered into a course of protectionism and cartel formation after 1869 (seventy-six cartels were created between 1879 and 1885). Great Britain suffered the repercussions of these crises: exports to those countries affected by the depression became more difficult, market competition increased, industrial activity slowed, wholesale prices fell, and unemployment among unionized workers reached 10 percent. This depression took until 1886–87 to come to an end.

At this time new prospects for profit making opened up: the discovery of gold in South Africa, the French project for a canal through Panama, the opening of new railroad lines in the United States, and the possibility of new economic developments in Argentina, Australia, and New Zealand. New speculations were begun, which gave rise to new blockages.

1889: in France the Metals Company and the company responsible for the construction of the Panama canal both went bankrupt. Credit crises were followed by a stock exchange panic, then a depression, which led to protectionism (the Méline tariffs).

1890: in Great Britain, the Baring Bank, which had become the financial agent of the Argentine Republic, became the victim of a crisis of confidence, due to Argentina's economic, financial, and political difficulties. The Baring Bank had to suspend payments, and the intervention of the Bank of England and other large English banks was needed to limit the banking panic. But a new depression began, which affected first the textile industry, especially cotton, and then naval construction and metallurgy. The depression was aggravated by the reduction in trade linked to the crises of 1893 which hit the United States, Argentina, and Australia.

Germany, which was increasingly oriented toward the conquest of foreign markets, was also affected by this crisis. The increased formation of cartels (137 by this time) opened the way to a new means for regulating the economy.

1893: until this time, the United States had experienced a period of prosperity, with excellent harvests and a resumption of work in the building trades and railroad construction. The great trusts exercised their power (Rockefeller, Carnegie, Morgan) and the protective McKinley tariff was established in 1890 for industry. But once more the railroad companies saw their profits fall, and some of them suspended payments. The stock exchange prices for railroad securities collapsed, and 491 banks failed. The depression grew worse in 1894, with more unemployment and an effort to reduce wages.

The most conspicuous indications of each of these crises occurred either on the stock exchange (price collapses, panics), or among the banks (failure of a large bank or chain failures). The same fundamental crisis was revealed in each case: when costs rise (a rise in wages, for instance, or in the case of the American railroads, an increase in the price of rails); when market outlets are reduced (a reduction in the buying power of rural populations or of workers in other sectors, a reduction in public investment, or difficulties on foreign markets), when sales go down (price competition, tariff wars between the American railroad companies), then profitability declines or drops drastically, realizing the value produced by each company becomes more difficult, competition stiffens, and the position of the companies in any one sector becomes increasingly precarious. Crisis can then be triggered by anything: a stock exchange rumor, a lost market, a company or a bank which discontinued payments—and an uncontrollable chain reaction follows.

In the crises of the first half of the nineteenth century, regulation operated through a double movement:

—a fall in prices and a large drop in realized value, thus the elimination of the most vulnerable companies: a radical form of the periodic "purge" of capital;
—unemployment and reduction of real wages, resulting in a lowering of workers' consumption, which contributes to enlarging the crisis (and thus the "purge") and allows the period to get going again with a labor force available at a lower cost.

In the crises of the nineteenth-century depression, a lowering of prices accompanied the reduction of production. This lowering constitutes a "heavy trend" during these twenty years; thus, from 1873 to 1896 wholesale prices fell by 32 percent in Great Britain, 40 percent in Germany, 43 percent in France, and 45 percent in the United States (see Table 4.1). This movement affected some products more than others: the price of Scottish cast iron, for instance, fell by 60 percent between 1872 and 1886.[4]

Increasing unemployment can also be observed: in Great Britain the percentage of unionized workers affected by unemployment rose sharply with each crisis: from 1 percent in 1872 to more than 11 percent in 1879,

TABLE 4.1   Changes in Wholesale Prices, 1860–1913

	Great Britain	France	Germany	United States
Period maximum	152 (*1873*)	144 (*1872, 1873*)	136 (*1873*)	213 (*1865*) 136 (*1873*)
Period minimum	83 (*1896*)	82 (*1896*)	82 (*1895, 1896*)	75 (*1896, 1897*)
Prewar maximum	116 (*1912, 1913*)	116 (*1912, 1913*)	115 (*1912, 1913*)	113 (*1910, 1912–13*)

Base index: 100 = 1901–10.
Source: From Frédéric Mauro, *Histoire de l'économie mondiale* (Paris: Sirey, 1971), p. 400.

from 2 percent in 1882 to more than 10 percent in 1886, and again from 2 percent in 1889–90 to 7.5 percent in 1893.[5]

In the United States, real salaries tended to go down in the affected sectors, which gave rise to harsh struggles. But this phenomenon was less clear in Great Britain and in France. In Britain, considering the real wage of the full-time worker to be 100 in 1850, this rose to 128 in 1873 and to 176 in 1896, though it dropped during the crises: from 137 in 1876 to 132 in 1878, from 137 in 1879 to 134 in 1880, from 136 in 1881 to 135 in 1882, and from 166 in 1890 to 163 in 1892. For the period as a whole, however, the real wage rose by 37 percent.[6]

In France, real wages grew about 25 percent between 1873 and 1896, but this movement as a whole fluctuated with the crises: stagnation in 1873, a retreat in 1876–77, and stagnation again in 1883 and in 1887–92.[7] The increase in real wages as a whole remained less than the increase in productivity.[8]

In all of this can be seen the beginning of a transformation in the means of capitalist regulation, for in the countries where the working class had succeeded in establishing themselves with sufficient strength, they reacted severely to the reduction in real wages during periods of crisis. At the same time, the employers were organizing capitalism through the formation of large companies or groups (in the United States and Great Britain), cartels (in Germany), and professional organizations (in France).

The elements for the establishment of a new means of regulating the capitalist economy were also present in this development. Certainly it would be excessive to contrast too radically the mode of economic regulation which can be observed during the great depression of 1873–96 to the regulation which took place during the first two-thirds of the nineteenth century. It must be noted, however, that during this great depression the form of economic regulation sustained a fundamental transformation.

How, then, can the depression at the end of the nineteenth century be characterized?

All capitalist crises result from the interaction of four fundamental contradictions:

1. the contradiction between capital and labor, that is, concretely, between capitalist companies and the working classes;
2. the contradiction between capitalists (either in the same sector or between sectors);
3. the contradiction between national capitalisms;
4. the contradiction between dominant capitalisms and dominated peoples, countries, or regions.

During this period, the first and third contradictions appear to be determining: the working classes organized and asserted themselves, and by the end of this period had a discernible effect in the functioning of national capitalisms; the rise of German and North American capitalisms challenged the hegemony of British capitalism, until then undisputed.

The second contradiction acted in a complex way, for on the one hand, new capitalist structures were established (concentration and centralization of capital and the formation of finance capital), and on the other hand, the development of new sectors made it possible to compensate for the decline of first-generation industries.

The fourth contradiction did not act here as a factor in crisis; it acted rather as a factor in its solution, with the expansion of capitalism on a world scale, capital exportation, and colonization.

THE END OF BRITISH HEGEMONY

What gentleman could doubt the British superiority? The craze for Englishness saturated the wealthy classes of Europe. British fashion was the mark of masculine elegance. The sports of Britain were more and more copied or adapted: baseball, basketball, football, lawn tennis, rugby. The era of matches and fair play opened up: the British influence was undeniable, though it was a Frenchman, Pierre de Coubertin, who launched the reborn Olympic Games in Athens in 1896. British troops and bureaucrats

TABLE 4.2   Coal, Cast Iron and Steel Production in Great Britain, Germany, and the United States (millions of tons)

	GREAT BRITAIN Coal	GERMANY Coal	UNITED STATES Coal
1871	117	29	42
1880	147	47	65
1890	182	70	143
1900	225	109	245
1913	292	190	571

	GREAT BRITAIN		GERMANY*		UNITED STATES	
	Cast iron	Steel	Cast iron	Steel	Cast iron	Steel
1880	7.9	3.7	2.7	1.5	4.8[†]	1.9[†]
1890	8.0	5.3	4.7	3.2	10.1	4.7
1900	9.1	6.0	8.5	7.4	20.4[‡]	17.2[‡]
1910	10.2	7.6	14.8	13.1	30.8[**]	31.8[**]

* Including Luxembourg.   [†] Average, 1881–85.   [‡] Average, 1901–05.   [**] Average, 1911–15.

Sources: J. H. Clapham, *The Economic Development of France and Germany (1815–1914)* (Cambridge: The University Press, 1923), pp. 281, 285; S. B. Clough, *Histoire économique des Etats-Unis, 1865–1952* (Paris: PUF, 1953).

were present everywhere in the world; British tourists invaded the most attractive sites along the Mediterranean and explored the most distant countries. Rudyard Kipling wrote of the "white man's burden": the greatness and responsibility of the white man, of whom the Englishman is the most eminent representative. Lord Baden-Powell, after taking part in the Boer War, founded scouting and in 1908 published *Scouting for Boys*. Fifteen years earlier, Sir Arthur Conan Doyle had created the character of Sherlock Holmes, an elegant synthesis of pragmatism and rigor, intuition and deduction.

The power, prosperity, and wealth of Britain were undeniable. London was the capital of the world, and sterling was the international currency. British domination extended over five continents, and British capitalism extracted considerable income from this domination (see Table 3.10).

And yet a relative decline had begun, of which the crises of 1873–96 were the first tremors. These crises did not in fact have the same impact on the different national capitalisms: in the United States and in Germany they accompanied the vigorous growth of the railroads, coal, steel, and

TABLE 4.3   Production Growth Rate

	TOTAL PRODUCTION			
	Great Britain	France	Germany	United States
1885–94 to 1905–14	23.8	15.7*	322.9‡	44.7
1905–14 to 1925–29	14.0	18.4†	17.7**	36.7‡
1925–29 to 1950–54	16.3	11.5	26.5	32.2

	PER CAPITA PRODUCTION				
	Great Britain	France	Germany	United States	Japan
1885–94 to 1905–14	11.4	13.5*	17.0‡	20.1	25.5
1905–14 to 1925–29	5.2	16.1†	7.3**	16.5‡	32.8
1925–29 to 1952–54	11.3	10.0	12.5	19.2	9.9

* 1861–70 to 1890–1900.   † 1896–1929.   ‡ 1880–89 to 1905–13.   ** 1895–1904 to 1925–29.

Source: Compiled from Rostow, *The World Economy*, pp. 378, 388, 395, 405.

naval construction, while in Britain they indicated the waning of a fully mature capitalism at the height of its powers.

The evolution of the base industries of the first industrialization, coal and steel, provide evidence of this. In 1871, and even in 1880, Britain produced more coal than the United States and Germany together, but by 1913 Britain's production was hardly more than half that of the United States. Britain was very quickly surpassed by the United States in steel, and after 1900 by Germany as well.

More generally, the new German and North American capitalisms were benefiting by this time from a dynamic of growth which allowed them quite clearly to prevail over the "old" French and English capitalisms. From the depression to the eve of the Great War, growth was two times more rapid in Germany than in France, and almost two times more rapid in the United States than in Britain. And, on average, the superiority of U.S. growth was maintained until the period directly following World War II. Thus the relative declines of British and French capitalisms began in the last third of the nineteenth century at the same time as the power of German and North American capitalisms increased (see Tables 4.2 and 4.3).

TABLE 4.4   Share of Major Industrial Countries in World Industrial Production (percent)

	Great Britain	France	Germany	Russia	United States	Japan	Rest of world
1870	32	10	13	4	23	–	18
1881–85	27	9	14	3	29	–	18
1896–1900	20	7	17	5	30	1	20
1906–10	15	6	16	6	35	1	22
1913	9	7	12	4[†]	42	3	23
1936–38	9	5	11	19[†]	32	4	20
1963	5	4	6[*]	19[†]	32	4	30

[*] West Germany.   [†] USSR.

Source: Rostow, *The World Economy*, pp. 52–53.

The share of Britain within world industrial production fell from 32 percent in 1870 to 14 percent just before the Great War to 9 percent on the brink of the crisis of 1930, while the share of the United States at the same time rose from 23 percent to 38 percent to 42 percent (see Table 4.4). Also during this period, the share of Belgium fell from 3 percent to 1 percent, the share of Italy rose from 2 percent to 3 percent, and then fell back to 2 percent; and the share of Scandinavia rose from 1 percent to 2 percent, as did that of Canada.

Britain represented one-fourth of world trade in 1880, one-sixth in 1913, and one-eighth in 1948 (see Table 4.5). This decline, it must be repeated, was only relative; on the whole, production and trade kept increasing, foreign investments grew, and Britain was present, active, and influential throughout the world. But in the face of the "leaps forward" of German, North American, and then Japanese capitalism, it no longer had the means which would enable it to stay ahead of these other nations.

The "weakening of the spirit of enterprise and innovation," the development of a "mentality common to those living off of an established income": these attitudes, no doubt linked to the advantages provided by regular and considerable foreign revenues, then manifested themselves.

English agriculture, after a prolonged depression, survived at the price of transforming its most proven methods, but became incapable of satisfying more than 40 percent of the alimentary needs of the country, and, without experiencing

TABLE 4.5   Distribution of World Trade (percent)

	Great Britain	France	Germany	Rest of Europe	United States	Rest of world
1880	23	11	10	27	10	19
1913	16	7	12	29	11	25
1928	14	6	9	22	14	35
1930	14	4	9	20	10	43
1948	12	5	2*	22	16	43
1958	9	5	8*	26	14	38

* West Germany.

Source: Rostow, *The World Economy*, pp. 72–73.

a true decline in its income, had to resign itself to a secondary role. It lived in the hope of governmental aid, which it received only progressively during the war, and which was cut off after 1921. The large base industries operated more and more with already acquired techniques, and closed themselves to the most promising innovations: the steelmakers were too loyal to the Bessemer and Siemens processes; the cotton producers after 1900 hesitated to adopt circular weaving, and later, automatic machines. The chemical industries, and the new companies producing electricity, rubber, bicycles, and automobiles developed at a slow speed.[9]

In summary, during the period preceding World War I, the old English and French capitalisms were overtaken and surpassed by the new German and North American capitalisms. This process occurred partly through the crises which affected the end of the nineteenth century.

THE AFFIRMATION OF THE WORKING CLASSES

The other underlying movement which marked this period was the rise of the working classes. Indeed, this was the most fundamental movement, for it indicated the passage of a phase in which capitalism was able to develop by utilizing a labor force that was uprooted, dependent, subjugated, and crushed. The new phase was one in which the capitalist bourgeoisie had to contend with a working class which was increasingly conscious of its own position, which organized itself, and which finally imposed a new balance of forces.

The working-class movement developed within the framework of a more encompassing transformation of the whole society, which was also caused by capitalist industrialization. Notable were the following:

—The continuation of the process of *paying wages*: 80 percent of the active population in Britain at the end of the nineteenth century received wages; while in the United States in 1880 the figure was 63 percent; in Germany in 1902, 66 percent; and in France in 1911, 58 percent. From this time on, wage earners in the capitalist world numbered in the tens of millions, outweighing the small independent producers in agriculture, trade, and craft work.

—The prominence of *urbanization*: at the beginning of the twentieth century, London had more than 4 million inhabitants, while Glasgow, Manchester, Birmingham, and Liverpool each had 1 million, and more than forty British cities had populations exceeding 100,000. The percentage of the U.S. population living in cities larger than 8,000 people rose from 23 percent in 1880 to 32 percent in 1900, and to 44 percent in 1920, while in Germany the percentage of the population living in towns larger than 2,000 people rose from 41 percent in 1880 to 60 percent in 1910, by which time this percentage was 78 percent in Britain, 46 percent in the United States, and 44 percent in France. Through this process of urbanization, the new conditions for collective action were created.

In this context, the development of the working classes can be grasped with a few figures:

—In Britain the number of industrial workers grew from 5.7 million in 1881 to 8.6 million in 1911 (divided between 6.2 million in manufacturing industries, 1.2 million workers in the mines, and 1.2 million in construction), to which must be added 1.5 million wage earners in transportation.

—In the United States the population employed in the secondary sector rose from 23 percent of the active population in 1870 to 31 percent in 1910, while the number of wage earners in industry (factories only) increased from 2 million in 1870 to 4.5 million in 1899, to 6.2 million in 1909, and to 8.4 million in 1919.

—In Germany the percentage of the population working in industry grew from 41 percent in 1895 to 43 percent in 1907, while the number of workers increased from 5.9 million to 8.6 million, including 300,000 home workers throughout this period.

—In France the numbers in the working classes increased from 3 million at the end of the nineteenth century to 5 million just before World War I. The transformation of manufacturing employment was significant between 1850 and 1910, during which time employment in craft work fell from 2.5 million to 900,000, while the numbers working for industrial companies rose from 1.2 million to 4.5 million.

Thus in the four large capitalist countries the working classes represented about 30 million men and women. When one adds the workers in other countries affected by capitalist industrialization, this figure rises to around 40 million. Along with this growth in numbers, these workers became aware of their solidarity, and, little by little, of their force.

There are always many forms of resistance to oppression and exploitation. Consider the observations of Frederick W. Taylor, who was a worker before becoming a supervisor and then the prophet of the "scientific organization of labor."

When he was eighteen, Taylor decided to forgo a Harvard education and instead become an apprentice machinist, then an unskilled laborer at Midvale Steel, where he was promoted to gang boss. "Within six years he went from gang boss to foreman of the machine shop, to master mechanic in charge of repairs and maintenance throughout the works, to chief draftsman, to chief engineer."[10] Along the way he changed his work habits. As long as Taylor was a worker he "obeyed the social code and restricted output"—not working too hard to break the rates, i.e., the standard amount paid for each piece.

> We who were the workmen of the machine shop had the quantity output carefully agreed upon for everything that was turned out in the shop. We limited the output to about, I should think, one-third of what we could very well have done. We felt justified in doing this, owing to the piecework system—that is, owing to the necessity for soldiering under the piecework system—which I pointed out....
>
> As soon as I became gang boss the men who were working under me and who, of course, knew that I was onto the whole game of soldiering or deliberately restricting output, came to me at once and said, "Now, Fred, you are not going to be a damn piecework hog, are you?" I said, "If you fellows mean you are afraid I am going to try to get a larger output from these lathes," I said, "Yes; I do propose to get more work out." I said, "You must remember I have been square with you fellows up to now and worked with you. I have not broken a single rate. I have been on your side of the fence. But now I have accepted a job under the management of this company and I am on the other side of the fence, and I will tell you perfectly frankly that I am going to try to get a bigger output from those lathes." They answered, "Then, you are going to be a damn hog."[11]

Taylor made workers' resistance a key element in his analysis:

> Underworking, that is, deliberately working slowly so as to avoid doing a full
> day's work, "soldiering," as it is called in this country, "hanging it out," as it is
> called in England, "ca canae," as it is called in Scotland, is almost universal in
> industrial establishments, and prevails also to a large extent in the building
> trades; and the writer asserts without fear of contradiction that this constitutes
> the greatest evil with which the working-people of both England and America
> are now afflicted.[12]

Particularly during these periods of crisis, strikes broke out, and these
became longer and stronger. A series of strikes in the United States culmi-
nated in the "commune of Pittsburg" and the railroad workers' strike in
1877. In France there was a strike at Anzin in 1884, and in Decazeville in
1886; in the United States there were more than 3,000 strikes and more
than a million strikers between 1881 and 1886. These strikes included the
railroad strike of 1884–86 and the May 1886 strike for the eight-hour
working day in Chicago: there were 80,000 strikers, and following the
Haymarket Square riot the movement leaders were arrested, condemned,
and hanged. During this same period there was also a dockers' strike
which paralyzed the port of London in 1885.

Miners in the United States went on strike in 1893, and in 1894 the
Pullman strike was broken by the application of the Sherman Antitrust
Act and the imprisonment of the strike leaders. In France there was a
strike by the weavers in Roanne and by the glass makers of Carmaux,
both in 1895, and in Germany during this same year a new strategy was
established which concentrated the workers' organization within a single
body.

American miners staged new strikes in 1899 and 1902, as did workers
in Creusot in 1899, dock workers in the port of Marseilles in 1900,
miners of Montceau-les-Mines in 1901, and miners throughout France in
1902. In Germany textile workers and miners struck in 1905, the same
year in which miners in the French department of Nord went on strike.
The year 1910 saw a strike by the railroad workers in France and the
woodcutters of Louisiana in the United States, followed by a textile
workers' strike in the United States in 1912–13.

At the same time workers' organizations began to develop: trade unions,
work exchanges, mutual insurance companies, parties. In Britain, where
the workers' movement had benefited from long experience, despite being
weakened during the 1870s, the number of unionized workers increased
markedly: from 1.1 million in 1876 to 2.2 million in 1900 to 4.1 million
in 1913. The socialist movement had regained vitality during the 1880s,

and the first workers' representatives were elected in 1892. But it was only in 1900, when the unions decided to participate in a Labour Representation Committee, that the Labour Party was able to be organized: in 1914, out of 1,600,000 members, 1,570,000 were union workers. During these early years the Labour Party was not able to exert a strong influence within the British two-party system, however.

The workers' movement in France at the end of the nineteenth century was organized within a context of permanent debates and schisms, an abundance of different schools of thought, and various sects and traditions. When the diverse socialist forces collected into the French Section of the Workers International (SFIO, 1905), the General Congress of Workers (CGT) affirmed the total autonomy of a trade union movement at the Congress of Amiens (1905), which, with the weapon of the general strike, contained the potential force to overthrow capitalism. The number of union workers surpassed 1 million in 1912, and the number of SFIO members grew from 30,000 in 1905 to 90,000 in 1914. The number of socialist votes rose from 880,000 in the elections of 1906 to 1,400,000 in the elections of 1914.

In Germany, after the 1878 Socialist Law prohibiting all organization, meetings, or publications by socialists or social democrats, and the subsequent period of semi-clandestine action, social democracy gained some initial success in 1884, with 550,000 votes and twenty-four elected representatives. Its influence widened considerably in the elections of 1903, with 3 million votes and 81 representatives, and again in the 1912 elections, with 4 million votes and 110 representatives. The trade unions developed at the same time: there were 300,000 union members in 1890, 680,000 at the turn of the century, and 2.5 million in 1913. The agreement about parity, adopted by the Congress of Mannheim in 1906, obliged the party and the trade union organization to make essential decisions together.

In the United States the trade union movement was formed through a series of crises, strikes, and repression. The Knights of Labor grew from 110,000 members in 1885 to 729,000 in 1885, but fell back in 1890 to 100,000. Some organizations swelled in numbers following a successful campaign: for example, the American Railway Union (150,000 members in 1893) and the Federation of American Miners (100,000 members in 1897); while the American Federation of Labor (AFL) developed more gradually and prudently: 100,000 members in 1886, 250,000 in 1892, and 2 million in 1912.

Throughout the world, there were about 15 million unionized workers in 1913. The effect of mass protest and electoral influence of street protests, strikes, and spilled blood, of trade union organizations, work exchanges, cooperatives, mutuals, parties, and movements was to shift the balance of forces in each country, according to each country's specific historical development. The working class from then on carried weight, though it was still excluded in many ways from local and national life. It is this new balance of forces, and this alone, which explains the conquests and new benefits which came to the working world at the end of the nineteenth and the beginning of the twentieth centuries.

The tendency toward a rise in real wages in the four principal capitalist countries resulted from this new balance of forces. Between the 1870s and the period preceding World War I, real wages rose on the average by one-fifth in Germany and two-fifths in France.[13] A parallel movement was the tendency toward a *reduction in the length of the working day*. Some authors have emphasized here that during this period gains in productivity were sufficiently large to "make possible" these concessions, from the point of view of capital. Now, while there is some truth in this, it is also true that without the new balance of forces these concessions in all probability would never have been made.

The new balance of forces explains also the importance of the social laws which were voted at this time. In Britain the Employers and Workmen Act of 1875 replaced the Master and Servant Act of 1867. Laws of 1875 and 1876 authorized nonviolent strike pickets, and granted legal status to the trade unions. In Germany, Bismarck initiated laws with the aim of checking the demands of the workers: laws about medical insurance (1883), accident insurance and old-age benefits (1884), and retirement at sixty years of age (1889). France passed a law granting freedom of association (1884), laws regarding the length of the working day (1874, 1892, and 1900), cleanliness and safety (1893), work-related accidents (1898), retirement (1905), and weekly rest (1906). In Britain a 1906 law facilitated union action, a 1908 law dealt with workers' retirement, and another regulated work in the home, and a 1911 law established unemployment benefits and widened medical insurance. In the United States, many states adopted social laws concerned principally with an eight-hour working day for minors, child labor, and work-related accidents.

This new balance of forces brought the Catholic church to "concern itself" with the social question: in 1891 Leon XIII published his encyclical *Rerum novarum*, in which he addressed himself to "the rich and the employers": "They must not treat the worker as a slave; it is just that they respect in him the dignity of man, which is heightened still further by his being Christian. Labor of the body ... far from being a reason for shame, honours man.... What is shameful and inhuman, is to use man as a vile instrument of lucre, and to value him only in proportion to the strength of his arms."[14] Leon XIII addressed himself also "to the poor man, to the worker": "He should provide completely and faithfully all the work for which he has been engaged through a free and equitable contract. He should harm neither his employer's goods, nor his person. His demands must be free from violence and must never take a seditious form. He must avoid the perverse men who, in their lying speeches, suggest to him exaggerated hopes." For, "in society the two classes are destined by nature to unite harmoniously and to hold each other in perfect equilibrium. They have an imperious need, one for the other; there can not be capital without labor, or labor without capital." For the shrewd reader, this advice penetrates through the discretion: "We believe, however, that it is more appropriate to the present conditions of social life to temper the work contract, so far as this is possible, with elements borrowed from the social contract."[15]

This new balance of forces explains finally the conviction of innumerable socialists, anarchists, and communists that the overthrow of the capitalist system was imminent. Lafargue wrote in 1882: "The revolution is near; the collision of two clouds will suffice to cause the human explosion." Kropotkin wrote in 1883: "Gentlemen, believe me, the social revolution is close at hand. Within ten years it will burst out. I live among the workers and I affirm this." Emile Pouget wrote in 1889, in *Le Père Peinard*: "Can you see what would happen if, in fifteen days, there were no more coal? The factories would stop, the large cities would have no more gas, the railroads would sleep.... And then, the common people would rest. This would give them time to think; they would understand that they are nastily cheated by the bosses, and so they might well come to shake the living daylights out of them!" Guesde wrote in 1897: "The beginning of the next century will be the beginning of the new era."[16] More prudent, it was in the year 2000 that the American writer Edward Bellamy situated the socialist society which he described in *Looking Backward* (1888).

A NEW AGE OF CAPITALISM

Competition between capitalists stiffened, especially in the sectors of the first industrialization; the rivalry between the great national capitalisms hardened; the working classes became organized and forced capital to grant appreciable concessions; crises widened; and some people saw the death of capitalism close at hand. But already capitalism was adapting itself, transforming itself, opening new prospects, and modifying the areas of dispute. And this occurred in the face of the organized working classes.

Social laws? There were always employers to condemn them, such as Henri Schneider, interviewed in *Le Figaro* in 1897:

> State intervention in workers' problems is very bad, very bad.... I don't accept a prefect by any means in a strike.... It is the same as regulating labor by women and children.... They set up useless impediments which are too strict. As for the working day of eight hours, that is just another fetish.... In five or six years everyone will have forgotten it; something else will have been invented.... For me the truth is that a healthy worker can very well do his ten hours of work, and he should be left free to do more if it pleases him to do so.[17]

Some employers were ready to twist the laws around. But increasingly the employers were resigned to the social laws, or accepted them, some through calculation, some through philanthropy.

Strikes? Strikes were combated vigorously. In France the employers appealed to the force of the police and the army; in the United States they called out detectives (especially from the Pinkerton agency) and militia, Orientals, and federal troops.[18] In 1907 the French Supreme Court of Appeal still confirmed that the employer was not obliged to rehire striking workers, "since the worker who strikes willingly renders impossible the continuation of the execution of the labor contract which bound him to his employer; this act of striking, though not forbidden by penal law, constitutes on the part of the worker, whatever his motives, a breach of contract."[19]

But the right to strike was not often acknowledged, as Jaurès was asking for it in *L'Humanité* in 1904, as "the exercise of one of the implicit and essential clauses of the modern labor contract." The strike was gradually integrated into the institutionalized terms of collective bargaining.

Production slow-downs? The effort by employers to combat this was unceasing, affecting for a long time the system of wages. At the end of the nineteenth century, wages paid by the piece lost their efficiency. "It remains true," noted economist Leroy-Beaulieu, "that however useful and however necessary piece work may be, it can easily multiply the difficulties between workers and employers, and a great spirit of conciliation and justice on both sides is indispensable to its peaceful functioning."[20] "Now," he went on to observe, "popular hostility toward piece work seems to increase everyday instead of diminishing with the advance of instruction."[21] Frederick Taylor, who had experienced the application of piece work, was more realistic: "After a workman has had the price per piece of the work he is doing lowered two or three times as a result of his having worked harder and increased his output, he is likely to lose sight of his employer's side of the case and become imbued with a grim determination to have no more cuts if soldiering can prevent it." And again: this system "involves a deliberate attempt to mislead and deceive his employer, and thus upright and straight-forward workmen are compelled to become more or less hypocritical. The employer is soon looked upon as an antagonist if not an enemy, and the mutual confidence which should exist between a leader and his men ... is entirely lacking."[22]

Various wage systems were invented: bonus systems such as the "Lallemand wage rate," applied in 1888, again briefly in 1899, and more systematically in 1912, about which its creator said, "My system is, I believe, the first which attempts to remunerate not the time or the pro-duced labor—two elements, which, all in all, leave the worker rather indifferent—but the effort which he must display at every moment."[23] Regressive wage rates were applied in armories, but they led to poor results; progressive wage rates were used in different sectors of the economy during the second half of the nineteenth century, and in some automobile factories at the beginning of the twentieth century. Some employers already extolled workers' participation, and in 1889 the "Society for the Practical Study of the Participation of Personnel in Profits" was created: by 1911, 114 companies in France had put this to work, with 77 in England, 46 in Germany, and 43 in the United States.

It was the organization of work which gave the employers the weapon they needed at this time. Monsieur Fayol, a French mining engineer and general director of the Commentry-Fourchambault Company, presented his ideas regarding general industrial administration in 1916 in the *Bulletin de la Société de l'industrie minérale.* He distinguished the "professional ability" of the inferior agents from the "administrative ability" of the directors, and encouraged a clear definition of roles and systematic organization. Taylor, who had become a "consulting engineer and specialist in the systematic organization of workshops," as his business card announced, was the stubborn champion of the scientific organization of labor: the break-down of labor into separate tasks, organization and definition of movements, norms, and remuneration encouraging respect for the norms. He outlined the steps for establishing his new organization of production:

> *First.* Find, say, 10 or 15 different men (preferably in as many separate establish-ments and different parts of the country) who are especially skilful in doing the particular work to be analyzed.

Second. Study the exact series of elementary operations or motions which each of these men uses in doing the work which is being investigated, as well as the implements each man uses.

Third. Study with a stop-watch the time required to make each of these elementary movements and then select the quickest way of doing each element of the work.

Fourth. Eliminate all false movements, slow movements, and useless movements.

Fifth. After doing away with all unnecessary movements, collect into one series the quickest and best movements as well as the best implements.[24]

Taylor's results were often spectacular: he found that where a worker was loading a cart with 12.7 tons of cast iron molds per day, he could load it with 47 to 48 tons, with happiness as a bonus, since he was sure the workers were "happier and better contented when loading at the new rate of 47 tons per man per day in place of 12½ tons, at which rate the work was then being done."[25]

But these were only pioneering efforts; it required the war and the development of mass production for these principles of scientific labor organization to be systematically put to work.

In the face of the accentuation of intercapitalist competition, reactions, offensives, and initiatives again multiplied. These took the form first of all of protectionism through higher tariffs: in Germany in 1879, and again following 1902; in the United States in 1857; in France in 1892, 1907, and 1910. The only country to escape this trend was Britain, whose essential strength lay precisely in its preeminence on the world market.

Cartels and trade agreements followed, particularly numerous and organized in Germany: producers agreed to fix levels of production, co-ordinate investments, divide the market among themselves, and determine prices. In 1903 the Rhine-Westphalia coal cartel controlled 98.7 percent of this region's coal production; in 1905 an official inquiry recorded the existence of 17 mining cartels, 73 in the metallurgy industry, and 46 in the chemical industry. In the United States these agreements, in multiple and changing forms, affected many sectors: railroads, gunpowder, tobacco, and oil, most notably. In 1914, 114 international cartels were functioning, including 29 in coal production and metallurgical industries, 19 in the chemical industries, and 18 in transport.

In a related development, there was an extraordinary proliferation of scientific and technical advances, inventions, and innovations. The number of patents granted each year surpassed 30,000 in Britain between 1880 and 1887, and there were still more than 16,000 granted in 1908. In the United States the number rose from 14,000 in 1880 to more than 36,000

TABLE 4.6   Leading Second-generation Industries in Five Countries

	Steel	Electricity	Motor vehicles	Sulfuric acid
GREAT BRITAIN				
(a)	1870–79	1900–10	1900–10	1870–79
(b)	1870–1929	1900–59	1920–69	(c)
UNITED STATES				
(a)	1870–79	1880–89	1900–10	1870–79
(b)	1870–1929	1900–59	1910–59	(c)
GERMANY				
(a)	1870–79	1900–10	1870–79	1900–10
(b)	1870–1959	1900–69	1920–69	(c)
FRANCE				
(a)	1870–79	1920–29	1945–50	1900–10
(b)	1870–1959	1900–69	1920–79	(c)
JAPAN				
(a)	1900–10	1920–29	1930–39	1930–39
(b)	1900–69	1920–59	1930–79	(c)

(a) Period of greatest expansion.
(b) Period in which sector played a leading role in national industry.
(c) Sector not sufficiently developed to play leading role.

Source: Compiled from Rostow, *The World Economy*, pp. 379, 393, 400, 408, 422.

in 1907; in France, from 6,000 in 1880 to 12,600 in 1907; and in Germany, from 9,000 in 1900 to 12,000 in 1910.[26]

Many of these inventions involved the various possible uses of electricity: in 1869 Gramme took out a patent for a direct current generator; in 1883 Deprez succeeded in transporting energy from Vizille to Grenoble; in 1891 Frankfurt was using the 15,000 volts produced 140 km away on the Neckar. Electric lighting became possible after 1879 with the carbon filament bulb invented by Edison; the use of electric lighting extended after 1910 with the tungsten filament bulb. Equipment for electricity generating stations— water- or combustion-dependent—became available at the same time as cables were strung or laid, cities were illuminated, public transport was electrified, and electric motors were developed; equipment for factories, offices, and homes was also electrified. Powerful companies developed rapidly in this new sector.

In a parallel development, the construction of the internal combustion engine in 1862 led, with the invention of the carburetor (1889), to the gasoline engine, and then to the diesel engine (1893–97), which used gas-oil. Innumerable manufacturers built automobiles which were modernized from year to year, while other industrialists manufactured rubber tires. Roads had to be constructed, enlarged, and improved; and the first Automobile Exposition opened in Paris in 1898. A few years later the first airplane flights took place; the English Channel was crossed in 1909, as was the Mediterranean in 1912. This burgeoning aeronautical industry, together with the automobile industry, were given a powerful spur by World War I.

The new sources of energy developed mainly after 1900, though coal retained an indisputable supremacy. Steel pipe lines were built after 1875, particularly in the United States; the first tanker was put into service in Russia, on the Caspian, in 1877; in 1890, sixty oil tankers crossed the seas. And in 1914, 2 million automobiles were in circulation throughout the world, half of them in the United States.

Chemistry developed, with new processes, new products, and a great increase in quantities. Within a few decades the production of aluminum reached an industrial level (from 175 tons in 1890 to more than 50,000 tons in 1912). Electro-chemistry and electro-metallurgy permitted the fabrication of new products. New sectors of production developed, whose products dramatically changed living conditions: rayon, photographic papers, nitroglycerin, cement, telephones, telegraphs and soon radio, pharmaceutical products, and products for agriculture. All these developments led to high profits and allowed for the rapid establishment of a few powerful companies.

The armaments industries experienced a renewal with the development of steel, engines, and new explosives: repeater rifles (Lebel and Mauser), machine-guns, cannons, armor plates, steel turrets, armored ships, the first submarines—all the more since one of the aspects of the renewal of capitalism was expansion on a world scale, which exacerbated national rivalries.

THE AGE OF IMPERIALISM

A weakening in the first-generation industrial sectors; strengthening and organization of the working classes in the developed capitalist countries; stiffening of intercapitalist competition; violent crises; some people saw in these things the symptoms of the impending collapse of capitalism. But already new and important industrial sectors were unfolding; new means of domination over the workers and new relations with the working class were made ready; beyond defensive reactions (protectionism, cartels), and within their shelter, a fundamental mutation of capitalism was beginning: concentration and centralization of industrial capital, formation of trusts and national monopolies, and, inevitably, expansion onto a worldwide scale of the sphere of influence of the dominant capitalisms, by means of trade and the exportation of capital, the formation of multinational groups, and colonization.

Everywhere, the average size of business establishments and industrial companies increased; in Britain the average size of the spinning mills doubled between 1884 and 1911, with a similar increase for blast furnaces between 1882 and 1913; in France in 1906 one-tenth of the wage-earning labor force was employed in companies having more than 500 wage earners; in the United States the average number of wage earners for each industrial company rose from twenty-two in 1899 to forty in 1919. In times of crisis, mergers took place which benefited the most powerful companies; thus during the period 1880–1918 in Britain, 655 companies "disappeared" into 74 merger companies.[27]

Above all, unprecedented concentrations of capital occurred, under the direction of a capitalist or of a family; trusts or groups very quickly came to dominate an entire industrial sector within a nation, especially in the United States and in Germany. In the United States in 1908, the seven largest trusts owned or controlled 1,638 companies.[28] By 1900, the percentage represented by the trusts included 50 percent of textile production, 54 percent of the glass-making industry, 60 percent of the book and paper industry, 62 percent of the food industry, 72 percent of the liquor industry, 77 percent of nonferrous metals, 81 percent of the chemical industries, and 84 percent of iron and steel.[29] These included companies such as the United States Steel Corporation, founded by J. P. Morgan and E. H. Gary, which incorporated the Carnegie steel mills, and Standard Oil, founded in 1870 by J. D. Rockefeller, which in 1870 refined only 4 percent of American petroleum but by 1879 controlled 90 percent of the American refineries, and by 1904 controlled 85 percent of the domestic business and 90 percent of the export business as well.

In Germany the Krupp industrial empire employed 7,000 workers in 1873, and 78,000 in 1913; the AEG electrical industry, through an astonishing process of concentration, by 1911 controlled 175 to 200 companies, and employed more than 60,000 workers. After 1908 it cooperated with the other German company, Siemens, and divided up the world market with the U.S. company General Electric (Europe for the former and North America for the latter).[30] In Britain this movement was less marked, but even so there was a considerable degree of concentration within the banking world: 250 private banks in 1880 reduced to 48 in 1913; 120 Joint Stock Banks in 1880 went to 43 in 1913. The same process occurred in Germany: at the time of the crisis of 1873, 70 banks failed, and there was another round of bank failings during the 1890–91 crisis. The crisis of 1901 was a true "cleaning-up crisis": the Deutsche Bank absorbed 49 others, the Dresdner Bank absorbed 46, and the Diskonto Bank 28. Out of this there remained 5 or 6 very large banks, "each bank being the financial core for a set of companies. In order to share the risks, however, several banks associated to sponsor the same company."[31] In the same way in the United States two "financial empires" were founded: one formed by the First National Bank (of Morgan), General Electric, Rubber Trust, U.S. Steel, Vanderbilt's railways, and various electrical companies; the other formed by Rockefeller's National City Bank, Standard Oil, the Tobacco Trust, the Ice Trust, Gould's railways, and telephone companies.[32]

"The Concentration of production; the monopoly arising therefrom; the merging or coalescence of banking with industry—this is the history of the rise of finance capital and what gives the term 'finance capital' its content,"[33] wrote Lenin in *Imperialism: The Highest Stage of Capitalism.* Like Bukharin, he took up the concepts developed by Hilferding: "Finance capital signifies the unification of capital. The previously separate spheres of industrial, commercial and bank capital are now brought under the common direction of high finance, in which the masters of industry and of the banks are united in a close personal association."[34] And elsewhere:

> Thus the specific character of capital is obliterated in finance capital. Capital now appears as a unitary power which exercises sovereign sway over the life process of society; a power which arises directly from ownership of the means of production, of natural resources, and of the whole accumulated labour of the past, and from command over living labour as a direct consequence of property relations. At the same time property, concentrated and centralized in the hands of a few giant capitalist groups, manifests itself in direct opposition to the mass of those who possess no capital.[35]

Imperialism develops indissociably with finance capital, as Hilferding made clear:

> The policy of finance capital has three objectives:
> (1) to establish the largest possible economic territory;
> (2) to close this territory to foreign competition by a wall of protective tariffs, and consequently
> (3) to reserve it as an area of exploitation for the national monopolistic combinations.[36]

Bukharin made a similar observation: "The policy of finance capital is imperialism."[37]

As exports increased from capitalist countries, international competition became still more severe; capital was exported and overseas holdings and affiliates were created. Within this same movement there was a second, powerful wave of colonizations, accompanied by rivalries, conflicts, and wars.

From 1875 to 1913, despite protectionism, German exports rose by a factor of four and U.S. exports by a factor close to five. British exports were multiplied by only 2.2, and French exports by 1.8, but in both these countries the effort to export increased: in Great Britain the percentage of the physical product exported, which had risen from 26 percent in 1851 to 46 percent in 1871 and had then fallen after 1881, rose again after 1900 to reach 50 percent in 1911. In France this figure advanced more gradually, from 17 percent in the last third of the nineteenth century to 21 percent in 1905–13.[38] Britain exported 13 percent of the coal it produced in 1870, but 21 percent in 1890 and 33 percent in 1913; it exported 35 to 40 percent of the cast iron and steel which it produced in the second half of the nineteenth century, and 50 percent of what it produced in 1905–07.[39] In this, British industry continued to benefit from an advantage present in its industrial structure, since the proportion of the production of the means of production increased still more, from 47 percent in 1881 to 58 percent in 1907.[40] Essential outlets for these exports were the new countries that were industrializing, urbanizing, and equipping themselves.

The export of capital was one of the means for making sure of these outlets, and it assumed a growing importance at the end of the nineteenth and the beginning of the twentieth century. Foreign investments, in annual flows, doubled in Britain from 1880–84 to 1890–94, and then quadrupled between 1890–94 and 1910–13. In Germany they doubled once between 1883 and 1893, and again between 1893 and 1914. In France they tripled between 1880 and 1914.[41]

These three countries together represented more than three-fourths of the capital invested abroad in 1914: 43 percent from Britain alone, 20 percent from France, 13 percent from Germany, 12 percent from the Belgian, Swiss, and Dutch investments together, only 7 percent from the United States, and 50 percent from all other sources.[42]

As for the zones of "investment," Europe represented the largest share (27 percent), followed by North America (24 percent), Latin America (19 percent), Asia (16 percent), Africa (9 percent), and Oceania (5 percent).[43] Britain was clearly the chief world investor, though the direction of its investments underwent a profound change, becoming oriented less toward Europe, the United States, and India, and more toward the rest of the Commonwealth and Latin America.

French assets remained principally in Europe (nearly three-fifths), with a strong orientation toward Eastern Europe and especially Russia. They were not yet strongly invested in the colonies. German capital was also mainly invested in European countries (especially Austria, Russia, Hungary, and Rumania), though it was also in some other countries, such as Japan, Mexico, and the Ottoman Empire. Capital from the United States stayed mainly in the Americas: Canada, Mexico, and Cuba.

These overseas assets assumed many different forms: subscriptions to public loans (of which French savers were very fond), government loans, loans to banks and companies, share holdings or purchases in the various sectors of activity, or, for the trusts and groups, the creation of foreign affiliates. Thus Westinghouse created an English affiliate in 1903, and before 1912 AEG had affiliates in London, Petrograd, Paris, Genoa, Stockholm, Brussels, Vienna, Milan, and many cities in America. The banks played a decisive role in this movement. In 1913 the assets of the Société Générale de Belgique were divided between national stocks (three-fifths) and foreign stocks (two-fifths), especially in Austria, Russia, Canada, Argentina, and New Caledonia. The Deutsche Bank had subsidiaries in South America (Argentina, Peru, Bolivia, Uruguay, and Brazil) and Spain; holdings in Switzerland, Iraq, and China; and interests in Austria, the Ottoman Empire, Central America, East Africa, and southern Africa. The Diskonto Bank had affiliates in Britain, Rumania, Bulgaria, Brazil, and China; holdings in Belgium, Italy, Argentina, Brazil, the Cameroons, Guinea, and Asia; and interests in Europe (Britain, Finland, Austria, Rumania, and Russia) and Africa. In 1910 British banks had more than 5,000 branch offices or agencies throughout the world, while French banks had 140, German banks had 70, and Dutch banks had 68.[44]

The various national strivings for colonization of this period took place within this expansion of national capitalisms, as indicated by what Cecil Rhodes said in 1895:

> I was in the East End of London yesterday and attended a meeting of the unemployed. I listened to the wild speeches, which were just a cry for "bread," "bread," and on my way home I pondered over the scene and I became more than ever convinced of the importance of imperialism.... My cherished idea is a solution for the social problem, *i.e.*, in order to save the 40,000,000 inhabitants of the United Kingdom from a bloody civil war, we colonial statesmen must acquire new lands for settling the surplus population, to provide new

TABLE 4.7   Colonial Expansion, 1876–1914

	COLONIES				MOTHER COUNTRIES	
	1876		1914		1914	
	Area (million km²)	Population (million)	Area (million km²)	Population (million)	Area (million km²)	Population (million)
Great Britain	22.5	251.9	33.5	393.5	0.3	46.5
Russia	17.0	15.9	17.4	33.2	5.4	136.2
France	0.9	6.0	10.6	55.5	0.5	39.6
Germany	–	–	2.9	12.3	0.5	64.9
United States	–	–	0.3	9.7	9.4	97.0
Japan	–	–	0.3	19.2	0.4	53.0
Total	40.4	273.8	65.0	523.4	16.5	437.2
Small states*	–	–	9.9	45.3	–	–

* Belgium, Holland, etc.

Source: Nikolai Bukharin, *L'Economie mondiale et L'impérialisme, 1915–1917* (Paris: Anthropos, 1969), p. 81.

markets for the goods produced in the factories and mines. The Empire, as I have always said, is a bread and butter question. If you want to avoid civil war, you must become imperialists.[45]

And Joseph Chamberlain, minister of the British colonies, in a speech before the Birmingham Chamber of Commerce in 1896, stated: "If we had remained passive ... the largest part of the African continent would have been occupied by our commercial rivals.... Through our colonial policy, as soon as we acquire and develop a territory, we develop it as the agents of civilization, for the growth of world trade." And Jules Ferry: "Colonial policy is the daughter of industrial policy."

When Leroy-Beaulieu, a member of the Institute, a professor at the Collège de France, and director of *L'Economiste français*, published in 1891 his *De la colonisation chez les peuples modernes*, he placed this sentence from John Stuart Mill at the very beginning: "It can be affirmed, in the present state of the world, that the founding of colonies is the best business in which the capital of an old and rich country can be invested." Leroy-Beaulieu went on to write:

Colonization is the expansive force of a people; colonization is the reproductive power of a people, it is the people's expansion and multiplication through space; it is the submission of the universe, or a large part of it, to this people's language, ideas, and laws. A people who colonize cast the foundations of their

TABLE 4.8   Military Spending Increase, Principal Capitalist Countries

	Per capita increase (percent)		Percentage of state total	
	1875 to 1908	1908 to 1913–14	1875	1908
Great Britain	62	29	38.6	48.6
France	63	14	29.0	37.0
Germany	95*	28	28.5	28.3†
United States	67	n/a	33.5	56.9

* 1881–82.   † Not including "extraordinary temporary expenditures."

Sources: O. Schwarz, cited in Bukharin, *L'Economie mondiale*; W. Sombart, *Le Capitalisme moderne*.

greatness and supremacy into the future.... It is impossible not to consider [colonization] as one of the tasks which is imposed on civilized States.[46]

Here economic realism and racism support each other:

It is neither natural nor just that the civilized people of the West should be indefinitely crowded together and stifled in the restricted spaces that were their first homes, that they should accumulate there the wonders of science, art, and civilization, *that they should see, for lack of profitable jobs, the interest rate of capital fall further every day for them*, and that they should leave perhaps half the world to small groups of ignorant men, who are powerless, who are truly retarded children dispersed over boundless territories, or else to decrepit populations without energy and without direction, truly old men incapable of any effort, of any organized and far-seeing action.[47]

The clear conscience of civilization or religion blessed this movement; racism and the certitude of superiority removed the last scruples; interests compelled; the mysticism of bright sun and open spaces was sometimes an inspiration; modern weapons gave the necessary courage. These were the colonial expeditions of Britain, France, Germany, Belgium, and Holland. When necessary, whole populations were massacred: the mad scramble was on. On a smaller scale and in a different way, Russia and the United States took part in this movement as well[48] (see Table 4.7).

Friction arose between nations due to their expansionism, as did a hardening of economic and financial competition, national rivalries, alliances and the breaking of alliances. All these took place against a background of nationalism, chauvinism, and racism, of military parades and universal expositions. Military spending increased, providing the industrialists of each country with enlarged markets, and the military with the means for new conquests (see Table 4.8). Military spending was particularly important among the four dominant capitalist countries of this period.

A "new capitalism," which many people called by the name of "imperialism," developed at the beginning of the twentieth century. It included many factors, among which the following were prominent: concentration of capital, cartels, trusts, and monopolies; interpenetration of industrial capital and banking capital within the new reality of finance capital; the renewed role of the state, through social legislation, its major role in large public works projects, territorial expansion, and militarism; export of capital, colonization, and the dividing up of the world. Thus Hobson wrote in 1902:

> The new imperialism differs from the older, first in substituting for the ambition of a single growing empire the theory and the practice of competing empires, each motivated by similar lusts of political aggrandisement and commercial gain, secondly, in the dominance of financial, or investing, over mercantile interests.[49]

Thanks to imperialism, finance capital was able for a while to surpass the contradictions inherent in the national framework. Hilferding wrote in 1910:

> [The imperialist] observes with a cold and steady eye the medley of peoples and sees his own nation standing over all of them. For him this nation is real; it lives in the ever increasing power and greatness of the state, and its enhancement deserves every ounce of his effort. The subordination of individual interests to a higher general interest, which is a prerequisite for every vital social ideology, is thus achieved; and the state alien to its people is bound together with the nation in unity, while the national idea becomes the driving force of politics. Class antagonisms have disappeared and been transcended in the service of the collectivity. The common action of the nation, united by a common goal of national greatness, has taken the place of class struggle, so dangerous and fruitless for the possessing classes.[50]

And Otto Bauer stated in 1913: "Imperialism is in fact a means for extending the limits of accumulation."[51]

If the world economy is a system of relations of production and corresponding relations of exchange encompassing the whole world, then imperialism is the widening onto a worldwide scale of capitalist relations of production and exchange. This widening of capitalist relations functioned at the beginning of the twentieth century under the domination of the capitalisms and bourgeoisies of Britain, Germany, France, and the United States.

The "peace" which reigned at this time—some consider that the *pax germanica* succeeded the *pax britannica*—was an imperialist peace, already marred by outbursts of war. During this period there were many signs of imperialism, including colonial expeditions: the French in Dahomey, Madagascar, Chad, Morocco; the British in South Africa and the Sudan; the Italians in Abyssinia and Tripoli. The period also saw U.S. intervention in Hawaii, Puerto Rico, Samoa, the Philippines, and in Panama; Japanese expansionism in China and Korea; and an international expedition to China. Rivalries led to explosive situations in Fachoda in 1898, in Morocco in 1905 and 1911, and to such wars as the Boer War (1899–1902), the Spanish–American War (1898), and a Russian–Japanese war (1904–05)—the first warnings of another forthcoming upset, since European powers were twice defeated by "overseas countries." There were national wars between Greece and Turkey (1897) and in the Balkans (1912 and 1913), in which the interests of the great powers were not absent.

Rivalries, competition, friction, and confrontations, industrialist and financial interests, as well as patriotic spirit—while it was not the only cause, the imperialist expansion of national capitalisms at the end of the nineteenth century and beginning of the twentieth century was a fundamental cause of the Great War of 1914–18, a gigantic charnel made bearable only by the thought that it was "the war to end all wars."

SUMMARY

In every period of their formation and development, national capitalisms drew from foreign countries: gold from the Americas, pillage, forced labor, slavery, colonial levies, commercial profits. Imperialism, then, is characterized neither by the existence nor even by the importance of these foreign resources.

Imperialism is the functioning and the development of a national capitalism on a world scale. The extortion of value at the time of production, the realization of the produced value at the time of the sale of the commodities, and the development in the form of new capital of previously materialized profits: these are no longer conceived and organized on a strictly local and national level, but are considered from the start on a national and worldwide scale. This new attitude was due to capitalist entities of great size: oligopolies, taking many forms, large companies, trusts, groups. It depended increasingly upon the alliance and sometimes the interpenetration of industrial capital and banking capital in the form

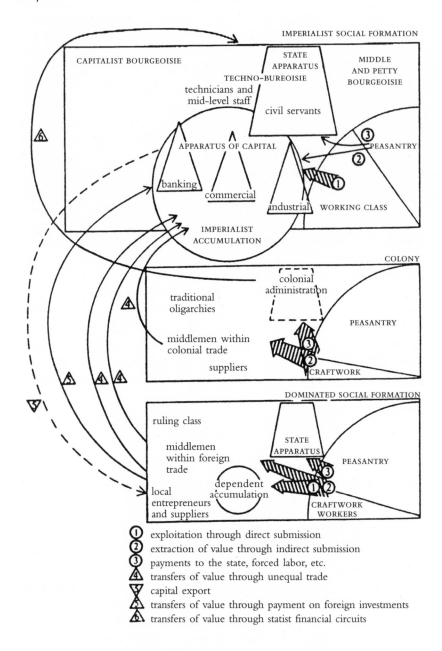

IMPERIALIST SOCIAL FORMATION

CAPITALIST BOURGEOISIE

STATE
APPARATUS
TECHNO-BUREOISIE

MIDDLE
AND PETTY
BOURGEOISIE

technicians and
mid-level staff

civil servants

APPARATUS OF CAPITAL

PEASANTRY

banking
commercial

industrial   WORKING CLASS

IMPERIALIST
ACCUMULATION

COLONY

colonial
administration

traditional
oligarchies

PEASANTRY

middlemen within
colonial trade

suppliers

CRAFTWORK

DOMINATED SOCIAL FORMATION

ruling class

middlemen
within foreign
trade

STATE
APPARATUS

PEASANTRY

local
entrepreneurs
and suppliers

dependent
accumulation

CRAFTWORK
WORKERS

① exploitation through direct submission
② extraction of value through indirect submission
③ payments to the state, forced labor, etc.
④ transfers of value through unequal trade
▽ capital export
⑤ transfers of value through payment on foreign investments
⑥ transfers of value through statist financial circuits

DIAGRAM 12   SOCIAL FORMATIONS, CLASSES,
AND EXTRACTION AND CIRCULATION OF VALUE
IN PRE-1914 IMPERIALISM

of finance capital; it was given life by fractions of the bourgeoisie who, overcoming local and national horizons, planned and gave impetus to projects on a national and worldwide scale, and who, within this dynamic, obtained the support, diplomacy, and weapons of the state. That is, with imperialism:

—The contradictions pertaining to the movement of enlarged reproduction of capital develop henceforth in a national/worldwide framework.

—New contradictions appeared and developed. For the period under consideration, these contradictions were principally related to realization of the produced value, and to control of various world regions.

We may analyze these phenomena more closely by considering Diagram 12, and by considering the four historically developing contradictions of capitalism which were identified above (see p. 140).

The contradiction between capital and labor manifests itself above all in its direct form (real submission) within the framework of each national capitalism. Progress by workers, along with national legislation, have both helped reduce the brutality of this contradiction, compared to capitalism's early phases.

At the same time, on an international level, this contradiction tends to develop in its indirect form (formal submission) between dominant capitalisms and traditional producers of the dominated, particularly the colonized, countries.

Is there a link between the direct and indirect forms? This question has been hotly debated within the intellectual and political circles of the workers' movement. There are those who see no link whatsoever: what has been won by the workers in the advanced capitalist countries has been made bearable to capital by productivity increases due to technical progress, the rise in worker training and skill levels, and increased intensity of labor.

From an opposing viewpoint, others argue that the dominant nations and the dominant capitalisms profit from the transfer of value originating in the dominated nations. Such profit arises from income tied to foreign investments, interest on debt, and transfers involved in unequal exchange. Within this view, the concessions made by employers and by the states of the dominant nations are thus made less onerous. At the same time, the working classes of these nations, whose material position is improved by the transfer of value, become *volens nolens* beneficiaries of, and even accomplices to, domination over other peoples.

The contradiction between national capitalisms intensified considerably during this period, mainly between dominant (or those trying to become dominant) national capitalisms. The intensifying struggle affected access to raw materials and new markets (for consumption or equipment), as well as credit and foreign investments. The effects of this contradiction were visible in tensions and confrontations in different parts of the world; the struggle between dominant national capitalisms contributed to setting off the First World War.

During this period, however, the contradiction between dominant and emergent capitalisms remained of minor importance.

The contradiction between capitalists also became more pronounced during this period, especially at an international level. As we have described, professional organizations, cartel agreements, and trusts all multiplied rapidly within each nation, though this phenomenon remained limited at an international level. This contradiction thus reinforced the contradiction between national capitalisms; the contradiction between capitalists grew to form an important piece of the contradiction between national capitalisms.

Finally, *the contradiction between dominant capitalisms and the dominated peoples and nations* became more important on a world scale with the new wave of colonization, the dividing-up of the world, and the establishment of areas of influence. These processes involved not only the old nations of Europe, but also new nations, especially the United States, and modernizing nations, such as Japan and Russia. The establishment of domination often took place through extremely violent military measures. In this period a new contradiction is forming, which will leave a deep mark on the whole second half of the twentieth century, and whose reverberations will likely endure past the year 2000.

This new reality was designated by the word "imperialism." Strangely, this word had served as a positive slogan for those who advocated the domination of the world by Great Britain and the United States. Now it returned as a term of denunciation within the workers' movement and within Marxism. Later on, the word will be used frequently within the struggles for independence, and within the third world movements. In this later period, some will see imperialism less and less as a form or stage of capitalism and more and more as the domination of the great powers pursuing their own ends.[52]

The use of this word in the singular, which occurs very frequently, tends, however, to globalize its meaning, at the risk of emptying the word of some of its content. Whether it is a matter of capitalisms, great powers, or states, these are always *national* actors extending their domination, clashing and conflicting with rivals. The formation, assertion, and rise of imperialisms at the end of the nineteenth century took place from strong national bases and led at the beginning of the twentieth century to the collision between imperialisms, the conflict between nations which led to the Great War.

Thus, the imperialisms of this period were doubly anchored. They were anchored first within the need for expansion of the developed national capitalisms, and second within the logic of domination of their states. When the war broke out, it was the national dimension which prevailed: the internationalism and anticapitalism of the workers were shattered in the confrontation with nationalism.

Chapter 5

THE GREAT UPHEAVAL
(1914–45)

Our century, hardly passed, will have seen two radically dissimilar eras succeed one another with no transition between them other than the war. Our contemporaries must try to imagine the years of the past: a time of stability, economies, prudence; a society of acquired rights, traditional politics, trustworthy businesses; a regime of fixed incomes, secure salaries, tightly calculated pensions; an era of the "3 percent," old tools, and the standard dowry. Competition aided by technics chased away this wisdom and killed this quietness.... The war has enlarged the natural course of things into a torrent and has transformed the range of needs. In order to satisfy these needs as they are—diverse, imperious, and changing—the activity of men becomes multiplied and hurried.... Every day machinery and the division of labor force the retreat of eclecticism and illusion.

—Charles de Gaulle[1]

Carried away by the logic of accumulation and enlarged production, national capitalisms searched throughout the world for space in which to expand, confronting one another with increasing severity. National reactions became sharper, and with the spirit of conquest and revenge, nationalist feelings became more pronounced. The world war resolved nothing—very much to the contrary. The need for expansion on a world scale endured, although the previously existing system of international payments had been destroyed. And during the 1920s this world which had been split apart experienced the coexistence of both prosperity and crisis, and after 1929 was dragged into a new huge crisis and then another huge war.

FROM WAR TO CRISIS

"Capitalism brings war, as the rain cloud brings the storm," Jaurès had said. In fact, capitalism brings crisis above all and the imperious necessity to conquer new territory. What makes capitalism bring war is its concrete development in national social formations and the conflict of national capitalisms.

World War I turned Europe upside down, heightened the British decline, and strengthened the United States, without resolving the underlying contradictions present before 1914. And the war opened a long period of crisis, which, though masked and taking many forms during the 1920s, became general despite its diversity after 1929.

The Upheaval of the Great War

The broken spirit of the workers' movement, the aggravated decline of European capitalism, the hardening of nationalism—and yet, with World War I the great upheaval had only begun.

The beautiful myth of proletarian internationalism was shattered. The general strike should have prevented the war; the working classes should have refused to kill one another for the sake of the capitalists. The Confédération Générale du Travail stated in 1910: "In every strike, the army is for the employers; in every European conflict, in every colonial war and every war between nations, the working class is duped and sacrificed to the profit of the parasitic and bourgeois possessing class. This is why the Congress of the CGT approves and recommends all antimilitaristic and antipatriotic propaganda action...."[2] And again: "In the event of war between the European powers, the workers will respond to the declaration of war with the declaration of a revolutionary general strike."[3] After a two-year campaign the December 16, 1912, general strike against the war was a failure, despite its size and its moments of strength. Then in 1914, the July 29 Manifesto of the CGT stated: "The leaders ... will have the French people with them, if, as is proclaimed, these leaders sincerely work for peace. "[4]

There were some who remained loyal to their pacifist convictions to the end, but many were strongly divided within themselves. A few took up the struggle for peace in the midst of the conflict. Nevertheless, the proletarians of all the European countries killed each other by the millions, while the bitterness and harrowing divisions continued.

European workers suffered another defeat. Just before the war, workers opposed the introduction of new methods for organizing work, with strikes at Renault in 1912 and 1913, and at de Dietrich in Argenteuil and Brasier in Ivry in 1913. The workers in these companies refused to be timed:

> The application [of timed work] in the Renault factories clearly demonstrated the intolerable situation and the exhausting labor this system would bring to any workers naive enough to accept it … ; the worker is reduced to the position of a brute, in which he is forbidden to think or reflect; he is reduced to a machine without a soul, producing intensely and excessively, until his premature exhaustion, by turning him into a non-value, throws him out of the workshop. Taylorism is pitiless; it eliminates the non-values and those who have surpassed the age of full muscular strength.[5]

And Merrheim, in the *Vie Ouvrière* of March 31, 1913, wrote: "Intelligence is chased away from the workshops and factories. What remain are only arms without brains and robots of flesh adapted to the robots of iron and steel."[6]

But the war allowed for the implantation of scientific methods for organizing work. The army used these methods in its central automobile repair shop. Louis Renault emphasized in 1919, before the members of the automobile manufacturers' trade association, that "the advantage of the scientific organization of labor is that it permits the most delicate fabrications to be carried out without a specialized labor force." In a memorandum to his engineers as early as 1918, Renault stressed that "almost all the necessary elements for a complete organization exist." At the same time, the *Bulletin des Usines Renault* warned the workers that their efforts, far from becoming lighter, had to continue and intensify: "You can be sure that when this war is over, the other war, the economic war, will begin.… In this other war, you will be the front-line soldiers."[7] In the end, like the other classes, the working class was decimated: 10 percent of the men active in industry in 1913 were killed in World War I.[8]

We must note here the attempt at communist revolution in Germany, which was drowned in blood (January–March 1919); the crushed Hungarian revolution (July 1919); and then the break between communists and socialists at the Congress of Tours in France (1920). At the time when for innumerable workers the Soviet revolution had just given socialism a homeland, the workers' movement in the large capitalist countries of Western Europe found itself weakened, battered, and divided.

These countries themselves were lifeless and in ruins, though some industries did develop during and because of the war. The war caused approximately 8 million deaths: 2.7 million in Germany, 1.7 million in France, 1.7 million in Russia, 1.5 million in Austria-Hungary, 930,000 in Britain, and 150,000 in the United States. In Germany as in France, 10 percent of the men of active age were killed, and in Britain, 5 percent. The cost of the war for England represented 32 percent of its national wealth; for France, 30 percent; for Germany, 22 percent; and for the United States, only 9 percent. Each state involved in the war contracted an enormous public debt: the total public debt of all the belligerent countries rose from $26 billion before the war to $225 billion in 1920. This was in addition to foreign debts: Britain borrowed about $4 billion from the United States, and France borrowed $3 billion from the United States. In 1921 the Allied reparations commission exacted payments of $33 billion from Germany.

Giving the value of 100 to the index of industrial production in 1913, the level of industrial production in 1920 was 141 in the United States, 100 in Britain, 62 in France, and 61 in Germany. The gold reserves of the United States more than quadrupled during the war, and in 1921 these reserves surpassed a value of $2.5 billion, nearly 40 percent of all world reserves.

Besides this, the October revolution cut off the European powers for several decades from a promising market in which they had invested: the socialist ideal inspired the rupture with capitalism as well as the West. New national dynamics arose in Turkey after the Ottoman Empire was divided up. New movements began in Persia and Afghanistan too. In Egypt, which had been occupied since 1882 and had become a British protectorate in 1914, there were strikes, boycotts, and attacks on trains. These actions led the British government to proclaim Egypt's independence in 1922, an independence which the British hoped would remain quite theoretical. And during the war Japan greatly increased its industrial production, its foreign trade, and its foreign assets: a new industrial power was gaining strength in Asia.

It is impossible to dissociate the weakening of European capitalism and the "decline of Europe." The United States was from this time on the leading economic power; Germany rebuilt its industrial strength; the USSR and Japan both began tremendous efforts to industrialize, though along different roads; Britain and France still retained great assets with their industrial apparatuses, their banking and financial networks, and their empires. As Louis Renault had foreseen, hardly had the peace treaties been signed than a formidable economic war began.

THE CRISIS OF THE 1920S

Traditionally, this period is divided into four phases: the boom immediately after the war, the reconversion crisis of 1921, the period of "prosperity," and then the crisis of 1929 and its continuation into the 1930s. Very often the monetary aspects (international debts, international payments, inflation) are dissociated from the economic aspects (production, commercial exchanges).

I propose the contrary hypothesis that it was a single crisis which developed under different forms during the 1920s. While the fundamental contradictions did not disappear (is it necessary to say this?), with the working class on the one hand and the dominated social formations on the other, it was in fact the contradictions between national capitalisms which give the key to the great crisis of this period.

War damages? Huge public debts? Foreign debts toward the United States and Great Britain? In France the answer was always the same: "Germany will pay." France had "paid" enough after the defeat of 1871. But the reparations demanded from Germany forced the industrialists of that country to export increased quantities of goods, particularly of coal, steel, metallurgical products, and mechanical products, which stiffened competition between Germany and Britain.

During the war American economic power was strengthened, along with its financial power: American foreign investments rose from $3.5 billion in 1913 to $6.5 billion in 1919, while British foreign investments fell from $18.3 billion to $15.7 billion. At the same time American gold reserves greatly increased, from $700 million in 1913 to $2.5 billion in 1921—a far greater increase than occurred in Britain, where reserves rose from $200 million to $800 million. The exchange rate of the pound fell from $4.78 in 1914, before the detachment of gold, to $3.78 in January 1921. But the idea was deeply rooted that to be able to regain its status as international currency, the pound should be able "to look the dollar in the eye"—that is, regain prewar parity and return to gold convertibility. However, insofar as British industry did not achieve productivity increases greater than its competitors, this policy made its exports more costly, thus more difficult, and its commercial reestablishment more problematic. The choice, though, was between this policy and the reduction of domestic consumption, particularly the reduction of workers' buying power, leading to harsh social conflicts.

The payment of German reparations; the return to parity and to the gold convertibility of the pound, and more generally, the very widespread

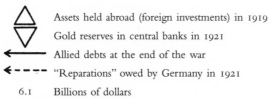

Assets held abroad (foreign investments) in 1919
Gold reserves in central banks in 1921
Allied debts at the end of the war
"Reparations" owed by Germany in 1921
6.1   Billions of dollars

Source: Adapted from A. Sauvy, *Histoire économique de la France entre les deux guerres*, vol. I (Paris: Fayard, 1965). Figures should be interpreted as "orders of magnitude."

DIAGRAM 13   THE NETWORK OF INTERNATIONAL FINANCIAL
OBLIGATIONS IN THE PERIOD AFTER WORLD WAR I

concern to return to an international monetary system founded on gold; the attempts to resolve the inextricable problem of international debts: all these monetary and financial problems which dominated the 1920s had an economic and social dimension.[9] A prophet who at the time was not widely listened to, J. M. Keynes, understood this very well:

> In truth, the gold standard is already a barbarous relic. All of us, from the Governor of the Bank of England downwards, are not primarily interested in preserving the stability of business, prices, and employment, and are not likely, when the choice is forced on us, deliberately to sacrifice these to the outworn dogma, which had its value once, of £3.17.10½ per ounce.[10]

Keynes wrote this in 1923 in *A Tract on Monetary Reform*. But in 1925, after five years of efforts in this direction, the pound regained its prewar parity and its convertibility was reestablished.

The price paid for this was heavy: the crisis of 1921 affected Britain with particular severity. Exports plummeted, while unemployment rose sharply—there were 1 million unemployed workers in January 1921 but 2 million in June 1921. The fall in exports, at constant values, affected not only coal and steel but also the cotton and wool industries and machine manufacturing (while German exports by 1923 had regained their 1913 volume levels). Throughout the 1920s more than 1 million British workers remained unemployed. But the City of London had recovered its position.

It was only in 1928 that the French franc officially returned to gold convertibility, and at a fifth of its prewar value. As for the German mark, after the collapse of 1922–23, it was rebuilt with the help of foreign credits, especially from Britain, in the same movement which developed and modernized its industrial apparatus. During the period 1924–30, the foreign credits obtained by Germany had a value two and a half times greater than the reparations which it actually paid, which allowed Germany not only to supply itself with raw materials, but to restock its reserves of gold and foreign currencies, and to develop foreign investments.[11]

The massive value of the international network of debts required a great expansion in production and international trade in order to be absorbed: these alone would allow the necessary balances to be established. But the choice of the persons responsible for the monetary system at the time was to return to a system based on gold, a decision which burdened the resumption of British trade and made vulnerable any country incapable of balancing its trade. At the same time, there was no one financial center which assumed responsibility for the whole: the American banks were not yet competent for the task, while the City of London, still

TABLE 5.1 Share of Global Exports of Manufactured Goods (percent)

	1913	1929	1937
Great Britain	30.2	22.4	20.9
France	12.1	10.9	5.8
United States	13.0	20.4	19.2
Germany	26.6	20.5	21.8
Japan	2.3	3.9	6.9
Others	15.8	21.9	25.4
Total	100	100	100

Source: Harry Magdoff, *The Age of Imperialism* (New York: Monthly Review Press, 1969).

preoccupied with rebuilding its leadership, did not at the time have the necessary power. On this point, C. P. Kindleberger's diagnosis is accurate:

> The international economic system was rendered unstable by British inability and United States unwillingness to assume responsibility for stabilizing it in three particulars: a) maintaining a relatively open market for distress goods, b) providing counter-cyclical long-term lending, and c) discounting in crisis.... The world economic system was unstable unless some country stabilized it, as Britain had done in the 19th century and up to 1913. In 1929, the British couldn't and the United States wouldn't. When every country turned to protect its national private interest, the world public interest went down the drain, and with it the private interests of all.[12]

It was in this fragile international context that the different national capitalisms developed, each following its own path: British capitalism, caught between the combativity of a working class which refused the demanded sacrifices and the pugnacity of its foreign industrial competitors; German capitalism, concentrated, dynamic, expansive, and supported by a national will to surmount humiliation; French capitalism, more disparate than ever, torn between large industry and craft work, between the calm of the provinces and the adventure of empire; American capitalism, carried away in a frenzy of mass production, mass consumption, blockages, and speculation; and then all the other capitalisms: the various European capitalisms, and Japanese capitalism, and new productions by the "new countries" for whom World War I gave initial opportunities.

The struggle for foreign markets became fiercer: thus while the pound returned to gold convertibility, British exports fell in value from 1924 to 1926, and from 1927 to 1929 remained below the level they had reached in 1924. French exports had benefited from the devaluation of the franc during the first half of the 1920s, but with the financial stabilization of 1926 and the return to the gold standard in 1928, exports in numerous sectors fell after 1928. In this struggle the old capitalisms fell back before the rise of the new capitalisms.

Thus foreign outlets became increasingly closed off. But American capitalism had just experienced an exceptional period of expansion and accumulation, as had Japanese, German, and French capitalism. Besides this, the crisis that had been shaking world agriculture since the end of World War I—overproduction, falling prices, falling incomes for farmers—reduced another essential outlet for industrial products. It is by returning to these fundamental economic realities, and not by being content to follow the ups and downs of stock market speculation, that the great crisis between the two wars can be understood.[13]

Crisis was chronic in Britain throughout the 1920s, and latent in most of the other capitalist countries, especially the United States and France, at the end of the decade. The speculation and the panic of Wall Street were the fascinating catalyst of the American economic crisis. The knowledge of this crisis, its banking and financial repercussions throughout the world, and the effects it had through the drop in American commercial trade: all these precipitated in each country crises which in fact were already at work or in gestation.

A WORLD SPLIT APART

In 1929 in the United States the index of security prices stood in the neighborhood of 200–210. In 1932 it had fallen to 3–40. Commodity prices in general fell in the same period by 30 to 40 percent; the fall in particular commodity markets was even more catastrophic. Production in the chief manufacturing countries of the world shrank by anything from 30 to 50 percent: and the value of world trade in 1932 was only a third of what it was three years before. It has been calculated by the International Labour Office that in 1933, in the world at large, something like 30 million persons were out of work. There have been many depressions in modern economic history but it is safe to say that there has never been anything to compare with this. 1929 to 1933 are the years of the Great Depression.[14]

The potential for crisis was at work in the heart of each national capitalism in which the very model of postwar accumulation was being exhausted. This potential was aggravated by a situation in which protectionist pressures and the absence of an established system for international payments limited the expansion of trade. It was in the United States that the potential for crisis was definitively released and became a Great Crisis.

AMERICA FIRST...? BUSINESS FIRST!

The United States was the world's leading economic power immediately after World War I. National income rose from $33 billion in 1914 to $61 billion in 1918. Industry was particularly strengthened, acquiring a worldwide predominance in most domains: 75 million long tons of iron ore and 555 million short tons of coal extracted in 1917; 60 million tons of oil extracted in 1920 (two-thirds of world production); electricity production equivalent to the whole of Europe; approximately 40 million tons of steel produced in 1920 (more than half of the world's production); and the advance of modern industries: automobile, electrical, chemical. Although in spite of its strong growth, the American fleet had not yet surpassed the British fleet, American commerce benefited from the needs and difficulties of other countries and attained record levels in 1920: $5 million worth of imports, and $8 million worth of exports. And though American foreign investments in 1919 were still less than half of Britain's ($6.5 billion compared to $15.7 billion), American gold reserves were worth $2.5 billion in 1921, and the value for America of Allied war credits was on the order of $12 billion.

Moreover, American military intervention had been decisive to the outcome of the war; the participation of President Wilson in the negotiations for peace, and the part which he played in these negotiations, confirmed the rise of the United States to the first rank of world powers.

But the U.S. Senate refused to ratify the Treaty of Versailles, and even rejected U.S. membership in the League of Nations, the organization to whose creation President Wilson had greatly contributed. In the 1918 elections the Republicans won a majority in the House of Representatives, and in 1920 it was a Republican, W. G. Harding, who was elected to the presidency. To the ideals of democracy and international cooperation which had inspired Wilson, Harding opposed his nationalist convictions: "I have confidence in our America that requires no council of foreign powers to point the way to American duty.... Call it the selfishness of nationality if you will, I think it an inspiration to patriotic devotion. To safeguard America first—to think of America first—to exalt America first."[15]

America first! From 1922 to 1924 the United States protected itself against foreign commodities and—a people composed of immigrants—against immigration. Though the principal American banks had already

TABLE 5.2   U.S. Subsidiary Banks and Foreign Investments

	Subsidiary banks		Foreign investment ($ billion)	
	1918	1939	1924	1940
Latin America	31	47	4.0	4.0
Overseas territories	4	8		
Canada			2.5	3.8
Europe	26	16	1.9	2.0
Asia	0	18	}0.7	0.6
Other	0	0		0.4
Total	61	89	9.1	10.8

Sources: Magdoff, *The Age of Imperialism*, p. 72; Christian Palloix, *L'Economie mondiale capitaliste et les firmes multinationales* (Paris: Maspero, 1975), p. 126; Faulkner, *American Economic History*; Claude Julien, *America's Empire* (New York: Pantheon, 1971), pp. 125, 172.

begun to internationalize, banks in the United States felt neither obliged nor able to control a worldwide system of payments.[16] And American growth during the 1920s was able to take place largely on the basis of American resources and for American markets.

America first! Although American capitalism was already an imperialism, its horizon for the most part was limited to the Americas. During the war the ties between British and Canadian capitalisms became slack, and Canada fell under American influence: in 1904–14, eight times more Canadian debentures were placed in Britain than in the United States, but in the period 1921–30, twenty times more Canadian debentures were placed in the United States than in Britain.[17]

From this time on, Canada and Latin America became the principal fields for the investment of American capital. And it was in Latin America that United States intervention and domination were most intense, with dollar diplomacy, the "big stick" policy, and the cover slogan of "America for Americans" (see Table 5.2).

America first! The United States experienced tremendous growth and astonishing prosperity during the 1920s. And for this the American working class bore the major part of the burden. During the war the number of American workers grew from 10 million to 13 million in 1920 (of whom 5.5 million were specialized workers), and by 1930 the number had reached 14 million (of whom 6.3 million were specialized workers). From 1913 to workshops at Highland Park, 95 percent of the pattern makers and smelters were "unskilled, or to put it more accurately ... skilled in exactly one operation which the most stupid man could learn within two days."[22] In 1926, 79 percent of the workers employed in the Ford factories went through a training period of less than one week.

The assembly line, by dividing up work operations to the greatest possible extent and by imposing a uniform speed upon all the workers, produced considerable increases in productivity. For example, the assembly of a magnetic fly wheel, when carried out by one worker, required twenty-five minutes; with a conveyor belt and twenty-nine "specialized" workers, each one performing a single operation, this assembly took at first only thirteen minutes, then, with the conveyor belt speeded up, seven minutes, and finally, with yet another increase in both the speed of the belt and the tempo of the work, five minutes. Productivity increased by a factor of five. In order for this increase to take place, however, each worker had to repeat the same motion every ten seconds: in a working day of nine hours, this amounted to over 3,000 repetitions of the same movement, performed on an equal number of magnetic fly wheels.

Like Charlie Chaplin in *Modern Times*, there were many who did not accept this, who could not bear it, and who refused it: absenteeism and turnover reached record levels. In 1913 "Ford required between 13,000 and 14,000 workers to run his plants at any one time, and in that year over 50,000 workers quit."[23] At the end of this same year, in order to add 100 persons to the work force in one factory, the company found it was necessary to hire 963 workers.[24] Moreover, the secretary of the Detroit Employers' Association was getting worried: "There is at this time more restlessness, more aggression among the workmen of Detroit and elsewhere than there has been for several years past.... There is a lot of inflammable matter scattered about the plants and it is up to you ... whether or not a spark ignites it, or it is cleared away before damage results."[25]

Henry Ford had an idea of what this "something" might be, and it was somewhat audacious: while the wages in the automobile industry ranged from $2 to $3 per day, Ford decided to raise wages to $5 per day on January 1, 1914. He moved also to reduce the working day from nine to eight hours. This was the "five-dollar day." Its effect was immediate: turnover fell to less than 5 percent and absenteeism followed suit. Long waiting lines formed in front of the Ford hiring offices. Production was able to rise rapidly: 200,000 cars in 1913, 500,000 in 1915, 1 million in 1919, 2 million in 1923, and more than 5 million in 1929. The production cost dropped and the base price of the famous Model T (produced until 1927) fell from $1,950 to $290. Ford wrote: "The payment of five dollars a day for an eight-hour day was one of the finest cost-cutting moves we ever made, and the six-dollar day wage is cheaper than the five."[26] And Ford did bring daily wages to $6 on January 1, 1919, and to $7 on December 1, 1929.

But it was not only a question, for Ford, of ensuring for himself a disciplined and loyal labor force. It was primarily a question of opening breaches in the midst of the working class and of widening the differences between the workers: between those who worked for Ford and those who worked for other employers; and among Ford's workers, between those who were able to benefit from the $5 per day and those who were not (yet) worthy of it. For not all of Ford's workers received this wage; among those who did not have the right to the five-dollar day were (a) workers having less than six months' tenure, (b) young workers less than twenty-one years of age, and (c) women (since they were called upon to marry).

Moreover, "good morals" were necessary: "cleanliness and discretion," no smoking, no drinking, no gambling, no frequenting of the bars. The five-dollar day was thus an instrument of control and, in a way, of "breaking in" the workers.

But it was also a question of allowing these "good workers" to reach a "good level of consumption" (thus assuring market outlets for the Ford factories) and of creating "sturdy children" (thus assuring for the future a labor force in "good health" for the Ford factories). In Ford's words:

> I believe in the first place that, all other considerations aside, our own sales depend in a measure upon the wages we pay. If we can distribute high wages, then that money is going to be spent and it will serve to make storekeepers and distributors and manufacturers and workers in other lines more prosperous and their prosperity will be reflected in our sales.[27]

In 1929 a survey carried out in Detroit at the request of the Ford Company found that out of 100 working families, 98 owned an electric iron, 76 a sewing machine, 51 a washing machine, 49 a phonograph, 47 an automobile, 36 a radio, and 21 a vacuum cleaner. During this same year there were 23 million automobiles in circulation in the United States (19 for every 100 inhabitants, compared to 2 for every 100 persons in France and Britain at this date). More than 4 million jobs were linked to the automobile through tires, supplies, gasoline, repairs, and so on. In a parallel movement, the construction of roads and highways and the extraction of oil developed. Towns sprawled and housing construction progressed at an unprecedented speed. Electrical and telephone equipment advanced also, and the production of electricity doubled within ten years.

There was at this time, then, the exploitation of a part of the working class using pre-1914 methods (low wages, brutal methods of management and regimentation, the factory system and the sweating system); but there was also mass production, the rational organization of work, and a policy of high wages for a certain group among the workers, and consequently mass consumption reached by a fraction of the working class: these were the bases for the "prosperity" in the United States during the 1920s.

The years 1921 to 1929 saw the following developments:

—an increase of 90 percent in industrial production;
—a rate of investment which exceeded 20 percent of the GNP;
—an increase of 47 percent in the hourly productivity of labor (whereas during the first two decades of the century hourly productivity increased respectively 17 percent and 11 percent).

One of the slogans of Calvin Coolidge, the Republican president elected in 1924, was "the business of America, is business." But this model became exhausted toward the end of the decade. Although it had been accepted thanks to the "carrot" of high wages and access to certain consumption spending, assembly-line work remained extremely fatiguing, and the effect of Ford's innovations became less pronounced. Productivity increases slowed down. Some segments of the market became saturated. Besides these factors, the agricultural crisis, which brought a reduction in prices and incomes, affected an important outlet. Foreign markets were bitterly disputed. During the second half of 1929 the profits of the automobile industry went down. Stock market speculation became feverish, and was inflamed by the thirst for gaining more and more. The infernal spiral began, and then came the crisis.

This was the crisis which, in the euphoria of the 1920s, the American economists were convinced could never happen again. For example, Irving Fisher, in 1928: "Nothing resembling a crash can occur." In 1929: "There may be a recession in the price of stocks, but nothing in the nature of a catastrophe." In 1930: "For the immediate future, at least, the perspective is brilliant." And the Harvard Economic Society, in November 1929: a "severe depression like that of 1920–21 is outside the range of probability." In January: "There are indications that the severest phase of the recession is over." In November 1930: "We are now at the end of the declining phase of the depression." And in October 1931: "A stabilization at [present] levels is clearly possible."[28]

Wholesale prices, which had been relatively stable after 1922, with a slight falling tendency after 1925, dropped by one-third between 1929 and 1932. The index of industrial production which, on the base of 100 for the period 1923–25, had reached 126 in May 1929, fell to 105 in May 1930, 89 in May 1931, and 61 in May 1932. The number of unemployed workers in all sectors of activity reached 3 million in 1930, exceeded 6 million in 1931, 10 million in 1932, and 13 million in 1933. Labor productivity continued to increase (by 23 percent between 1929 and 1933), but wages went down by one-third to one-fourth, depending on the source, from 1929 to 1933. Expressing the opinion of one part of U.S. employers, Treasury Secretary Mellon saw the "positive" aspects of this drama: "People will work harder, live a more moral life."[29] This was the same Mellon who, by caricaturing them, had recalled the chief components of the "purge" inherent in all capitalist crises: "Liquidate labor, liquidate stocks, liquidate the farmers."[30]

It was also felt necessary to protect the country against foreign competition: this was done in 1930 with the Hawley-Smoot tariff. Imports fell from $4.4 million in 1929 to $1.3 million in 1932, and exports fell too, from $5.2 million in 1929 to $1.6 million in 1932. But the United States still held close to 40 percent of the world's gold reserves.[31]

In 1932 President Hoover was beaten by the Democratic candidate Franklin D. Roosevelt. Making wide use of the new radio audience, Roosevelt denounced "industrial dictatorship," the "kings of the economy," and the "new despotism." He criticized the Republican administration and announced a new policy: "Sacrificed by the political philosophies of the previous government, citizens from one end of the nation to the other are turning their hopes toward us. They want their fair share in the distribution of the national wealth. I pledge to give to the American people the New Deal, the new pact, the opportunity it has been waiting for." Elected thanks to a wide range of heterogeneous votes—conservative Democrats from the South, dissatisfied farmers, union workers, unemployed workers, blacks, ethnic and religious minorities—Roosevelt probably did not know exactly what this New Deal would be. He elaborated it little by little, with pragmatism and tenacity, relying on the social forces which were able to help its advance (especially the union movement), and confronting powerful opposition (which crystallized principally around certain Supreme Court rulings).[32]

Looking back on the New Deal, three factors stand out.

1. The reorganization and the resurgence of fundamental sectors of economic activity. The banks were first, in the wake of the banking crisis

at the beginning of 1933, followed by industry, with the National Industrial Recovery Act (NIRA) of June 1933; agriculture, with the Agricultural Adjustment Act (AAA) of May 1933; electric energy, with the Tennessee Valley Act (TVA) of May 1933 and the Public Utilities Holding Company Act of 1935; and transportation, with the Railroad Emergency Act of 1933 and the Wheeler Lee Transportation Act of 1940.[33]

2. A policy aimed at restoring the United States' favorable position on the world market. Measures included abandonment of the gold standard (April 19, 1933), progressive devaluation of the dollar in relation to gold, and a policy of commercial accord based upon the Reciprocal Trade Agreements Act of 1934.

3. Finally, and this is probably the essential aspect of the New Deal, a search for a new social compromise about which the principal social forces could agree. This was not, of course, a matter of overthrowing capitalism: "It is my administration," Roosevelt declared during his campaign of 1936, "which has saved the system of private profit and free enterprise." Rather, this involved imposing a group of reforms upon the most reactionary forces and the most egoistic interests.

Thus, in liaison with the NIRA, the Democratic administration proposed to the employers a formula they could stick to: child labor was forbidden, the work week was set at forty hours in the offices and thirty-five hours in industry, and a minimum wage was established (40¢ per hour in industry, $12 to $15 per week in other jobs). The NIRA guaranteed to workers the right to organize themselves freely and to choose their representatives, which facilitated the development of unions.

In 1937 strikers resorted to the occupation of factories on a large scale. And after the Supreme Court declared the NIRA unconstitutional, Roosevelt reintroduced its main points in the Fair Labor Standards Act. On May 24, 1937, he addressed Congress on behalf of a quick passage:

The time has arrived for us to take further action to extend the frontiers of social progress.... The overwhelming majority of our population earns its daily bread either in agriculture or in industry. One-third of our population, the overwhelming majority of which is in agriculture or industry, is ill-nourished, ill-clad, and ill-housed.... A self-supporting and self-respecting democracy can plead no justification for the existence of child labor, no economic reason for chiseling workers' wages or stretching workers' hours.[34]

In a related development Roosevelt launched great public works projects, created a system of "work exchange" for certain unemployed workers, and promoted bonds for the construction of low-cost housing. For workers having a sufficiently long period of wage-earning employment, the Social Security Act of 1936 systematized their right to unemployment payments and retirement benefits.

Union membership increased during this period.[35] Many of these agreements were made collectively within a company, bringing to light the inadequacy of the old system of unions-by-trade on which the AFL was founded. The system of industrial unions continued to develop, and led to the creation of the Congress of Industrial Organizations (CIO) in 1935. In 1938 the CIO had 4 million members, more than the AFL. Some employers pursued a systematic fight against the unions, with private police, strike-breakers, infiltrators into the unions, intimidation of union workers (from clubbings to attacks to bombings of union halls and homes of union members), and the use of corrupt sheriffs or judges. But courage, resolution, and solidarity won decisive victories for collective trade union action: in 1937, after the strike at General Motors and Chrysler, the CIO was recognized as a representative union and signed a collective contract with the automobile industry. Ford, however, did not give in until 1941. In the steel industry, U.S. Steel, reversing its traditional policy, signed collective contracts with the CIO, contracts which the "independent" producers continued to refuse for several more years.

American capitalism, this enormous mechanism for accumulation, could not be started up again by the New Deal: only the war could accomplish this task. Though unemployment did decline, the rate of unemployment was still 10 percent in 1940. But the average length of the working week was in fact reduced from around fifty hours to about forty hours, and real wages of employed workers rose. Collective contracts covered an increasing number of economic sectors. And finally, the decisive contribution of the New Deal to American capitalism lay in these tendencies:

—it led one segment of the employers to accept the concessions which would allow for the integration of the working class as a whole into the system of consumption;

—it marked a rupture with the old Republican principle: "Less government in business and more business in government," and opened the way for a "fruitful cooperation" between government and business.

For, from the moment when it came to be said that "What's good for General Motors is good for America," the slogan *America first!* could just as well be pronounced *Business first!*

STERLING FIRST...

The corollary to the rise of American power was the decline of Europe, a decline which particularly affected the two oldest capitalisms: the British, which had dominated the world in the nineteenth century; and the French, which had never succeeded in breaking away completely from its provincial and rural roots. Both persisted unremittingly after World War I in restoring their currencies, which were both instruments and symbols of their power. The price for accomplishing currency restoration was paid largely by the working classes and by drawing resources and wealth from overseas empires.

The British economy was engaged in the immediate postwar period in a policy of bringing the pound back to its former parity and to gold convertibility. Then it was profoundly affected by the crisis of 1920–21, and remained caught up in a masked crisis throughout the 1920s. Keynes had clearly criticized the implications of such monetary policies:

> The policy of improving the foreign-exchange value of sterling up to its pre-war value in gold from being about 10 percent below it, means that, whenever we sell anything abroad, either the foreign buyer has to pay 10 percent *more in his money* or we have to accept 10 percent *less in our money*. That is to say, we have to reduce our sterling prices for coal or iron or shipping freights or whatever it may be, by 10 percent in order to be on a competitive level.... Thus, Mr. Churchill's policy of improving the exchange by 10 percent was, sooner or later, a policy of reducing everyone's wages by 2 Sh. in the £.... Deflation does not reduce wages "automatically." It reduces them by causing unemployment.... Woe to those whose faith leads them to use it to aggravate depression.[36]

And Keynes proposed another policy: "What we need to restore prosperity to-day is an easy credit policy. We want to encourage business men to enter on new enterprises, not, as we are doing, to discourage them."[37]

In 1925 the pound recovered its prewar parity and gold convertibility was reestablished. But at what a price for the working class! Directly after the war the working class appeared to be at the height of its powers, with more than 8 million union members and a Labour Party which was winning votes from the Liberal Party with each election. But the employers were resolute and relied upon a powerful Conservative Party: faced with the railroad workers' strike in 1919, the London *Times* wrote: "as was the war with Germany, this must be a war to the end."

In 1920 the striking railroad workers did not obtain nationalization of the mines, but they did get a work week of forty-eight hours and wage increases. But the crisis of 1920–21 raised the number of unemployed workers: 1 million in January 1921, 2.5 million in July; unemployment hit one-half the workers in metallurgy, and one-third in naval construction. Mine owners tried to reduce wages, sometimes by as much as 35 percent. The workers' movement came up against the determination of the employers (who used lockouts) and the government which, resolved "to confront a situation analogous to civil war," sent in the armed forces. The workers were divided, suffered from the indecision of their leaders, and finally were defeated. The minority Labour government of 1924 was unable to begin the slightest social reform. And when, after the return of the pound to gold convertibility, the employers attempted a new reduction in wages, the miners went out on strike again (1926); the general Trades Union Congress decided to support them with a general strike, but the Conservative government had the king decree a "state of exceptional circumstances" and declared the strike to be illegal. Once more the workers' movement was divided and was defeated. Confidence in the unions weakened and the number of union workers fell to fewer than 5 million.

After 1927 the Conservatives consolidated their advantage by passing a law which limited the rights of unions. Civil servants were forbidden to strike, and were no longer allowed to be members of the Trades Union Congress. Solidarity strikes were prohibited, as were strikes aiming at bringing pressure to bear upon the government. The general strike was declared illegal, and the exercise of the right to strike was itself strictly controlled. In addition, the payment of membership fees to the Labour Party was made more difficult.

The working class was fundamentally weakened, most of all by unemployment, which throughout the 1920s was felt by more than 1 million British workers (12 percent of the active population) and which reached 3 million wage earners at the beginning of the 1930s. The working class was also weakened by its considerable heterogeneity, corresponding to the great diversity of British capitalism, its wage inequalities, status differences, and trade traditions. For example, in 1926 the majority of the railroad workers, the public service workers, and mine workers were paid by time, but half the textile workers (and two-thirds in the cotton industry) were paid by the piece, as were forty percent of the mine workers and the ready-made garment workers, and one-third of the workers in the mechanical, chemical, pottery, and glass-making industries. Moreover, multiple systems of regressive or progressive wages, of bonuses and penalties, worked to expand specificities and divisions to a very high degree.[38]

This explains the strong drop in nominal wages from 1920 to 1922, and their quasi-stagnation from 1922 to 1929; and the parallel increase in productivity (12 percent from 1924 to 1930 and 10 percent from 1930 to

1934), and thus "the slow but constant reduction" in wages considered as a proportion of net production in the processing industries. But the reduction of wholesale prices, especially of food commodities, suggests that some wage earners were able to maintain their buying power; some even were able to improve their buying power: from 1924 to 1939, real wages rose by 15 percent. Besides, during the 1930s such measures as the eight-hour day and an annual week of holiday were accomplished and became widespread. The poorest citizens were able to receive something, though it was often very little: less than half the old people received a pension at all, and those who did found that it rarely assured a decent minimum; heads of households who became ill could receive slim compensation and the conditions for allocating unemployment benefits remained differentiated and restrictive throughout the 1930s. Out of this situation arose the hunger marches, particularly in 1932, which were put down harshly by the police.

Unemployment, pressure on buying power, increased productivity, misery for the weakest: the British working class paid heavily for the policy of restoring the pound during the 1920s, and they paid again for the effects on British capitalism of the world crisis of the 1930s.

It can be seen then, underlying the muffled debates of the British economists, what huge stakes were at issue for the ruling class. While Keynes and a few isolated thinkers called for an increase in public spending, less restrictive credit policies, and public works projects, and were opposed to the systematic attempt to reduce nominal wages, the economists in authority saw in this latter course the key solution. For example, A. C. Pigou, a student of Marshall and tutor of Keynes, wrote that "with perfectly free competition among work-people and labour perfectly mobile … there will always be at work a strong tendency for wage rates to be so related to demand that everybody is employed. Hence, in stable conditions everyone will actually be employed. Thus in a stable situation, everyone will in fact find employment."[39] And Robbins used even more explicit terms:

> But in general it is true to say that a greater flexibility of wage rates would considerably reduce unemployment…. If it had not been for the prevalence of the view that wage rates must at all costs be maintained in order to maintain the purchasing power of the consumer, the violence of the present depression and the magnitude of the unemployment which has accompanied it would have been considerably less.[40]

Keynes' *General Theory* was designed to refute and replace the classical vision:

I have criticised at length Professor Pigou's theory of unemployment not because he seems to me to be more open to criticism than other economists of the classical school; but because his is the only attempt with which I am acquainted to write down the classical theory of unemployment precisely. Thus it has become incumbent on me to raise my objections to this theory in the most formidable presentment in which it has been advanced.[41]

As an alternative to one capitalist solution to the crisis which forced huge sacrifices upon the working class and which thus ran the risk of leading to disquieting conflicts, Keynes proposed another capitalist solution which, through a resurgence of activity, would allow for the reduction of unemployment without cutting off workers' buying power. In this sense, and twenty years after Ford's five-dollar day, Keynes stated an economic theory which helped to justify new policies by means of which the integration of the working world into capitalist society would be sought and in part accomplished. This is already going on in the United States, but still appears largely unrealistic in Europe.

The lengthy crisis of the 1920s and 1930s struck particularly at the economic sectors of the first industrialization which had formed the strength of British capitalism in the nineteenth century: coal, metallurgy, and textiles. On the other hand, second-generation industries were given impetus to develop: the electrical industry (which doubled the number of its wage earners between 1924 and 1937), the automobile industry (which doubled its production between 1929 and 1937), highway transportation, artificial silk, and food industries. This restructuring was strengthened by considerable operations of sectorial organization and concentration: the coal industry included more than 1,000 companies; after 1930 a Reorganization Commission was given control over production and exportation and a central Council of Coal Mines facilitated reorganizations and mergers. In the steel industry the Reorganization Comittee provided the merger of 2,000 companies into the one British Iron and Steel in 1932. The textile industry remained dispersed and inefficient: for example, in 1927 there were 57 million spindles in Britain compared to 38 million in the United States and 6 million in Japan. Yet British production was only half that of the United States, and Japan was on the way to equaling its British competitors. In the modern industries, powerful companies were formed: in chemistry, the Imperial Chemical Industries (ICI), with the participation of the English Nobel Company; in the automobile industry, Rootes Motor Ltd. was created in 1932 from the merger of eight companies; Courtauld dominated rayon; and Lever (soap) in 1929 linked with the Dutch company United Margarine to form the Unilever group, of which Unilever Ltd. (British) held 46 percent of the capital and Unilever NV (Dutch) 54 percent.

In 1935 the three leading companies in each sector controlled, respectively, 83 percent of the railroads, 82 percent of the oil industry, 71 percent of steel piping, 71 percent of sugar, 48 percent of the chemical industry, 43 percent of mechanical industries, and 43 percent of the automobile industry, but only 23 percent of the textile industry. At the same time, 30,000 companies employed between ten and one hundred persons (one-fifth of industrial workers), while 130,000 companies employed fewer than ten workers. The heritage of a prestigious past weighed heavily on the destiny of British capitalism.

This heritage contained also an important asset: the empire of colonies and dominions, which was enlarged after World War I by authority over German East Africa and by a sphere of influence in the Middle East. Each dominion had a vote in the League of Nations, which assured Anglo-Saxon predominance. At the Imperial Conference of 1926, equality was affirmed between Britain and its dominions in matters of foreign policy, though Britain assumed "special responsibilities" for defense. Britain's commercial trade with its empire better resisted the crisis than its other foreign trade. And when in September 1931 the pound was detached from gold, a protectionist tariff was immediately put into effect. At the Ottawa Conference in 1932 the empire was renamed the British Commonwealth of Nations, and an agreement of "reciprocal preference" was concluded: Britain gave tax immunity to most Commonwealth products, while Australia, New Zealand, India, Canada, Newfoundland, the Union of South Africa, and Rhodesia granted considerable preferential tariffs to English products. Britain in 1939 received 38 percent of its imports from the Commonwealth countries (against 26 percent in 1929), and sold 45 percent of its exports to these countries (against 40 percent in 1929).

In a parallel movement, British foreign investments, which declined in the United States and stagnated in Canada, progressed in Europe, Argentina, Mexico, and above all in the Commonwealth countries: Australia, New Zealand, and India, particularly.[42] The income from these investments formed an essential resource for Britain's foreign accounts throughout the period between the two wars (see Table 3.10).

Besides this, the terms of exchange improved, in large part because of the large drop in the relative prices of base products, particularly agricultural products from the "new countries": for Britain, the relation of export prices to import prices rose from an index of 60 in 1881–85 to 82 in 1926–30 and to 100 in 1931–35.[43]

Hidden levies by means of unequal exchange accentuated by this improvement in the terms of exchange and levies by means of income from foreign investments both signified a widening and an intensification of exploitation on a world scale. In forms adapted to each production, to each social formation, and to each type of presence in the mother country, the compulsion to extract surplus labor was at work more and more on all five continents. New forms of misery and new injustices sprung up. There were also new movements toward liberation and independence: often the spokespeople for these movements came from the well-off strata of society and from among the intellectuals, and sometimes from the clergy and the religious orders. At the same time that the empire was becoming more necessary than ever for British capitalism, it was already marked by innumerable rifts.

THE FRANC FIRST?

Certain fractions of French capitalism had also favored the "development" of the empire in the 1920s: thus the Sarraut plan of 1921, the creation of the Bank of Syria and Lebanon (1919), the State Bank of the Afrique occidentale française (1925), and the Bank of Madagascar (1925). In the face of sharpened competition for the world market, a customs law in 1928 organized imperial preference, and essentially suppressed tariffs between the mother country and the colonies. In 1931 the colonial Exposition of Vincennes was arranged. In 1934–35 the imperial conference barely succeeded in proposing that the word "overseas" be used instead of "colonies" and "colonial."

It was during the crises of the 1930s that the innermost recesses of the French empire appeared most clearly: trade with the colonies represented only 12 percent of French imports and 19 percent of exports in 1928–30, but these figures grew to 27 percent and 30 percent, respectively, in 1936–38. In 1913 only one-tenth of French capital invested abroad was invested in the empire; this proportion did not change a great deal between the two wars, despite the active presence of a few large financial groups, such as the Compagnie Française de l'Afrique de l'Ouest (a capital group principally from Marseilles), the Société Coloniale de l'Ouest Africain (a capital group from Lyons, linked to the Demachy bank), the Parisian Union Bank (associated with capital from Bordeaux), the Bank of Indochina, and the Bank of Paris and the Netherlands. Expressive of the state of mind of French capitalists, investments in the empire were made primarily in commerce (39 percent) and banking and real estate (10 percent),

TABLE 5.3   Foreign Investments of Leading Capital-Exporting Countries
(as a percentage of total)

	1914	1930	1960
Great Britain	50.4	43.8	24.5
France	22.2	8.4	4.7
Germany	17.3	2.6	1.1
Netherlands	3.1	5.5	4.2
Sweden	0.3	1.3	0.9
United States	6.3	35.3	59.1
Canada	0.5	3.1	5.5
Total	100.0	100.0	100.0

Source: Magdoff, *The Age of Imperialism*, p. 56.

but relatively little in industry (10 percent) and mining (7 percent). This investment in the colonies ultimately had little impact, for from this period onward France's foreign investments declined.

Cracks had already appeared in the French empire—though it is easier to understand their importance in retrospect. There were troubles in Tunisia in 1920–21, a revolt by Abd El Krim in Morocco (1925–26), an uprising at Yen Bay and peasant revolts in Indochina (1930–31), and movements, again put down, in Tunisia and Morocco in 1937–38. These movements were not tolerable—not only because they conflicted with colonial interests, but because French opinion to a high degree mixed colonial ideas with ideas of legitimate government in a way which today may appear strange. The following remark by a high official offers an example:

> It is the Republic which in less than 40 years has restored colonial France and which has spread the ideas of liberation and social progress over the French world.... This colonial policy has a double task ...: to create the rights of colonial populations, and to develop and encourage the social and economic evolution of indigenous peoples.... [Thus] the indigenous peoples which France rules and instructs could become partners in her life, freed from their customs and evolution, but federated as a part of Overseas France.[44]

Although the empire allowed for the partial absorption of the effects of the 1930s crisis, the expansion which French capitalism enjoyed during the 1920s was not based primarily upon exploitation of the empire. This expansion was indeed undeniable: on the base of 100 in 1913, industrial production was 57 in 1919, 55 in 1921, because of that year's crisis, 109 in 1924, and 127 in 1928. Between 1922 and 1929, the rate of growth of

TABLE 5.4   Industrial Production in Britain and France
(percentage of total)

	GREAT BRITAIN		FRANCE	
	Consumer goods*	Means of production	Consumer goods*	Means of production
1875–84			78	22
1881	53	47		
1905–13			72	27
1907	42	58		
1920–24			66	34
1924	47	53		
1935–38			59	41

* Includes construction and public works.

Source: T. K. Markovitch, *Cahiers de l'ISEA*, November 1966, p. 287.

production was 5.8 percent per year, a rate comparable to that of Germany (5.7 percent), inferior only to that of Japan (6.8 percent), and greater than the growth rates of the United States (4.8 percent), Great Britain (2.7 percent), and Italy (2.3 percent). This growth was stronger for capital goods industries (which surpassed their prewar levels by 50 percent) than for consumer goods industries (which rose above their prewar levels by only 10 percent).

Thus, while the place occupied by the sector of the means of production was strengthened in French industry, a movement in the opposite direction took place in British industry, which had been very much ahead in this sector before World War I (see Table 5.4). This growth was above all due to second-generation industries. The production of electricity quadrupled between 1920 and 1928; Ernest Mercier, supported by the Rothschilds, regrouped the companies in the Parisian region into an electrical union and strengthened the bonds with companies which manufactured electrical matériel: between the general company of electricity and Alsthom (formed in 1928 from the merger of the mechanical construction Alsatian Company with Thomson-Houston, affiliated with the American General Electric). The automobile industry built 250,000 vehicles in 1928, which was a large number for Europe, though small in comparison to the United States; more than half of these automobiles were built by Renault, Peugeot, and Citroën. The rubber industry, whose production in 1929 was eight and a half times greater than in 1913, was dominated by Michelin. There were important advances also in the chemical industry, which was dominated by Kuhlmann, but several newcomers arose as a result of "reparations": the National Office of Nitrogen (public capital), the Rhône Company (Swiss capital), and Progil (textile capital from Lyons—Gillet—and from the department of Nord—Motte). There was rapid progress in aluminum and electrometallurgy, with Pechiney and Ugine. Even the production of iron and steel products, always dominated by Schneider and Wendel, increased during this period.[45]

This growth was stimulated by a strong rise in exports, encouraged by the devaluation of the franc until 1926–28: the percentage of manufacturing production exported stood at 7 percent at the end of the nineteenth century and at 8 percent in 1905–13, rising to 10 percent in 1920–24, and falling back to 4 percent in 1935–38. In 1930, 10 percent of France's coal production was exported, with the following percentages for other industries: rubber, 15 percent; automobiles, 17 percent; chemical industries, 25 percent; and steel products, 29 percent. Exports were more important still for the traditional industries: leather and hides, 30 percent; cotton fabrics, 32 percent; wool fabrics, 38 percent; ready-made clothing and lingerie, 50 percent; pharmaceutical products, 50 percent; musical instruments, 50 percent; perfumes, 60 percent; clocks and jewelry, 60 percent; fine leather goods, 60 percent and silk and rayon fabrics, 65 percent.[46] This growth was then partially supported by a relative devaluation of French labor in relation to American or British labor. This devaluation occurred through a relative fall in the franc, which encouraged the maintenance or development of exports.

Such growth was supported also by considerable increases in productivity. In 1905–13 francs, the value of production per worker grew from about 2,500F (the same level as in 1905–13) to 3,500F in 1925–34 and to 4,250F in 1935–38. The increase in productivity was particularly strong during the period 1925–35 (37 percent). While productivity per worker in industry declined from 1913 to 1920 at an average rate of 1.8 percent per year, productivity increased at a very fast pace during the 1920s (5.8 percent per year), and continued to increase from 1930 to 1937 (2.8 percent per year). On the basis of 100 in 1913–14, industrial productivity had fallen to 84 in 1920, but rose to 136 by 1929. Taking into consideration the fact that during this period the length of the work week was reduced, and annual vacations became widespread, the increase in hourly productivity was even greater: it nearly doubled between 1920 and 1938.[47]

The increase in productivity was linked to an accentuation of mechanization and motorization, and of modernization and rationalization of the industrial apparatus: the rate of investment rose from 15 percent in 1896–1913 to 19 percent in 1928–31. At the same time various methods for the intensification of labor were developed in different sectors, and measures leading to a greater stability of the working class were taken by the directors of large companies. For example, in steelmaking: "The reduction in the number of workers due to war losses and the rise in wages," wrote Eugène Schneider in 1931, "forced the development and the perfecting of tools by substituting them for the former manpower in manufacturing as well as in handling." The number of blast furnaces rose from 73 in 1921 to 154 in 1929; at Wendel as well as at Schneider, it was already a tradition to insert part of the labor force into cities or towns where everything, from housing to cemeteries, and from stores to schools to clinics, belonged to the factory.

In the coal mines the number of jack hammers grew from 1,400 in 1913 to 13,300 in 1925. At the same time the "Bedeaux system," which defined labor norms, was established: workers were penalized if they did not attain the norm, and rewarded if they exceeded it. From time to time the norms were raised; here again, a policy of stabilization and integration was followed, supported by "the pride of being a miner." The neighborhoods of the miners' row houses included schools and churches, and coal was provided free.[48] In the automobile and other mechanical industries, assembly-line work served as the basis for increases in productivity: at Renault the number of machine tools rose from 4,250 in 1914 to 5,210 in 1920, and at Citroën from 3,450 in 1919 to 12,260 in 1927. The number of work days required for the manufacture of one car fell from 563 in 1920 to 129 in 1929 (160 days at Renault, where the models were more varied and the organization "more flexible," but 100 days at Citroën).[49] At Pechiney, before World War II approximately 40 percent of the workers lived in "Pechiney housing," and often in towns where everything was controlled by the company.

Progress in productivity between the two wars resulted, then, from mechanization/motorization/rationalization of production as well as from an intensification of labor. This intensification took place under the pressure of various methods of organization and remuneration which in the large companies often included a paternalistic policy aiming at the stabilization and integration of the workers. But large companies remained an island within French capitalism: companies employing more than 500 wage earners represented only 20 percent of French workers in 1926 and 1936, while companies employing fewer than 10 workers still accounted for 40 percent of the workforce. Within the small companies, traditional methods for extracting surplus labor continued.

By 1926 this phase of accumulation began to encounter its own limits: disposing of what was produced became increasingly difficult. This was due on the one hand to divergences in sectorial growth, and on the other hand to weakness of worker and peasant buying power. Moreover, competition on the world market became more difficult, and hardened still further with the financial stabilization of 1926 and the reattachment of the franc to gold in 1928. Wholesale prices began to fall in 1926: on the base of 100 in 1913, for 94 industrial materials, they fell from 793 in 1926 to 697 in 1928 to 579 in 1939, the year in which the "American crisis" is supposed to have begun to affect France. This fall in wholesale prices was especially marked in minerals and metals, textiles and leather, chemical products, and rubber. In a parallel movement, the value of exports began to decline: for wool and silk fabrics, lingerie and clothing, automobiles and metal tools, this decline had begun by 1926. For cotton fabrics and wool yarn, it began in 1927. And in 1926 profit rates for all sectors climbed to levels which would not be reached again for the next fifteen years.[50]

A crisis, then, was already very much at work in France by the time the French economy felt the after-effects of the American crisis. The stubborn policy of maintaining the gold convertibility of the franc and of attempted deflation contributed to making the crisis a lengthy one. The maximum number of unemployed workers receiving aid was attained in 1935–36 (more than 400,000). There was a slight but constant lowering of nominal wages until 1936, and prices fell until 1935 (more among wholesale prices than for retail prices). There was a continuing stagnation of industrial production at levels 10 to 25 percent less than those of 1928, and exports also dropped, in volume until 1932, and in value until 1936.[51] With these came protectionism, Malthusianism, the rise of the Right, 1934—and then, in the face of the mounting fascist movement, came the Popular Front.

Twice during this period the French workers' movement found itself in a position of strength: first, directly after the war (1919–20), when the Confédération Générale du Travail (CGT) recovered its 1913 membership levels (900,000 workers) and the working class proved to be combative; and again at the time of the Popular Front, with the great movement of 1936, and the unprecedented pressure for unionization (800,000 union members in 1935, 4 million in 1937). But by 1919 serious differences at the heart of

BASE INDEX 100 = 1900

Source: *Statistiques et études financières*, 40, 1979.

DIAGRAM 14   CHANGE OVER TIME IN
NUMBER OF HOURS WORKED PER YEAR IN FRANCE

the workers' movement came to light: some workers struck basically for the eight-hour day, while others struck for a radical change in society. Another breach developed between those who saw the USSR as the homeland of socialism (the victory of socialism throughout the world being from then on conditioned by Soviet successes) and those who saw the matter differently. These divergent views led to a break within the French Section of the Workers' International (SF 10), and then within the CGT, and a subsequent long period of conflicts and weakening of the workers' movement. This division continued to be an important part of the difficulties encountered by the Popular Front as World War II approached.

However, as a whole, the French working class (and more generally, the wage-earning world) during this period succeeded in maintaining a balance of power which enabled them to benefit in part from the productivity increases they endured. This occurred in two forms: (a) as a reduction in the length of the working day, and (b) as a defense and advance of real wages.

In 1919 the law on the eight-hour working day was passed, leading to a distinct drop in the length of the working day in 1920 and 1921. The slowdown in economic activity brought a new and noticeable reduction in the annual duration of labor after 1929. The forty-hour work week and the annual week's vacation in 1936 caused still another reduction. Compared to the slow diminution of the period between 1896 and 1913, and the grudging reductions (after a clear rise) in the 1960s, the reductions of the 1930s were marked. One can imagine the satisfaction that might have been experienced by the workers (except the unemployed) when they recovered "some time in which to live."

Between 1920 and 1930 real wages per worker increased by 2.2 percent per year, and between 1930 and 1937 they increased by 1.5 percent per year. In 1930 the buying power of different categories of workers had advanced from 14 percent to 50 percent over 1914; the structure of food consumption among working families changed: the percentage of cereal-based products went down from 19 percent in 1905 to 12 percent in 1930, while the share of poultry and pork products increased from 9 percent to 10 percent, and the percentage of fruits and vegetables rose from 10 percent to 16 percent. The proportion of egg, dairy, and fat products remained the same (19 percent), as did the share of beverages (13 percent).[52] In the industrial towns, the ladies of the house among the middle bourgeoisie were offended: imagine that—workers' wives are beginning to buy chickens!

The 1919 law on collective bargaining hardly applied for long. The 1928 law on social insurance led to an initial enlargement of indirect wages which represented one-fourth of the mass of wages in 1937. In 1936, besides the rise in wages, the forty-hour week, and paid vacations, the rights of unions became broader and stronger, the system of collective bargaining became generalized, and company delegates were created.

Thus, for the period as a whole, the working class managed to obtain the institutionalization of important "gains" at the same time as it benefited (in the form of a reduction in the length of work and an increase in buying power) from one part of the increase in production which this class sustained. As for the employers, although they had to make these concessions, they also obtained an intensification of labor within the framework of modernization and rationalization. Besides this, their paternalistic policies enabled them to insert—though not integrate—fractions of the working class in numerous regions or industrial zones. Although everyone in France rejected social democracy, those on the Left as well as those on the Right, the bases for a social-democratic compromise were in fact established between the two wars. Such a compromise was not achieved at this time in Germany, the cradle of social democracy.

Deutschland Über Alles!

An amputated imperialism blocked in its expansion; a mutilated capitalism, heavily penalized to the profit of its rivals. Indeed. However, not everything can be reduced to capitalism, to its manifestations and jolts. There was a defeated army and its military caste. There was a humiliated people and there was nationalism. The uncontrollable ferment of racism mixed with chauvinism and xenophobia. And then there was the encounter of an uncommon demagogue with this wounded people and these greedy interests—and their enchantment through radio, propaganda, monumental staging, and mass violence. Ideology had its impact: for men, "Arbeit macht frei" ("Work makes you free"—and how could it be denied when one has experienced unemployment?)—and for women, "Kinder, Küche, Kirche" ("children, kitchen, church"—and what could the Church have to say against such healthy ideas?). There were fierce attacks, strokes of luck, unrestrained and threatening violence, and various different factions.

On the other side there were errors of judgment, a succession of cowardly acts, and poor calculations. But wasn't there also a large share of complicity on the part of the ruling classes as a whole? From the moment when evil became synonymous with the USSR, communism, the Reds— couldn't Nazi Germany serve as a useful counter? Wouldn't Germany find useful compensations for a new thrust toward the East? For a time, the German–Soviet pact broke that dream—and the conflagration set the world on fire.

The program of the National-Socialist Party in 1920 had certain distinctly anticapitalist features. It recommended the nationalization of stockholding companies, which would become "goods of the national community." Gregor Strasser, who inspired this line of thinking, wrote:

> To see German industry and the German economy in the hands of international finance capital is the end of any possibility of social revolution, the end of a socialist Germany.... We, the young Germans of the war generation, we national-socialist revolutionaries, will engage in the struggle against capitalism incarnate in the Peace of Versailles.[53]

The Nazi hymns kept traces of this thinking:

> We are the army of the swastika;
> Raise the red flags,
> For the German workers, we want
> To smooth the paths of freedom.

And Hitler, in *Mein Kampf* (1925–27):

> As National Socialists we see our program in our flag. In the *red* we see the social idea of the movement, in the *white* the national idea, in the *swastika* the mission of the fight for the victory of Aryan man, and at the same time also the

victory of the idea of creative work which in itself is and will always be anti-semitic.[54]

And Goebbels, in *Revolution of the Germans*:

What is the aim of the German Socialist? He wants the future Germany to have no proletariat. What is the aim of the German Nationalist? He wants the future Germany no longer to be the proletarian of the universe. National Socialism is nothing but the synthesis of these two concepts.[55]

The national-socialist movement took root in the middle and petty bourgeoisie, and among the middle and petty "bureoisie."[56] As it approached closer to large financial and industrial capital, the Nazi movement moderated the anticapitalist dimension (1927), and the supporters of that tendency were eliminated by the time power was seized (1933–34).

From then on the mysticism of nation, race, blood, and force prevailed. Hitler: "It is not hair-splitting intelligence which has pulled Germany from its distress, but our faith…. Reason would have advised you against coming to me, and only faith commanded you."[57] And Goebbels to Hitler: "In our profound despair, we have found in you the one who showed the road of faith…. You were for us the fulfillment of a mysterious desire. You addressed to our anguish words of deliverance. You forged our confidence in the miracle to come."[58] Hysteria was inflamed with the words: "Germany, wake up!"—"Deutschland über alles!" ("Germany above all!"). "A people who give up maintaining the purity of their race give up, by the same token, the unity of their soul." "The role of the strongest is to dominate and not to blend in with the weakest."[59]

These were simple ideas, shock formulas—hammered at and repeated again and again by the propaganda. Hitler: "I have always been extraordinarily interested in the activity of propaganda, an art which has remained almost unknown among the bourgeois parties." And again: "Propaganda must be maintained at the level of the masses, and one must not measure its value except through the results obtained." And Goebbels: "Propaganda has only one goal: the conquest of the masses. And all means which serve this goal are good." There was violence—organized, systematized, and programmed—by the SA, the SS: persecutions and then attacks against the Jews, attacks against union workers, against the (evil) Reds. The SS eliminated the SA, and then arrived the SS state…

One must of course consider Germany's defeat, and its humiliation: there were war debts, the occupation of the Ruhr, absolute inflation which destroyed the currency, the burden of reparations, the austerity efforts. And the crisis in the United States struck directly at Germany's extremely fragile economic revival, domestically as well as in its foreign relations: the gold reserves of the Reichsbank melted away, and industrial production, on the base of 100 in 1928, fell to 59 in August 1932. The number of unemployed workers rose from 2.5 million to 6 million in 1932. The workers' movement was weakened by its failures at the beginning of the 1920s, and by the deep division which opposed the German Communist Party, strictly linked to the USSR, as an irreducible adversary of the social democrats.

The ruling class was itself divided, with the industrial and financial employers opposed to the landed property owners, the manufacturing industries opposed to heavy industry, and the middle employers (wanting to negotiate a compromise with the working class) opposed to the large employers (anxious to revenge themselves against the workers' movement and to regain absolute power). As early as 1919, Stinnes, an industrial magnate, foresaw a moment to come: "One day the great industrialists and all the leaders of economic life will recover their influence and their power. They will be called back by a sobered, half-starved people, who will need bread and not words." And Fritz Thyssen, in 1924: "Democracy, for us, represents nothing." In 1929 the German National Party and the *Stahlhelm* steel helmets (movements inspired by Hugenberg, president of Krupp's administrative council and a press magnate) joined together in a "united national front" with the Pan-Germanist League and the National Socialist Party.

The middle classes—entrepreneurs and individual employers of the petty and middle bourgeoisie—and civil servants and employees of the petty and middle "bureoisie": these groups were traumatized and suffered in the crisis. The buying power of the farmers was decreased. Among the working class, as Reich emphasized, certain strata "became bourgeois" and the women of the working class remained for the most part obedient to the Catholic church. Nazi party membership in the early thirties was drawn from the following sections of the German population: 21–26 percent from the salaried workers (12 percent of the total); 13 percent from the civil servants (5 percent of the total); 20 percent from shopkeepers and artisans (9 percent of the total); but "only" 11 percent from the farmers (23 percent of the total); and 28–32 percent from the working class (45 percent of the total). In 1940, one-third of the SS cadres came from "intellectual" milieux: school teachers, professors, and graduate students (see Table 5.5).[60]

The social base for the rise of national socialism was, then, principally the petty and middle "bureoisie"; but the alliance with large capital was

TABLE 5.5   Class Structure and Ideological Structure in Germany, 1928–30 (millions)

Class	Ideology		
	PROLETARIAN (14.4)	PETTY-BOURGEOIS (20.1)	BOURGEOIS (0.7)
PROLETARIAT (21.8)	Workers in industry, transport, trade, etc. 11.8 — Farm workers 2.6 — TOTAL (14.4)	Housework — Domestic servants — Pensioners — Junior employees — Junior civil servants and pensioners — TOTAL	0.1 1.3 1.7 2.8 1.4 (7.4)
MIDDLE CLASSES (12.8)		URBAN — Small employers (≤ 2 employees) — Small employers (≥ 3 employees) — Clerks or middle-level officials — Professionals and students — Small property owners and people living off private income — RURAL — Small peasants and farmers (≤ 3 ha.) — Middddle farmers (5–50 ha.)	(6.2) 1.9 1.4 1.8 0.4 0.6 (6.6) 2.4 4.2
BOURGEOISIE (0.7)			Including large farmers and landowners 0.7

Derived from W. Reich, *The Mass Psychology of Fascism*, 1933.

the necessary condition for the accession to power. The organized workers' movement was very quickly broken by violence and by sending those who resisted to the camps. But after power was seized the buying power of the working class seemed to be maintained, and even seemed to increase for some categories—while buying power decreased for civil servants, the small shopkeepers, and artisans, a number of whom had to close their shops and become wage earners. The great strength of Hitlerian power

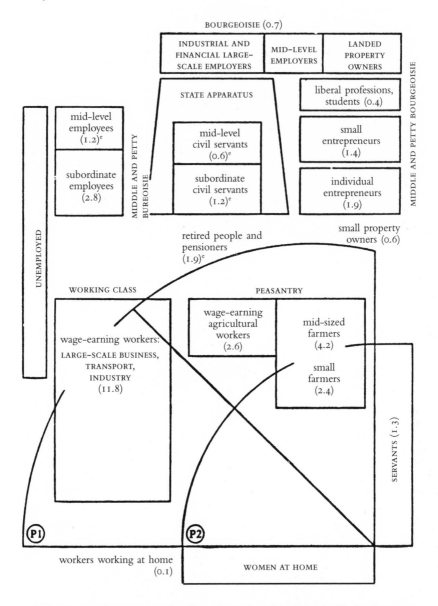

BOURGEOISIE (0.7)

INDUSTRIAL AND FINANCIAL LARGE-SCALE EMPLOYERS

MID-LEVEL EMPLOYERS

LANDED PROPERTY OWNERS

STATE APPARATUS

liberal professions, students (0.4)

MIDDLE AND PETTY BOURGEOISIE

mid-level employees (1.2)ᵉ

MIDDLE AND PETTY BUREOISIE

mid-level civil servants (0.6)ᵉ

small entrepreneurs (1.4)

subordinate employees (2.8)

subordinate civil servants (1.2)ᵉ

individual entrepreneurs (1.9)

UNEMPLOYED

retired people and pensioners (1.9)ᵉ

small property owners (0.6)

WORKING CLASS

PEASANTRY

wage-earning workers:

LARGE-SCALE BUSINESS, TRANSPORT, INDUSTRY (11.8)

wage-earning agricultural workers (2.6)

mid-sized farmers (4.2)

small farmers (2.4)

SERVANTS (1.3)

(P1)

(P2)

workers working at home (0.1)

WOMEN AT HOME

Numbers in parentheses represent, in millions, the number of people involved in the given category or activity in 1928–30. (P1) = sphere of material production; (P2) = sphere of subsistence production; ᵉ = estimate.

Source: Adapted from W. Reich, *The Mass Psychology of Fascism*, 1933.

DIAGRAM 15 SOCIAL CLASSES IN GERMANY AROUND 1930

came from the reduction of unemployment, the totalitarian state, and the affirmation of a Great Germany.

There were 5.5 million unemployed workers in 1933, 2 million in 1935, fewer than 1 million in 1937, and a few tens of thousands in 1939. Production more than doubled between 1933 and 1939, at which time it had surpassed its record level of 1929 by 26 percent. There was a policy of large public works projects—highways, railways, airports (all of which entailed strategic considerations)—as well as such urban projects as constructing prestigious buildings for the regime. Armaments were emphasized: by 1935 German armaments spending surpassed French armaments spending by 50 percent, and the Krupp factories were working at the limit of their capacities. Between 1935 and 1939 armament production capacity was multiplied by a factor of six. A policy of ersatz manufactures stimulated the chemical, metallurgical, textile, and food industries. All this took place within the framework of a rigorous policy of price and credit control and neutralization of excess buying power. Nazi Germany's foreign trade strategy was based upon bilateral accords and mechanisms for payment by compensation, which allowed for a strengthening of trade, especially with Latin American countries and countries in central and Mediterranean Europe.

But the resurgence and the policy of state control relied upon and reinforced the powerful industrial and banking groups within German capitalism. Even foreign companies—General Motors (Opel), Ford, Unilever, Shell, Schroeder—were respected: they simply had to reinvest all of their profits in Germany. Participation by the state in banking, steel production, and naval construction was transferred to private interests, and municipal control of electrical production was discouraged to the benefit of private industry. And though Hermann Goering Reichswerke joined public capital together with private capital, this was because public support was necessary to develop marginally profitable production from poor iron ores.

Above all, the process of cartel formation within German capitalism was strengthened still further. The number of cartels grew from 1,500 in 1923–24 to 2,100 in 1930; IG Farben dominated the chemical industry after 1926; by 1926–27 the Vereinigte Stahlwerke had reassembled the four largest steel producers; and after the merger in 1929 of the Deutsche Bank with the Diskonto Gesellschaft, three banks dominated the entire banking system. A 1933 law systematized this "organization" of German capitalism by requiring companies to participate in the cartel of their sector, reflecting a concern for simultaneous horizontal and vertical rationalization. Thus the industrial effort necessary to the Reich became organized and systematized.

Powerfully supported and strongly structured by the state, German capitalism was reinforced in a form which was without doubt the most extreme ever assumed by state capitalism. This development took place at the heart of a society caught in the tight grip of an intricate network woven by the state and the party. Goebbels had announced: "The state will be the leading organization of public and private life.... All the forces of the nation will be subject to the state, in such a way that it will be impossible for them to exercise any activity outside the state. The state will put into effect the totalitarian principle." The spearhead and organ of surveillance, control, and state repression was the police. After 1933 all local police were unified; in 1934 the Gestapo (the political police) were joined with the SS under the direction of Himmler; in 1936 all police units became subject to the Gestapo–SS apparatus. From 1933 to 1938 more than 400,000 Germans were arrested and many of them were put into the camps. All aspects of life became ensnared together. Workers were organized into a Labor Front created in May 1933, at the same time as the trade unions were dissolved. For leisure there was *Kraft durch Freude* (strength through joy). For everything, for everyone, there were organizations: for young people, students, teachers, artists, women, parents. Radio, the press, cinema, and schooling were totally at the service of the national-socialist ideology and propaganda.

Hitler offered to the humiliated Germans the possibility of a triumphant Germany. In *Mein Kampf* he wrote that all men "of the same blood should belong to the same Reich." Once united, what can be done with a "people without space"? The national-socialist movement must "find the courage to gather together our people and their power in order to launch them on the road which will lead them out of their present narrow habitat toward new territories." Of course, it was necessary to annihilate France: "Never allow the formation in Europe of two continental powers. In any attempt to organize a second military power on German borders, you must see an attack against Germany." The Reich had to expand in Europe toward the East: "Be careful that the source of our country's power is not in the colonies, but in Europe, in the soil of the homeland.... The gigantic state of the East is ripe for collapse." And finally, why be limited to Europe? "A state which, in a time of racial contamination, jealously watches over the preservation of the best elements in its own race, must one day become the master of the earth. May the members of our movement never forget this."

The year 1935 saw the reestablishment of military service in Germany; the following year reoccupation of the Rhine. In 1938 Hitler became commander-in-chief of the Reichswehr; the same year saw the occupation of Austria, the Prague ultimatum, the Munich accords; 1939 saw the occupation of Czechoslovakia, the capture of Klaipeda (Memel), the Italian–German military alliance, the German–Soviet nonaggression pact, and the invasion and then the division of Poland with the USSR, which occupied Finland. The inferno of World War II was then lit. Germany dominated Europe. But the attack by the USSR and the U.S. entry into the war (1941) reversed the balance of forces. But three more years of pitiless war and mass destruction (the military continuation of mass production and mass consumption) and 50 million deaths (six times more than in World War I) were required before the German capitulation, and the use of the first atomic bomb before the Japanese capitulation.

From then on, two great powers dominated a devastated world: the United States, leader of the capitalist camp; and the USSR, at the center of a new bloc which invoked the name of socialism.

SUMMARY

The crisis of the 1920s and 1930s resulted from the same combination of contradictions that essentially led to the 1914–18 war: the loss of energy in industries of the first industrialization; accentuation of competition between national capitalisms; pressures by the workers' movement to obtain a less unequal division of produced values. These contradictions acted within a world which had been divided up between the zone of American influence, the British Commonwealth, the French, Dutch, and Belgian empires, and—both surrounded and turned back upon itself—the USSR. Aided by protectionism, it was within each zone of influence that these contradictions intensified and that the path toward crisis—helped or hindered by the policies of each great power—developed.

But industries of the second generation were at this time in full development. And, in a striking dialectical reversal, the rise in buying power of some fractions of the working class, which in the eyes of most capitalists should have ruined the system, revealed itself to be an element of economic dynamism and social integration: on the whole, the length of the working day was reduced and real wages increased for workers in the leading industrial countries. But unemployment remained an unrelenting burden, especially at times of crisis.

Through foreign investments, unequal exchange, and price scissoring and improvement in the terms of exchange, a considerable transfer of values occurred from the colonies—as well as from the new countries, producers of minerals and agricultural products—toward the large, industrialized capitalist countries.[61] Thus, the relative improvement in the buying power of the European and American working classes was in part provided from or compensated by, from the point of view of capital, a levy upon primary-sector producers, especially the peasantries, of the entire world.

During this period industrial concentration increased in many forms: large companies, groups, combines, and cartels. Industrial plants making use of several thousand workers were no longer rare, and some employed tens of thousands. The role of the state widened and deepened, especially in times of war, as well as for large public works projects and the development of indirect wages.[62] More generally, duties of direction, organization, and administration increased. Alongside the peasantry, the petty and middle bourgeoisie, and the working class, a new class was developing: the "techno-bureoisie"; though it was essentially a wage-earning class like the working class, it did not directly confront material production like the peasantry and the working class; and in its way of life it was often closer to the petty and middle bourgeoisie.[63]

These evolutions took place in a world split apart. It was split primarily because state collectivism in the USSR was developing as a wedge firmly sunk within the world market.[64] Moreover, the previously dominant imperialism of Great Britain no longer had the means for regulating a system of world payments, while the leading economic power, the United States, did not take charge of this task. Each great power was focused upon a national objective: American prosperity, the pound, the franc, the recovery of German power. Finally, during the difficulties of the crisis each great power withdrew into its own cocoon (the Commonwealth for Britain, the empire for France) or its own project (the American New Deal), while Hitler's Germany was mobilizing for national greatness, rearmament, conquest, and the mastery of Europe and the world.

In this fragmented world, each protectionist retreat expanded the crisis. Supply countries were affected, and, because they purchased fewer goods, the leading industrial nations and the newer nations also contributed to the developing crisis. The nations which considered themselves deprived of their "vital space," an area of influence for adequate economic and commercial growth, chose expansionist policies which led to the war.

	Decolonization	Capitalist bloc	East–West relations	Socialist bloc
1943	Independence of Korea guaranteed by the United States, Britain, and China.	Keynes' plan; White's plan. Allied landing in Sicily and Italy.		Dissolution of the Comintern.
1944	Conference of Brazzaville. Manifesto of Istiqlal.	Allied landing in France. Bretton Woods Conference.		Russian troops in Bulgaria and Hungary.
1945	Independence proclaimed in Indonesia, Laos, Cambodia, and Vietnam; French interventions. Uprisings in Constantine and Sétif (Algeria); repression. Creation of the new State of Libya. Independence of Syria and Lebanon. Creation of the Arab League in Cairo.	Advance of Allied troops in Western Europe.	Yalta conference. Russian troops in North Korea. U.S. troops in South Korea. Meeting of Russian and U.S. troops in Germany. U.S. atomic bomb exploded on Hiroshima. Charter of the United Nations.	Advance of Russian troops in Western Europe. Republics proclaimed in Yugoslavia and Bulgaria.
1946	French troops in Tonkin. English troops in Indonesia. Independence of Transjordan recognized by Britain. Independence of Philippines. Failure of negotiations between France and Vietnam. General insurrection of Tonkin. Dutch–Indonesian accords	Beginning of civil war in Greece.	U.S. atomic testing on Bikini.	Popular Republic of Albania. Favorable elections for the Communist Party in Czechoslovakia

	Decolonization	Capitalist bloc	East–West relations	Socialist bloc
1947	Insurrection in Madagascar. Dutch military operations in Java. Independence of India and Pakistan; war in Kashmir. French offensive in Tonkin. Independence of Burma. Continuation of Indochina war.	Marshall Plan. Communists are no longer in the governments of Belgium, France, and Austria. The Cummunist Party is forbidden in the State of New York, in Brazil, and in Greece. U.S. aid pact with Greece and Turkey. Anti-strike laws in the United States. Inter-American defense pact in Rio. Split between the CGT and the Force Ouvrière (FO). Communist electoral defeats in Finland and Norway.	Truman doctrine. Refusal by the USSR and Czechoslovakia to participate in the Marshall Plan. Failure of the Conference on Korea.	Popular Republic of Rumania; dissolution of the peasant party. Prohibition of the agrarian party in Bulgaria. Constitution of the Cominform. Strengthening of the economic ties between the USSR and the popular democracies.
1948	Dutch–Indonesian truce. Assassination of Gandhi. Ceylon receives the status of a dominion. First Arab–Israeli war. New Dutch intervention in Indonesia. Continuation of the Indochina war.	Split in the Italian CGT. Dissolution of the Communist Party in Chile.	Beginning of the Soviet blockade of Berlin.	Resignation of non-Communist ministers in Czechoslovakia. Conflict between Tito and the Cominform; Yugoslavia excluded from the Cominform. East Berlin riot; Russian tanks shoot into the crowd. Arrest of Cardinal Mindszenky in Hungary. Advance by the Communists in China.
1949	Evacuation of Djakarta by the Dutch. Formation of the states of Jordan and Israel. Vote by the U.N. on the independence of Libya. Continuation of Indochina war; accords on the "independence" of Laos and Cambodia; creation of the "state" of Vietnam (Bao Dai).	North Atlantic treaty at Washington; NATO. Constitution of West Germany. Excommunication of communist and communist-inspired, Catholics. Fight against Communist activities in the United States. Nationalist Chinese in Taiwan.	End of the Berlin blockade. Russian atomic explosion.	Trial condemning Rajk in Hungary. Popular Republic in China. A Russian marshal becomes chief of staff in Poland.

	Decolonization	Capitalist bloc	East–West relations	Socialist bloc
1950	Uprisings in the Ivory Coast. Continuation of the Indochina war.	Institution of the European payments union. U.S. laws regarding anti-American activities; beginning of McCarthyism. End of the civil war in Greece.	U.S. decision to manufacture the H-bomb. Beginning of the Korean War.	East German–Polish accords on the Oder–Neisse border. Russian generals are chiefs of staff in Czechoslovakia and Hungary.
1951	Nationalization of oil in Iran; Mossadegh government. Riots in Casablanca. Anti-English riots in the Suez Canal zone; British military intervention. Independence of Libya. Continuation of the Indochina war.	European community of coal and steel. Peace treaty and alliance between Japan and the United States. Invitation to Greece and Turkey to join NATO.	Continuation of the Korean War.	Arrest of Slansky in Prague. Chinese intervention in Tibet.
1952	Riots and strikes in Tunisia; arrests of the neo-destourian and Communist leaders. Bloody riots in Cairo. Neguib takes power. State of alert against the Mau-Mau in Kenya. Rupture of diplomatic relations between Iraq and Britain. Riot in Casablanca. Continuation of the Indochina war.	Bonn accords between the Allies and West Germany. First British atomic bomb.	Continuation of the Korean War.	
1953	Deposition of the Sultan of Morocco. Fall of Mossadegh; U.S. aid to Iran. Grave attacks in Casablanca. Continuation of Indochina war.		First U.S. atomic artillery shell. Korean armistice. The USSR declares itself to possess the H-bomb. Refusal of the U.N. to admit Communist China.	Death of Stalin. Nagy replaces Rakosi in Hungary. Strikes and demonstrations in East Germany.

	Decolonization	Capitalist bloc	East–West relations	Socialist bloc
1954	Dien Bien Phu Conference in Geneva on Indochina. Nasser president of the cabinet in Egypt; removal from office of Neguib. Principle of internal autonomy of Tunisia. Abolition of the Dutch–Indonesian Union. Insurrection of Aures; beginning of the Algerian war. Revolt of the Mau-Mau in Kenya.	U.S. military accords with Japan, Pakistan, and nationalist China; Conference in Manilla; establishment of SEATO. Failure of the European Defense Community. Membership of West Germany in NATO.	First H-bomb explosion.	
1955	Attacks in Casablanca; return of the Sultan to Morocco. Continuation of the Algerian war. Afro-Asian conference in Bandung.		Conference of the four great powers in Geneva.	
1956	Independence of Morocco, Tunisia, the Sudan, Malaysia, and Ghana. Nationalization of the Suez Canal; French–British intervention. Second Israeli–Arab war. Continuation of the Algerian war.	U.S. pressure on France and Britain to impose a ceasefire.		Report by Khrushchev; the 20th Congress, CPSU. Russian tanks shoot into the crowd in Poland; the return of Gomulka. Rehabilitation of Rajk; uprising in Hungary; Russian tanks in Budapest.

Chapter 6

CAPITALISM'S
GREAT LEAP FORWARD
(1945–80)

Whatever those who see in each war, in each crisis and hint of crisis, a new aggravation of the "general crisis of capitalism" may think, what has been accomplished in the present period is in fact capitalism's new "leap forward." Of course, in a considerable part of the world capitalism reigns no longer; a new mode of accumulation and industrialization, another class society, and a tremendous concentration of state power have brought to these regions new means for production and resource appropriation. But World War II, the reconstruction and the period of prosperity which followed, decolonization, the internationalization of capital, and new industrialization in the third world all testify to a new thrust by capitalism on a world scale. And the crisis of the 1970s was in some ways the means by which this new expansion of capitalism and its accompanying mutations were carried out.

FROM WAR TO CRISIS

Faced by a considerably enlarged state collectivist bloc, and within a world context marked by the historic movement of decolonization, the developed capitalist countries, once they had arisen from the ruins of the war, experienced a period of exceptional prosperity. But the seeds of the present crisis were already developing in the very conditions of this prosperity.

THE THREE WORLDS

Directly following the first victory by a new country (the United States) over an old country of Europe (Spain), Jaurès foresaw in 1898: "The

United States will have an increasingly large impact on the destiny of the world.... The wealth and power of the United States are one-fourth of the wealth and power of the globe." At the end of World War I, the United States was the leading power in the world, although the expansion of American territory took place on American soil and the extension of American power within the Americas. At the end of World War II the United States was a great industrial, monetary, and military power: U.S. industrial production in 1945 was more than double that of annual production between 1935 and 1939; in 1945 the country produced half the world's coal, two-thirds of the oil, and more than half of the electricity. That year, U.S. production capacities reached 95 million tons for steel, 1 million tons for aluminum, and 1.2 million tons for synthetic rubber. The United States was able to produce great quantities of ships, airplanes, land vehicles, armaments, machine tools, chemical products, and so on. It held 80 percent of the world's gold reserves and had not only a powerful army but also the atomic bomb.

Facing the USSR, whose power had also strengthened and whose territorial influence had expanded, the United States assumed the role of leader of the capitalist camp. After 1943 U.S. representatives studied with their British counterparts the reconstitution of what had been so cruelly lacking between the two wars: a system of international payments which would allow for the simultaneous imposition of the necessary equilibria and the possible expansion of exchange and payments. In 1944 at Bretton Woods a system was established based upon the definition of each currency in relation to gold and fixed exchange parities; known as the gold exchange standard, this system used the dollar as its keystone for at least its first fifteen years. In 1945 Roosevelt and Churchill prepared the postwar era by negotiating with Stalin at Yalta about respective zones of influence; this same year American and Russian troops joined together in Germany and confronted one another in Korea.

Once Germany and Japan were defeated, two movements developed which came to dominate the immediate postwar period; for the period as a whole, they were to determine (a) the division of the world into two blocs, one dominated by the United States, the other dominated by the USSR; and (b) decolonization.

Through Stalin's industrialization effort before and during the war, the USSR had become a great industrial power; the sacrifices and destruction of the war were enormous (perhaps 20 million deaths, some 10 percent of the population), but in 1950, at the end of the fourth five-year plan, the index of industrial production surpassed by 71 percent that of 1940 (by 60 percent for machines and equipment and by 80 percent for chemical products). Coal production reached 250 million tons, and steel production reached 25 million tons. The Red Army was large, powerful, and well-equipped; the first Russian atomic bomb was exploded in 1949. Through its army, the USSR was present in all the central European countries, and the United States was afraid that Russian influence would extend into Turkey and European countries where communist parties were powerful (Greece, Italy, and France). A planetary chess game then began, with each of the two superpowers placing their pawns, reinforcing the zones in which they dominated, and threatening those in which the other appeared weak. Exceptional periods of tension established the points which were not to be surpassed. In 1947 the Marshall Plan was launched and the Cominform was established; in 1948–49 the Americans organized the "air bridge" in response to the Soviet blockade of Berlin. In the West communists were expelled from the governments they participated in, communist parties were sometimes forbidden, and a terrible civil war led to the crushing of the partisans in Greece. In the East communists took absolute control over state apparatuses and Soviet generals were named commanders in Poland, Czechoslovakia, and Hungary. The Korean War demonstrated each side's desire for victory as well as their shared interest in avoiding widening the conflict, which would bring the risk of a new world war. The United States institutionalized its military alliances in the Americas (1947), the North Atlantic (1949), and Southeast Asia (1954); while the Soviet Union had established solid political, economic, and military ties with the popular democracies of Europe by the end of the 1940s. Thus two worlds face to face became organized economically, monetarily, and in matters of defense: the capitalist world, yesterday hegemonic, discovered today that the Earth belonged to it no longer, that some raw materials and markets were no longer accessible to it, and that another mode of accumulation and industrialization also existed, founded upon the collective appropriation of the means of production, central planning, state direction, and state force.

At the same time the third world was being born. It arose principally through the powerful decolonization movement which had been engendered during the war by the strengthening of new bourgeoisies and intelligentsia, by the awareness of the unbearable and avoidable character of colonial domination, and by the desire for independence (which most often took the form of national independence). The weakening of the European mother countries, the Japanese occupation of Asia, the participation by third world peoples in the battles of the European mother

countries, the influence of Marxist analyses and perspectives opened by
the Soviet revolution, and liberation movements growing out of specific
national and religious situations—all these, under different forms and
following various pathways, presented an alternative: the possibility of
liberation from colonial domination, administration, and exploitation, from
paternalism, racism, persecution, or oppression. Independence was achieved
in Syria, Lebanon, the Philippines, India, Pakistan, Burma. The independence process in Indonesia was strewn with pitfalls, there was war in Indochina, and riots accompanied movements of the people in North Africa
and Black Africa. Even before political decolonization was achieved
throughout the world, the new independent states sought to recover
control over their natural wealth (nationalization of Iranian oil in 1951) or
their economic assets (nationalization of the Suez Canal by Egypt in 1956).
Third world chiefs of state met and attempted to organize into a force
which would weigh in the destiny of the planet. In 1955 an Afro-Asian
Conference was held at Bandung; over thirty countries representing more
than half the earth's population voiced with new power a language which
until then had been stifled by Western domination. Typical was the
statement by C. P. Romulo: "We have experienced, and some among us
experience still, the stigma of being belittled in one's own country, of
being systematically reduced to an inferior condition, not only politically,
economically, and militarily, but racially as well.... In order to fortify his
power, in order to justify himself in his own eyes, the Western white man
considered as an established fact that his superiority resided in his genes
themselves, in the color of his skin." Indonesia's President Sukarno echoed
the same feeling: "For generations our peoples have been without a voice
in the world.... We have been those to whom no attention was granted,
those whose fate was decided by others according to their own interests
which overwhelmed ours and made us live in poverty and humiliation."
He asked: "How can one say that colonialism is dead so long as vast
regions of Asia and Africa are not liberated?" And India's Nehru stated:
"Asia wishes to help Africa."

It was in this world context that the reconstruction of the capitalist
countries devastated by the war took place, and in this context that an
exceptional period of prosperity flourished.

AN EXCEPTIONAL PROSPERITY

After reconstruction the capitalist countries as a whole went through a
remarkable period of growth. Never had the world experienced such a
simultaneous advance in industrial production and world trade.

TABLE 6.1   Average Annual Growth Rates in World Industry and Trade

	World industry	World trade
1860–70	2.9	5.5
1870–1900	3.7	3.2
1900–1913	4.2	3.7
1913–29	2.7	0.7
1929–38	2.0	−1.15
1938–48	4.1	0.0
1948–71	5.6	7.3

Source: Rostow, *The World Economy*, pp. 49, 69.

The war effort, the widened mobilization of workers for production, the systematization of methods for organizing work, and advances in productivity were such that, whatever had been the extent of destruction in World War II, the rate of industrial growth during the ten-year period from 1938 to 1948 equaled the highest growth rates attained since the middle of the nineteenth century, that is, during the period from 1900 to 1913. And on this already high base, a new and exceptional phase of growth began. For nearly a quarter of a century growth rates averaged 5.6 percent per year for industrial production and 7.3 percent for commercial trade (see Table 6.1).

Within this general movement the developed capitalist world remained predominant: three-fifths of industrial production and two-thirds of world trade originated here. The United States dominated even further; one-third of world industrial production came from this country. Nevertheless, another mode of accumulation and industrialization was at work, effective in its own way, in the socialist countries. And a trend toward industrialization arose in the third world countries, in part as an effect of the internationalization of industrial groups in the developed capitalist countries, and in part as the result of initiatives—private or state—in these countries themselves.

In this period of general growth, inequality on a world scale increased; even when higher growth rates seem to indicate that the third world was beginning to catch up, in absolute values the gap widened between per capita production in the developed capitalist countries compared to third world countries (see Table 6.3).

Postwar growth was the greatest that had ever been experienced by the capitalist countries as a whole. Slower in Britain, appreciable in the United

TABLE 6.2   Share of World Industrial Production and Trade (percentage)

| | CAPITALIST WORLD | | SOCIALIST WORLD | | THIRD WORLD |
	Total	U.S.	Total	USSR	
Industrial production					
1936–38	76	(32)	19	(19)	5
1963	62	(32)	29	(19)	9
1971	61	(33)	26	(16)	13
World trade					
1938	64	(10)	1	(1)	35
1948	59	(16)	5	(2)	36
1963	63	(11)	12	(5)	25
1971	68	(13)	10	(5)	22

Source: Rostow, *The World Economy,* pp. 52–53, 72–73.

States (taking into account the high level of production at the end of the 1940s), this growth was especially marked in France and Germany, and still more so in Japan. It was based relatively little on an increase in labor power, and much more on a rise in labor productivity, which itself depended on an increase in the means of production put at the disposal of each worker, and which called for an intensification of individual labor.

The rise in productivity was obtained by using the various means for pumping out surplus labor which capitalism had perfected during its development:

1. Various pressures were exercised through the indirect submission to capital of farmers, "independent" transporters, and an increasing number of artisans and small shopkeepers; thus the farmers were "caught" between the price of what they bought from industry and the price of their own sales. Added to this was the burden of indebtedness; they were obliged each year to sell more and more.

2. When automation was impracticable, the old methods of piece work, work in the home, the sweating system, and so on were employed. These methods have been used, for example, in the ready-made garment trade, which employs women, recent immigrants, and even illegal immigrants (Mexicans in Los Angeles, Turks in Paris).

3. Subcontracting, which enables a large company wanting to retain its brand name to demand low cost prices from a small entrepreneur, was also utilized. The small entrepreneur is forced to require high produc-

TABLE 6.3   Per Capita Gross National Product in the Developed and
Developing Countries

REGION	POPULATION	PER CAPITA GNP		
	(million) 1975	Growth rate (percent) 1950–75	Value (1974 U.S.$) 1950	 1975
South Asia	830	1.7	85	132
Africa	384	2.4	170	308
Latin America	304	2.6	495	944
East Asia	312	3.9	130	341
China (PR)	820	4.2	113	320
Middle East	81	5.2	460	1,660
Developing countries	1,912	3.0	187	400
Developed countries*	654	3.2	2,378	5,238

* OECD countries excluding Spain, Greece, Portugal, and Turkey.

Source: Morawetz, *Vingt-cinq années de développement économique*, p. 13.

tivity from his own workers and from those he employs as temporary
workers.

4. New equipment, with greater capacities, higher speeds, and benefiting
   from advances in automation, has changed the nature of work (less
   physical fatigue and confrontation with materials, more nervous tension,
   monotony—and responsibility in case something happens), especially in
   the metallurgical, chemical, and textile industries.

5. The "classic" methods for organizing labor were put in effect anywhere
   possible. This occurred in places where these methods had been only
   slightly developed, particularly in Europe and Japan. In this way Taylorism, Fordism, and wage systems which spurred productivity became
   more widespread (in France in 1973, 6.5 percent of the workers worked
   on an assembly line).

6. In order to extract more profits from increasingly costly equipment,
   continuous labor was utilized, using shift work, which permitted
   production to be carried on for fourteen, sixteen, or twenty-four hours
   in a day. This system, which in prewar France was limited to production which the technology required to be unceasing (continuous fire
   processes), developed particularly after 1957: the percentage of shift
   workers among the working population grew from 14 percent in 1957
   to 31 percent in 1974.

TABLE 6.4 Economic Growth in the Developed Countries (average annual rates, 1950–75, in percent)

	United States	Great Britain	France	West Germany	Japan
Gross domestic product (by volume)	3.3	2.5	4.9	5.5	8.6
Employment	0.9*	0.3†	0.9	0.7	1.2‡
Labor productivity	1.5*	2.3†	4.6	4.7	8.6‡
Capital (per capita)	2.7*	3.1†	4.5	5.2	9.0‡

* 1952–75.   † 1949–76.   ‡ 1955–75.

Sources: *Statistiques et Etudes financières*, 1980, p. 30; J. H. Lorenzi et al., *La Crise du XXᵉ siècle* (Paris: Economica, 1980), pp. 104, 327, 330, 332, 334; J. J. Carré et al., *La Croissance française* (Paris: Editions du Seuil, 1980), pp. 104, 115, 211.

7. Finally, labor was intensified in offices, banks, insurance companies, the post office, and so on. Advances in calculating instruments and then computers produced an intensification of labor and an increase in the pace of work in these fields as well.

The increase in productivity of the decade of the 1950s, then, occurred through forced surplus labor, and on the basis of a considerable accumulation effort that allowed the use of modern equipment. In some cases this meant a longer working day, with or without an intensification of labor (farmers, truck drivers, workers in the home); in other cases it meant principally intensification of labor (assembly-line work, Taylorism, wages based upon productivity). Sometimes it implied a disqualification/intensification of labor, and sometimes a degradation in living conditions (night work, shift work), including all possible combinations.

For two decades this effort has been generally accepted. It has been accepted in Europe and Japan by a generation of workers who lived through the war and who experienced privation and destruction. Through increased buying power these workers have been offered entry to the "consumer society," and to the "mass consumption" which the United States had experienced between the two wars. And workers in the United States have accepted this effort because the choice remained between an always very "energetic" repression and access (through credit) to still greater consumption.

Studs Terkel records the words of some American workers. Phil Stallings, a welder at Ford:

> I stand in one spot, about two- or three-feet area, all night. The only time a person stops is when the line stops. We do about thirty-two jobs per car, per unit. Forty-eight units an hour, eight hours a day. Thirty-two times forty-eight times eight. Figure it out. That's how many times I push that button. The noise, oh it's tremendous. You open your mouth and you're liable to get a mouthful of sparks. (Shows his arms) That's a burn, these are burns. You don't compete against the noise. You go to yell and at the same time you're straining to maneuver the gun to where you have to weld.... You *have* to have pride. So you throw it off to something else. And that's my stamp collection.[1]

Hobart Foote, a utility man at Ford:

> Phil Stallings. He's grown to hate the company. Not me. The company puts bread and butter on the table. I feed the family and with two teen-aged kids, there's a lot of wants. And we're payin' for two cars. And I have brought home a forty-hour paycheck for Lord knows how long. And that's why I work.... Thirteen more years with the company, it'll be thirty and out. When I retire, I'm gonna have me a little garden. A place down South. Do a little fishin', huntin'. Sit back, watch the sun come up, the sun go down. Keep my mind occupied.[2]

Gary Bryner, president of Local 1112 of the UAW, whose members are employed at the General Motors assembly plant in Lordstown, Ohio:

> My dad was a foreman in a plant. His job was to push people, to produce. He quit that job and went back into a steel mill. He worked on the incentive. The harder you work, the more he made. So his knowledge of work was work hard, make money.... My father wasn't a strong union advocate. He didn't talk management, he was just a working-man. He was there to make money.... I took on a foreman's job, some six or seven weeks and decided that was not my cup of tea.... I went back as an assembly inspector—utility.... I don't give a shit what anybody says, it was boring, monotonous work. I was an inspector and I didn't actually shoot the screws or tighten the bolts or anything like that. A guy could be there eight hours and there was some other body doing the same job over and over, all day long, all week long, all year long. Years. If you thought about it, you'd go stir. People are unique animals. They are able to adjust.[3]

And Mike LeFevre, a steelworker: "Who you gonna sock? ... You can't sock a system."[4]

Always more. Always faster. Non-stop. All day long. For the whole week. For the whole year. For years. Workers as a whole benefited in part from the additional production they had been induced to provide. Per-capita hourly wages rose by 7.9 percent per year in Japan between 1955

TABLE 6.5   Automobiles in Circulation in the Major Capitalist Countries

	United States	Great Britain	France	West Germany	Japan
TOTAL NUMBER (million)					
1947	30.7	1.9	1.5	0.2	0.03
1957	55.7	4.2	4.0	2.4	0.2
1975	106.8	14.2	15.3	17.9	17.2
NUMBER PER 1,000 PEOPLE					
1975	500.0	255.0	290.0	289.0	154.0

Sources: W. W. Rostow, *Stages of Economic Growth* (Cambridge and New York: Cambridge University Press, 1960), pp. 109–10, 202–03; *Annuaire statistique de la France*, 1979.

and 1975, by 6 percent per year in West Germany during the 1950s, by 2.8 percent per year in Britain between 1949 and 1971, while the rise in hourly real wages in the United States was 2.5 percent per year between 1948 and 1970. In France, weekly real wages increased on the average by 4 percent per year between 1949 and 1973, while in the most "favorable" periods of the past (between 1870 and 1895 and between 1920 and 1930) this wage rose on the average by 2 percent per year.[5] After this time consumption levels rose; the structure of consumption changed; the purchase of new durable goods, symbols of the "consumer society," became widespread.

This growth was expressed by an increase in housing construction, a new thrust of urbanization, development of road and highway networks, an increasing number of weekend outings and annual vacation trips, an increase in health expenses, a generalization of credit use, not only for home mortgages, but for buying cars and durable goods. Though the "more"—the growth—was undeniable, the "better"—the improvement—was less easy to grasp. For example, the car became a necessity for commuting to work, and it often became a burden and a worry. Leisure, vacation, and health expenses were also made necessary by a more intense rhythm of living and working.

Once again, however, the conviction arose that an era of plenty had finally arrived.[6] Economists worked at establishing growth as a model, either in a Keynesian perspective (transposing the equilibrium between savings and investment into a dynamic), or in a neoclassical perspective (systematizing the relations between the product and the factors in production).[7] Some of them, notably W. W. Rostow and W. A. Lewis, established chronologies and extrapolations.[8] And while a few obstinate Marxists saw in each downturn in the economic situation signs of the fulfillment of the inexorable general crisis of capitalism, economists for the most part conferred with one another in an atmosphere of reassuring euphoria. Paul Samuelson, for example, has been declaring since the late sixties that the post-Keynesian era has developed currency and taxation policies which can create the necessary buying power for avoiding great crises as well as chronic recession.[9]

A NEW GREAT CRISIS

The 1960s: crisis appeared inconceivable. The 1970s: crisis had arrived, with its accompanying consequences, uncontrollable and ungovernable.

There was a slowdown in growth, a rise in unemployment, an increase in inflation, a fall in workers' buying power; uncertainty, disquiet, latent anxiety; and an advance by the Right in Europe and the United States. World War I had followed the first "great depression" and World War II was engendered by the second "great world crisis": there are fears that this third "great crisis" may result in a third world war.

How have we arrived at this point? The logic of capitalist growth implies it: the very movement of accumulation produced the obstacles which accumulation encountered. The seeds of the crisis of the 1970s were present in the prosperity of the 1960s.

Depending on which indicators and methods of calculation are used, disparities may appear. But it is clear that the rates of profit of the chief capitalist countries began to decrease during the 1960s. In Britain, profit rates went down throughout the 1960s until 1975; in Germany, profit rates stagnated, with a slight decline after 1960 and a fall from 1968–69 to 1975; in France, the rate of profit declined after 1968–69, and fell from 1973 to 1975; in the United States, the rate of profit fell from 1965–66 until 1974. It was only in Japan that the rate of profit increased throughout the 1960s, with a downturn which occurred, depending on the sources, in 1970, 1971, or 1973.[10]

In fact, from the point of view of capital, the conditions for the production and realization of value and surplus value were eroding. On the

TABLE 6.6   Growth, Inflation, and Unemployment in the Major Capitalist Countries

	United States	Great Britain	France	West Germany	Japan
GROSS DOMESTIC PRODUCT (annual growth rate by vol.)					
1960–70	3.8	2.8	5.6	4.7	11.2
1970–73	4.7	4.3	5.6	3.9	8.1
1973–78	2.4	0.9	2.9	2.0	3.7
CONSUMER PRICE INDEX (base 1970 = 100)					
1973	114	128	120	119	124
1977	156	249	183	146	204
UNEMPLOYED (million)					
1968	2.8	0.6	0.3	0.3	0.6
1973	4.3	0.6	0.4	0.3	0.7
1977	6.8	1.5	1.1	1.0	1.1
1979	6.2	1.3	1.2	0.8	1.1

Sources: *Economie prospective internationale*, January 1980; *Annuaire statistique de la France*, 1979; United Nations, *Statistical Directory*, 1978; ILO, *Directory of Labor Statistics*, 1979.

production side, there was first of all the pressure by the workers' movement for higher wages; this permitted a clear rise in real wages for workers as a whole throughout this period. In accordance with the deep intuition that Henry Ford had had several decades earlier, this rise in wage earners' buying power facilitated the sale of commodities in the consumption goods sector. This helped to sustain growth, but nonetheless, for some sectors and some companies, the rise in buying power impeded the sharing of the added value and contributed to a fall in capital profitability.

Within production itself there was a growing refusal of certain forms of work organization: a refusal of fragmented, repetitive work; revolts against "infernal work rhythms" and the speed of assembly-line work which tires the nerves and causes accidents. There were explosive strikes by specialized workers, especially in the automobile industry (at Renault in France); there were also strikes by white-collar workers, who have been, in their turn, affected by automation, disqualification, and mandatory work speeds (in post offices, banks, insurance companies, etc.). There was a movement toward self-organized control of work speeds within the workshop, as in Italy. There was also a simple refusal to work: absenteeism rates grew in German industry as a whole from 4 percent to 11 percent between 1966 and 1972; they grew from 6.5 percent to 9.5 percent between 1964 and 1973 in French mining and metallurgical industries. Absenteeism grew from 4 percent to 8.5 percent between 1961 and 1974 at Renault and from 7.6 percent to 9.7 percent between 1970 and 1975 at Chrysler. Turnover exceeded 100 percent at the Fiat works in Italy, stood at 40 percent at Ford in Britain, 25 percent at Ford in the United States, and grew from 40 percent to 60 percent in eight American processing industries between 1966 and 1972. Lack of interest in work, carelessness, manufacturing defects: as Gary Bryner, an American union worker, told Studs Terkel, monotony, boredom, and fatigue combine to the point where a worker says: "Aw, fuck it. It's only a car ... he'll let a car go by. If something's loose or didn't get installed, somebody'll catch it, somebody'll repair it, hopefully."[11]

Finally, the development of mass production has led to worsening pollution; the first to be affected—farmers, fishers, nature-lovers, locals—have protested, organized, and increasingly succeeded in getting anti-pollution devices installed. Sometimes the workers, fearful of losing their jobs, have been distrustful or hostile to the ecologists; sometimes they have realized that they are first to be polluted, and have obtained an improvement both in hygiene and in their conditions of work. In any case, these devices are extra expenses for businesses.

The reduction in yields and the increase in costs have taken place at a time when competition is stiffening and the consumption model of the 1950s and 1960s has largely disintegrated. The great wave of reconstruction and the surge in the construction of new housing have begun to be absorbed; equipping the "nonequipped" households has become a saturated market. Of course, after the refrigerator there is the freezer, and after the black-and-white television there is color television. But a certain stage has been reached.

Moreover, consumers' movements denounce products which wear out too quickly; many buyers carefully consider the quality and product life of their prospective purchases. At this point, only a massive and lasting rise in the buying power of the most disadvantaged strata could give new impetus to consumption. But inequality appears to be inherent in capitalist society. In the United States, even according to United States administration measures, there are 35 million poor people, one-fifth of the population; in

TABLE 6.7   Invested Capital and Foreign Subsidiaries,
by Country of Origin

	United States	Great Britain	France	West Germany	Switzer- land	Japan
Percentage of total capital invested abroad:						
1976	55.0	16.2	5.5	2.8	3.9	1.3
1971	52.0	14.5	5.8	4.4	4.1	2.7
Number of foreign subsidiaries:						
1969	9,691	7,116	2,023	2,916	1,456	n/a
Distribution of subsidiaries (%):						
Other capitalist countries	74.7	68.2	59.7	82.2	85.7	n/a
Third world	25.3	31.6	40.3	17.8	14.4	n/a
Distribution of subsidiaries within third world (%):						
Africa	8.3	40.0	66.6	21.8	15.8	
Asia	18.8	31.5	9.2	28.3	23.9	
Latin America	72.8	28.5	24.1	49.9	60.3	

Sources: C. A. Michalet, *Le Capitalisme mondial* (Paris: PUF, 1976), p. 30; Christian Palloix, in *La France et le tiers monde*, ed. M. Beaud et al. (Grenoble: PUG, 1979).

France in 1970, 10 million people, one-fifth of the French population, were caught in the vicious circle of poverty. In the United States in 1966, the richest tenth of the population had an income twenty-nine times greater than the poorest tenth; in France this same year the corresponding figure was eighteen times.[12] Thus the capitalist development of the economy, which produces and sustains this inequality, once more stumbles under its weight.

Within each of the chief capitalist countries, the general trend is toward heavier costs, market saturation, and increased competition: these explain the tendency toward lower profitability observable during the 1960s. Foreign markets, of course, still remained. For each national capitalism, the effort to export appeared at least to be able to palliate the progressive saturation of domestic markets: from 1967 to 1971, exports increased at an annual rate of 9 percent for the United States, 12 percent

TABLE 6.8   Foreign Branch Offices of U.S. Banks

	1950	1960	1969	1975
Latin America	49	55	235	419
Overseas territories	12	22	38	–
Europe	15	19	103	166
Asia	19	23	77	125
Middle East	0	4	6	17
Africa	0	1	1	5
TOTAL	95	124	460	732

Sources: Magdoff, Age of Imperialism, p. 74; Palloix, L'Economie mondiale, p. 126; O. Pastré, La Stratégie internationale des groupes financiers américains (Paris: Economica, 1979), p. 280.

for Britain, 16 percent for both France and West Germany, and 23 percent for Japan. For the mechanical and metallurgical industries, the percentage of business devoted to exports rose between 1960 and 1970 from 18 percent to 25 percent in France, 31 percent to 37 percent in West Germany, and 41 percent to 76 percent in Italy. In France between 1963 and 1973 the percentage of production which was exported rose from 16 percent to 23 percent for industry as a whole, and from 22 percent to 33 percent for capital goods industries.[13] Thus competition pitting industrial producers in one country against foreign producers became more intense—not only for national markets, but for foreign markets as well. The French manufacturers of electrical appliances complain about the Italians, and then about the Japanese; the American automobile manufacturers complain about the Europeans and the Japanese, and Europeans complain about the Americans and the Japanese. Buy American! Achetez français! The Japanese have no need to say it: the Japanese buy Japanese.

In order to sell, it appeared more and more that it was necessary to be present in the country: to do product assembly there, and even production. Thus there developed what had until then been only an exceptional form of the internationalization of capital: the implantation of affiliated companies or taking control of foreign companies. From 1967 to 1971 foreign investment rose at an annual rate of 8 percent for Great Britain, 10 percent for the United States, 12 percent for France, 24.5 percent for West Germany, and 32 percent for Japan. During this same period, capital invested abroad grew from $108 million to $165 million (see Table 6.7).

As can be seen, the American, German, Swiss, and Japanese groups invested mainly in other capitalist countries, while the "old" French and

British capitalisms kept a larger part of their assets in the third world. If one considers investments in the dominated countries, Great Britain is present in the three large zones of influence, but the United States, Switzerland, and West Germany preferred Latin America, and France preferred Africa. The American banks strengthened their foreign presence simultaneously—in Latin America first of all, but in Europe and Asia as well (see Table 6.8).

The establishment of more effective technology and the use of more costly tools, the accentuation of competition, the search after and the conquest of foreign market outlets, the internationalization of production: these related processes accompanied a strengthening of concentration. In the United States, after the waves of concentration in 1897–1903 and during the 1920s, a new great period of concentration occurred during the 1950s. At the beginning of the 1960s there were around 1,000 mergers per year. In 1929 the 100 largest companies controlled 44 percent of U.S. industrial assets; in 1962 the figure was 58 percent. Huge U.S. financial and industrial powers dominated the production and commercialization of oil (Standard Oil, Mobil, Texaco, Gulf), the automobile industry (General Motors, Ford, Chrysler), electrical construction (General Electric, Western Electric), computers (IBM), and teletransmissions (ITT).

In France the number of mergers increased after 1960 and particularly after 1963: there were 850 mergers between 1950 and 1960, but more than 2,000 between 1961 and 1971. Toward the end of the 1970s, many mergers of French companies took place: Saint-Gobain with Pont à Mousson, Pechiney with Ugine Kuhlmann, Wendel with Marine Firminy, BSN with Gervais Danone, Empain with Schneider, Mallet with Neuflize Schlumberger, as well as the strengthening of two large financial groups, Suez and Paribas.[14] In West Germany, concentration strictly speaking was doubled by the "strong concentration of powers within the administrative boards of large companies and banks"; thus in 1973, 35 representatives of the 3 great banks held no fewer than 324 mandates in the supervisory councils of German companies.[15]

Throughout the world, the powerful industrial and financial groups observe, coexist, confront, and ally themselves with one another.

CRISIS OF THE INTERNATIONAL MONETARY SYSTEM AND
PRESSURE FROM THE THIRD WORLD

In this combat among Titans, U.S. groups had an advantage which considerably influenced the game: the U.S. currency, the dollar, was in fact the world currency. What had been established at Bretton Woods was of course in principle a gold exchange standard, with each currency defined in relation to gold and fixed parities of exchange; but what in fact functioned throughout the 1950s was a system of payments based on the dollar, in which all currencies were defined in relation to the dollar, itself convertible into gold, and above all, "as good as gold."

For in the immediate postwar period and the 1950s the dollar "shortage" and the dollar "famine" dominated the economic and monetary relations of the capitalist countries. From 1946 to 1955 there was a surplus of $38 billion in the U.S. balance of current payments (total world gold reserves in 1951 were $34 billion, of which $24 billion were held by the United States). From this time onward, "U.S. aid" was necessary not only to reconstruct and restart activity by U.S. partners but to maintain U.S. exports as well. From 1945 to 1952 U.S. aid reached $38 billion ($26.5 billion in gifts and $11.5 billion in loans; $33.5 billion in economic aid and $4.5 billion in military aid), divided between $29 billion for Europe and $7 billion for the countries in Asia and the Pacific.

But as the economies of the chief capitalist countries were rebuilt and became modernized, their commercial trade picked up, their currencies became stronger, their account balances improved, and their relative importance compared to the United States increased. The U.S. share of production within the capitalist world as a whole fell from 70 percent in 1950 to less than 66 percent at the beginning of the 1960s and less than 50 percent at the beginning of the 1970s. During the same period the share of the United States within "Western" trade fell from one-half to one-third to one-fourth. Overall, the American economy benefited abroad from two major assets: (a) its trade surplus (greater than $70 billion for the period 1950–70); and (b) the net income of its foreign assets (around $36 billion from 1950 to 1970).[16]

To this must be added the fact that the dollar was the world currency, which gave any U.S. investor, trader, or speculator the means for purchasing throughout the world, with no impediments other than those established by the U.S. banking and monetary authorities. Professor James Tobin acknowledged this with great simplicity before a congressional committee in 1963:

> Under the reserve currency system properly functioning, the initial beneficiary of an increase in the supply of international money is obviously the reserve currency itself. It is pleasant to have a mint or printing press in one's backyard, and the gold exchange standard gave us, no less than South Africa, this privilege. We were able to run deficits in our balance of payments for 10 years because our IOU's were generally acceptable as money.[17]

And the financial secretary, C. D. Dillon, stated that

> we have a very real benefit in that we have been allowed to finance our deficits through increased foreign holdings of dollars. If we had not been a reserve currency, if we had not been a world banker, this would not have happened. It would have been the same situation as other countries face; as soon as we got into deficit we would have had to balance our accounts one way or another even though it meant restricting imports, as Canada had to do last year, or cutting back our military expenditures much more drastically than our security would warrant.... I would say that is the chief area of benefit although there is one other very important one and that is that somebody had to be the world banker and provide this extra international liquidity. It has been the United States, which is proper, because we are the most powerful financial country and we had the most powerful currency.[18]

During the 1960s, in fact, U.S. expenses overseas became heavier: there were governmental expenses, military expenses (particularly with the increasing burden of the Vietnam war, military spending reached some \$35 billion between 1961 and 1970), and economic and military aid to regimes which the United States chose to support (\$56 billion between 1957 and 1967). Moreover, the commercial surplus dwindled in the late 1960s (with the accentuation of international competition), and commercial deficits appeared for the first time since 1935: \$2.7 billion in 1971, and \$6.9 billion in 1972. Thus assets in dollars overseas grew tremendously, and some governments preferred to convert them into gold—sometimes spectacularly, as in the case of General de Gaulle's government. The crisis of the dollar then issued from a two-sided movement: (a) the rise in assets in dollars belonging to partners of the United States; and (b) the fall in U.S. gold reserves.

Assets in dollars outside the United States surpassed American gold reserves after 1960; by 1968 they were three times greater in value than the U.S. gold reserves, and by 1972, eight times greater (see Table 6.9). Possessing dollars, the European banks opened credit accounts in dollars: this mass of "Eurodollars" approached 100 billion at the end of 1971. The United States suspended the convertibility of the dollar on August 15, 1971; the dollar was devalued by 8 percent in relation to gold in December 1971, and devalued again in 1973. This improved the situation of American industrialists in relation to their European and Japanese competition. Strong, the dollar had been the means for domination; once devalued, it facilitated commercial competition. All the more so since American prices, which had risen very little at the beginning of the 1960s (2 percent per year approximately until 1965), began after 1965 to rise more quickly (approximately 5 percent per year).

TABLE 6.9   U.S. Gold Reserves versus Dollar Liabilities to Foreigners

	U.S. gold reserves	Assets held by foreigners
1955	22	12
1960	18	19
1965	15	25
1968	11	32
1972	10	82

Sources: Magdoff, *Age of Imperialism*, p. 108; Beaud et al., *Lire le capitalisme* (Paris: Anthropos, 1976), p. 177; Samir Amin, *Accumulation on a World Scale* (New York: Monthly Review Press, 1974), p. 461.

But oil, especially from the Middle East, was paid for in dollars, at prices fixed in dollars. The devalorization, and then devaluation, of the dollar crystallized the uneasiness of the oligarchies in the producing countries who saw the wealth under their lands being reduced and their assets growing in a currency which appeared suddenly to be no longer "as good as gold." More deeply, a new stage appeared to have been reached in the long struggle for the control of national resources and for a more favorable sharing of the value these resources contain. Recall a few dates:

1958   Nationalization of Mexican oil; boycott by the American companies.
1948   50/50 sharing of profits by the Venezuelan government, which was then overthrown by a coup d'état.
1951   Nationalization of Iranian oil by the Mossadegh government; boycott of Iranian oil, followed by the fall of the Mossadegh government.
1950s The producing countries gradually obtain a 50/50 division of profits.
1960   Creation of the Organization of Petroleum Exporting Countries (OPEC).
1960s Creation of national companies (Venezuela, Kuwait, Saudi Arabia, Algeria, Iraq, Libya).
1970   Syria, by blocking the Tapline, prevents the transport of part of the oil from Saudi Arabia; Libya reduces its deliveries and increases its extractions.

When the fourth Israeli–Arab war broke out in October 1973, the decision to reduce deliveries and raise oil prices joined the unceasing pressure to lessen the advantages of imperialism. And the rise in the price of oil in 1973 compensated in large part for the fall in its relative price: at the beginning of the 1970s a barrel of oil allowed the importation of only two-thirds of the amount it had allowed in 1949.[19]

But paradoxically, the interests of the American companies at this time converged with the interests of the oil-producing countries. American oil companies had an interest in raising oil prices: on the one hand because they were increasingly led to make use of more costly wells (offshore oil wells, Alaskan oil), and on the other hand because the oil companies were in the midst of becoming energy companies: a clear rise in energy prices was needed to ensure the profitability of new energy forms (especially nuclear). Similarly, American industrialists had an interest in this price rise: 80 percent of their oil supply in fact came from American crude oil at $3 per barrel, while the Europeans and the Japanese were 100 percent supplied with crude oil bought at $2 per barrel; in addition to the devaluation of the dollar, the rise in world oil prices contributed still more to improving the position of American industrialists in relation to their European and Japanese competitors.

Secondarily, then, the rise in oil prices strengthened the United States in relation to its principal capitalist competitors. Primarily, however, the rise in oil prices considerably increased export revenues for the oil-producing countries.

The capitalist countries reacted in various ways, according to specific social tensions and political situations. West Germany chose to reflect back the effects of the oil price rise in a rough manner: the cure was harsh (a sudden rise in unemployment, hundreds of thousands of foreign workers sent back to their countries, forceful pressure on buying power); but the rise in prices remained moderate, the Deutschmark remained solid, and the balance of trade quickly became positive. On the contrary, in France, Italy, and Great Britain (which nevertheless was benefiting from the development of its own oil resources), the choices were different, and the pressure on workers' buying power was exercised largely through inflation and unemployment.

Those who thought they could "make up for" the rise in oil prices with a subsequent rise in the price of industrial products for the most part lost their money: from 1974 to 1978 the price of oil roughly followed industrial prices, and in 1979–80, oil prices increased still more (the price of oil rose from $2 per barrel in 1973 to $10 in 1974, to $13 at the end of 1978, and to $30 in 1980). Rise in the prices of oil and gold; disorder in the international monetary system leading to adoption of floating rates of exchange; weakening of the dollar, whose principal strength lay in the fact that no other currency was able to replace it as a world currency; a great flood of monetary creation, as each great multinational bank was in a position to grant credits in different currencies, and thus to contribute to the creation of these currencies on a world scale; international speculation; national and world inflation; companies or whole sectors caught in the whirlwind of crisis; unemployment, anxiety, fear for the future—in short, crisis.[20]

The essential outlines of the crisis may be summarized as follows:

1. Exhaustion of the models for accumulation of the 1950s within each capitalist country (saturation of markets and resistance by workers), and a fall in the rate of profit during the 1960s.
2. An intensified search for foreign outlets; the development of exports and foreign investments; and increased intercapitalist competition.
3. The increasing burden of U.S. imperialism on the third world; the gradual questioning of the dollar and the international monetary system; and then the crisis of the dollar, which had to be detached from gold (1971).
4. The U.S. response to European and Japanese competition through devaluation of the dollar (1971 and 1973), and the rise in the price of oil.
5. Within the dynamic opened by the postwar process of decolonization, the successful attempt by the oil-producing countries to obtain a more favorable sharing of produced value (1973).
6. The attempt to make up for the effects of the oil price rise, either by recycling the capital of the oil countries or by raising industrial prices; moderate indexation (1974–78) and then a strong rise in the price of petroleum products (1979–80).
7. A demand by the other (non-oil-producing) third world countries for a "new international economic order"; and especially the determination of the third world to industrialize, which conflicted with the interests of some industrial sectors in the developed capitalist countries.

Thus the current crisis results simultaneously from (a) internal contradictions inherent in the process of capitalist accumulation, which develop differently within the different national capitalisms; (b) competition and rivalries which oppose the principal developed capitalist countries; and (c) conflicts of interest, even antagonisms, between the developed capitalist countries as a whole (with each country taking part in specific ways, according to its resources and its history) and the countries of the third world as a whole, as well as conflicts which oppose the capitalist countries against those countries producing oil and other raw materials, those in the midst of industrialization, and those with strategic importance. The succession of these different contradictions and their constant interaction result in the particular seriousness of the present crisis.

THE NEW MUTATION OF CAPITALISM

There is nothing to prevent the hope that socialism may be born out of a crisis of capitalism. To think that this may yet be possible requires—for anyone who does not identify concrete socialism with the countries having collective appropriation of the means of production and centralized planning, such as they have developed—taking up once again a radical reflection on socialism.[21] Is a considerable rate of accumulation compatible with the journey toward socialism? Who will decide the scope and application of accumulation? Who will support the burden of accumulation? How can the attitudes of fear, dependence, and submission, present from time immemorial, be pushed back? How can the perpetuation or restoration of class domination be avoided? All these problems are posed in different ways according to the history, nature, and current situation of each national social formation.

There is nothing to prevent the fear that the present crisis may give rise to the worst: to absolute modern tyrannies, to a multiplication of conflicts and even a World War III with the risk of total destruction of our planet. What is most probable is that in this as in other crises, capitalism will undergo profound mutations and achieve new advances. This future is already here: in current trends one can see the main lines of change as well as the zones of uncertainty.

The East and the West

Let us begin with a certainty—which will open out into several major questions. The world increasingly tends to be divided in two: the capitalist camp and the socialist camp, with two superpowers—the United States and the USSR—two groups of intermediate powers, and two groups of slightly developed and dominated countries.

Since the beginning of the 1950s, the socialist camp has been expanding; although in Europe the borders appear to have stabilized following the line defined at Yalta, the USSR now has strongholds in Asia, the Middle East, Africa, and even in Latin America. In order to extend its influence it has three assets at its disposal: (a) the real determination on the part of countries dominated by Western imperialism to free themselves of this domination and to achieve national independence; (b) a mode of accumulation which has proved itself in the slightly developed countries, most precisely called state collectivism (not yet socialism); and (c) a mode of political organization (state, party, mass organizations) and ideological mobilization (making large use of socialist themes) which has also proved itself.

In the face of this advance the United States has generally, and especially in Latin America and Asia, relied upon dictatorial regimes dominated by narrow oligarchies supported by the army: police states having recourse to a greater or lesser degree to police terror, torture, and murder. These apparently strong states can suddenly reveal themselves to be extremely fragile, as in the case of the shah's regime in Iran or the Somoza dictatorship in Nicaragua.

Beyond these few observations, a series of questions appears. Will the socialist camp continue to advance during the crisis? Will it not also find itself in difficulty in certain countries, involving the necessity for direct military intervention, as in Afghanistan in 1980? Will localized wars burst out again? Will a country or group of countries be able to succeed for long in belonging to neither of the two camps—and if so, what means might they have to avoid being at the mercy of an eventual "new dividing-up of the world"? For won't the United States and the USSR reach a point where a new worldwide Yalta will appear to them preferable—an "acceptable" equilibrium having been achieved—to pursuit of an endless conflict?

There are other uncertainties. Will relations between the two camps tend to harden—with localized military confrontations—or relax—with a development of commercial and technological trade? In a sense, the socialist camp, with its immense equipment and consumption needs, could constitute an enormous market for the large industrial groups of the West.[22] But with borrowed technology and a relatively underpaid working class, this camp could also be a formidable competitor, as has begun to occur for the Western automobile market.

Thus two main questions remain open and decisive. Will one camp expand to the detriment of the other? Will the principal tendency between the two camps be toward conflict or toward the development of exchange?

The interrelation between the two great productive systems—capitalist and state-collectivist—will depend on answers to these questions. But the answers themselves depend on the history of the coming decades, and on the bonds which will be formed between these two peoples, these two nations, these two social systems, these two superpowers, the USSR and the United States.

THE BREAK-UP OF THE THIRD WORLD

During the period of prosperity the development of the industrialized countries resulted in "the development of underdevelopment" in the dominated countries.[23] In the course of the crisis, disparities and inequalities increased on a worldwide scale, but also within the third world itself.

First of all a rift has deepened between the oil-exporting countries with small populations and the rest of the countries of the third world; through the "oil crises" the oil-producing countries have obtained a new share in the value of their now strategic commodity. These oil countries have become in a way the *nouveaux riches* of the planet: the average income per person in these countries has surpassed that of the industrialized countries. Fabulous fortunes are amassed and handled by the oligarchies in power; on the whole the populations benefit from wealth which filters down, and these countries use immigrant laborers who have come from neighboring countries and from Europe.

The inequalities are huge: the inhabitants of the developed capitalist countries and of the oil-producing countries (16.5 percent of the world population) dispose of two-thirds of the world's production, while the countries of the third world (more than half the population) dispose of

TABLE 6.10   Worldwide Growth and Production

	Annual growth GDP 1960–76	Per capita GNP ($US) 1976	Percentage of total 1976		
			POP.	PROD.	EXPORTS
Oil-exporting countries	9.5	6,691	0.3	1.1	5.7
Other third world countries	5.7	538	52.2	15.3	22.6
Developed capitalist countries	4.3*	6,414	16.2	64.6	63.9
Socialist countries	5.0*	1,061	31.3	19.0	7.8

* 1960–77.

Source: World Bank, *World Development Report 1979*, pp. 4, 14, 16, 144–45.

TABLE 6.11   Third World Growth and Production

	Annual growth GDP		Per capita GNP ($US) 1976	Percentage of total 1976		
	1965–74	1974–77		POP.	PROD.	EXP.
Oil-exporting countries	9.5*		6,691	0.3	1.1	5.7
Low-income countries						
in Africa	4.1	2.4	157	3.8	0.3	0.5
in Asia	3.9	5.5	158	25.5	2.1	1.4
Middle-income countries						
Sub-Saharan Africa	5.9	1.6	523	4.6	1.5	2.9
Latin America and Caribbean	6.5	4.0	1,159	7.8	5.0	5.7
East Asia and Pacific	8.3	8.0	671	4.0	1.4	4.3
Southern Europe	6.9	4.0	1,948	3.0	3.2	3.4
Middle East and North Africa	7.0	7.5	989	3.5	1.8	4.4

* 1960–76.

Source: World Bank, *World Development Report 1979*, pp. 12, 13.

only 15 percent of the world's production; among the latter, the poor countries of Africa and Asia (nearly 30 percent of the world population) dispose of only 2.4 percent of world production—an "other world," crushed and doomed to misery and famine. This world inequality, already distinguishable when one examines averages, is widened and multiplied still further by national inequalities (see Tables 6.10 and 6.11).

Between the richest and the poorest countries emerge groups of countries or countries where the average income is rising—in southern Europe, Latin America, Africa, and Asia. A new wave of industrialization is forming and becoming larger.

At the end of the nineteenth century and the beginning of the twentieth century, capitalist industrialization extended mainly across Europe and North America. Between 1914 and 1945, capitalist industrialization intensified, while the Soviet Union instituted the new methods of state socialism. Capitalist industrialization spread into Mediterranean Europe, Australia, and Latin America. Since 1950 industrialization has progressed through the methods of state collectivism in Eastern Europe and China, and through capitalist methods of accumulation in southern Europe and Latin America. Since the end of decolonization, new zones of industrialization,

TABLE 6.12   Worldwide Growth of Production and Employment
(base index 1970 = 100)

	World*	Soviet bloc	Western Europe	North America	Latin America	Middle East, Asia, S.E. Asia
PRODUCTION						
1960	52	42	60	62	54	51
1977	142	174	122	129	151	170
EMPLOYMENT						
1960	79	72	92	87	73	73
1977	112	112	97	102	139[†]	138[†]

* Not including Albania, Mongolia, China, Vietnam, and North Korea.   [†] 1976 figures.

Source: United Nations, *Statistical Yearbook 1978*.

capitalist or state-collectivist, have formed in East and South Asia, around the Mediterranean basin, and in some countries in Africa. And the industrialization of these countries has continued, and even increased, during the current crisis period—for one aspect of the current crisis is the redistribution of industries on a world scale (see Table 6.12).

From 1970 to 1977 annual rates of industrial growth were particularly high in the countries of East and South Asia: South Korea (17 percent), Indonesia (13 percent), Taiwan (12 percent), Thailand (10 percent), the Philippines, Singapore, and Malaysia (9 percent), and Hong Kong (7 percent). Of course, high growth rates must be considered in their actual dimensions when the point of departure is low. Besides, these growths are known to be determined by establishment of, or orders from, large Western (and Japanese) industrial groups. Nevertheless, new bourgeoisies and new "techno-bureoisies" have formed in these countries, and along with them, new working classes; authoritarian and dictatorial states may hold these countries, but they too must take into account that the balance of power and the relations of force in a society are never fixed and settled once and for all.

During the same period (1970–77) industrial growth has also been high in various Latin American countries: the Dominican Republic (14 percent), Ecuador (13 percent), Brazil (11 percent), Paraguay (8 percent), Guatemala, Nicaragua, and El Salvador (7 percent), Mexico (6 percent).

This is a continent oppressed by U.S. domination; the countries here are already rich in revolutions, peasant and worker struggles, popular conquests, and breakthroughs of democracy. It is a continent holding many promises which in recent times has been especially battered, crushed, and ravaged by bloody repressions. These countries bear many hopes and much mourning.

During the whole period from 1970 to 1977, there were high rates of industrial growth in a few countries in Africa (Nigeria, 10 percent; Ivory Coast, 8 percent), North Africa (Tunisia, 9 percent; Morocco, 8 percent; Algeria, 6 percent), the Middle East (Iraq, 12 percent; Syria, 11 percent), and Mediterranean Europe (Yugoslavia and Turkey, 9 percent). The rate of industrial growth in Iran, which had been 13 percent during the 1960s, fell to 3 percent from 1970 to 1977; similarly, the growth rates of Greece, Spain, and Portugal, which had been 9 percent during the 1960s, fell to 5 percent after 1970.

Thus from the point of view of the leaders of the capitalist West, one of the more interesting aspects of recent history—and the crisis in various ways has contributed to this—is that the third world has been fractured and split apart. Henceforth there are countries "attached" by their regimes to the capitalist camp, countries "attached" to the socialist camp, and countries which attempt—the expression has already aged—to remain "nonaligned." There are cultural and religious differences which stand out more now than they did at the time when the colonizer and colonization were an obvious target and permitted the formation of a united front. From an economic point of view, there are now (a) the oil-producing countries; (b) the mineral-producing countries; (c) the countries which are mainly islets of welcome for the Western industrial groups; (d) the countries which are beginning the second stage of their industrialization; (e) the countries which are beginning to industrialize; and (f) the poor, agricultural countries of Asia and Africa.

Besides, there is a great variety in the political regimes and in the class alliances they rest upon—a diversification which crosses the lines of the previous division. Thus third world countries are characterized by (a) domination by a traditional oligarchy supported by the army; (b) a military dictatorship (whose relations may be more or less good with the various parts of the possessing classes); (c) domination by a "techno-bureoisie" of the state supported by the army; (d) an alliance of a "techno-bureoisie" of the state with, for example, the petty bourgeoisie, a part of the peasantry, or a budding bourgeoisie; or (e) a populist regime (of progressive or religious character). And in each case the types of relations that the capitalist countries can establish, and the points of support they can find, are extraordinarily various.

A MULTIPOLAR CENTER?

In the present crisis, the rivalry between the chief capitalist countries has played its part: international competition has intensified with the progressive saturation of national markets; exports and foreign investments have increased, in large part reciprocally; there has been a refusal of the absolute leadership defended by the United States after the war; an international monetary system founded on the dollar has been called into question, and so on.

But no other country wishes or is able to take over this role. Europe, forever divided, cannot be a power, and probably will never be one, so long as it remains split by the division decided at Yalta. Japan moderates its ambitions, and for the moment keeps principally to Asia—somewhat as the United States kept mainly to the Americas after 1918. The only rival of the United States is the USSR; its ambition today is to push back, and gnaw away at, the American sphere of influence.

Thus the capitalist camp will remain dominated by the United States; but the United States has had to make concessions and compromises with the other capitalist powers: by recognizing their "particular zones of influence" (though nonexclusive) in the world; by accepting (out of realism or weakness?) that each of these other countries may have the potential for greater autonomy in defining its positions, especially toward the USSR; by gradually establishing a monetary system in which each strong currency can be better acknowledged and have a greater impact.

As a counterpart, the United States finds allies and assistance among the industrialized capitalist countries. For example, it is through IBM-France that IBM is present in many of the countries of Africa and Latin America; in 1975 U.S. banks held only 5 affiliates or branch offices in Africa directly, but they held 500 through their own European affiliates. The American financial group, Morgan, is tied in many ways to the French financial group, Suez; and its British affiliate Morgan Grenfell, together with Suez, has created subsidiaries in Hong Kong and Singapore. Thus within the banking and industrial domain a hierarchical system has been established, such as has already been functioning in the political and military domain, principally by means of state relations. It is a supple hierarchy, multiform and shifting, in which one can observe four main levels:

1. DOMINANT IMPERIALISM
United States

2. ANCILLARY IMPERIALISMS
Britain,   France,   West Germany,   Japan,   Others

3. PRIVILEGED SUPPORTING COUNTRIES
(a) for the U.S.   (b) for each ancillary imperialism

| around the Mediterranean | in the Middle East | in Asia | In Latin America | in Africa |

4. OTHER COUNTRIES

| around the Mediterranean | in the Middle East | in Asia | In Latin America | in Africa |

Membership in the "corps" of ancillary imperialisms implies not only sufficient economic power (at once banking, industrial, commercial) but also a capacity to exert force and intervene, both politically and militarily. Ideological or cultural influence and scientific or technical prestige are also important.

Membership is furthermore never acquired once for all time. The force exerted depends on the balance of power, and this is forever shifting. One more aspect of what is at stake in the crisis is found here. Each developed capitalism, if it wishes to remain within the dominant group, must not let itself be overtaken within this group, and in certain domains, must take the lead. For those in charge, publicly or privately, within each national capitalism it is a question of (1) "managing" the decline of activities judged to be unprofitable and unnecessary; (2) maintaining and modernizing agricultural potential, which will be an element in the balance of power in coming decades; (3) modernizing and adapting second-generation industries—fabricating consumption goods as much as equipment goods—to their new possibilities (at a slow pace in the developed countries and more quickly in the countries undergoing industrialization); and (4) giving a good start to the technical and industrial development of third-generation industries, for these industries will be the basis for the new model of accumulation which is being established.

In the eyes of the ruling classes of the imperialist countries, a condition for this new model of accumulation is the restructuring of productive activities to ensure greater competitiveness and thus the closing of some companies and the total or partial liquidation of some productive sectors. The new model of accumulation may also involve increased pressure on workers to help companies recover their profitability: inflation and unemployment may be means to this end (they are not, then, signs of this policy's failure, but rather characterize it). The many efforts to limit wage increases and, more generally, the questioning or restriction of workers' gains—social security, public services, the nationalized sector, the right to strike and the rights of unions—may also be a means of recovering profitability. Movement in this direction has been particularly strong in Mrs. Thatcher's Britain and in the France of Giscard d'Estaing. More fundamentally still, there are the ceaseless efforts by the employers to bring the workers to breaking point—either through the development of precarious job forms (time-limited contracts, use of substitute workers, part-time work, temporary work, subcontracting, use of home workers, etc.) or through calling into question the acquisitions which "unify" workers (minimum wage, normal work week of forty hours, guaranteed unemployment compensation, etc.). Through these means the decline in the share of company revenues within the total national value added may be progressively slowed down.[24] These measures also reestablish improved profit conditions for the most successful companies and help create a favorable context for the workings of a new model of accumulation.[25]

A NEW MODEL OF ACCUMULATION

Already, the chief components of this new model of accumulation can be perceived. They include (a) new leading industries; (b) new mutations in the work process; (c) a considerable upheaval in the way of life which will give impetus to a "new mass consumption"; and (d) a still greater diversification in the forms of worker mobilization. The new leading industries will be new energy forms (nuclear, solar) and new technologies which enable the saving of energy in transportation, production, and habitation; new techniques for the fabrication of materials, substances, and elements (biochemistry and bio-industries, new syntheses); and above all, the application of electronics (computers, teletransmissions, or, to use recent terms, telemation, techtronics).

Electronics particularly will cause profound changes in the process of production, the organization of work, daily life, and the model of consumption. The level of research, the efficiency of production, and thus the place of each country in the "international hierarchy" will largely depend on the mastery of electronics.

With these new technologies, especially teletransmissions and electronics, the direct process of production and the work process will be deeply transformed—in industry, of course, but also in offices, post offices, banks, educational and health systems, and agriculture. In effect, the following will become increasingly possible: (a) storage of and access to necessary information; (b) teletransmission of information, orders, and images; (c) treatment of complex problems involving large quantities of information, limits, and factors; and (d) command over complex productive systems and their simultaneous coordination in space, between themselves, and according to customers' orders and available stocks.

In these areas France is clearly behind the United States and Japan. For instance, in 1979 there were nearly 10,000 industrial robots in the world, compared to 4,000 in 1975. Three thousand of these were in the United States, several thousand were in Japan (the estimate varies according to the definition used), and five hundred were in France. These devices have been in use for several years in the automobile industry. For example, at General Motors:

> When they took the unimates on, we were building sixty an hour. When we came back to work, with the unimates, we were building a hundred cars an hour. A unimate is a welding robot. It looks just like a praying mantis. It goes from spot to spot to spot. It releases that thing and it jumps back into position, ready for the next car. They go by them about 110 an hour. They never tire, they never complain, they never miss work. Of course, they don't buy cars. I guess General Motors doesn't understand that argument.[26]

Any repetitive work—so denounced through strikes by specialized workers during the 1960s—and systems of assembly-line work can be replaced during the next two decades with robots. Robots will certainly be used in places where the cost of labor power or the attitudes of workers render the use of living laborers unsuitable or unprofitable, although this will not prevent the development of Taylorized work and assembly-line production in other zones of the world. Moreover, robotization will most often be used for one part of productive procedures, with disqualified jobs subsisting, or developing, upstream or downstream.

With computers, telecommunications, and the automation of large productive procedures will come the development of work by "autonomous teams" and "autonomous workshops," which will be described by some people as "self-managed." In cases where industrial robots will be unsuitable or too costly, workers will be able to organize themselves in an autonomous way—provided they respect the objectives, norms, and limits transmitted to them by computer. In some cases they will be able to discuss and to express objections, but it is probable that the mass of available information and the combination of constraints will leave a very small "margin of freedom."

244

DIAGRAM 16   THE IMPERIALIST HIERARCHY
AND THE CIRCULATION OF VALUE ON NATIONAL
AND WORLD LEVELS IN THE 1970S

Moreover—the psychosociologists have approached the new perspectives thus opened—the individuals and the teams will be put into competition against each other.

> The authoritarian organization based on relations of superior to subordinate must disappear.... In the new model, no individual would depend on a superior. He would quite freely negotiate his concurrence with a continually changing structure of reciprocal relations between himself and those with whom he exchanges goods and services.... A nonauthoritarian structure implies the exercise of internal competition.... Each individual would then be in a situation identical to that of an owner managing his own business.[27]

In the same way, new forms of subcontracting will develop (with teletransmission of orders and technical information provided by the computer of the "main client"). There will also emerge new forms of dispersed workshops, workshops in the countryside, and work in the home (already going on in France for telephone information workers). In group work situations, flexible scheduling will be able to develop, with a computer helping to indicate the limits (thus a greater or smaller margin of choice),

---

KEY

 National social formation (with the sphere of material production: agriculture and industry). To keep the drawings as clear as possible, social classes have not been included (see preceding diagrams for social classes).

 National state apparatus

 Apparatus of finance capital

 RC   Ruling class

 Apparatus of industrial capital

 Apparatus of industrial capital mainly dominated by foreign capital

 Capital export, loans, government aid*

 Circulation of produced value on national and world levels (as much through trade of commodities and invisible values as through profit repatriation, interest payments, dividends, etc.).*

* For these flows, departure and arrival points only have been indicated, as the actual network of connections, interwoven and dense, cannot be represented on a diagram of this scale.

and to coordinate and carry out controls. These new technologies and this new organization of work will develop a new way of life and new mass consumption.

Let us caricature things, starting only from what already exists. Nurseries are functioning where the children are under electronic surveillance (Japan); schools are multiplying where each child, instead of a wooden table and a blackboard, has in front of him a video screen and a keyboard to question the computer (Japan and the United States); an "electronic house" has been conceived and built which wakes up the occupants (after having prepared coffee and toast), controls the level of food supplies, can heat up meals, answer the phone, record television programs on demand, "watch" and deter unexpected or undesirable visitors (United States). A system for the individual programming of an "optimal urban path" is being developed which would allow each driver, after having indicated his destination, to have his itinerary programmed and his driving guided— take the right lane, turn right, slow down (Japan); soon an "electronic guardian angel" will give advice to the driver (be careful; you're not driving smoothly; you're driving too fast; you're being "energy-greedy"). United States firms are researching an electronic driving system which would permit each vehicle to enter individually onto the highway, after which the cars would form into "automobile trains," so that each car would restart its engine only when leaving the highway.

Electronic games multiply and diversify. Experiments with the first newspaper on an electronic screen have just occurred in the United States. Electronics and telecommunications will profoundly change modes of access to various sorts of information: telephone (railroad, weather, tourist), daily news (general or specialized), scientific or technical data, mail order catalogues, and even mail.

A profound change in the way of life will thus occur, followed by the gradual and then massive diffusion of electronic products. This will be accompanied by a renewal of the stock of traditional second-generation goods (automobiles, telephones, televisions, stereos); and a diffusion of new goods (surveillance and remote control systems, individual terminals with video screens, individual computers).

There will be new technologies, a new organization of work, new consumption, and new ways of living. One may imagine that this could lead to the establishment of a permanent control over each worker, whose training, work, and leisure would be systematically analyzed and programmed. Most probably, there will be an extreme split in the way workers are mobilized, with at one pole, the strata and the categories who are perfectly integrated, totally at ease in a universe of programs, keyboards, screens, synthetic voices, and robots; and at the other pole, the groups and strata who refuse and reject this world, becoming quite totally marginal. Between the two will remain the traditional modes of work mobilization, joined for the most part to the dominant pole: work in the home, work at the craft level, dependent individual businesses, small subcontracting companies, new forms of piece work, substitute work, temporary work, and contractual work.

If one considers that through multinational industrial and financial groups, this system will function on the five continents, at the four levels of the imperialist hierarchy, and in over one hundred countries (each one having its own laws, traditions, and balance of power), one realizes that there will be a whole range of situations, diversified still further by national, cultural, and religious specificities: a capitalism multiple *and* unique, deformed *and* coherent, split apart *and* structured.[28]

A Diversified and Hierarchical Multinational System

John F. Kennedy stated in 1962: "Foreign aid is a method by which the United States maintains a position of influence and control around the world, and sustains a good many countries which otherwise would definitely collapse, or pass into the Communist bloc."[29] The essential has been spoken. Economic, military, food aid; loans; gifts; industrial and commercial investments; exchange of goods; cultural and military presence: there are so many bonds which reinforce dependence. And in addition to the directly established bonds, there are those which go through the secondary imperialist countries and continental points of support.

The system first of all serves to prevent too many countries from turning to the socialist camp. It also forms a tremendous system for draining off produced value on a world scale. This draining of value is carried out in a perceptible and measurable way through income from foreign investments. For example, from 1970 to 1976, American industrial and financial groups made $67 billion worth of foreign investments, of which $27 billion came out of the United States. At the same time these groups received $99 billion in income from these investments (of which $42 billion were reused outside the United States, and $57 billion returned to the United States): this represents a net excess of $32 billion for these groups and a net return of $30 billion for American foreign accounts.[30]

The draining of value occurs first through the payment of interest and the burden of foreign debt. The indebtedness of the dominated countries

TABLE 6.13   Debt Burden of Dominated Countries

	Total	Low-income countries		Middle-income countries
		Africa	*Asia*	
Current medium- and long-term debt ($ billion)				
1965*	38	11		27
1970	68	17		51
1977	260	49		211
1985†	740	124		616
Debt service– export ratio				
1970	–	13‡		10.3
1977	11.8	*9.6*	*13.5*	11.8
1985†	18.1	*11.6*	*17.0*	18.3

*1965 figures were obtained from a different series to the others, but the order of magnitude remains significant.   † Forecast.   ‡ Estimate.

Sources: Fitt et al., *La Crise de l'impérialisme et la troisième guerre mondiale* (Paris: Maspero, 1976); World Bank, *World Development Report 1979*, p. 83.

has in fact become massive during the recent period, and constitutes a new "bondage," a new form of dependence. The current debts of the developing countries rose from $40 billion in 1965 to $70 billion in 1970 and to $260 billion in 1977; it has been forecast that they will rise to $740 billion by 1985.

Indebtedness represents four to five times the currency reserves of the "low-income" countries, and two to two and a half times the currency reserves of the "middle-income" countries. Debt servicing represents, on the average, one-tenth of export revenues; in 1977 this proportion reached higher levels for some countries: more than 20 percent for Bolivia, Mauritania, and Egypt; 28 percent for Uruguay; 30 percent for Peru; 32 percent for Chile; 43 percent for Guinea; and 48 percent for Mexico; up to one-third, even one-half, of export revenues are devoted to debt servicing (see Table 6.13).

The draining of value also occurs through the international exchange of goods and services. A major aspect of diversified capitalism on a worldwide scale, of "deformed capitalism," is an extreme disparity in labor

TABLE 6.14   Wages in the Developed and Underdeveloped World

	Imperialist countries		Support countries		Dominated countries	
MONTHLY WAGES						
(US$), 1970–72	USA	500	Mexico	157	S. Korea	50
	W.Ger.	400	Brazil	157	Ghana	39
			India	30	Philippines	38
AVERAGE HOURLY WAGE (at comparable level, US$)						
Electronics	USA	3.13			Hong Kong	0.27
production	USA	2.3–2.6	Mexico	0.53	Taiwan	0.14
Office equipment	USA	3.67			Taiwan	0.38
manufacture	USA	2.9–3.0	Mexico	0.48	Hong Kong	0.30
Semiconductor	USA	3.36			S. Korea	0.33
manufacture	USA	3.32			Jamaica	0.30
	USA	2.23			Trinidad	0.40
Textile industry	USA	2.49				
	USA	2.28	Mexico	0.53	Honduras	0.45
	USA	2.11			Costa Rica	0.34
	USA	2.11			Br. Honduras	0.28
INDEX OF						
HOURLY WAGE	W.Ger.	144	Australia	97	S. Korea	21
(100 = France)*	Belgium	143	Austria	95	Hong Kong	19
	Sweden	142	Italy	93	Singapore	19
	Netherlands	139	Finland	87	Taiwan	15
	Denmark	136	Spain	79		
	Switzerland	129	Ireland	67		
	Norway	127	Greece	42		
	USA	118	Brazil	40		
	Canada	110	Mexico	33		
	Japan	103	Portugal	26		
	France	100				
	Britain	74				

* In Philips Industries, 1979.

Sources: Michalet, *Le Capitalisme mondial*, p. 144; Fitt et al., *La Crise de l'impérialisme*, p. 215; *L'Expansion*, July 4, 1980.

costs. Between the cost of labor power of an American or European worker which includes—taking into account urbanization, a generalized wage-paying system, and separation from the rural world—an equipped house, a car, the costs of health, leisure, training of children, and so on, and the cost of labor power of a worker in Southeast Asia, living at the limits of the biological minimum, or of a worker in the third world, still attached for the most part to a rural community (in which a large portion of the production/reproduction of labor power is ensured by non-commodity production and by self-subsistence), the separation is very great. Differences in wages serve as indicators of this (see Table 6.14).

The range goes from 1 to 9 for the third indicator (cost of a working hour to a company in 1979, including indirect costs), from 1 to 16 for the first indicator; for the second indicator, the separation often exceeds 1 to 10 and once reaches 1 to 17. Since these are averages, these indices are sufficient to illustrate the gap: we know that the difference is enormous between a well-paid technician in an imperialist country and a laborer in Africa or Asia—or a child living on one of these continents (for currently there are about 100 million children throughout the world working in conditions comparable to those of nineteenth-century Europe in the course of industrialization, and sometimes worse).[31]

The present world capitalist system operates on a scale never attained before, at once *unique* (the world market, the multinationalization of production) and *heterogeneous* (disparity in the costs of labor power, a wide range of "national values" for the same commodity). It is then unimportant whether we think in terms of average world values and "extra profits," or in terms of unequal national values—the fundamental phenomenon is this: just as low-priced oil from the third world allows the capitalist countries to benefit from part of the oil income, in the same way the labor power of the third world, bought at a low price and put to work in productive segments integrated within a multinational productive process dominated by industrial and financial groups, allows the capitalist countries to benefit from part of the value produced in the third world. This may occur either through the multinational groups and their price transfers, or through the world market and the system of world prices (the variation in the terms of exchange being only the sign of an improved or deteriorated division).

This phenomenon is not marginal or limited; it is massive. There were 35 to 40 million workers in the world just before World War I; today there are more than 160 million in the capitalist world: around 110 million in the imperialist and developed capitalist countries, and 50 million in the countries of the third world.[32] And several hundred million peasants are becoming proletarians: chased from their lands and villages and forced to sell their labor power in order to live, these people live in the *barriadas* and *favelas* of Latin America, the shantytowns throughout the third world, and the overcrowded cities of Asia. These are the "free workers" unconditionally available for new industrializations.

And one must insist that the imperialist system be grasped and understood as simultaneously unique (the principal domination of the United States, with the dollar as the world currency; the world market and world prices of basic products and major manufactured products) *and* diversified (a great variety in situations on the five continents; an extreme diversity in national and local situations; the coexistence of very different modes of utilizing labor power, since this labor power is reproduced under varying conditions). It is a hierarchical system with the United States as the dominant imperialism in the economic, monetary, technical, military, political, and ideological domains, as well as in its way of life and diffusion of information.

This system also includes the ancillary imperialisms—former colonial powers (Britain and France) and more recent powers (West Germany and Japan)—which have their own specificities, assets, weaknesses, and particular zones of influence. These are threatened powers whose rank in the hierarchy of nations in the twenty-first century—a rise, preservation of their current position, or a decline—is at stake in the crisis. Within this system there are also "support countries," which are not imperialisms (though they might become imperialisms in the future), but which, through their geopolitical situation, their impact (demographic, economic, military, ideological, political), and their capacity for influence and intervention, constitute key elements within a world region. Among these support countries, the oil countries will occupy a special position for at least the next few decades. This system includes finally the "dominated countries"—the most numerous, the most disparate in their impact and potential, and whose importance may depend on the mineral wealth they conceal, on a particular strategic or political situation, or on their populations, among whom are found the most disinherited and forgotten people of the earth.

The hierarchical character of this system is extremely supple, which makes it both vulnerable and adaptable. Beyond the diversity of peoples, cultures, languages, religions, and ways of living and dying, what creates the system's unity is a complex network of bonds: economic bonds (commercial exchanges, loans, gifts, and various forms of "aid" and "assistance"), as well as class alliances on a world scale in which the ruling classes of the imperialist countries rely upon classes or organized forces (the army, the police) in the support countries and dominated countries (from which comes the importance of military aid, police assistance, and the presence and intervention of secret services). At the limit, countries may be wholly created, with artificially supported regimes and strata or

252

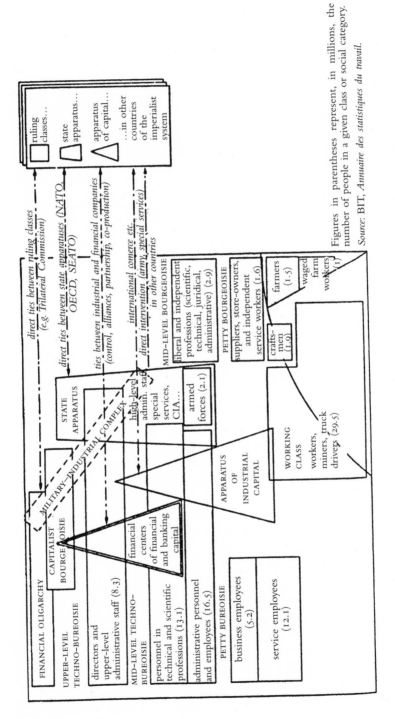

DIAGRAM 17   SOCIAL CLASSES IN THE UNITED STATES IN THE 1970S

FINANCIAL OLIGARCHY

CAPITALIST BOURGEOISIE

UPPER-LEVEL TECHNO-BUREOISIE

directors and upper-level administrative staff (8.3)

MID-LEVEL TECHNO-BUREOISIE

personnel in technical and scientific professions (13.1)

administrative personnel and employees (16.5)

PETTY BUREOISIE

business employees (5.2)

service employees (12.1)

financial centers of financial and banking capital

MILITARY–INDUSTRIAL COMPLEX

STATE APPARATUS

high-level admin. staff

special services, CIA...

armed forces (2.1)

APPARATUS OF INDUSTRIAL CAPITAL

WORKING CLASS

workers, miners, truck drivers (29.5)

direct ties between ruling classes (e.g. Trilateral Commission)

direct ties between state apparatuses (NATO, OECD, SEATO)

ties between industrial and financial companies (control, alliances, partnership, co-production)

international commerce etc.

direct intervention (army, special services) in other countries

MID-LEVEL BOURGEOISIE

liberal and independent professions (scientific, technical, juridical, administrative) (2.9)

PETTY BOURGEOISIE

suppliers, store-owners, and independent service workers (1.6)

crafts-men (1.9)

farmers (1.5)

waged farm workers (1)

ruling classes...

state apparatus...

apparatus of capital...

...in other countries of the imperialist system

Figures in parentheses represent, in millions, the number of people in a given class or social category.

Source: BIT, *Annuaire des statistiques du travail.*

TABLE 6.15 Occupational Structure in the Countries of the Imperialist System (percent)

	DOMINANT IMP.	ANCILLARY IMP.			SUPPORT			DOMINATED		
	USA 1978	France 1975	W. Ger. 1978	Japan 1978	Brazil 1970	Egypt 1977	India 1971	Bolivia 1976	Thailand 1976	Cameroon 1976
Scientific, technical and social science professional personnel	14.3	15.5	12.8	7.2	6.4	7.7	2.8	5.7	2.6	2.4
Directors and upper administrative staff	10.1	3.3	3.1	3.7	1.1	1.4	0.9	0.6	1.1	0.1
Administrative and comparable personnel	17.3	14.0	18.9	15.7	4.7	6.6	2.9	4.0	1.6	1.9
Tradespeople, shopkeepers, salespeople	6.1	7.3	8.5	14.3	7.5	7.4	4.2	6.1	10.4	3.2
Service workers	13.5	8.0	10.8	8.8	7.7	8.9	3.3	8.6	2.9	2.0
Farmers, ranchers, forestry, fishing, and hunting workers	2.8	9.6	5.7	11.3	42.7	41.9	72.1	46.4	62.1	73.7
Workers, laborers, transport workers	33.0	36.0	35.3	36.6	19.4	21.7	13.4	24.7	18.7	11.3
Others	2.1*	1.1*			1.5					
Not classified	0.8	5.2†	4.9†	2.4†	8.0	4.4	0.4	3.9	0.6	5.4
TOTAL (millions)	102.5	21.8	27.0	55.3	29.6	9.5	180.5	1.5	13.9	2.8

* Members of the armed forces.   † Includes the unemployed.

Source: ILO, Directory of Labor Statistics, 1979.

TABLE 6.16 Socioeconomic Indicators in the Imperialist System

	DOMINANT IMP.	ANCILLARY IMP.			SUPPORT			DOMINATED		
	USA 1978	France 1975	W. Ger. 1978	Japan 1978	Brazil 1970	Egypt 1977	India 1971	Bolivia 1976	Thailand 1976	Cameroon 1976
Population, 1977 (million)	220	53	61	113	116	38	632	5	44	8
Per capita GNP, 1977 (US$)	8,520	7,290	8,160	5,670	1,360	320	150	630	420	340
Per capita energy consumption, 1976 (kilos of coal/equ.)	11,554	4,380	5,922	3,679	731	473	218	318	308	98
Income of richest 10 percent (% of total income)	26.6*	30.4†	30.3‡	27.2**	50.6*	n/a	35.2††	n/a	n/a	n/a
Income of poorest 20 percent (% of total income)	4.5*	4.3†	6.5‡	7.9**	2.0*	n/a	6.7††	n/a	n/a	n/a
Adult literacy rate, 1975 (percent)	99	99	99	99	76	44	36	63	82	n/a
Number of inhabitants per doctor, 1976	600	680	500	920	3,600	1,190	3,140	2,120	8,460	13,980
Life expectancy at birth, 1977	73	73	72	76	62	54	51	52	61	46

* 1972.   ** 1969.   † 1970.   ‡ 1973.   †† 1964–65.

Source: World Bank, *World Development Report 1979*, p. 142.

ruling groups "fabricated" by the intervention of industrial and financial groups, states, and special services of the dominant countries (see Table 6.15).[33]

And this unifying network of bonds creates new inequalities and new disparities: the prior deduction of value occurring from production in support countries and dominated countries increases the power of industrial and financial groups, and the enrichment of the dominating classes, in the imperialist countries. At the same time this process increases the poverty of the poorest people in the poorest countries. The support given to ruling classes in the third world has allowed for the creation of fabulous fortunes, as well as for the development of new strata linked to the apparatus of the state or multinational capital.[34] New inequalities have developed and added to the earlier inequalities. Thus the richest 10 percent of the population in the developed capitalist countries disposes of 25 to 30 percent of national income, but in countries of the third world this percentage rises to 35 percent (India, Venezuela, Mexico, Argentina) and even to 50 percent (Brazil, Honduras).[35]

And these disparities create new "solidarities." The ruling families of the third world place their wealth in "safe" countries of the imperialist sphere (the United States, Switzerland, fiscal paradises), buy shares and interests in the industrial and banking groups of the dominant countries, and consume the highly sophisticated and luxury products produced by the dominant countries.[36] The industries of many dominated countries have not the slightest autonomy, integrated as they are into the productive processes established and coordinated by powerful industrial groups. The transformation of national productive structures must henceforth be analyzed in relation to the world imperialist system. For example, consider the development of the "tertiary" sector in the United States.[37] In part this corresponds to productivity gains in agriculture and industry and an increase in the division of labor (into management, forecasting, planning, information, coordination, research, education, control, surveillance) which partially supports these productivity gains. But in part the development of the tertiary sector corresponds to the fact that material production is now growing more quickly in the supporting and dominated countries. This process in turn develops the working classes in these countries (see Table 6.16).

Finally, this unity of the imperialist system is undermined by conflicts, rivalries, and relations of force. This is not merely a question of interventions by the armies, police, secret services, private militia, and mercenaries of the dominating countries. It is also a question of new rivalries, new

TABLE 6.17   Third World Military Expenditure

	Annual growth rate (percent)		Percentage of total third world arms imports
	1968–75	1973–78	1950–78
Middle East	25	4	43
Far East*	8	8	22
South Asia	5	4	10
Central America	2	4	2
South America	8	3	9
North Africa	8	15	6
Sub-Saharan Africa			8

* Not including China, Laos, Cambodia, Vietnam.

Source: P. Fabre, in *L'Economiste du tiers monde*, December 1979.

hatreds, and new expanionism: not only national, but religious, ethnic, and clan related. One can count 130 civil or regional wars since 1945, in which eighty-one countries, almost all of them belonging to the third world, have participated. In real terms the military budgets of third world countries have quadrupled in the last twenty years (see Table 6.17). And already some third world countries (India, Pakistan, the Philippines, Brazil, Argentina) are equipping themselves with an armaments industry.

In the last analysis, the unity of the imperialist system is based largely on the rivalry and tension with the socialist bloc dominated by the USSR. More than $400 billion were spent throughout the world in 1978 for armaments, and nearly $500 billion were spent for this purpose in 1980. This is around 6 percent of gross world product, while the modest objective of allotting "1 percent" of the gross national product of the rich countries to the aid of the poor countries is not attained in most of the richer countries.[38] In 1968 and 1978 world military spending was distributed in the following way (in percent):

	NATO	WARSAW PACT	CHINA	THIRD WORLD	OTHERS
1968	56	25	9	6	4
1978	43	29	10	14	4

In 1978 world arms exports were 47 percent from the United States, 27 percent from the USSR, 11 percent from France, 4 percent from Italy, 4 percent from Britain, and 2 percent from West Germany.[39] Forty percent of world research is organized within the perspective of "national defense" and war. Some 400,000 high-ranking scientists work on armaments research, two-fifths of all scientists in the world. Since 1950 "the total destructive power of world arsenals has been multiplied several million times.... The present increase in military spending occurs at a time when 1.5 billion people do not have access to adequate medical service, 570 million people are seriously undernourished, and 3 billion people lack safe drinking water."[40]

Thus the world is caught in a spiral of terror and devastation: on the one hand the means of destruction accumulate, enough to destroy the planet several times over, while on the other hand, 500 million human beings are threatened with death from hunger during the 1980s.[41] There is an economic crisis which—because of huge international indebtedness, speculation, and the seriousness of what is at stake for each nation—no one is able to master. And new technological advances further strengthen the power of the powerful and the crushing of the weak.

And how can one help thinking that the worst is possible: that the great depression at the end of the nineteenth century opened the way for World War I, that the crisis of the 1920 led to another world war, and that this third great crisis is still far from being overcome? At the same time, there are many possibilities developing which could be progressive factors.

SUMMARY

And then I told myself that all this unorganized violence was like a blind man armed with a pistol.

—Chester Himes

Manufacture of cotton cloth in the sixteenth to eighteenth centuries; large metallurgical companies and then steel companies in the nineteenth century; automobile and electricity companies, and then computer and teletransmission groups—through these, the same logic is always at work: forced surplus labor, realization of produced value and surplus value, enlarged capital leading to increased production; more commodities and more surplus value. This is a logic, then, of growth, but it is also a logic of crisis; for the increased production leads in one way or another toward saturation (taking into account distributed buying power), toward a stiffening of competition, and toward a decline in profitability. Crisis, available capital, a larger reserve of labor power: these also signify the search for new markets, new processes, and new production.

How can one deny the fascinating creativity of this system which in a few centuries has passed from mechanical looms powered by running water or steam to industrial robots capable of carrying out a series of complex operations; from printing to teletransmissions; from the discovery of America to the exploration of space? And how can one not be haunted by the destructive capacity of this dynamic at work (often intermingling with others: cupidity, religious faith, national sentiment, the "civilizing mission," racism, etc.)? Its work has included the massacre of the Indians of the Americas and pillage of their treasures; destruction of the traditional rural way of life and the proletarianization of poor peasants, beginning in England; the wasteful use of such nonrenewable resources as coal, oil, and minerals; the degradation of the environment and the earth's biological cycles, especially through air and water pollution; the risk of damages from nuclear power which will be a burden for generations to come; the unbounded use of labor power, both muscular and nervous, leading to fatigue, premature exhaustion, and accidents.

Creation and destruction of resources, people, and landscapes. Creation and destruction of societies as well. A few centuries ago rural societies were ruled by narrow aristocracies and the absolute power of the princes: in their midst were formed the embryos of the bourgeoisies and the working classes which developed with industrialization. Today in the United States a narrow oligarchy of powerful industrial and financial groups is linked to a diversified range of the high, middle, and petty bourgeoisies (industrialists, businesspeople, workers in the liberal professions, individual entrepreneurs), as well as to the higher strata of the salaried "techno-bureoisie" (directors and high technicians of the apparatus of capital and administration, "directors" of research, education, health). Urbanization and the establishment of a system of wage payments have been largely accomplished, and the working class and the "petty bureoisie" have been for the most part integrated into the cycle of consumption through credit. And this U.S. oligarchy is tied to the ruling classes of the other capitalist countries, either through international proceedings by which governments agree to act together, through alliances and controls established between industrial and financial groups, or finally, through such authorities as the Trilateral Commission in which high private or public leaders meet and agree to act together. This oligarchy has woven or allowed the establishment of multiple ties between the United States and the ruling classes or strata (including the armed forces, the police, and the special services) of the support countries and dominated countries.

Against this logic, the idea of socialism was given life in the nineteenth century by indignation at injustice, by generosity and obstinate hope. This was the hope that the ideas of solidarity, fraternity, equity or equality, social justice, security, and democracy might be realized on this earth. All of the early ruptures with capitalism were made in the name of socialism.

Today, against the capitalist logic, against imperialism, an alternative mode of production and accumulation exists and functions: state collectivism. For in the countries where a revolution which could be thought of as socialist was carried out, the economic and social constraints and the necessity to industrialize—and therefore to extract a surplus, force surplus labor, and transform former rural inhabitants into workers—were determining: it was by seizing the state apparatus that the core of the new ruling class asserted itself. And it was through the use of state force that the new ruling class imposed both work discipline and social discipline upon the productive classes.

State collectivism, like capitalism, encountered the national reality and combined with it: the Russian power, exalted by socialist ideology and sustained by the vigor of anti-imperialist struggles, managed to attain through state collectivism the economic and military apparatus which makes it the second power in the world. And in third world countries an alliance of classes has enabled former oligarchies to be overthrown and provided the means for emancipation from imperialism: these countries find in state collectivism the possibilities for developing equipment and industry.[42]

In each epoch, capitalism has functioned simultaneously on a national/regional/local scale *and* on a worldwide scale. This is particularly true at the present time, with a hierarchical system which covers the five continents, a world market, multinational groups, and international indebtedness.

In each epoch capitalism has been both a factor for unification, even standardization, *and* a factor for accentuating differences, disparities, and inequalities. This is particularly so today, with the colossal strengthening of the means of transport, exchange, communication, and information. Capitalism has brought proletarianization, the wage payment system, urbanization, and the unification of consumption objects with productive processes and ways of living. Yet century after century, the most varied ways of mobilizing labor power and of extracting surplus labor have been superimposed upon one another in infinitely diverse social contexts.

In each epoch, capitalism has been both creative *and* destructive, but today it is the very existence of humanity and the planet which is at stake. In the imperialist countries the workers have succeeded in organizing themselves. Partly because of the advantages the ruling classes drew from imperialism, workers have obtained important concessions and reductions in the rigor of capitalist logic. They now have effective ways of influencing decisions and a more favorable sharing of produced wealth. Henceforth this must be said and all of its implications must be considered—the working classes and, more widely, the working world of the dominant countries, are simultaneously in solidarity with the peoples and countries of the third world, for both groups are subject to the logic of production for profit, and dependent, for employment, for their standard of living, and for life itself, on the production of "their" national capitalism, sharing in this a common interest with "their" ruling class.

Were the working classes to liberate themselves from "their" capitalist bourgeoisie, what is most probable—taking into account precedents and inertia—is the passage to a new class society, dominated by a "new ruling class" (constituted in part from the high "techno-bureoisie" and the managements of party and union apparatuses), with the establishment of a system combining state collectivism and a market economy. It is not that the advance toward socialism is impossible, but that it is more complex than the great visionaries of the nineteenth century ever imagined; it involves not only the socialization of the means of production, but also liberation from the millennia-long habits of dependence and submission. In a positive sense, it involves the invention of relations and pathways which will permit the collective mastery of crucial decisions.

And here democracy is a fundamental achievement. A victory against the bourgeoisie insofar as the bourgeoisie would have preferred democracy to remain the affair of a narrow minority of owners and experts, democracy is the fundamental condition for any advance toward socialism. The history of the last century has taught us this. Democracy, individual freedoms, and human rights are essential achievements that we have the responsibility to protect, and if possible, to widen, strengthen, and deepen.

In the third world countries, the dominated countries, everything remains to be done. There must be a fight against the overlapping dominations of imperialism, of old exploiting classes and new exploiting classes—nascent bourgeoisies and "techno-bureoisies." At the same time there must be a fight against the effects of having been crushed for a thousand years and against the effects of modern pillage: poor production, nourishment, and health; mortality and illiteracy. The recovery of independence—national or "continental"—appears necessary; and this is not a matter of becoming liberated from one domination in order to fall under another: the formation of a large group of nonaligned countries is here fundamental.

In this framework, the methods of state collectivism may be efficient for developing certain types of production and carrying out certain processes. Perhaps new forms of production will be invented that will permit productive forces to be developed at the same time that social relations are transformed in the direction of socialism. Here we may hope that in their traditions of village community or popular solidarity, their wisdom of life, and their philosophical and religious traditions, some of the peoples who are today crushed may be able to invent a new art of producing, living, working, and deciding which will bring to light what the young people of so many countries understood in 1968: the absurd and slimy bloatedness of modern capitalist society.

At the end of the 1970s, the transformative power, both creative and destructive, of capitalism, was directly or indirectly at work throughout the world. The massive statist edifice of the USSR and the Soviet bloc, with bridgeheads on the different continents of the fragmented third world, continued to confront capitalism. The socialist hope for something other than the two harsh realities of capitalism or statism remained alive. But the path toward realizing socialism, "a new way of producing, living, working, and choosing," appeared far more difficult than the nineteenth-century socialists had imagined.

In the last twenty years of the century, generalized statism suffocated, while capitalism found new life through its mastery and control of science's contributions. The USSR and its empire fell apart. The most dynamic nations of the ex-third world, as well as wide regions of China, joined the game of private enterprise, the market, and insertion into the world capitalist system.

"One country, two systems," promised the Chinese leaders at the time of Hong Kong's return to their fold. "Two hundred countries, one system": such appears to be the unspoken slogan of the capitalist rulers at the turn of the century. This message is driven home both by the powerful resurgence of liberal ideology sweeping the entire planet and by the friendly-sounding allegory of globalization. Globalization in fact covers up the deepening abyss of inequality as well as the growing power of the giant transnational corporations to play mindless games with the fate of the world.

Chapter 7

THE END OF THE
TWENTIETH CENTURY

AN ACCELERATING TRANSFORMATION
OF THE CONTEMPORARY WORLD?[1]

At the end of the twentieth century we are at the center of a crucial change.[2]

Beyond the jolts and bumps of American hegemony, are we not witnessing the beginning of the end of Western preeminence, as evident in the decisive advances of India and China, along with advances too by most of the other countries in Asia? Hidden behind the industrialization of countries in the South, and behind the debates about deindustrialization in the North, are we not witnessing also the beginning of the eclipse of "industrial capitalism," which dominated the nineteenth century and the first half of the twentieth century? And, accompanying the retreat of industrial capitalism, is there not visible a new form of capitalism, "techno-scientistic" capitalism, affecting all capitalist domains and social life as a whole?

Though the years following the Second World War consolidated the preeminence of statist and capitalist systems of accumulation over tributary systems, the collapse of the Soviet empire at the end of the 1980s marked the overall failure of statism. Certainly, this collapse was not the End of History, but it did mean that capitalism imposed itself on a world scale— and no one knows for how long—as the most efficient system of accumulation, commodity production, and social transformation.

At the same time, with multinationalization, the rise in interdependencies and the whole process described by the word "globalization," the centuries-old period in which economic life could be analyzed in "national" and "international" terms drew to a close. At the same time, however, not all phenomena can be reduced to "the global," for many differences and disparities, far from diminishing, are in fact increasing in many domains. And the fact that money and commodity relationships are becoming dominant in the quasi-totality of the world's societies, at the same time as these societies are increasingly caught up in monetary and financial globalization, insidiously creates profound changes, entrenches inequality, and contributes to the rise of a-cracy.[3]

Finally, while all societies are working toward economic growth, the growth which has already been achieved and which is in progress has begun to harm essential balances and the stability of the Earth. And the ceaseless creation of new needs, joined with demographic growth and the destruction of natural resources, will all force future generations to face increasingly difficult choices.

More than ever, because of the importance of these changes, it is necessary to understand the forces now at work. Through the current great change, which in many aspects resembles the great depression at the end of the nineteenth century, a complex process of decomposition/recomposition of the world is taking place. The word "globalization" gives an inadequate image of this process. Several trends operating together appear to us to form the outlines of a "turning point in world history,"[4] an immense acceleration of historical change.[5]

THE GREAT CHANGE AT THE END OF THE TWENTIETH CENTURY

The years from 1973 to 1990 offer many points of comparison with the great depression of 1873–1895. We note:

—the crisis in the West;
—the economic morass of many parts of Africa and South America;
—unprecedented growth in many parts of Asia;
—the emergence of new technologies;
—"globalization."

But with the collapse of the Soviet system, the renewal of American economic power, the advances of European unity, the resurgence of "liberal" ideology, and the formation of huge corporations, capitalism, whose tentacles extend into nearly all parts of the world, has once again demonstrated its ability to adapt and bounce back.

A New "End-of-the-Century Depression"?

As was the case at the end of the nineteenth century, the period of crises
and economic instability which began in 1973 can be understood only by
considering together the interaction of the four great contradictions of
modern capitalism: 1) between corporations; 2) between capital and labor;
3) between national capitalisms; and 4) between dominant capitalisms and
dominated countries, including industrializing nations.[6]

Within this perspective, the "long crisis" of 1973–90 presents remarkable
similarities to the "great depression" of 1873–95.[7]

As had occurred during the "great depression" at the end of the nineteenth century, a redistribution of power and control on a planetary scale
has begun. A century ago the predominant economy, Great Britain, though
in attitude quite self-sure, had nonetheless to confront the rising economic
power of Germany and the United States. During the decade from 1970
to 1980, the U.S. appeared in control of the game relative to Japan, which
remained closely linked to the U.S., and relative to Europe, tied up in an
interminable attempt at unification. As for the major nations of the third
world—Brazil bogged down in crises, India and China weighed down by
their population growth—none appears able to assume a position of power.
However, didn't the United States require a half-century, between 1895
and 1945, to achieve its status as hegemonic power of the Western world?
Who can say what will happen between now and the year 2040?

As had occurred during the "great depression" at the end of the nineteenth century, many formerly powerful economies began to run out of
steam. This process took place to a certain degree throughout Western
Europe, and in countries such as Argentina which had begun, between
the two world wars, a rapid rise in economic power. But this process also
took place in all the nations of the Soviet bloc, pushed as they were to
economic suffocation by the weight of the statist system. At the same
time, new capitalisms rose up: in Asia's "four dragons," in several Southeast
Asian countries, in the petroleum kingdoms of the Middle East, and in
several other islands of success scattered throughout the former third world.
And within the two "continent-nations," India and China, powerful economic dynamics are at work, without having yet borne full fruit.

As had occurred during the "great depression" at the end of the nineteenth century, economic advances were affected by the decline of traditional industries: coal, iron and steel; naval construction; manufacture of
domestic durable goods and appliances.... Economic advances in the leading nations were slowed too by industrialization in other nations, and by

TABLE 7.1   Comparison between the "Great Depression"
at the End of the Nineteenth Century and the "Long Crisis" of 1973–90

	"Great Depression" of 1873–95	"Long Crisis" of 1973–90
Questioning of the predominant power and its currency	Great Britain: sterling	USA: the dollar
Fading of many formerly powerful economies	France, Belgium, Holland	Countries of Western and Eastern Europe
Rise of new national capitalisms	USA, Germany	Japan, newly industrialized countries (NICs), India, China
Previous industries in decline	Coal, iron and smelting, textiles	Steel-making, naval construction, automobile production, electric appliances
New technologies and new industries	Electricity, gasoline-powered internal combustion engine, telephone, automobiles, airplanes	Energy-saving processes, computerization, telecommunications, space technology, biotechnology
Internationalization and globalization	Imperialism, international credit, capital export, dividing-up of the world	Multinational corporations, offshore credits, offshore currencies, global finance, recomposition of the world

the relocation of production from North to South: many of these traditional industries took root and gathered strength in countries of the former third world where production costs were lower.

At the same time, Fordist wage arrangements, which had been at the heart of postwar prosperity in the leading capitalist countries, underwent a two-sided attack. From one direction, workers facing the most difficult working conditions (assembly-line work, around-the-clock "3 × 8" shifts, piecework) have, since the end of the 1960s, increasingly rejected the forms of labor compulsion which, in light of advances in their own and in society's overall living standards, appear to them less and less bearable. From this same direction the Consumption Society and its accompanying waste have been heavily critiqued and rejected by ecology and consumer movements, and by the "1968 generation." From another direction, the powerful rebirth of liberal ideology undermined union power, collective bargaining, and intervention by the state in general; this ideology advocated instead returning to a simple reliance on market mechanisms.

The dismantling of Fordism became visible, in the countries where liberal ideology dominated (U.S., Britain), in the rise of insecure jobs paying low and even sub-minimal wages, and, throughout these societies as a whole, in the massive increase in inequality. In Continental Europe, efforts to preserve essential features of socialized protection for workers have been accompanied by high levels of unemployment,[8] and the formation of large regions of poverty. In Japan, solutions have been sought first of all within the business company itself, through relentless pressure to be flexible and adaptable.

Nonetheless, countertrends are visible. The United States has been forced to maintain a certain minimum of social protection, while Europe has sought to hold unemployment below critical thresholds, and Japan's worsening difficulties have led the nation to question one of its sacrosanct symbols: "employment for life." Throughout the capitalist world as a whole, three tendencies are apparent:

—a tendency toward increasing fragmentation, in the kinds of work, in the levels and modes of payment, and ultimately in societies worldwide;
—a tendency toward increasing worker insecurity and precariousness;
—a tendency toward the lasting formation of populations and regions which are simply left out and excluded from community and economic life.

Simultaneously with these developments, and similar to what took place during the "great depression" at the end of the nineteenth century, many new technologies and new industries are emerging:

—New energy sources, including nuclear energy, natural gas and renewable energy sources, along with energy-saving processes.
—New techniques for the storage, access to, and processing of information; new techniques allowing mastery of life-forms and biological processes, with all possible applications implied, from animal and plant production to production involving the human life-form; finally, new techniques allowing man's exploration of and profiting from outer space.
—New materials and new frontiers, including the oceans, outer space, the core of matter itself, and life.
—New activities, affecting all these domains, including activities which, up to the present, had escaped economic logic.

Though instances of multinational and transnational cooperation have increased, it is clear that each individual nation has embarked on these paths by following its own strengths. The U.S. makes use of its ability to mobilize, for large projects, public financing, technical knowledge from the university community, and business dynamism. Germany and Great Britain call on the power of their industrial corporations and their banking systems. France relies on its statist tradition and the centralized plans carried out by state agencies. Japan uses its ability to create dialogue and cooperation between public and private bodies, and its accelerating pursuit of highly technological development. In 1990, as in 1980, these five nations alone accounted for 75 percent of worldwide high-technology exports.[9]

We note a final similarity between the present crisis and the "great depression" at the end of the nineteenth century: new advances are taking place which lead in the direction of increased internalization and globalization. Technological progress in telecommunications and computerization have immensely increased the ability to store, process, disseminate, and utilize information. This change has brought about a profound transformation of all human activity, from material production to "communication," and has affected all domains of culture, management, and finance. New forms of consumption, and widened possibilities for communication, of which the Internet is the symbol, have thus become available to population groups whose size has swelled in successive waves from tens of thousands to hundreds of millions at a time.

At the same time, international financial and monetary relationships—which have also been transformed by the telecommunications and computerization advances—have become less and less governable, following the abandonment of regulatory agencies, the rise of liberal ideology, and the multiplication of financial centers and dealers. Corporations, and especially the huge transnational corporations, now have the means to initiate extremely supple and mobile operations—encompassing sales, production, and finance—on a planetary scale.

Whatever similarities exist, then, between the present and the end of the nineteenth century, we are not now simply witnessing an end-of-the-century "great depression." We are living through a profound change, which is moving us into a new historical period.

CRISES OF THE 1980S: ASYMMETRIC INTERACTIONS
IN AN UNEQUAL WORLD

In analyzing the crises of the 1980s, several factors must be kept in view:

—Commercial, production, monetary, and financial relationships as a whole.

—The movement and flow of people, information, and representations.

—The dynamics of cultures and various ways of living.

—The variety of plans, projects, and strategies.

Given the interaction of these factors, no nation, no society, and not even any micro-society, may be considered to exist in isolation, as an entity having only secondary relations with the outside world.

The interweavings of mutual dependence keep multiplying and diversifying. Each nation's weight, power, strategies, and overall position within the world system expand or limit its room to maneuver. Out of this context arise the many discussions about dependence, compulsion from foreign sources, de-linking, and, most broadly, the ability of any one country or group of countries to master their destiny.

The American economy has become more and more integrated into the world economy. The share of imports and exports within its GNP rose from 7–8 percent to 18–21 percent during the 1970s. Export percentages then fell back, but have stabilized around 20 percent for imports. Dollar assets held by foreigners doubled from 1980 to 1985, from 500 billion to one trillion dollars. Dollars held by Americans outside the U.S. rose slightly less quickly during this same period, from 600 billion to 950 billion dollars.[10] Investments by American corporations overseas increased markedly, from 100 billion dollars in 1973 to 220 billion in 1980 and 455 billion in 1990. Investments in the U.S. by non-American corporations increased even more steeply during this time period, going from 20 billion dollars in 1973 to 60 billion in 1980 and 435 billion in 1990.[11]

The relative weight of foreign trade, the degree of penetration by transnational corporations, and the level of foreign debt have all become increasingly important for each national economy. This situation has bred the powerful and occasionally brutal interdependence visible during the 1980s.[12]

Policies of economic "stabilization" (reducing inflation, limiting social protection, reducing purchasing power) put into effect at the beginning of his term in office by Ronald Reagan, and carried out in several other Western nations, including West Germany and Mrs. Thatcher's Great Britain, produced noticeable effects on the world economy. Overall domestic spending (consumption, government spending, and investment) went down in the U.S. in 1980 and 1982, in the European Community in 1982 and 1983, and in Japan in 1980, 1981, and 1983.[13]

Effects on "developing" countries were brutal. While exports from these countries to the capitalist nations as a whole had risen on average by 21.5 percent per year from 1975 to 1980, exports fell by 7.4 percent in 1981, by 14.5 percent in 1982, and by 6.7 percent in 1983.[14] The reduction in payments for exports weighed heavily on third world nations: the gross domestic product for the countries of South America and the Caribbean, which had risen by 5.4 percent per year from 1973 to 1980, fell three years in a row, in 1981, 1982, and 1983. Similar statistics described the countries of sub-Saharan Africa: their gross domestic product had risen from 1973 to 1980 by 3.6 percent per year, but fell for three successive years, in 1982, 1983, and 1984.[15] This situation formed one of the sources of the third world foreign debt crisis in the 1980s.

This was not the only realm where the effects of interdependence between national economies were evident. Once he became President, Reagan's economic policy reduced much federal and social spending, while maintaining military and research spending at high levels. The objective was to assure the strategic superiority of the U.S., while at the same time sustaining the leading technological, scientific, and industrial sectors of the economy. U.S. military spending went up from 134 billion dollars in 1980 to 227 billion dollars in 1984. These figures represented, respectively, 22.6 percent and 26.7 percent of the federal budget. During this same period the federal budget deficit deepened from 74 billion dollars in 1980 to more than 200 billion dollars in 1983, 1985, and 1986.[16] Simultaneously, the foreign trade deficit of the U.S. worsened from 1982 to 1987. These two movements together increased borrowing by the American government and within the financial world, and led to sharp increases in nominal interest rates. Real interest rates, which had been negative in the U.S. in 1979 and 1980, became positive in 1981 and remained at high levels between 1982 and 1985.[17] The rate of exchange of the dollar against other currencies as a whole rose to a maximum in 1985.[18]

This rise of the dollar, which encouraged imports to the U.S. while making exports more difficult, increased the trade deficit as well as the deficit in the ongoing balance of payments of the U.S. The balance of payments, which had been positive in 1981, showed a deficit of 41 billion dollars in 1983, 102 billion in 1984, and 113 billion dollars in 1985.[19] From this time on, the foreign debt of the U.S. grew markedly; from 130 billion dollars in 1980, it rose to 300 billion at the end of 1983.[20] The overall foreign financial position of the U.S. became negative in 1987, and continued to decline during the 1990s.[21]

The rise of the dollar produced a strong effect on the economies of nations which paid in dollars for a significant share of their imports. This was especially true for the indebted nations of the former third world, for whom the weight of foreign debt relative to their own production and income from exports quickly assumed crushing proportions. The outstanding foreign debt of these countries rose from 481 billion dollars in 1980 to 552 billion in 1982, and 711 billion in 1985; these figures represent, respectively, 90 percent, 116 percent, and 136 percent of the value of their exports.[22] The real interest rates these nations had to pay on their foreign debts reached unbearable levels in the 1982 to 1985 period: 20 percent for Nigeria, 18 percent for Argentina and Chile, 17 percent for Mexico, 16.5 percent for Brazil, and 10 percent for South Korea.[23] The cost of servicing their debt steeply rose for each of these nations. In 1977 it represented on average 10 percent of payments received for exports; this figure reached 16 percent in 1980, and was approximately 20 percent after 1982. Among the most heavily indebted nations the percentages were far worse, as in Chile (55 percent), Mexico (49 percent), Brazil and several other countries in South America (35 percent), Burma (37 percent), Egypt (34 percent), Algeria and numerous countries in sub-Saharan Africa (34 percent).[24]

The huge increase in foreign debt produced disastrous effects within the economies of nations in the South. Their growth was suddenly slowed down or blocked entirely. This in turn produced serious risks for the banks which had lent money in the first place, and more generally, for the capitalist economy as a whole. The specter of the great crisis of the 1930s revived. A flurry of negotiations took place, giving rise to the rescheduling of many debt payments. Under pressure from experts at the IMF, numerous countries were subjected to policies of "structural adjustment."[25] The average real wage went down by 15 percent in Chile from 1981 to 1985; by 36 percent in Mexico from 1982 to 1985; by 40 percent in Peru from 1980 to 1985; by 9 percent in Brazil from 1982 to 1983. Officially counted unemployment rose by a factor of four in Singapore between 1980 and 1983, and in Thailand between 1980 and 1982. Unemployment also rose noticeably in Burma and in Indonesia between 1980 and 1982, and in India from 1980 to 1984.[26]

Thus, the high rate of exchange of the dollar created an unacceptable situation, not only for the principal trading partners of the U.S., but also for American producers and exporters. Once the rate of exchange reached levels which were clearly excessive, speculators and careful money managers made good their gains and then sought to reduce their holdings in dollars.

There was risk of a collapse. The controllers of the central banks managed in the winter of 1985 to craft a "soft landing" for the dollar—the only problem being that no one knew exactly at what level of exchange the landing platform floated.[27] Within this situation the Baker plan, announced in the fall of 1985, allowed the U.S. to slightly soothe the open wounds of the indebted nations of the South, especially those in South America.

However, the fall in the dollar went along with a fall in the price in dollars for oil. Since 1973, OPEC had lost its preeminent position, and by 1981 its production was surpassed by that of other countries. Additionally, its own member nations were divided among themselves. Saudi Arabia, trying to gain back market share and to make the most expensive oil production facilities less profitable or even unprofitable, exerted pressure toward lowering prices. The price of oil, which had reached a peak in 1979, at more than 80 dollars a barrel for "Arabian light," decreased during the early 1980s to 38 dollars a barrel in December 1985, to 10 dollars a barrel at the end of July 1986, and then leveled off at around 20 dollars a barrel. During the Gulf War in the summer of 1990 the price briefly went up to 40 dollars a barrel, and then fell back to less than 20 dollars a barrel.[28] Overall the reduction in price was a windfall for the oil-consuming nations (Japan, the consuming nations of Europe and of the third world). At the same time the drop in prices represented a serious problem for oil-producing countries in northern Europe and in the Persian Gulf. And for several heavily populated countries whose economies were largely dependent on oil—including Mexico, Nigeria, Algeria, and Egypt—the price drop placed them in very difficult, and sometimes desperate situations.

In real prices oil fell back to pre-1973 levels. The overall price of all raw materials fell sharply—so much so that their real prices ended up at their lowest level in a century, comparable to 1932–33 prices.[29] It is clear, then, that the burden of the current phase of the crisis is carried by those at the bottom of society in both North and South. In the industrialized North the crisis is for the most part borne by the unemployed, the marginalized social groups, certain categories of aging workers, and, increasingly, by the younger generations, who face unemployment and insecure and unregulated work situations. In the South the effects of the crisis are felt most acutely by the direct producers of the third world: farmers, wage-laborers (as well as workers within the informal sectors of the economy), and all those without jobs and without resources, who have often had to relocate themselves in an attempt to survive. In the South the worst effects of the crisis are borne by the poor within the poor countries. This has created a striking and explosive situation within an unstable and profoundly unequal world system.

The current world situation is thus characterized by a remarkable interdependence, though this is a highly asymmetric interdependence in which the influence of the U.S. and the other countries of the North is preponderant. It is an interdependence which makes itself felt through repeated shock waves and counter-shock waves, where reduction as well as amplification of effects are possible. This is an interdependence whose effects spread out further and further into the world, leaving no person and no place untouched. Workers in the mines and straggling villages at the end of the world, fishermen on distant islands, peasants in the most remote villages: all have become dependent on world events.

This is an interdependence which the most powerful actors work into their strategies, in order to come out on top. Those on the bottom, without resources, most often must simply submit to such interdependence and suffer whatever effects it brings.

THE RISE OF LIBERALISM, GROWTH, AND CRISES OF THE 1990s

The reassertion of liberal ideology in the 1980s might have been nothing more than a fashion affecting only Great Britain, the former dominant power, and the U.S., dominant power of the second half of the twentieth century. But in fact the liberal reassertion represented much more than that: it was a top-to-bottom change in the ideological and political climate comparable to the interventionism which arose first in reaction to the crisis of the 1930s, then on a worldwide scale during the war of 1939–45, and finally during the later 1940s and 1950s as an ideology accompanying reconstruction, growth, and development, in a context where the nations calling themselves Communist presented a serious challenge.[30]

It was in Great Britain, under Mrs. Thatcher, that the most radically "liberal" policies were put into effect during the 1980s. These policies included reduced state intervention generally, privatization, deregulation, reduction in social protection, and attacks on unions, and were pursued in diluted form by the following Conservative government of John Major. Citizen sentiment about such policies led to the Labour Party's victory under the very pragmatic Tony Blair, but once in power, Blair revealed himself as a promoter of social liberalism.

In the United States Reagan's policies were a mixture of significant cuts in social spending, tax reductions, and a major increase in the federal deficit. Under George Bush's presidency (1988–92), federal spending remained high, while the defense of American interests remained priority number one in negotiations on world trade. The election in 1992 and re-election in 1996 of Bill Clinton, also highly pragmatic, brought no radical change: the federal deficit was reduced through economic growth and budget cuts, while the liberal discourse simply took on a more social tone. Economic nationalism continued to dominate the scene, including particular stress on defense of the national interest, on the need for remaining competitive, and on the establishment of "strategic trade policies."

In Europe, liberalism gained recognition largely through ideological debate, and managed to penetrate the corridors of power and even to impregnate the discourse of the Left. State interventionism remained many-sided, however. Established organizational solidarities were not seriously attacked, and many social benefits, if defended, remained intact. It was thus by way of "cuts and alterations" that the bend toward liberalism was made. In France, for example, the "plural Left" government put into place by Lionel Jospin in June 1997 succeeded better than had Rightist governments in establishing privatization and deregulation. Jospin's economic minister appears very close to the social-liberal positions formulated together by Tony Blair and the German Gerhard Schröder, two government leaders under the socialist umbrella who state that "most people no longer have a vision of the world in terms of Right and Left." These leaders apply against social democracy the same accusations which for decades the Right leveled against the Left.

In Asia, the liberal credo had for a long time been part of the obligatory international stance. In certain sectors, competition may be merciless. In all the countries which benefit from strong growth, however, it is state action, along with action by certain corporations or families, which is determining. In China the state apparatus, in particular the army, acts with family groups and secret networks; when crisis strikes, national and statist reflexes again spring into action.

In Russia, and throughout the former Soviet empire, a wildly un-fettered liberal discourse, often propagated by irresponsible Western ideologues, spread in the wake of the collapsed statist system. Where this discourse took form in practical measures undertaken without foresight—and this was the case especially in Russia—enormous chaos developed, in which sanctioned power networks and Mafia-like organizations together divided up and shared the "juiciest" economic booty. And the International Monetary Fund prescribed, as it has for all nations facing economic

TABLE 7.2   Growth of the World Economy (average annual percentage)

	World as a whole	High-income economies	Medium-income economies	Low-income economies
1980–90	3.1	3.2	2.8	4.3
1990–97	2.3	2.1	2.5	4.2

Sources: World Bank, *World Development Report 1998–1999*; *Le Savoir au service du développement* (Paris: ESKA, 1999), p. 233.

difficulties, a doctrinal liberalism as a condition of economic aid. The IMF has not in fact helped reconstruct a solid and viable economy.

The ideology extolling the virtues and merits of liberalism functioned at a deep level in all cultural domains throughout the 1990s. Evident in the salesman-like smiles of the political leaders, it was dictated by the leading international financial institutions, and was diffused by university teachings, television, and the so-called information media. And wide segments of public opinion accepted without resistance the idea that liberalism assures growth and prosperity.

Yet if one examines the first eight years of the 1990s, the fact is that world economic growth slowed down and fell back relative to the 1980s. This was true not only for the world as a whole, but for the rich nations of the North as well as those countries trying to modernize and catch up.

Within the "high-income economies," the rich capitalist nations, the economic growth rates of the United States and Great Britain appear to outdistance the performance of the other rich nations. In part this split is attributable to time-lag differences between the American and the European economic cycles: 1990 represented a low spot for the U.S. and a peak period for Europe.[31]

The major difference between Anglo-American growth rates and Western European growth rates during the 1990s may be explained as follows. In Great Britain and in the United States, a livable minimum wage has been practically abolished: in real terms, the lowest wages have dropped even lower, while social protection has regressed and inequalities have deepened. In Europe, on the other hand, the bottom has not fallen out of the minimum wage and social protection, in its essentials, has been maintained. Where inequality has increased in Europe, this has principally occurred through the establishment of significant levels of long-duration unemployment, which has in turn excluded from social life a growing

TABLE 7.3   Growth in the Rich Nations (average annual percentage)

	USA	Great Britain	France	Japan
1980–90	2.9	3.2	2.4	4.0
1990–97	2.5	1.9	1.3	1.4

Source: World Bank, *World Development Report 1998–1999*.

segment of the population. In both cases, job insecurity and "flexibility" have increased—not only for young people and unskilled workers, but for many experienced workers as well.

As for Japan, the first signs of difficulty became brutally apparent during the series of explosions which marked the Asian fiscal crises.

For the first eight years of the 1990s, what is in fact most spectacular is the growth of the Asian nations and the economic collapse of the former Soviet empire.

After the USSR came apart and the Soviet empire was dismantled, from 1989 through 1991, most of the nations in Eastern Europe went through a difficult transition from statism to a more or less controlled market economy. Following the lead of the Russian Federation, most of the countries of the former USSR experienced a real meltdown after becoming independent, for free enterprise and the market could not be put into place without rules and without an effective state able to assure the rule of law. While the old centralized system was no longer working, the main sources of wealth had been captured and the principal positions of power had been taken over by former apparatchik groups relying on nationalist, and occasionally liberal, ideology. These groups were more or less closely tied to the Mafia-like networks, linked closely to elements of the Party apparatus, which had flourished right within the heart of the Soviet regime.

The miracle this time—insofar as capitalism has achieved miracles each decade of the second half of the century—took place in Asia. Immense India registered 5.9 percent annual growth rates during the first eight years of the 1990s; Cambodia grew at more than 6 percent annually; South Korea, Indonesia, and Thailand at more than 7 percent; Malaysia and Vietnam at more than 8 percent; and China recorded more than 12 percent growth annually during this time period. The economic magazines

TABLE 7.4   Growth in Eastern Europe and Asia (average annual percentage)

	East Asia and the Pacific	China	India	Eastern Europe	Russia and Central Asia
1980–90	7.8	10.2	5.8	2.9	2.8
1990–97	9.9	11.9	5.9	−5.4	−9.0

Source: World Bank, *World Development Report 1998–1999*.

were full of such news, while most commentators had eyes only for this new growth, in which they saw the promise of a world in which Asia's full weight would make itself felt.

Such a promise is not false, but to found it upon a single period of growth shows a lack of historical understanding, for capitalism has always progressed by alternation of growth and crisis. Additionally, the current crisis has revealed the weaknesses within the economic dynamics of the emerging Asian nations. The model is immoderately oriented toward insertion into the world market, through production for export, as well as through foreign investment and finance. Given that background, the excessive levels of indebtedness and the lack of prudence on the part of the banks easily prepare the speculative whirlwind. All that is needed for crisis to begin is for a few foreign speculators to make good their profits, with foreign investment capital and national financiers following suit. Such crisis will probably be tonic and healthy for the financial and banking systems of these countries; it will probably have severe effects on the productive systems; and it will probably be socially devastating, with effects reaching clear into the middle classes. But such lessons will just as probably be forgotten in a few decades.

The Asian crisis, which began with a massive drop in the value of the Thai Baht in July 1997, quickly spread to Malaysia, Indonesia, and the Philippines.[32] By the end of the year the crisis had brought to light the financial and banking weaknesses of both South Korea and Japan. While in Asia the crisis made itself felt through a sharp drop in production,[33] it expanded and took on new aspects in the summer of 1998 with the crisis in Russia and upheaval in Argentina and Brazil. All these events taken together brought out the limits and fragility of the world financial system, which in fact went through a severe correction in September–October 1998. The weaknesses of its own banking and financial system, and the inflexibility of its production apparatus, revealed the fragile nature of Fortress Japan; if Japan were caught up in the crisis, this would directly threaten the United States, and thus the system as a whole.[34] The Japanese government thus decided on a vast clean-up of their banking system. At the same time, other developments were taking place: the measures prescribed by the International Monetary Fund, especially the high interest rates it imposed, tended to worsen the crisis. From another direction, the crisis was in part contained by China, which, by not devaluing the Renminbi, received recognition for contributing positively to world economic stability.

China, with its staggering population of 1,200 million people, did not spurn contradiction; under the firm authority of the Party apparatus, the most diverse forms of production coexisted, ranging from small family production to huge state enterprises, from statist and collective production to all forms of capitalism, with many sectors affected by corruption and Mafia-like organizations.

The decade of the 1990s, which unfolded under the sign of liberalism, was a decade of hot and cold, of growth and crisis, and of routine and chaos. While some worried about the risks of inflation, others worried about the threat of deflation. Some analysts were concerned about the limits to speculation in the stock market, where the proportion between payments per share to prices fell to the lowest level ever recorded.[35] Other analysts saw instead a new stock market logic where profit gains would give rise not only to speculation, but to increases as well in consumption spending by shareholders. While many people were concerned about the physical limits to growth (dangers on a global level, water...) others sang the praises of a "new economy" based primarily on information.

If there is liberalism at the end of the century, it is a liberalism unfolding within a unitary yet diversified system, a liberalism where inequality has been pushed to unheard-of levels. This might be called, in a world already flagrantly unequal, the liberalism of the super-powerful.

REALITIES AND IDEOLOGIES OF GLOBALIZATION

Throughout the 1990s the word "globalization" cropped up everywhere— not only within the media, and as an argument within political discourse, but also within learned debates, where scholars were forced to modify the terms of their analyses...

Though some authors, such as Robert Boyer, cast into doubt not only the importance but even the reality of globalization,[36] the fashionable use of the word can be explained in part by the emergence within the closing decades of the century of some new phenomena:

—the end of the tripartition of the post–Second World War world;
—financial globalization and the planetary reach of shock waves sent out by monetary and stock market tremors;
—damage to the ozone layer, and indications of climatic change due to human activity;
—the Internet.

Plump and round, smooth and slippery, the word "globalization" is an all-purpose word. It can be substituted for terms such as "imperialism," "world capitalism," or "dependence," as well as for the whole group of phrases which express forward progress toward a unified and happy humanity. Nonetheless, the growing use of the term is not neutral, but takes place within the neoliberal flood, where, once again, extreme positions are being stated. Within this context the word is used to justify certain choices and to cover up certain sacrifices.

In the absence of a generally accepted definition, the use of this word to designate so many different objects contributes to the ambiguity of the discussions in which it figures. The ambiguity may be partially clarified by recognizing that the word "globalization" is used to describe three different levels of process:

—An increasing number of phenomena take place on a planetary scale.
—Interactions and interdependences multiply and mutually reinforce each other throughout the world.
—New realities, organically formed and dispersed, make their effects felt on a worldwide scale.

Three uses of the word "globalization" thus coexist:

1. Globalization as the attainment of a worldwide dimension by any given reality: in the past, globalization of mankind's presence or of certain techniques of production on the different continents; today, globalization of instantaneous information or of consumption of certain products.
2. Globalization as multiplication and intensification of interdependences on a world scale. This includes interdependences which for a long time had remained minimal and weak, because they were played out over long time frames. Globalization as intensification strengthens such interdependences, in part due to changes in transport and communication.

3. Globalization as an organic, encompassing movement. This sense of contemporary globalization is strongly linked to the dynamics of capitalism.

Given these distinctions, the globalization now taking place represents the first time that the three levels of process are all occurring together. We are witnessing the simultaneous expansion onto a world level of diverse realities, the intensification of a whole range of world interdependences, and an organic movement—dominated by the development of capitalism on a world scale—which propels, deepens, and accelerates the whole process. And, for each of these dynamics, resisting and countervailing forces also exist. Current globalization is anchored in the long transformation begun in the fifteenth and sixteenth centuries during the formation and emergence of capitalism. The globalization at the end of the twentieth century extends and continues certain dynamics—national expansions, internationalizations, multinationalizations, continentalizations—which have been spurred on by the dominant national capitalisms.

Contrary to the idea of a sphere denoted by the term "globalization," the worldwide process now taking place is polarized, unequal, and asymmetric. All human beings will be affected by one aspect or another of globalization. This will occur in their lifestyle and consumption patterns, in the areas of culture and information, through sales and marketing, or through the destruction of natural resources, pollution, and climate changes. Rather than the neighborly charms, the reciprocity and mutual support implied by the image of a "global village," the vast majority of the six billion inhabitants of the Earth must instead simply put up with developments and changes they are unable themselves to influence.

The geopolitical entity composed of the rich capitalist countries—which Kenichi Ohmae describes as a "Triad"[37] and which geographer Olivier Dollfus describes as a "world/metropolitan archipelago"[38]—is by far the most decisive element within the process of globalization. The rich capitalist countries are the center of numerous crucial activities:

—The concentration of the greatest masses of buying power, consumption, savings, investment, research and development, financial instruments, and military might.
—The initiation of planetary strategies, not only by the powerful nations (with the United States leading the pack), but also by huge transnational corporations and by the world's leading financial players, all of which exert definite influence on the principal international economic and financial institutions.

—The invention and development of new techniques, and, along with them, new procedures, new products, and new forms of consumption and lifestyle.

—New technoscientistic threats, just as these countries were the main source, up through the 1980s, of industrial pollution.

Each of these areas merits closer attention, and we will examine several of them in the second section of this chapter. For the moment, consider monetary and financial globalization.

This aspect of globalization is certainly real. Technological advances in telecommunications and computerization have made possible the instantaneous execution of any monetary payment or financial order, anywhere on the globe. These advances have also allowed the creation of increasingly abstract and sophisticated financial products: futures and options on rates, currencies, and stock market levels.[39] As part of the same movement, the number of exchange operations has multiplied, monetary relationships have proliferated, while financial and stock market activity has ballooned. Speculation has become endless and arbitration acute. New financial markets have arisen and a monetary/financial sphere has developed where players from around the world carry out financial operations which also affect the entire planet. This swollen monetary/financial sphere is increasingly subject only to its own impulses and logic.[40] And the ever-present possibility of panic-driven movements within this sphere appears less and less controllable by the major national and international monetary and financial institutions.

For all this, it is important not to lose sight of the preeminence, within this "global financial sphere," of the dominant national capitalisms, first and foremost that of the United States. At the end of 1998, stock market capitalization of the New York Stock Market was close to 10 trillion dollars, while the eight major European markets were capitalized at 6.7 trillion dollars, and the major markets of Asia and the Pacific represented 3.6 trillion dollars.[41] At the beginning of 1999, 65 percent of all payments for world exports were carried out in dollars, while 20 percent of these payments were made in a currency of the European Union. Of the world's currency reserves, 56 percent are held in dollars, and 26 percent are held in a currency of the European Union.[42] Some qualifications are needed here: some of these dollars are Eurodollars, the result of credits in dollars allocated outside the United States by banks which are not necessarily American. And the Euro, created at the beginning of 1999, is not yet the standard currency in Europe, and so has not yet showed its capabilities as a world currency. Furthermore, the Japanese banking system had to go through a very vigorous housecleaning in order to climb out of its difficulties. Nonetheless, the major monetary and financial actors remain those in the U.S., the European Union, and Japan, while the international lender of last resort remains the American Federal Reserve, which works closely with the International Monetary Fund and the major banks of G7 nations.

The paradox is that American monetary and financial imbalances are an integral part of the world financial sphere: American imbalances contribute to the functioning of this sphere, but at the same time they are at the heart of the crisis which numerous signs indicate is looming. Back in 1989 we wrote:

> The unstable balance of the world economy in the 1980s is due in large part … to the imbalances of the United States, which themselves eventually produce … grave dysfunction within the world economy.[43]

Ten years later, the American foreign deficit has deepened further, going from 155 billion dollars in 1997 to 233 billion in 1998.[44] The net foreign balance of the U.S., which has been negative since 1987, reached −620 billion dollars (8 percent of GDP) in 1995 and −1.55 trillion dollars (17.8 percent of GDP) in 1998.[45] Revenue from investments abroad became negative in 1997, and recorded a deficit of 23 billion dollars in 1998.[46]

Paradoxically, the rest of the world contributed to financing American growth during the last two decades of the twentieth century. Today, the United States needs this financing, which helps explain the importance of what happens on Wall Street. Yet the sharp rise in stock prices creates a growing gap between the price of shares and their dividend income. Increasingly, the sought-after returns from stocks focus on capital gains. However, the race for capital gains for the sake of capital gains alone leads eventually to a severe stock market correction, which itself carries the potential for wider crisis.

Will Europe demonstrate sufficient unity, strength, and credibility to form another pole of stability?

Elsewhere in the world, the two great nation-continents, China and India, represent regions large enough to allow them to maintain some autonomy. Russia, too, will fall in this category once she manages to settle down and reestablish herself.

Some of the small and medium-sized nations, once they achieve sufficient internal unity and a state able to implement a planned strategy, will be able to navigate through the continuing upheavals, by aiming to satisfy the needs of their populations rather than production for export. After the 1997–98 crisis the leaders of at least some of the Asian nations began to understand this distinction.

At the same time, however, many of the small and medium-sized nations, along with the vast majority of the Earth's inhabitants, find themselves in a position of simply having to endure processes—and crises, when they occur—being played out on a planetary scale.

Inequality on a world level is profound, though the word "globalization" tends to mask or even make us forget this fact. Over several decades, and developing along with capitalism in a "liberal" environment where monetary and market relationships have expanded their domains, inequality has increased within nearly all nations, just as it has increased between nations. The result is a deepening of world inequality between the well-off, rich, and extremely rich, compared to the poor and very poor. On a worldwide level, the poorest 20 percent of the world's population possessed 2.3 percent of world resources in 1969, and 1.1 percent in 1994. The richest 20 percent possessed 69 percent of the resources in 1969, and 86 percent in 1994. A Swiss citizen earns in one day what an Ethiopian earns in a year. Some of the very wealthiest families spend for their family alone in a year sums which would allow hundreds of thousands of poor families to live for the same period.

Beyond these incredible differences in wealth, globalizing processes and increasing interdependence have placed whole regions and countries in tenuous and sometimes unbearable situations. Globalization and interdependence have led to increasing manifestations of identity, along national, regional, ethnic, and religious lines, as well as to social regression and increasing disparities. Just as capitalism is both creative and destructive, globalization—at the same time as it unifies—also brings out and creates differences.

To the extent that the word "globalization" in fact corresponds to a definite entity, it refers to a group of processes which are played out in a radically unequal and asymmetric way. This is all the more true in that globalization is indissociable from other profound changes, such as the powerful extension of the domain open to market and money relationships, the increase in inequality brought about by the creation of new forms of poverty, the increasingly systematic corporate use of technoscience, and the imperilment, both locally and globally, of biodiversity and the fundamental stability of the Earth.

Beyond the search to control the economic, monetary, and financial processes, what is at stake most importantly is whether a lasting and stable balance will be established between the expansion of human activity and the bio/physical/chemical reproduction of the Earth. And can such a lasting balance be found, given the incredibly deep inequalities dividing humanity?[47] This is the crucial problem of our globalized world, a problem left off the agenda by most of those now talking about globalization.

FORCES GUIDING THE ACCELERATING TRANSFORMATION OF THE CONTEMPORARY WORLD

In order to describe the "great changes" of the years 1980–90, there exist numerous similarities to the great depression at the end of the nineteenth century, including linked processes of growth and crisis, recovery and setback, as well as the unification and diversification implied by the word "globalization." An economist might be tempted to go no further than these similarities.

Yet there is more involved, not only for the history of capitalism but for human history as a whole, as can be seen in the terms occurring in some recent works: "great disorder," "shake-up," "turning upside down," "end of worlds," and "end of history."[48] For our part, we speak of the accelerating transformation of the contemporary world, in which there is evident both a swift passage from one state to another and a movement of the whole which is in many respects irreversible.

Contemporary capitalism ties together economies and societies in an increasingly dense network. This is evident in the weaving together of international ties into multinational spaces, in the proliferation of commercial, technological, and informational relations, and in monetary and financial globalization. The collapse of the Soviet system and the statist plurinational domain organized around it; the dazzling advance of money and market relationships into the quasi-totality of the world's societies; dynamics relying on wealth and enterprise extending into all countries, including India and China: the flows and waves of world capitalism are starting to submerge all dikes and dams, not only those constructed in the last few decades, but also those dating from ancient times.

Whether it is a question of the decline of industrial capitalism, of the weakening of Western predominance, of the growing submission of all societies to the economy, of the dangers to the Earth from human activity, or the chain reaction of accelerating radical changes, many different facts lead to the conclusion that we have begun to tip into a new stage of world history.

The New Structuring of the World

It was only yesterday: hardly a quarter of a century ago. Three worlds appeared to exist:[49]

—The first world, capitalist, industrialized, and rich, with the United States still predominant but increasingly obliged to take into account the rising power of Japan and the major nations of Europe.

—The second world, communist, bent upon industrialization and productive growth, dominated by a Soviet Union which was itself deeply scarred by the logic of statism and the policies carried out by Stalin.

—Finally, the third world, a heterogeneous collection formed out of the final phase of decolonization affecting countries which, through domination and colonization, had experienced various forms of exploitation, destructuring, backwardness, and impoverishment.

At the junction-point between the first and third worlds lay several countries hosting military bases; along with other newly industrializing and modernizing nations, these countries all found a place within the hierarchical national/world capitalist system. At the intersection between the second and third worlds there were two huge nation-continents: China and India. After its rupture with the USSR, China was tempted to become the leading power of a new communist grouping, while at the same time it sought to be seen as the first and most influential of the poor nations. During this period, India, while remaining clearly a part of the third world, also maintained firm ties to the USSR.

This period witnessed levels of wealth which became more and more unequal. A succession of "economic miracles" was seen, and while the sparsely populated oil-producing nations became wealthy, elsewhere rates of growth and modernization varied widely from country to country. The third world was the first to come apart, and from the 1980s onward it became necessary to speak of the former (or ex-) third world. Then, in the transition from the 1980s to the 1990s, the Soviet bloc and the USSR itself came apart, on the ruins left behind by the double failure of totalitarianism and the statist management of the economy.

In an article published in *The National Interest* in the summer of 1989, Francis Fukuyama proclaimed "the end of history," a claim which the author further developed in a book in 1992 and which provoked lively reaction and discussion. In 1999 he reconfirmed his basic beliefs: "Nothing causes me to doubt my conclusion: liberal democracy and the market economy are the sole viable possibilities for modern society."[50]

In this article is evident the deeper meaning of globalization as ideology: the world being united through the market, a market bearing no trace of inequality or asymmetric power relations. Within the words themselves— "liberal democracy" and "market economy"—everything appears to be stated. And yet: has the ideal of liberal democracy been in fact accomplished in today's world? Do not the Western democracies suffer from what we have called a "lack of framework and orienting principles"?[51] Besides, can what is triumphing today truly be called "a market economy"? And has the link between capitalism and liberal democracy been in fact clearly established? Does not history demonstrate that capitalism adapts itself to liberally scented democracy as well as to social democracy, and that it can prosper perfectly well under dictatorship or totalitarian regimes? Finally, we must not forget the deeply rooted forces concealed within national pride, religious conviction, and the thirst for wealth and domination.

Because capitalism represents a transforming potential which develops by setting into motion nearly all aspects and facets of society, its development necessarily brings into play new terrain, new conflict, and new power relations. The end of history—along with the global village, happy globalization, and the reign of the market economy—are all false ideas aiming to silence critical discussion.

In fact, at the conclusion of the 1990s, if anything is triumphing, it is capitalism, and, more precisely, the rich capitalist group—composed of the leading states and huge corporations of the Triad—whose influence far outweighs any other presence on the planet. This group continues to control not only the major share of market production, but also the essential means of finance, scientific and technological research, and innovative power.

Within the Triad, the United States is the major actor. The U.S. is predominant in practically all domains, answers to no one, and attempts to impose its laws on everyone else. The U.S. is the only country able to maintain a lasting trade deficit, thanks to foreign financing. Some of this financing arrives in the form of returns on its own investments, but significant quantities come as investment flowing in from all corners of the globe—from countries possessing strong economies, and from oligarchies among the poor and modernizing nations—as well as from money linked to racketeering and Mafia-like activity.[52] The United States has increased its domestic market through the North American Free Trade Agreement (NAFTA), which bring in Canada and Mexico, and has multiplied its connections in nearly all direction as well: toward the other sectors of the Americas, toward Europe, and toward Asia and the Pacific. The U.S. makes

TABLE 7.5　Relative Weight of the Triad within the World in 1997 (percent of world total)

	U.S.	Japan	European Union	Total
Population	4.6	2.2	6.2	13.0
Gross production	25.7	15.9	28.4	70.0
Stock market capitalization	42.0	15.3	23.1	80.4

On the relative weight of R&D spending, see Table 7.8.

Source: World Bank, *World Development Report 1998–99*.

use of international organizations in order to impose its own views, and, in case of failure, the U.S. falls back on various forms of pressure and blackmail.

Foreign trade, along with capital and credit transfers, link together the three poles of the Triad, and the other parts of the world back to the Triad. These connections operate in the present period more tightly than ever. The states within the Triad appear to have less and less ambition and fewer and fewer plans. Instead, it is the world capitalist oligarchy which now provides goals and gives direction. With its banks and financial organizations, it is at the heart of monetary and financial globalization. The oligarchy's huge corporations overwhelmingly determine not only productive and trading activity, but research, investment, and consumption patterns as well.

Gross sales by the two hundred largest corporations represented 17 percent of world production in 1960, 24 percent in 1984, and 31 percent in 1995.[53] In 1995 the 500 largest corporations in the world[54] employed more than 35 million workers.[55] With more than 32 trillion dollars in assets, their gross sales represented nearly 11.4 trillion dollars: nearly half (47 percent) of world production.[56] These corporations made 320 billion dollars in profits:[57] this sum represents more than the gross product of the 43 poorest countries where all together more than a billion people live.[58]

According to available estimates, multinational corporations were responsible in 1980 for half of world trade, though 30 percent of their trade was intra-firm trade,[59] taking place between multinationals and thus not to be considered "true" trade between distinct partners. During the 1990s these corporations carried out two-thirds of world trade, with 40 percent being intra-firm trade.

Another perspective on these developing tendencies appears in the following figures. In 1992, 37,000 multinational corporations controlled 170,000 foreign subsidiaries representing 2 trillion dollars in foreign productive assets. Overall foreign sales[60]—that is to say, outside of the home country of the primary corporation—represented 5.5 trillion dollars, an amount significantly more than international trade, which in that year represented approximately 4 trillion dollars.[61]

Yet nearly all of these huge corporations which dominate the world's production, exchange, and technological research are based within the three principal capitalist centers of the Triad.[62]

We are living through a period witnessing not at all a market economy bringing together actors of roughly equal weight, not at all a globalization such as that conjured up by the image of a global village. Instead, more than at any past time, we are in the presence of an entity which is simultaneously national, multinational, and global, very heavily unequal and hierarchical, and dominated by the power of the Triad's capitalist oligarchy. It is within the midst of this concentration of wealth that consumption patterns of the coming decade are determined, as well as the direction of research and the uses of knowledge,[63] the structuring and circulation of international exchange (and thus the form of the division of labor), and the ability to face (or not face) global environmental problems...

Confronting the Triad's power, and after the collapse of the Soviet empire and the crumbling of the USSR, the two great nation-continents of Asia, India and China, are beginning to emerge.

China and India are the only two countries containing more than a billion people. Each grows out of a past rich in history and accomplishments. Each has been dominated and humiliated, and each is trying to get rid of the bitter taste left by past domination. Both nations are able to join the market to administration, centralization to decentralization, manufacturing skill to scientific knowledge, and state to society. Under statist leadership, both nations have developed significant productive capacity, and have allowed the development of important capitalist enterprises.

It is true that, measuring production per inhabitant, these countries are still far away from the rich countries. However, both India and China have mastered nuclear and space technology, and their students and researchers are present within all important future technological domains. This is especially true of India in the area of computer science. Note, too, that the richest tenth of the population of either India or China is economically more significant than a major European nation. Additionally,

TABLE 7.6 Relative Weight of the Principal Powers at the Beginning of the Twenty-first Century

1997	World	U.S.	European Union	Japan	China	India	Russia	Brazil
POPULATION (million)	5,829	268	363	126	1,227	961	147	164
GROSS PRODUCTION								
by exchange rates (US$ billion)	29,926	7,690	8,510	4,772	1,055	374	403	773
by purchasing power parity (PPP$ billion)	36,951	7,690	7,466	2,951	4,382	1,587	618	1,020
GROWTH RATE (%)								
1980–90	3.1	2.9	2.6*	4.0	10.2	5.8	2.8	2.8
1990–97	2.3	2.5	1.5†	1.4	11.9	5.9	−9.0	3.1

* Twelve-nation Europe, 1981–90. † Estimate.

Sources: World Bank, *World Development Report 1998–99*; *RAMSES 1992*, Dunod 1991, p. 409; UNCTAD, *Trade and Development Report 1998*, p. 4.

measured by purchasing power parity and not by exchange rates, the gross production levels of both countries take on greater importance, especially in the case of China. For twenty years both India and China have been experiencing economic growth of such proportions that they are beginning to make themselves felt as influential actors within the world economy. This influence was noticeable during the Asian crises of 1997–98. Finally, both nations have available a huge potential domestic market, able to attract long-term foreign suppliers as well as to provide space for several decades of domestic production for consumption.

For all these reasons, failing the always-possible collapse or blockage, India and China will certainly be among the world's leading economic powers in the second third of the twenty-first century.

Russia, too, once she gets solidly on her feet, must be weighed in the economic balance. Several other nations of the ex-third world, such as Brazil, Pakistan, and Indonesia, though not on the same demographic scale as India and China, are all led by strong states and will have their say. At the same time, there is a large share of humanity which already lives in a state of destitution and whose living conditions are often declining even below that level. Nearly always, the young people of these societies face no future, and are placed before a Hobson's choice: either they wrangle a way to go live in one of the rich (or less poor) countries—which gives rise to a new wave of population migration, against which more and more nations are closing their borders—or else they turn against the rich strata and ethnic groups of their own region or nation. As part of this movement, they often focus their energy against the West, as the principal incarnation of wealth, and symbol of past and present domination.

Reaction against the West is evident in many areas, from opposition to Western choices (structural readjustment policies imposed on nations in economic difficulty, high interest rates imposed on Asian nations in the 1998 crisis, the return to American bombing of Iraq at the beginning of 1999, the NATO war against Serbia in the spring of 1999) to the more fundamental questioning of the West as such by populist regimes and by Islamic fundamentalism.

Robert Bonnaud, a knowledgeable observer of world history, has emphasized the deep asymmetry which marks the previous five centuries: "From the end of the fifteenth century to the beginning of the twentieth, it was the West which made history. Men elsewhere, more often than not, followed or submitted to the West."[64] And again, on Western dynamism:

> The period which begins near the end of the fifteenth century and which ends at the beginning of the twentieth century represents a wonderful and terrifying

concentration of progress, a regional hypertrophy and a worldwide atrophy, a localized flaring blaze within a wider darkness, a narrowing of the stage of human history which was at the same time an elevation of this stage.... To the progress of Western reason there corresponded a retreat of non-Western morality, to the progress of Western freedom there corresponded a backward movement of non-Western equality.[65]

The "great change" we are currently passing through certainly marks the end of the period Bonnaud describes. Will we move straightforwardly to a reequilibration of the world, in which the great civilizations and continents which were dominated and scorned for so long once again find their place? Or are we witnessing, with the emergence of Asian capitalisms, the beginning of the relative decline of Western capitalisms and of what François Perroux called "Worldwide Europe"? The game is still in play; the coming decades will be decisive.

The age when the world was dominated by Europe belongs to the past. Already the leadership of the West encounters increasing resistance to carrying out its will, except from the smallest, weakest countries. A new page has been turned, comprising many developments at once:

—The demographic and economic dynamics of Asia.
—The demographic growth of Africa and South America.
—The rise in nationalisms, regionalisms, and fundamentalisms.
—The collapse of numerous nation-states and the increase in the number of areas torn by unending and overflowing conflict, leaving in their wake considerable population migrations.

Given these developments, must not Europe and the West be prepared to harvest the storm whose seeds they sowed while conquering the world for the sake of progress, civilization, and Christian faith? A storm of which we have so far felt only the first squalls...

This is without a doubt one of the forces guiding the contemporary world's accelerating transformation.

MONETARIZATION AND COMMODIFICATION: SOCIETIES UNDER THE YOKE OF THE ECONOMY

Monetarization, commodification, and the extension of capitalism into all aspects of society: these are phrases—forbidding in their abstraction—which it would be helpful to bring down to earth.

A child and his father are out walking in the countryside. Suddenly the child stops and asks worriedly, "Who do we have to pay, Daddy?" Amusement parks, cross-country ski trails where one pays to ski, beaches where one pays to swim: fewer and fewer outdoor activities escape money relations.

Water from the well was free; water from the house faucet has to be paid for. While the sale of bottled mineral and spring water advances in all the opulent outposts of the world, control over a water spigot (even if the quality of the water is doubtful) in the shantytowns of the poor countries provides an opportunity for racketeering. In all countries, the production of potable water is becoming a significant economic activity in its own right. Where sufficient water is lacking, water becomes an import product. Water itself will be a major domain of economic activity at the beginning of the twenty-first century. Will we see a day when water is more expensive than oil?

A similar process has begun regarding air. Certain intersections in Mexico City feature coin-operated mechanical oxygen distributors guaranteeing a few breaths of pure air. More and more buildings rely upon air conditioning, while "artificial cities" (with prototypes such as "Biosphere 1" and "Biosphere 2") are proposed as future projects. The idea of air as a commodity is insidiously becoming accepted.

Consider health. At first glance, it appears we have always had to pay doctors and pharmacists. At a deeper level, however, everything has been transformed. Health systems are more and more costly, and there are enormous sums at stake in research, production, and marketing by pharmaceutical companies. Medical lobbies within the legislative process attest that medicine is big business, as does the recent scandal in France regarding contaminated transfusion blood. The principal explanations about this affair had to do with the national interest, the necessity of using up existing supplies, and competition between laboratories. These explanations relied then upon statist dynamics or the economic force of market dynamics. Another sign of medicine's conversion to a business is the proliferation of medical processes, such as those involving human reproduction and organ and tissue donation, in which money is a prime factor. In medicine, as in education, job-training, journalism, culture, and art, money has come to dominate the other aspects of these processes.

The same process is occurring in the area of data storage and electronic information processing, where we might have imagined free, "public service" access. Instead, market logic has dominated the development of this sector, involving monopolies, market control, and the creation of scarcity. Market dynamics and the search for profit lie behind the huge changes taking place within telecommunications and the electronic media.

New needs are being created, which can be satisfied only through spending money, and which thus rely upon consumer buying power. The business of furnishing equipment, as well as that of consumption, will take place within the framework established by the huge capitalist corporations which dominate these domains.

The reign of the commodity does not, then, present itself through an immense "accumulation" of material commodities alone, as was thought in the nineteenth century, and still into the twentieth, during the halcyon days of the consumption society. The commodity's reign is evident, rather, in the submission to market forces of all aspects of mankind's life, and all aspects of society's functioning. Even further: increasingly, all facets of the Earth itself, reduced to the meager status of mankind's "environment," also fall under the sway of market forces. In a word: the commodification of man, society, and the Earth.

In a related movement, in many of the poor regions of the world, subsistence production—family production for the family, village production for the village—has been forced to retreat, as public agencies or market middlemen have exerted pressure to expand production for cities or for export. Pressure in this direction has been generated also by competition from other products, often themselves subsidized, which are increasingly available as a result of improvements in transportation.

For anyone who keeps his eyes open, and who reads and travels, the overall process taking place can only appear enormously powerful. We are witnessing the generalization of the commodity, and most particularly, of the capitalist commodity, to the detriment of traditional domestic economies and economies not based on money. Social life as a whole has become monetarized, and is increasingly invaded and bewitched by money. The counterpoint of this development is the growth of "informal" economic sectors, new forms of poverty, expanded social marginalization, and the attempt by some societies under the thumb of money relations to create survival space by turning back upon themselves.

Such an expansion of the sphere of the market and of monetary relations is accompanied by profound social transformations:

—an increase in the importance of technology, research, and science;
—an ever-increasing division of labor;
—the continuous creation of new needs, along with new ways for these needs to be expressed and satisfied;
—the transformation of values, social structures, motivations, and behaviors;
—dispersion of decision-making authority along with a general dilution of responsibility.

Productive activities, which had been servants of society until the modern era, have now come to dominate other social activities as a whole: the economic realm has become autonomous relative to human society.

The economic realm has become autonomous through two separate movements: first, an expansion of the market system, and second, the development of capitalism. It is important to distinguish these two movements clearly.[66] Either one may very well be connected to a statist system. The economic realm has become autonomous, in addition, through the destruction, often violent, of previously existing social forms. These earlier forms had melded together many different levels and dimensions of social life: the religious; the economic and political; family ties; relations of dependence, submission, and allegiance; and systems expressing solidarity and redistribution. Such social forms wove together to make a complex, varied fabric.[67]

Karl Polanyi's analysis of this process remains highly pertinent. Traditional societies were broken apart by the generalization of the "self-regulating market," and its subsequent extension beyond produced commodities to land, labor, and money. Once this occurred, "society increasingly was seen as an auxiliary of the market. Instead of containing the economy within social relations, social relations themselves were contained by, and made to fit, the economic system."[68] Having become "the source and center of the system,"[69] the self-regulating system reduced human and social relations to simple money relationships.

From this time on, the economy came to dominate society as a whole. Confronting questions and problems which in other times would have been seen as political or ethical questions, economic arguments came to be seen as primary. Henceforth, one's existence as man, woman, or child is mediated by the money at one's disposal. Even in the most hidden valleys and faraway islands, families everywhere are subjected to the ups and downs of the world's markets. Within the study of economics, ever more powerful trends develop which claim to provide an answer for every question, based on economic calculations of maximization and optimization alone.[70] The tightening grasp of the economy on our societies is accompanied by the growing grip of economic reasoning on our minds, our ways of thinking, our judgments, and our decisions. And finally, not only an improvement of living conditions, but even happiness and existence itself now seem to depend on economic growth alone. Growth has in fact become the supreme goal of the quasi-totality of contemporary societies.

The societies of the developed capitalist world as a whole advance "to the rhythm of growth": they see solutions to their problems only through growth, and need growth to maintain whatever stability they possess, for nothing beside growth appears able to carry out this function. At the first signs of crisis, and at each stage of crisis, growth has appeared as the only possible way out. To take only one example: as a candidate for his first term, Bill Clinton proposed to overcome unemployment, poverty, and problems in the education and health care systems by doubling the GNP in a generation. He did so without asking why decade upon decade of growth had not been sufficient to wipe out these problems in the richest and most powerful nation in the world. As his second term in office draws to a close, a drop in unemployment has in fact accompanied economic growth, but inequality has deepened within American society. New forms of poverty have appeared, affecting low-wage earners, while among the poor populations, access to education and health has deteriorated.

In a similar vein, it was for the most part on the terrain of "growth" that the USSR and the nations of the Soviet bloc attempted to beat the capitalist West.[71] The results of that effort are well known: the transition from statism to a market economy was carried out with varying degrees of trauma and drops in production. Several countries, following Russia's lead, experienced widespread impoverishment and new inequality. To these populations, who had been suspicious for so long about claims for great collective change, the leaders promised more buying power and more consumer goods: in a word, growth.

Within the ex-third world,[72] a great diversity of trajectories is visible. At one pole lie the Asian nations, which, from South Korea to Southeast Asia and part of China, have set off on a forced march to industrialization and modernization. The goal is straightforwardly to catch up to the rich countries. Growth functions within this process both as engine and as goal. Growth is the motivation for a whole generation who believe growth offers them the possibility of escaping poverty, and, for the oligarchy and a small number of entrepreneurs who manage to succeed, of becoming fabulously wealthy. At the other pole lie the countries of South Asia and Africa where wealth, both from traditional and more recent sources, co-exists with the most extreme impoverishment. Many of the people in these areas battle simply to survive on a daily basis.

In between these two poles are those countries, for the most part in South America and the Arab-Islamic world, which went through the initial phases of industrialization and modernization, and which were seriously hurt by the crisis of the 1980s. Some of these nations appear to be mired in no-exit, explosive situations, while others have once again falteringly started off on the path toward growth.

Throughout these diverse predicaments, nearly all countries appear to be relying on economic growth alone, a growth which, through the proliferation of money-based relationships and the sheer number of commodities raining down upon them, corrodes and shakes any society still finding cohesion from other sources. This is the same growth, too, which is harming the environment to such an extent that the reproduction of the biosphere itself is endangered.

The truth is that growth by itself cannot resolve any of the social problems for which it is claimed to be a solution. Were growth a solution, then in the first place, the major share of growth-generated wealth would need to be controlled by strata other than the rich and powerful. In the second place, that share of growth-generated wealth received by poor populations would need to prevail over growth's destructive effects, insofar as any growth is also destruction. Third, a considerable share of the benefits of growth would need to be directed toward the solution of pressing problems, and this would require that the powerful and the leaders agree to direct resources in problem-solving directions. Even if all three of these conditions were met, another problem—which no one wants to admit— would have to be resolved: the powerful dynamics of capitalism, continuously bringing both growth and crisis, strongly contribute to the creation of new needs and to "discovering" the existence of these new needs among the classes and strata possessing sufficient purchasing power for their satisfaction. As part of this process, such new needs then filter down to the less rich strata, and eventually to the very poorest segments of the population.[73] The growth of needs is a problem which must be mastered, yet how can such a task be accomplished in a world as unequal as ours?

A fundamental problem is confronting mankind, the future of humanity, the world: we are more than ever caught up in an increasingly inexorable process which subjects us all to an expansion of market and money relationships, with all the risks such expansion carries.

This is another indication of the accelerating transformation of our present historical situation.

GROWTH WHICH IMPERILS THE EARTH

Since the first United Nations Conference on the Environment, held in Stockholm in 1972, more than a quarter of a century has gone by. Damage to the environment has worsened, while awareness of the dangers has increased. Legislation on national levels has progressed, as have international agreements: more than 150 world or regional accords have been reached, including three concerned with protecting the ozone layer, signed at Vienna (1985), Montreal (1987), and London (1990). The Basle Convention of 1989 dealt with the production and circulation of dangerous waste material, while the UN Conference on development and the environment at Rio de Janeiro in 1992 produced agreements on the Earth's climate, biodiversity, and rainforests, as well as Agenda XXI.[74] Following the 1995 Berlin meeting on the greenhouse effect, a 1997 conference in Kyoto outlined a plan for the industrialized nations to reduce their emission of those gases which increase the greenhouse effect.

During the same period, the 1975 Hammarskjöld report, *What Is To Be Done?*, the 1980 Brandt report, *North–South: A Plan for Survival*, and the 1987 Brundtland report[75] all took up the problem of interrelationships between development, inequality on a world scale, and preserving the environment. Though they did not develop a true world strategy, development and planning experts worldwide agreed on the idea of "sustainable development," an ambiguous formula acceptable to the North as well as the South, to nature-loving ecologists as well as to those advocating scientific/technical solutions. For this was a phrase which summed up a desirable goal but which at the same time avoided questioning growth too bluntly.

Population growth, production growth, growth of needs, growth of resource depletion, growth of waste material: every day we see more clearly the damage to our planet caused by growth. The rivers, soil, air, and oceans are polluted by chemical discharges; the forests are being destroyed while deserts gain ground; the ozone layer is threatened, and global climate change is possible. For the first time in human history, human activity is the process of damaging, and threatens to destroy, the fragile physical-chemical balance which has made life on earth possible.[76]

This is the heart of the problem: demographic growth appears unstoppable for several decades for the human population as a whole. And all societies, from the richest to the poorest, appear compelled to grow economically. The need to grow is constantly renewed and expanded by the growth of needs. Growth itself, in all its various aspects, threatens the environment, the quality of life, and ultimately, the planet.

Though some would have us believe a happy and decent life is possible for twelve, fifteen, or twenty billion humans on earth, we would suggest instead that people alive today, at the turn of the century, are caught up in an unprecedented, accelerating process of growth that is leading us, given current modes of production and ways of living, to the limit of what the planet can sustain on a continuing basis.[77]

Consider population growth: there were from 5 to 8 million humans in 20,000 BC, around 250 million at the beginning of the Christian era, around 600 million in 1600, 1 billion in 1800, 2 billion in 1927, 6 billion in 1999, with projections for between 8 and 13 billion in 2050.[78] These figures represent steeply accelerating growth. For a very long time it took thousands of years for the world population to double, and required the birth and death of more than a hundred generations. Within the twentieth century alone, however, the world population doubled between 1950 and 1987, and tripled between 1927 and 1999. These are increases which took place within a single human lifespan.

Consider growth in production. Though the problems encountered when trying to evaluate in money terms the production of non-money-based societies are well known, the following figures allow comparison of orders of magnitude. Different studies[79] estimate that average production per inhabitant grew only slightly for thousands and thousands of years; production per inhabitant was multiplied by about 10 between 2,000 BC and 1500 AD (a period of 3,500 years), by 1.3 between 1500 and 1820 (a period of 320 years), and by a little more than 6 between 1820 and 2000 (a period of 180 years). The economic growth of the last two centuries is thus an exceptional phenomenon within human history. Such growth may be the beginning of a lasting progression, or it may be an unusual transition which will lead to a new semi-stationary period. Such growth may also represent a blaze of glory preceding a descent into chaos.

It is important to note also that, while the slow growth from 2000 BC to 1500 AD did not create major differences between the Earth's various population groups, the growth begun by capitalist industrialization in Europe took place on a highly unequal basis throughout the world. Some populations became impoverished, while others experienced only moderate growth, often accompanied by a deterioration in living conditions. The population groups at the center of industrialization multiplied their per capita production by a factor ranging from 20 to 35. Growth rates such as these had never before been seen in human history, and brought profound changes for all those involved in the process of industrialization. The deep inequality between different regions of the world today has its historical source in the differential growth inherent to capitalist industrialization.

Growth took place on all fronts: population growth accelerated, while per capita production increased as well. Gross world production was multiplied by a factor of approximately 40 between 2000 BC and 1500 AD (3,500 years), by 3.25 between 1500 and 1820 (320 years), and by close to 37 between 1820 and 2000 (180 years). The growth of this most recent period, which appears "normal" to us, is in fact highly unusual within human history, and even more so within the history of the planet. Never have men extracted, transformed, modified, discharged, and polluted so much.

For a very long period of time, human societies more often than not worked to establish a balance with the surroundings in which they developed. But in some cases man's activity led to imbalance and local or regional destruction: degradation of soil conditions, deforestation, increase of desert lands, and pollution of rivers and waterways lying near population centers. The extent of such imbalance and destruction was closely tied to the number of people involved, as well as the technical abilities and activities of the societies concerned. Destruction was thus limited in scope, and usually led to population migrations.

In today's world, population migrations are less and less possible. The acceleration and globalization of growth processes, along with the increase in the effects of technology, have led to a situation where the effects of imbalance and destruction caused by man's activity are no longer limited to local, regional, river-system, continental, or oceanic levels, but reach planetary dimensions. The effects of resource extraction and industrial waste discharge are evident now on a planetary scale.

Consider world energy production. The world's annual commercial production of energy from primary sources rose from the equivalent of 10.6 million tons of coal in 1800 to 501 million tons in 1890, to 1.335 billion tons in 1913, to 2.496 billion tons in 1950, and reached 10.875 billion tons in 1990.[80] Accelerated growth is evident here, as is the case too with discharge into the atmosphere of products of combustion: annual emissions of CO_2 rose from less than 100 million tons in 1860, to 1 billion tons at the end of World War I through the middle of the 1930s, to around 1.7 billion tons in 1950, 2.5 billion tons in 1965, 5.3 billion tons in 1983, and 5.7 billion tons in 1987.[81] This figure may reach 10 billion tons annually in the year 2010.[82]

Whether it is a question of non-renewable resources, forests, soil, water, air, or the oceans, massive resource extraction and waste product discharge are reaching the limits of what is sustainable for countless micro-systems as well as for the planet as a whole. This is another sign of the world's shift into a new historical period.

It is true that the North, which without a doubt has been and remains the prime instigator of resource extraction, pollution, and environmental damage, has managed to reduce the worst negative environmental effects of industrial capitalism. At the same time, some of the polluting processes have simply been transported to the South. And while technoscientific

TABLE 7.7   World Population and Energy Consumption, 1994 (percent)

	Share of world population	Share of worldwide commercial energy consumption
High-income nations*	14.0	54.0
Middle-income nations†	28.6	30.8
China and India	37.5	12.3
Other low-income nations‡	19.9	2.9

* 24 nations, mainly Western Europe, North America, Japan, and a few other rich countries.
† More than 50 countries, mainly in Latin America, Asia, and the former Soviet bloc.
‡ 49 poor countries, mainly in Africa and Asia.

Source: World Bank, *World Development Report 1996*.

capitalism has reduced industrial pollution, the effects of some of the new technologies, especially those affecting life-forms, give rise to new concerns.

It is clear that, compared to the rich North, the South consumes only slight amounts of energy. If the lifestyle of the West were to extend around the planet, with current levels of technology and with each human being consuming as much energy as an inhabitant of the North, then world annual energy consumption would be multiplied by a factor of four. This would, of course, bring about a proportional increase in local and regional pollution, as well as gases increasing the greenhouse effect. Already, given its current energy consumption, China is the source of acid rains affecting its neighbors, especially Japan. India, likewise, in 1999 produced over the Indian Ocean a huge pollution cloud which threatens to disturb the climate throughout southern Asia.

For the present and for the next several decades, it is the South, with its huge populations and demographic growth rates, its industrialization and urbanization, its production and consumption increases, and its movement toward an agriculture relying on massive amounts of chemical fertilizers and pesticides, which will be the source of industrial era pollution.

We are confronting problems which affect the entire planet. The ramifications of these problems are difficult to forecast, often because the problems contain multiple levels of interaction. Given this situation, the principle of prudence should weigh more heavily than the commercial interests of a few corporations, a few countries, or the interests of a few million, or even a few hundred million, consumers. Unless some sort of sustainable development is established, we will face a lasting crisis between man and the environment. Signs of this crisis are present in shortages of potable water, in the shrinkage of cultivable land, in deforestation, in the advance of deserts, and in the various sorts of pollution, especially chemical and radioactive, which threaten health through air, water, and food-chain pathways. The crisis between man and the planet will worsen the difficulties already facing many of the poor and emerging countries, and will increase tensions between countries and between regions.

The rich countries of the North should bring their own needs under control. They should curb their wastefulness, and should above all bring their own lifestyles, production, and growth into sustainable balance with the Earth and its resources. At the same time, they should aid access to sustainable, modern technology for countries undergoing modernization and industrialization. If this is not done, the North will become guilty of a new category of crime: crime against the Earth, against those who are destitute, and against future generations.

At Rio, in 1992, or in the following years, a different direction should have been taken. Having at their disposal the world's main financial, industrial, technological, and scientific resources, the high-income countries should have expended the effort needed to research and promote the least damaging forms of energy and resource utilization. They should have developed a decades-long worldwide strategy for developing equipment made from energy-efficient, "clean" materials. The rich countries should have paid for the major portion of the cost of such development, either as compensation for damage they had already caused to the planet, or simply because of their greater financial reserves.

Instead of this scenario, a very different one continues to be played out: government leaders, as well as the directors of the huge corporations and the leading world organizations, have demonstrated neither the necessary vision nor courage.

What is needed today is to embark upon the alternative described above, as quickly and as thoroughly as possible, before more damage is done. We have the means to accomplish this goal. Twice within the twentieth century our nations managed, in only a few months, to mobilize 40 percent of productive capacity, toward war. Why would we not be able to mobilize half of our productive capacity now, for the future of the Earth, for life, for mankind? Yet, to accomplish such a task would require stepping beyond the selfishness, the irresponsibility, and the a-cracy which currently dominate the world.

BEYOND INDUSTRIAL CAPITALISM:
THE EMERGENCE OF TECHNOSCIENTISTIC CAPITALISM

The transition from agrarian society to modern industrial society occurred over a very long period. The effects of this transition profoundly affected the post-Second World War policies of countries in the Communist bloc as well as in the third world.

At the same time, however, a new movement was gathering steam within the leading edge of industrial society. During the 1930s and 1940s Colin Clark drew attention to the growing importance of the "tertiary," service sector of the economy.[83] Among the 16 nations of the Organization for Economic Cooperation and Development, the OECD, the share of tertiary employment within employment as a whole rose from 24.3 percent in 1870 to 38.7 percent in 1950, 53.4 percent in 1973, and 63.5 percent in 1987.[84] In the U.S., where this transition took place more rapidly than anywhere else, tertiary sector employment, which represented 17 percent of total employment in 1850, rose to 77 percent by 1992, and accounted for 70 percent of gross domestic product in 1991.[85] In France, more than two-thirds of the workers employed in 1991 worked in the tertiary sector, and this sector accounted for 71 percent of France's gross domestic product in 1997.[86] In France as well as in the U.S., the growth of the tertiary sector was the major component of the overall economic growth in the 1990s.[87]

However, the economies of the advanced countries are not adequately described by invoking the growth of the tertiary sector alone. If one examines the list of countries where the service sector accounts for more than 60 percent of gross domestic product, one finds not only the U.S., most of the nations of Europe, Japan, Hong Kong, and Singapore; one finds also nations such as Argentina, Bolivia, Colombia, Costa Rica, Croatia, Jordan, Mexico, Senegal, and Uruguay.[88] It is necessary to distinguish traditional service work from the new tertiary economic activity,[89] and also to take into account new tertiary employment within industry and agriculture. But this approach may not sufficiently emphasize the heart of the transformation now taking place: the growing importance of technoscience within all the dynamic sectors of capitalist production.

Reflecting in reverse the rise of the tertiary sector, entire branches of industry active in Western Europe and North America during the nineteenth and the first half of the twentieth centuries have declined, disappeared, moved elsewhere, or have been radically changed. Between 1950 and 1987, the proportion of industrial employment within total employment fell in Belgium from 46.8 percent to 27.7 percent, in Holland from 40.2 percent to 26.3 percent, and in Great Britain from 46.5 percent to 29.8 percent.[90] This transformation, which was felt throughout the West following 1973, expresses the beginning of the eclipse of industrial capitalism, and with it, of the working class, of workers' trade unionism, and certain forms of social conflict and social relations. At the same time, the idea of socialism, which had developed in the struggle against industrial capitalist exploitation, has also begun to fade, though its founding ideals of solidarity, equality, social justice, and fraternity survive. This conception of socialism held the working class as the prime force moving toward human emancipation, and the proletariat as the messiah of modern times.

The priority accorded to industry, which for so long had been at the center of the Communist project, has crumbled along with Communism. Yet industry continues to progress widely throughout the ex-third world, spearheaded by multinational corporations, entrepreneurial effort, or by national states. Though the rate of industrial development present in the 1970s has slowed in many countries of South America, Africa, and the Middle East, in Asia it has continued at a brisk pace. In the unabashedly capitalist countries of Southeast Asia and in the "four dragons," industry has progressed with open state support, while in China it has developed under the cover of "market socialism." From 1980 to 1997, the contribution of industry to gross domestic product rose from 49 percent to 51 percent in China, from 26 percent to 30 percent in India, from 40 percent to 43 percent in Korea, from 38 percent to 46 percent in Malaysia, and from 29 percent to 40 percent in Thailand, while remaining steady at 42 percent in Indonesia.[91] Nonetheless, on a world scale, the tide is turning. Debates proliferate in numerous directions: on deindustrialization;[92] on the emergence of "postindustrial society";[93] the neo-industrial economy;[94] the "hyper-industrial" economy;[95] the service economy;[96] the invisible economy;[97] the immaterial economy;[98] the information economy;[99] and the knowledge economy.[100] Peter Drucker goes so far as to glimpse the end of capitalism in his view of current transformations.[101] For him, knowledge is in the process of substituting itself for capital; a new socioeconomic reality is replacing capitalism.

We disagree with this view. We believe that capitalism is more powerful than ever, and that we are witnessing the opening of a new age of capitalism, in which corporations use technoscience to develop new products and new schemes, and in which a competitive struggle to create monopoly persists on a permanent basis.

Beyond the transition from industry to the tertiary sector, the essential process now taking place is the relative retreat of industrial capitalism—characterized by heavy investment in plant and equipment infrastructure and by massive energy inputs—at the same time as "postindustrial" capitalism gains ground. This postindustrial capitalism relies on the advances and potential of science and technology; by orienting research and development toward the invention of future needs and forms of consumption, it may be called a "technoscientistic" capitalism.[102] Some writers have interpreted current developments in terms of a third industrial revolution, or of a new scientific and technical revolution.[103] Richta claims the scientific and technical revolution to be the origin of an approaching change which will overcome the opposition between capitalism and socialism. In our view, capitalism's grip on scientific and technological development is an essential part of its current "leap forward," and of its recent victory in the countries having statist economies.

Similarly, some writers have interpreted contemporary developments as an entry into a new technological age.[104] While this approach illuminates certain aspects of the process, we believe the central dynamic lies in the submission of technoscience to the huge capitalist corporations, who then make use of it for their own ends.[105]

The powerful capitalist corporations provide the major impetus which calls into play new scientific and technical knowledge, in domains such as material handling, energy, life-forms, electromagnetic communication, and data storage and transmission. The effects of scientific knowledge are visible in every economic sector, from agriculture to transportation, and in various tertiary sectors such as health, culture, leisure, and administration. Huge technoscientistic systems—conceived and staffed by groups which each control a different side of the technoscientistic whole—then create and develop new markets and new commodities (products, materials, services) which are themselves produced by scientifically based technical knowledge. The way we live and the way our societies function are both profoundly affected by this process. The underlying dynamic remains dominated by the search for a profit which will assure the enlarged reproduction of capital. The dynamic is dominated as well by social logics which, more than ever, unceasingly project themselves toward the future.

At the heart of technoscientistic capitalism lies a new commodity, which is no longer a material product able to be used on its own, nor a simple service. The new commodity is complex and is composed of material products and services (software programs, subscriptions to networks, various connecting contracts) which could be purchased separately but would be useless without the other pieces. Linked together by a combination of technologies controlled and constantly updated by a small number of corporations, the new commodities are embedded into networks and systems which impose their own procedures and norms.

The "technical macro-systems" of the industrial era (electricity, railroads, telecommunications, air transport) opened the door in this direction.[106] The new networks and systems are based on technoscience, and are thus entirely dependent on the companies and huge corporations which themselves control technoscience.[107]

The process we are describing involves also a new phase of the division of labor and of commodification, which henceforth affects all activity involving the well-being of humankind, business progress, the functioning of information and decision-making systems, as well as the management of political issues, urban systems, the environment, and even nature. In all these areas there is a proliferation of increasingly specific and refined activities, a proliferation characterized by skilled living labor making use of diversified technological means. Within the advanced domains of research, knowledge, and technology, such activities are undertaken and controlled by large corporations which deal in communication, information, multimedia, biotechnology, space technology, leisure management, the antipollution market, etc.

Being on the crest of this new capitalism means mastering the new technological advances or the combination of these advances. Two strategic domains intersect: the domain of the mother technologies (computerization, telecommunications, biotechnology, especially genetic engineering, and material science, etc.), and the domain of their combination, conceived for markets in which expressed or potential solvent demand exists (space technology, globalized information and multimedia, health, anti-pollution, etc.). Within each of these domains, only the largest corporations (tied to powerful states), acting together with other highly specialized companies, are in a position to set into motion, master, and direct technoscience for the conception and production of new systems and their associated commodities. For the new productive process, and the new technological competition within which it takes place, require ever greater investment toward research, equipment, and training. Consequently, in each strategic sector a small number of corporations dominate.[108] Concentration has increased during the 1990s in nearly all these sectors, and agreements, alliances, and trade-offs take place within each pole of the Triad, and within the Triad as a whole.

Any country attempting to remain on the leading edge of this generalized capitalism must master the new technological advances. Technology's

TABLE 7.8   World Spending for Research and Development
at the Close of the 1990s

	% of worldwide R&D spending	R&D spending as % of GDP
North America	37.9	2.5
Western Europe	28.0	1.8
Japan and NICs of Asia	18.6	2.3
China	4.9	0.5
Former Soviet republics	2.5	1.0
India and Central Asia	2.2	0.6
Oceania	1.3	1.5
Central and Eastern Europe	0.9	0.8
Other nations of ex-third world	3.7	0.3

Source: Drawn from statistics given in a table published as part of an interview with Rémi Barré, director of the Science and Technical Observatory, in *Le Monde*, June 30, 1999.

contribution to Japan's economic growth rose from 20 percent in the 1970s to 40 percent in the period from 1980 to 1985, and to 60 percent from 1986 to 1990.[109] The importance of technology is generally acknowledged in the U.S., where debate focuses mainly on the extent of technology's influence.

Yet, as is evident from the data in Table 7.8, published at the time of the UNESCO conference on "Science in the Twenty-first Century," the three poles of the Triad concentrate more than 80 percent of world spending on research and development; the U.S. alone accounts for about one-third of total spending.[110]

When one examines research and development spending as a percentage of GDP, the U.S. and Japan lead, followed by Western Europe,[111] though the efficiency of Europe's research spending is reduced because it is dispersed throughout several nations.

On a worldwide basis, the only other countries which carry weight for R&D spending are China, India, and the much weakened former Soviet republics.

Within the United States, 70 percent of research and development spending in is controlled by private interests. In France the proportion is around 50 percent. Corporate spending for R&D in the U.S. increased by more than 5 percent per year from 1995 to 1998.[112]

Thus, the large technoscientistic corporations exert force not only on production and the market; they direct research, conceive products, structure systems, create demand, and ultimately determine the lifestyles and form of future society. They pursue these goals, guided only by the target of existing or anticipated money-connected needs. Capitalism's growing control over science can only accelerate the process which continuously projects us toward future needs, and which deepens the worldwide split between those who possess purchasing power and those who do not.

Of course, industrial capitalism has not disappeared with techno-scientistic capitalism's rise. As has always occurred through the stages of human social evolution, the preceding stages—manufacturing and industrial capitalism—become less important, while the new stage—technological capitalism—gains strength. At the same time, the preceding stages, and, more generally, the earlier forms of production, are reshaped: in the same way that agriculture and domestic life were profoundly transformed by the innovating power of industrial capitalism, all social activities—domestic life, agriculture, transport, industry, health care, and information—will be deeply changed by the innovating power of technoscientistic capitalism.

Consider, too, the breadth of activity of successive stages. While manufacturing capitalism applied itself primarily to textile production, industrial capitalism widened its scope to the production of a highly diversified range of material goods. Technoscientistic capitalism finds application in practically every domain, anywhere a combination of scientific knowledge, material goods, services, and technical know-how are able to satisfy a money-based need. In this sense, with the rise of technoscientistic capitalism, we are witnessing a widening and a universalization of capitalism's field of activity.

Thus, more than ever, capitalism dominates the world and its societies. A merchant economy and mercantile capitalism arose in Europe from the fourteenth through the sixteenth centuries. Manufacturing capitalism came in the seventeenth and eighteenth centuries, and was followed by industrial capitalism in the nineteenth and twentieth centuries. The twenty-first century promises to be the century of technoscientistic capitalism. Though we are far from having understood all its ramifications, this new stage of capitalism is a fundamental element of the "great transition" we are currently living through.

CHANGES WITHOUT END

An astonishing range of pronouncements has dealt with the diverse and contradictory dynamics of capitalism:

—From reflections ranging from the division of labor and the market to studies on the accumulation of capital.

—From studies of the industrial crises of the nineteenth century to debates about crises in the twentieth.

—From the possibility of a steady-state economy, or long-term stagnation, to a vision of economic waves taking place over centuries.

—From the ever-epeated analysis of cycles to theoretical modeling of growth.

—From the recurring talk about economic miracles to apocalyptic announcements about the return of a great depression.

So much has been said that we end by forgetting what is essential: capitalism is dynamic. It is in constant motion and is constantly regenerating itself. The appearance of capitalism marks a break with all previous history. Marx and Engels emphasized this break in 1848, in *The Communist Manifesto*:

> The bourgeoisie cannot exist without constantly revolutionizing the instruments of production, and thereby the relations of production, and with them the whole relations of society.... Constant revolutionizing of production, uninterrupted disturbance of all social conditions, everlasting uncertainty and agitation distinguish the bourgeois epoch from all earlier ones. All fixed, fast-frozen relations ... are swept away, all new-formed ones become antiquated before they can ossify. All that is solid melts into air, all that is holy is profaned....[113]

In his *Theory of Economic Evolution*, Joseph Schumpeter in 1912 also insisted on the significance of the historic break which capitalism inaugurates. Whereas all previous societies were based on repeating cycles—the cycle of the seasons, the cycle of good and bad years—capitalism's dynamic economy depends on constant innovation. Inseparable from the character of the entrepreneur, as well as from the search for profit and credit, such innovation destroys the past while preparing its own future.

As we have noted, during the last two centuries, production has massively increased, as have energy and technical capacities. Ways of producing, consuming, of moving about, of communicating, and of living in general have constantly evolved, and have undergone even more marked change during recent decades.

Of course, not all the changes visible over the past few centuries are due to capitalism alone. The desires for possession, power, knowledge, and useful action have all been a part of human life since time immemorial. Rational thinking and knowledge, instituted power, and commitment to values and ideals have been part of our lives for several thousand years.

Within recent centuries, the three main forces for change have been state power, scientific and technical knowledge, and the group of dynamics described by the term "capitalism." However, in the last few decades, state powers have been weakened twice over: by their loss of visions and projects for the future, and by liberal globalization. Similarly, scientific work is increasingly mobilized and directed by giant corporations which control the essential technological processes. In this situation, capitalism has become the primary force transforming our societies and the world as a whole.

In a way, the previous half-century of Soviet history illustrates our argument from an opposing position. The Soviet regime elevated the role of state power to an extreme level, while placing an extraordinary emphasis on science and technology. Together, these two forces made significant advances in several areas, especially nuclear weaponry and space technology. Yet in the race toward growth and permanent innovation (consumption, armaments, data, etc.) the Soviet regime was overwhelmed by the dominant capitalisms, which were supported by their own states and by scientific research.

We return then once again to the evolving and ceaselessly self-transforming reality designated by the word "capitalism."

The logic of capitalism was not constructed or instituted by any one agency. As was the case with other social logics and other social orders, capitalism developed and matured within history. Though it emerged out of mercantile logic and the dynamics of wealth, capitalism cannot be reduced to either one of these alone. The specific character of capitalism lies in the fact that the surplus acquired through production and trade is applied to expanding the means of production and trade in order to extract an additional surplus. Production or trade for profit; profit for accumulation; accumulation for new production or new trade … as well as increased profit. This is the continuous progression at the heart of all capitalist reality. In a word: the search for profit as a way to expand the field of profitable activity.

However, accumulation-for-profit is not the complete picture. Accumulation—shrouded within the circulation of commodities, stimulated by competition *and* by the quest for monopoly, and continuously supported by entrepreneurial innovation—gives rise to and nourishes a complex abundance of transforming dynamics. The establishment of a trading or producing activity; borrowing and credit; investment; innovation, research and development; activity affecting needs or the expression of needs: all these initiatives linked to the reproduction of capital are a wager about the future, and thus help produce the future. These initiatives transform the economy, man, and society.

Complex and oriented toward the future, the capitalist logic gives rise to ceaseless transformations. Some of these transformations concern the three fundamental human motivations—power, possession, and subsistence—which are sources of both separation and coherence.[114] On one side is visible the search after wealth and profit, power over other people, the concentration of capital, the dominating positions and the power of monopolies. On the other side lies subsistence, which, for an ever-increasing proportion of people, requires dependent employment, wage-labor, and the purchase of consumer goods which have been produced by capitalist machinery.

Thus, in its widest meaning, capitalism cannot be reduced either to a "mode of production,"[115] or to an "economic system."[116] And capitalism is not an actor capable of willing, planning, or choosing. At its heart, and through its various historical forms, transitions, and mutations, a complex social logic is at work. This logic is both structuring and destructuring, destructive and creative. The social logic of capitalism destroys other productive forms, and destroys formerly existing activities, social forms, and resources. At the same time, this logic creates new activities, new markets, and new needs. It gives rise to a totality which is simultaneously productive, trade-based, and monetary. This totality is both territorialized and worldwide, and is in a state of constant change; in addition, it demonstrates an increasing autonomy relative to the societies in which it has been formed. This is the totality we call "capitalism."

A growing proportion of the transformations which have taken place in Europe since the sixteenth century, as well as the bulk of changes which have taken place in the world since the nineteenth century, may be explained through the development of the reality of capitalism. And capitalism lies behind the breadth, increase, and acceleration of changes currently being experienced by societies throughout the world.

A century after Marx, Schumpeter emphasized in 1942 the importance of the "creative destruction" rooted within the dynamics of innovation:

> The fundamental drive which sets in motion, and maintains in movement, the capitalist machine is imparted to the new objects of consumption, the new methods of production and transport, the new markets, and the new kinds of industrial organization. These are all elements created by capitalist initiative.... This process of *Creative Destruction* constitutes the fundamental fact of capitalism.[117]

This capacity has today been multiplied many times over by the giant corporations' systematic use of science and research to help them create "new objects of consumption," "new methods of production and transport," "new markets," and "new kinds of industrial organization." To this list I would add: new money-connected demands based on new, or constantly renewed, needs. All these factors create new opportunities to make a profit on the basis of scientific advances.

Through their increasing control of scientific research and its applications, the huge corporations have vastly multiplied their creative and destructive potential. This is the source of the whirlwind-like changes affecting us all.

But what is at stake is not a cartoon or a video game. What is being played with here is mankind's life on the Earth.

For the first time in history, fundamental decisions affecting man, life, and the Earth are being made by corporations possessing enormous financial, scientific, technical, and industrial resources. These decisions are made with an eye on populations possessing purchasing power. The needs of these populations are anticipated, but not, of course, passively. Corporate decisions are based on the expectation and possibility of profit within the coming year or next few years.

Is it legitimate that the most important resources and effort of the world are directed toward the satisfaction of a minority of the planet's inhabitants, while another minority lives tenuously and in destitution?

Is it legitimate that satisfying the needs, for a few generations, of that proportion of humanity who possess purchasing power should threaten the resources and fundamental stability of our planet, to the point where the interests of future generations are irreversibly harmed?

Is it acceptable that choices which involve the future of the Earth and human society should be abandoned to deciding agencies which possess either a very restricted vision (a market or a slice of a market) or a short-sighted vision (the expectation of more or less short-term profit)?

We posed these same questions in a recent book.[118] Insofar as we are members of the human race, we all share responsibility for the world today, as well as for the effects of our actions on the world of tomorrow.

Confronting the accelerating spiral of changes in which we are all caught, our own effort is to travel in the direction marked out by Hans Jonas. Taking into account technology and the impact of technology, as well as "the orders of magnitude of long term actions, including the possibility they are irreversible," Jonas states emphatically: "All these factors place the idea of responsibility at the very center of ethics."[119] Yet, in order to carry out such responsibility, "what can serve as a guide?" he asks. His response: "the anticipation of the threat itself!" This is what Jonas describes as "the heuristics of fear."[120]

What then appears indispensable to Jonas (and the developments we have described give added weight to this sense of necessity) is the "Principle of Responsibility," by which he means that "in the enduring ambivalence of his freedom, which no possible change in circumstances could ever abolish, the integrity of man's world and his essence will be protected against the abuse of his own powers."[121]

Yet today we observe the exact opposite: misusing their potential, the powers which dominate human society threaten the integrity of man as well as the integrity of the world. The dynamics of capitalism contribute greatly to this process. Before time runs out, these dynamics must be restrained, as they have been during other periods, not only at the national level, but at the level of the continents and the world.

Otherwise, we face the massive destruction of resources and the balances of the Earth, the totalitarianism of a market dominated by a handful of giant global corporations, and the growing establishment on a planetary scale of a money-based apartheid. Such conditions threaten to become the lasting contours of a historical shift that will be increasingly difficult to control.

NOTES

INTRODUCTION

1. A great Austrian economist, Schumpeter was Finance Minister in Austria, a banker, a professor at Harvard, and published several major works.
2. J. Schumpeter, *Capitalism, Socialism and Democracy* (London: Allen & Unwin, 1942. *Capitalisme, socialisme et démocratie* (Paris: Payot, 1984), pp. 89, 223.
3. M. Beaud, "L'Avènement du système étatiste," *Le Monde diplomatique*, August 1985.
4. [*Trans. Note*: "Liberal" is used throughout in the French sense of advocating "free-market" policies, with minimized State intervention.]
5. The great French historian Fernand Braudel stated this position emphatically: "The worst error is ... to maintain that capitalism is an 'economic system' alone, while in fact it lives as part of the entire social metabolism, and is, whether as adversary or accomplice, on equal terms (or nearly equal terms) with the State, a weighty actor if there ever was one. All this has been true since capitalism's beginnings. And not only this: capitalism benefits as well from all the support which culture brings to the solidity of the social structure ...; capitalism contains the dominant classes, which, by defending it, defend themselves" (F. Braudel, *Civilisation matérielle, économie et capitalisme. XVe–XVIIIe siècle* [Paris: A. Colin, 1979], vol. III, *Le Temps du monde*, p. 540).
6. I. Wallerstein, "Les Etats dans le vortex institutionnel de l'économie-monde capitaliste," *Revue internationale de sciences sociales* 32, no. 4 (1980), pp. 797–805.
7. I systematically described this process in *Le Système national/mondial hiérarchisé (une nouvelle lecture du capitalisme mondial)* [*The Hierarchical Natiional/World System: a new interpretation of world capitalism*] (Paris: La Découverte, 1987).
8. See the present work, Chapter 7, section 2, part 4.
9. See the present work, Chapter 7, section 2, part 5.
10. See F. Fukuyama, *The End of History and the Last Man* (New York: Free Press, 1992); M. Beaud, *Le Basculement du monde. De la Terre, des Hommes et du capitalisme* (Paris: La Découverte, 1997); and the present work, Chapter 7, section 2, part 1.
11. R. Bonnaud, *Y a-t-il des Tournants historiques mondiaux?* (Paris: Kimé, 1992).
12. [*Trans.*] Beaud's term "basculement," from the verb "basculer," "to sway or topple over," has no exact equivalent in English. The author relies heavily on this word here and in Chapter 7, as well as in his 1997 book, *Le Basculement du Monde*,

where the word furnishes the key idea. We have generally translated the word as "the accelerating transformation of the contemporary world."

CHAPTER 1

1. See, for example, Herbert Heaton, *Histoire économique de L'Europe* (Paris: Armand Colin, 1952), vol. 1, p. 194. Heaton dates at 1450 the beginning of what he calls the "economic renewal."

2. "The rich man with his reserves, by keeping the poor man from starving without himself being put out, could he demand as reimbursement more than he had advanced? This would be making time pay, which, as opposed to space, was said to be the thing of God and not of men." (Georges Bataille, *La Part maudite, précédé de la notion de dépense* [Paris: Minuit, 1967], p. 166.)

3. Henri Denis, *Histoire de la pensée économique* (Paris: PUF, 1966), p. 82.

4. Adam Smith, *An Enquiry into the Nature and Causes of the Wealth of Nations* (1776; New York: Random House, 1937), pp. 528–29, cited in Andre Gunder Frank, *World Accumulation, 1492–1789* (New York: Monthly Review Press, 1978), p. 41.

5. Heaton, *Histoire économique*, pp. 197, 208. Using terms such as "the European expansion" or "the economic effects of the discoveries," Heaton brings together some useful material.

6. *The Log of Christopher Columbus' First Voyage to America the Year 1492*, quoted in Edwardo Galeano, *Open Veins of Latin America* (New York: Monthly Review Press, 1973), p. 24.

7. Cited in Frank, *World Accumulation*, p. 42.

8. Ramón Carande, a witness of this time, wrote: "Spain is like the mouth that receives the food and chews it only to send it immediately to the other organs, without retaining more than a passing taste or a few crumbs that accidentally stick to its teeth.... " Cited in Frank, *World Accumulation*, p. 51.

9. This was the first surge of peasants driven off of their land, of whom Thomas More wrote in *Utopia* (1516): "They leave their familiar hearths and can find no place where they may settle down. They sell their household goods, which would not bring much even if they could wait for a buyer, for little or nothing. When that little money is gone (and it will soon be spent), what is left for them to do but steal and so be hanged, doubtless justly, or to go about begging? And if they beg, they are thrown into prison as idle vagabonds. They would willingly work, but can find no one who will hire them." (Thomas More, *Utopia*, trans. H. V. S. Ogden [New York: Appleton-Century-Crofts, 1949], p. 10.)

10. J. Bodin, *Response to the Paradoxes of M. de Malestroit, Regarding the Increasing Expense of Everything*, 1568.

11. See P. Deyon, *Le Mercantilisme* (Paris: Flammarion, 1969), pp. 19ff.

12. *A Compendious, or Brief Examination of Certain Ordinary Complaints*, written in 1549 and published in 1581, no author given, cited in J.-Y. Le Branchu, *Écrits notable sur la monnaie* (Paris: Alcan, 1934), vol. II, p. 188. The British gentleman John Hales expressed similar ideas in his *Discourse of the Commonweal of this Realm of England*, also written in 1549 and first published in 1581 (Cambridge: The University Press, 1929).

13. More, *Utopia*, p. 25.

14. In tributary modes of production the subjection of a large productive mass of peasants or craftsmen allows for the imposition of a tribute, thanks to which an oligarchy possessing arms and controlling religion is able to live in ease, sometimes

even in luxury; this is the case in slave, feudal, Asiatic, and African modes of production. See, for example, Samir Amin, *Class and Nation, Historically and in the Current Crisis* (New York: Monthly Review Press, 1980).

15. Fernand Braudel, *Civilisation matérielle. Economie et Capitalisme* (Paris: Armand Colin, 1980), vol. III, *Le Temps du monde*, p. 18.

16. Immanuel Wallerstein and Andre Gunder Frank, among others, take this position, referring to Marx's statements in *Capital* that "the modern history of capital dates from the creation in the 16th century of a world-embracing commerce and a world-embracing market" (Moscow: Progress Publishers, 1954, p. 146) and that "although we come across the first beginnings of capitalist production as early as the 14th or 15th century, sporadically, in certain towns of the Mediterranean, the capitalist era dates from the 16th century" (ibid., p. 715). See, for example, Frank, *World Accumulation*, p. 256.

17. Cited in *Histoire générale des civilisations*, 7 vols. (Paris: PUF, 1953–56), vol. IV, p. 153.

18. Annual averages; Pierre and H. Chaunu, *Seville et l'Atlantique*, 1959, cited in Pierre Léon, *Economie et Sociétés pré-industrielles* (Paris: Armand Colin, 1970), vol. II, p. 32.

19. Artistic production flourished at the beginning of the century, however, with Cervantes (*Don Quixote*, 1605, and *New Examples*, 1613) and El Greco (*Assumption of the Virgin*, 1614) and later on with Lope de Vega and Calderón, Velasquez, and Murillo.

20. *Histoire générale des civilisations*, vol. III, p. 245.

21. Amsterdam largely profited from the destruction and decline of Antwerp, taken by the Spanish in 1585. The bourgeois of Amsterdam chose not to take back Belgium for fear of the competition Antwerp would give them once it was Dutch. See Heaton, *Histoire économique* and Violet Barbour, *Capitalism in Amsterdam in the Seventeenth Century* (Baltimore: Johns Hopkins Press, 1950). Information on the Bank of Amsterdam is taken from *Histoire universelle*, 3 vols. (Paris: Pléiade, 1958), vol. III, pp. 133–34.

22. Heaton, *Histoire économique*. The reader may imagine from Heaton's very "proper" expressions what the situation of these crews must have been.

23. As cited in Deyon, *Le Mercantilisme*, pp. 93–94.

24. Roland Marx, *L'Angleterre des révolutions* (Paris: Armand Colin, 1971), p. 87. Against these privileges and regulations, protests soon were raised; thus at the Long Parliament, Sir John Colepepper became indignant: "It is a pack of vermin which is crawling over the country. I mean the monopolists.... " (cited in *Histoire générale des civilisations*, vol. IV, p. 298).

25. Thomas Mun, *England's Treasure by Foreign Trade* (London, 1664), pp. 88, 71–72.

26. Hales, *Discourse of the Commonweal*, p. 15.

27. Barrington Moore, *The Social Origins of Dictatorship and Democracy* (Boston: Beacon, 1966), p. 23.

28. *The Leveller Tracts*, 1647–1653, ed. William Haller and Godfrey Davies (New York: Columbia University Press, 1944), pp. 151–53.

29. *La Lumière brillant dans le Buckinghamshire*, cited in *Histoire générale du socialisme*, 3 vols. (Paris: PUF, 1972), vol. I, p. 98.

30. "The Clothier's Delight, or the rich Men's Joy, and the poor Men's Sorrow, wherein is exprest the Craftiness and Subtility of many Clothiers in England, by beating down their Workmen's Wages," in P. Mantoux, *The Industrial Revolution in the 18th Century* (London, 1928), pp. 76–78.

31. John Locke, *Two Treatises of Government*, ed. Peter Laslett (Cambridge: The University Press, 1967), p. 430.

32. Ibid., pp. 351, 354.
33. Ibid., pp. 430, 433.
34. Sir Dudley North, *Difcourfes upon Trade, Principally Directed to the Cases of the Interest, Coynage, Clipping, Increase of Money,* 1691, in J. R. McCulloch, ed., *A Selected Collection of Early English Tracts on Commerce* (London, 1856), pp. 513, 514, 537, 540.
35. *Histoire générale des civilisations,* vol. IV.
36. He is quite explicit about the unity of economics and politics: "We can strongly affirm, against the opinion of Aristotle and Xenophon, that one cannot divide economics from politics without dismembering the principal part of the Whole, and that the science of acquiring goods, as they called it, is common to republics as well as to families." See Denis, *Histoire de la pensée économique,* p. 89.
37. Richelieu, *Memoirs* (1627), cited in Deyon, *Le Mercantilisme,* pp. 94–95.
38. Architectural signs of the period were the "arcs de triomphe" of the gate of Saint-Denis (1673) and the gate of Saint-Martin (1674), the colonnade of the Louvre (1667–74), and the Place des Victoires with the statue of Louis XIV (1686).
39. Jean-Baptiste Colbert, *Lettres, mémoires, et instructions,* cited in Deyon, *Le Mercantilisme,* pp. 100, 101.
40. *Histoire universelle,* vol. III, p. 142.
41. "Commerce," wrote Colbert, "is the source of finances, and finances are the sinews of war."
42. Cited in Deyon, *Le Mercantilisme,* pp. 102–03.
43. Boisguilbert, *Le Factum de la France,* 1707, cited in Denis, *Histoire de la pensée économique,* pp. 135–36.
44. Strong and conquering, Dutch capitalism was worldwide and followed free-trade doctrines. Forced to affirm itself, English capitalism was nationalist and protectionist; once allied, the monarchy and the bourgeoisie instituted mercantilist policies; after having obtained the first important successes, the free-trade and liberal ideas emerged. A sequence of the same kind occurred in France a half century later.

CHAPTER 2

1. The value of French foreign trade grew by a factor of 3.2 between the first five-year period following the death of Louis XIV (1716–20) and that of 1751–55; then it doubled between the latter period and 1778–89. The share of foreign trade within market production as a whole grew from 10 percent to 20 or 25 percent (J. Marczewski, "Some aspects of economic growth," *Economic Development and Cultural Change* 8, no. 3, p. 372). English foreign trade doubled between 1700–09 and 1750–59, and then multiplied 2.6 times between the latter period and 1795–1804 (Phyllis Deane and William A. Cole, *British Economic Growth 1688–1959* [New York: Cambridge University Press, 1969], p. 48). France saw a two-thirds increase in market production between 1701–10 and 1781–90, while considered at constant prices, the English national revenue went from £50 million in 1688 to £134 million in 1770, and £139 million in 1798 (Paul Bairoch, *Révolution industrielle et Sous-Développement* [Paris: CEDES, 1964], p. 271). Price rises were particularly noticeable in European agricultural products, and less so for "colonial products" and industrial products. See Camille E. Labrousse, *Esquisse du mouvement des prix et des revenus en France au XVIIIᵉ siècle* (Paris: Dalloz, 1932)

and William Beveridge, *Causes and Cures of Unemployment* (1931; New York: AMS Press, 1976).

2. European population grew from 120 million at the beginning of the century to around 190 million at the end of the century (*Histoire universelle*, 3 vols. [Paris: Pléiade, 1958], vol. III, p. 234). Wealth in circulation grew in France from 731 million francs in 1715 to 2 billion francs in 1788 (Pierre Léon, *Economies et Sociétés pré-industrielles* [Paris: Armand Colin, 1970], vol. II, p. 202).

3. Of all legal sugar imports to the mother countries these three countries enjoyed the following (annual averages in thousands of tons):

	FRANCE	ENGLAND	PORTUGAL	TOTAL
1741–45	65	41	34	150
1766–70	78	74	20	193

(Richard Sheridan, *The Development of the Plantations to 1950: An Era of West Indian Prosperity* [London: Ginn, 1970], pp. 22–23, cited in Andre Gunder Frank, *World Accumulation, 1492–1789* [New York: Monthly Review Press, 19781, p. 121.)

4. According to Simonson, 7 million slaves were transported to Brazil alone between 1700 and 1850; according to Frank Pitman, 2.1 million Africans were imported to the British colonies of America (the thirteen colonies and the Antilles) between 1680 and 1786. (See R. Simonson, *Historia económica do Brasil, 1500–1820* [São Paulo, 1962), p. 154, cited in Frank, *World Accumulation*, p. 91; and F. Pitman, *The Development of the British West Indies, 1700–1763* [New Haven, 1917], p. 67, cited in Eric Williams, *Capitalism and Slavery* [New York: Russell & Russell, 1961], p. 33).

5. Samir Amin, *Impérialisme et sous-développement en Afrique* (Paris: Anthropos, 1976).

6. Between 1700 and 1790 the production of export industries in England grew by a factor of 3.8, while national industries grew by a factor of only 1.4 (Deane and Cole, *British Economic Growth*, p. 59).

7. As tea drinking became popular in England in the eighteenth century tea imports multiplied by seventy in volume, though only by sixteen in value, because of the fall in price (Léon, *Economies et Sociétés*, p. 186).

8. Quoted by Henri Sée, *Modern Capitalism, Its Origin and Evolution* (New York, 1928), p. 28, cited in Williams, *Capitalism and Slavery*, p. 55.

9. L. A. Harper, "The Effect of the Navigation Acts on the Thirteen Colonies," cited in Frank, *World Accumulation*.

10. M. Vauban, *An Essay for a General Tax, or a Project for a Royal Tythe*, 1710, pp. iii–iv.

11. The entire nobility was estimated by Father Coyer in 1756 at 80,000 families, that is, around 400,000 persons. The major portion of them lived in ease on their estates, though some of them lived in poverty (Henri Sée, *La France économique et sociale au XVIIIe siècle* [Paris: Armand Colin, 1925]). Depending on the region, they owned between 11 percent and 40 percent of the land.

12. Sée, *La France*, pp. 36–37. See also *Histoire générale des civilisations*, 7 vols. (Paris: PUF, 1953–56), vol. V, p. 132 and *Histoire universelle*, 3 vols. (Paris: Pléiade, 1958), vol. III.

13. Cited by Sée, *La France*, p. 139.

14. *Registre paroissial de Lain* (Yonne), cited in *Les écrivains témoins du peuple* (Paris: Ed. j'ai lu, 1964), p. 67.

15. Cited in ibid., p. 89.

16. *Histoire générale des civilisations*, vol. V, p. 11.

17. Some of these were materialists and atheists: La Mettrie, *L'Homme machine* (1747), Helvétius, *De l'esprit* (1758); Baron d'Holbach, *Système de la nature* (1770); Diderot,

Pensées philosophiques (1746), *Lettre sur les aveugles* (1758). Other points of reference: Voltaire, *Histoire de Charles XII* (1731); *Lettres anglaises* (1734), *Le Siècle de Louis XIV* (1751), *Essai sur les moeurs* (1756), *Dictionnaire philosophique* (1764); Rousseau, *Discours sur les sciences et les arts* (1750), *Discours sur l'origine de l'inégalité* (1754), *Lettre à d'Alembert* (1758), *Le Contrat social* (1762).

18. From Turgot (*Discours sur l'histoire universelle*, 1750) to Condorcet (*Esquisse du tableau des progrès de l'esprit humain*).

19. *Histoire générale des civilisations*, vol. V, p. 75.

20. Montesquieu, *L'Esprit des lois* (1768; Paris: Ed. Garnier, 1949), vol. I, pp. 11–13.

21. Cited in Maxime Leroy, *Histoire des idées sociales en France* (Paris: Gallimard, 1946), vol. I, pp. 127–28.

22. Jean-Jacques Rousseau, *On the Social Contract*, ed. R. D. Masters (New York: St. Martin's, 1978), pp. 46, 50, 53, 56. Rousseau also made a remark upon which our leaders should meditate: "If I were a prince or a legislator, I would not waste my time saying what had to be done, I would do it, or keep silent" (p. 46).

23. Ibid., p. 79.

24. Ibid., p. 85.

25. "The larger the State grows, the less freedom there is" (ibid., p. 80).

26. Cited by Jean-Jacques Chevalier, *Les Grandes Oeuvres politiques de Machiavel à nos jours* (Paris: Armand Colin, 1949), pp. 92–93.

27. The first group includes Morelly, *La Basiliade*, 1753; *Le Code de la Nature*, 1775. As for the second, hasn't it been established for centuries that "God gives life to everyone, and 'the rich gives the poor his living'?" This idea survives today, since the rich "give work" and "create employment."

28. Cited in A. Chabert, "Rousseau économiste," *Revue d'histoire économique et sociale*, no. 3, 1964, p. 349.

29. Cited by A. Lichtenberger, *Le socialisme au XVIIIᵉ siècle* (Paris: Alcan, 1895), p. 147.

30. Jean-Jacques Rousseau, "Discourse on the Origin and Foundation of Inequality," in *The First & Second Discourses*, ed. Roger D. Masters (New York: St. Martin's, 1964), p. 181.

31. Ibid., p. 66.

32. Rousseau, article on "political economy" for *L'Encyclopédie*, cited by Henri Denis, *Histoire de la pensée économique* (Paris: PUF, 1966), p. 233.

33. Father Mably, *Des droits et des devoirs des citoyens*, 1758, cited in *Histoire générale du socialisme*, 3 vols. (Paris: PUF, 1972), vol. I, p. 243.

34. Father Mably, *Doutes proposés aux philosophes économistes sur l'ordre naturel et essentiel des sociétés politiques*, 1968, cited by Denis, *Histoire de la pensée économique*, p. 237.

35. Ibid., cited by Lichtenberger, *Le socialisme*, p. 229.

36. Diderot, *Principes de la philosophie morale*, cited in *Histoire générale du socialisme*, vol. I, p. 159.

37. Helvétius, *De l'homme*, 1772, cited in *Histoire générale du socialisme*, vol. 1, p. 161.

38. Holbach, *Ethnocratie, ou le gouvernement fondé sur la morale*, cited by Lichtenberger, *Le socialisme*, p. 267.

39. *Histoire philosophique des deux Indes*, 1770, cited by Leroy, *Histoire des idées*, p. 236.

40. Linguet, *Théorie des lois civiles*, Amsterdam, 1767, cited by Lichtenberger, *Le socialisme*, pp. 291–96, 303.

41. Linguet, *Lettre sur la théorie des lois civiles*, Amsterdam, 1770, cited by Lichtenberger, *Le socialisme*, p. 293.

42. Linguet, *Réponse aux docteurs modernes*, London, 1771, cited by Lichtenberger, *Le socialisme*, pp. 296–99.

43. Linguet, *Du pain et du blé*, London, 1974, cited by Lictenberger, *Le socialisme*,

p. 300.

44. *Annales*, vol. XIII, 1788, cited by Lichtenberger, *Le socialisme*, pp. 297, 302.

45. Voltaire, cited in Michel Foucault, *Madness and Civilization* (New York: Random House, 1964).

46. Rousseau, "Discourse on the Origin and Foundation of Inequality," p. 154.

47. Sée, *La France*, pp. 34–35.

48. Quesnay, "Grains," 1757, in *François Quesnay et la Physiocratie* (Paris: INED, 1958), vol. 11, 1958, p. 484.

49. "Homme," in ibid., p. 559.

50. Quesnay, *L'Analyse de la formule arithmétique du tableau économique*, 1766, in ibid., pp. 793–94.

51. M. Turgot, *Reflections on the Formation and Distribution of Wealth* (London, 1795), p. 55.

52. M. Turgot, "Questions importantes sur le commerce," 1775, in Turgot, *Textes choisis* (Paris: Dalloz, 1947), p. 106.

53. Turgot, *Reflections*, pp. 63–65.

54. Ibid., p. 65.

55. Ibid., p. 70.

56. Ibid., p. 73.

57. Ibid., p. 106.

58. Turgot, "Fondation," *Encyclopédie*, 1757, reproduced in Turgot, *Textes choisis*, p. 177.

59. Turgot, "Eloge de Vincent de Gournay," 1759, in ibid., p. 147.

60. They were represented by, among others, Mercier de la Rivière, *L'Ordre naturel et essentiel des sociétés politiques*, 1767; Dupont de Nemours, *De l'origine et des progrès d'une science nouvelle*; and Bigot de Sainte-Croix, *Essai sur la liberté du commerce et de l'industrie*, 1775.

61. Cited in Emile Levasseur, *Histoire des classes ouvrières et de l'industrie en France avant 1789* (Paris: A. Rousseau, 1900–01), vol. II, p. 855.

62. Cited in *Histoire économique et sociale de la France*, 6 vols. (Paris: PUF, 1976–80), vol. III, book I, p. 12.

63. Cited in Paul Mantoux, *La Révolution industrielle au XVIIIe siècle* (Paris: Génin, 1969), pp. 123–25. See also T. S. Ashton, *The Industrial Revolution, 1760–1830* (New York: Oxford University Press, 1948).

64. Mantoux, *La Révolution industrielle*, pp. 83–84.

65. Ibid., p. 81.

66. Ashton, *The Industrial Revolution*, p. 131.

67. Eric Williams, *Capitalism and Slavery* (New York: Russell & Russell, 1961), pp. 60–68.

68. Ibid., p. 82, cited in Frank, *World Accumulation*, p. 230.

69. Oliver Goldsmith, *The Deserted Village* (London, 1770), p. 15.

70. Mantoux, *La Révolution industrielle*, pp. 55–56.

71. Ashton, *The Industrial Revolution*, pp. 41–42.

72. Mantoux, *La Révolution industrielle*, p. 430.

73. Ibid., pp. 391–92.

74. The Darbys produced 500–600 tons per year around 1717, and 10,000 to 14,000 tons per year around 1790. Raw imported cotton, for the most part processed in England, rose from 5 million pounds in 1781 to 33 million tons in 1781 and 60 million tons in 1802.

75. Mantoux, *La Révolution industrielle*, pp. 419, 468.

76. David Hume, "Essays on Economics," in *Writings on Economics*, ed. E. Rotwein (Madison: University of Wisconsin Press, 1955), p. 13.

77. Adam Smith, *Theory of Moral Sentiments* (London, 1853), pp. 263–64.

78. Ibid., pp. 264–65.

79. Ibid., p. 265.

80. Adam Smith, *The Wealth of Nations* (New York: Modern Library, 1937), p. 651.

81. Ibid.

82. Ibid., p. 341.

83. Ibid., p. 344. When he speaks of the capital of the farmer, he expresses physiocratic ideas, which he criticizes later on: "No equal capital puts into motion a greater quantity of productive labour than that of the farmer. Not only his labouring servants, but his labouring cattle, are productive labourers. In agriculture too nature labours along with man; and though her labour costs no expence, its produce has its value, as well as that of the most expensive workman" (ibid.).

84. Ibid., p. 464.

85. Ibid., p. 347.

86. Ibid., p. 360.

87. Ibid., p. 128.

88. Ibid., p. 122.

89. Ibid., p. 674.

90. Thomas Paine, *Common Sense* (Philadelphia, 1776), p. 1.

91. Thomas Paine, *The Rights of Man*, Pt. II (London, 1792), pp. 7, 10.

92. See Marx, *Un Chapitre inédit du Capital* (Paris: Union générale d'éditions 10/18), 1971.

CHAPTER 3

1. William Godwin, *Enquiry Concerning Political Justice* (1793; Harmondsworth, Middlesex: Penguin, 1976), pp. 711–12.

2. Ibid., p. 716. The word "industry" is used here in the wide sense, current at the time, of activity or work.

3. Ibid., p. 732.

4. Thomas Robert Malthus, *Population: The First Essay* (Ann Arbor: University of Michigan Press, 1959), pp. 4–5.

5. Thomas Robert Malthus, *Essay on the Principle of Population* (London: John Murray, 1826), pp. 339, 343.

6. Ibid., 1803 ed., pp. 531–32.

7. Jean-Baptiste Say, *Cours complet d'économie politique, 1828–29*, cited by Henri Denis, *Histoire de la pensée économique* (Paris: PUF, 1966), p. 295.

8. David Ricardo, *On the Principles of Political Economy and Taxation*, vol. 1, *The Works and Correspondence of David Ricardo*, ed. Piero Sraffa (Cambridge: The University Press, 1951), pp. 105–06.

9. Say, *Cours complet*, in J. B. Say, *Textes choisis* (Paris: Dalloz, 1953), p. 195.

10. Ibid., p. 194.

11. Frédéric Bastiat, preface to *Harmonies économiques*, 1845, cited in Louis Baudin, *Frédéric Bastiat* (Paris: Dalloz, 1962), p. 24.

12. Frédéric Bastiat, *Jacques Bonhomme*, no. 1 (June 1948), in ibid., p. 161.

13. Bastiat, preface to *Harmonies économiques*, in ibid., p. 19.

14. The *Manifesto of the Equals* was not published at the same time because of two phrases that the Equals as a whole could not agree to: "Let all the arts perish, if necessary, so long as there remains to us real equality"; and "Let them disappear finally, these revolting distinctions between ... governors and governed." Cited in G. M. Braro, *Les socialistes avant Marx*, vol. I (Paris: Maspero, 1970), pp. 65–68.

15. Henri Saint-Simon, *Lettre d'un habitant de Genève à ses contemporains*, 1803.

16. Saint-Simon, *L'Industrie*, 1817–18; *Du système industriel*, 1821; *Henri de Saint-Simon à Messieurs les ouvriers*, 1821; *Nouveau Christianisme*, 1825.

17. See F. Fourier, *Traité de l'association domestique et agricole*, 1822; *Le nouveau monde industriel et sociétaire*, 1829; and *La Fausse industrie morcelée, répugnante, mensongère, et l'antidote, l'industrie naturelle, attrayante, véridique*, 1835–36.

18. See Michel Beaud, *Le Socialisme, à l'épreuve de l'histoire, 1800–1981* (Paris: Seuil, 1980), ch. 7.

19. See L. Le Van-Lemesle, "Les Méthodes de promotion de l'économie politique en France au XIXe siècle," *Recherches et Travaux*, UER d'histoire de Paris I, December 1977.

20. Jean-Baptiste Say, *Catéchisme d'économie politique* (1817; Paris: Mame, 1970), pp. 37, 41, 118.

21. David Ricardo, *Letters 1810–15*; vol. VI, *The Works and Correspondence of David Ricardo*, ed. Piero Sraffa, pp. 247–48.

22. Ricardo, *Principles*, pp. 93, 110.

23. Say, *Catéchisme*, p. 75.

24. David Ricardo, *Letters 1819–1921*, vol. VIII, *The Works and Correspondence of David Ricardo*, ed. Piero Sraffa, p. 171.

25. Ricardo, *Principles*, p. 388.

26. Ibid., p. 396.

27. See J. Marczewski, *Cahiers de L'ISEA*, no. 163 (July 1965), p. xlviii.

28. See T. J. Markovitch, *Cahiers de L'ISEA*, no. 179 (November 1966), p. 287.

29. *The Cambridge Economic History of Europe* (New York and Cambridge: Cambridge University Press, 1965), vol. VII, p. 141; and Phyllis Deane and William A. Cole, *British Economic Growth, 1688–1959* (New York and Cambridge: Cambridge University Press, 1969), pp. 106, 145.

30. A. G. Kenwood and A. L. Lougheed, *The Growth of the International Economy, 1820–1960* (Albany: State University of New York Press, 1971), p. 60.

31. Fourier, *Le Nouveau Monde industriel et sociétaire*, 1829, in E. Poisson, *Fourier* (Paris: Alcan, 1932), pp. 58–59.

32. Friedrich Engels, *The Condition of the Working Class in England* (London: Allen & Unwin, 1892), p. 21.

33. Ibid., pp. 24–25.

34. Maurice Lévy-Leboyer, *Les Banques européennes et l'industrialisation internationale dans la première moitié du XIXe siècle* (Paris: PUF, 1964), pp. 33–34.

35. J. Marchal and J. Lecaillon, *La Répartition du revenu national*, vol. I (Paris: Génin, 1958), pp. 81–82.

36. Engels, *The Condition of the Working Class*, pp. 79–80.

37. In *Past and Present*, Carlyle speaks of 1.4 million indigents and of 2 million persons forced to work in the workhouses.

38. Andrew Ure, *The Philosophy of Manufactures* (London, 1835), pp. 20–21.

39. Jean-Pierre Rioux, *La révolution industrielle, 1780–1880* (Paris: Seuil, 1971), p. 170

40. *Histoire générale du travail* (Paris: NLF, 1962–), vol. III, p. 83.

41. Ibid., pp. 78, 137.

42. Rioux, *La révolution industrielle*, pp. 162, 163.

43. A. Guépin, *Nantes au XIXe siècle*, 1825, cited in Edouard Dolléans, *Histoire du mouvement ouvrier*, 3 vols. (Paris: Armand Colin, 1936–53), vol. I, pp. 16, 17.

44. See particularly Barrington Moore, *Social Origins of Dictatorship and Democracy* (Boston: Beacon, 1966).

45. We will use the term "bureoisie" to identify the social layers of office workers: administrative and employed staff and, within the apparatus of the state, high

officials and functionaries. When these layers are technically specialized, we will speak of the "techno-bureoisie." If their function is tied to their function in the state, we will use the term "bureoisie of the state."

46. Duvergier de Hauranne, cited in *Histoire universelle*, 3 vols. (Paris: Pléiade, 1958), vol. III, p. 517.

47. Jean Lhomme, *La Grande Bourgeoisie au pouvoir, 1830–1880* (Paris: PUF, 1964), p. 71.

48. Nicos Poulantzas, *Political Power and Social Classes* (London: NLB and Sheed & Ward, 1973), p. 180.

49. See Marianne Debouzy, *Le Capitalisme sauvage aux Etats-Unis, 1860–1900* (Paris: Ed. Seuil, 1972), p. 32.

50. Bastiat, *Cobden et la Ligue*, 1846, in Baudin, *Frédéric Bastiat*, p. 58.

51. Rioux, *La révolution industrielle*.

52. European trade partners included Great Britain, first, and Germany, Belgium, Switzerland, Italy, and Spain. See *Histoire économique et sociale de la France*, 6 vols. (Paris: PUF, 1976–80), vol. III, p. 345.

53. R. E. Cameron, *France and the Economic Development of Europe, 1800–1914* (Princeton: Princeton University Press, 1961), p. 92.

54. Frédéric Mauro, *Histoire de l'économie mondiale* (Paris: Sirey, 1971), p. 13.

55. Cited in *Histoire générale des civilisations*, 7 vols. (Paris: PUF, 1953–56), vol. VI, p. 181.

56. Cited by Rioux, *La révolution industrielle*, p. 176.

57. Cited by J. Chatelain and J.-F. and J. Bacot, *Développement du capitalisme et alliances de classes en France* (Grenoble: Ther, 1978), p. 55.

58. *The Extinction of Pauperism*, 1844, cited in ibid., p. 86. Napoleon III made concessions to the working class, but from 1853 on, he let Haussmann open large avenues in Paris where army troops could maneuver.

59. Both cited in *Historie générale des civilisations*, vol. VI, p. 78 and vol. I, p. 507.

60. The number of voters in France grew from 90,000 to 166,000 in the period following 1830, and to 247,000 in 1846.

61. Marx, letter to Weydemeyer, March 5, 1852, in Karl Marx and Friedrich Engels, *Selected Works* (Moscow: Progress Publishers, 1969), p. 528.

62. Karl Marx and Friedrich Engels, *The Communist Manifesto* (New York: Monthly Review Press, 1949), p. 2.

63. Karl Marx, "The German Ideology," in L. D. Easton and C. H. Guddat, eds., *Writings of the Young Marx on Philosophy and Society* (Garden City, N.Y.: Doubleday, 1967), p. 414.

64. Karl Marx Preface to *A Contribution to the Critique of Political Economy* (Chicago: Charles Kerr, 1904), p. 13.

65. Marx and Engels, *Communist Manifesto*, p. 3.

66. Ibid., p. 14.

67. Ibid., p. 11.

68. Marx, "A Contribution to the Critique of Hegel's Philosophy of Right," in *Karl Marx: Early Writings* (New York: Vintage, 1975), p. 256.

69. Ibid., p. 254.

70. Karl Marx "The Holy Family," in Easton and Guddat, eds., *Writings*, p. 368.

71. Marx and Engels, *Communist Manifesto*, p. 22.

72. Ibid., pp. 38–39.

73. Ibid., p. 41.

74. Marx, *A Contribution to the Critique of Political Economy*, pp. 11–12.

75. Karl Marx *Capital*, vol. I (Moscow: Progress Publishers, 1954), p. 43.

76. Ibid., p. 181.

77. Ibid., p. 224.
78. On this point, see the very interesting thesis of H. Nadel, *Genèse de la conception marxienne du salariat* (Paris: VIII–Vincennes, 1979).
79. Marx, *Capital*, vol. III, p. 232.
80. Marx, *Capital,* vol. I, p. 542.
81. Ibid., p. 1592.
82. Ibid., p. 1604.
83. Ibid., p. 715.
84. Marx, *Capital,* vol. III, p. 1250.
85. Friedrich Engels, *Socialism, Utopian and Scientific* (New York: International Publishers, 1935), p. 53.
86. J. S. Mill, *Principles of Political Economy,* 1848.
87. On the last-named of these, see Marx, *Un Chapitre inédit du Capital.*

CHAPTER 4

1. Works on this period include Clément Juglar, *Les crises commerciales et leur retour périodique* (Paris: Guillaumin, 1889); Albert Aftalion, *Les crises périodiques de surproduction* (Paris: M. Rivière, 1913); M. Tugan-Baranowsky, *Les Crises industrielles en Angleterre* (Paris: Giard, 1913); J. Lescure, *Des crises générales et périodiques de surproduction* (Paris: Sirey, 1923); W. C. Mitchell, ed., *Business Cycles* (New York, 1913); A. C. Pigou, *Industrial Fluctuations* (London: Macmillan, 1929).
2. Oppenheim, cited in Charles P. Kindleberger, *Manias, Panics and Crashes* (New York: Basic Books, 1978), pp. 216, 251. See also M. Flamant and J. Singer-Kerel, *Crises et Récessions économiques* (Paris: PUF, 1968), p. 38, and Henri Heaton, *Histoire économique de l'Europe* (Paris: Armand Colin, 1952), vol. II, p. 241.
3. Cited in J. Bouvier, *Le Krach de l'Union générale* (Paris: PUF, 1960), p. 145.
4. Tugan-Baranowsky, *Les Crises industrielles en Angleterre,* p. 139.
5. Lescure, *Des crises générales,* p. 474.
6. From Pigou, *Industrial Fluctuations,* p. 385.
7. J. Lhomme, "Le pouvoir d'achat de l'ouvier français au cours d'un siècle: 1840–1940," *Le Mouvement social* (April–June 1968).
8. Cepremap, "Approches de l'inflation: l'exemple français," 1977, mimeo.
9. Roland Marx, *Le Déclin de l'économie britannique (1870–1929)* (Paris: PUF, 1972), p. 8.
10. Dan Clawson, *Bureaucracy and the Labor Process* (New York: Monthly Review Press, 1980), p. 211.
11. Frederick W. Taylor, "Testimony Before the Special House Committee to Investigate Taylor and Other Systems of Management," pp. 79–80, cited in Clawson, *Bureaucracy,* p. 212.
12. Frederick W. Taylor, *The Principles of Scientific Management* (New York: Norton, 1967), pp. 13–14.
13. See C. Kuczynski, *Die Geschichte der Lage der Arbeiter,* cited in J.-A. Lesourd and C. Gérard, *Histoire économique, XIXe–XXe siècles* (Paris: Armand Colin, 1963), vol. 1, p. 103. More recent national evaluations confirm these estimates, which in any case can only indicate tendencies.
14. *Encyclopédies et messages sociaux,* presented by H. Guitton (Paris: Dalloz, 1948), p. 64.
15. Ibid., p. 36.
16. See *Histoire générale du socialisme,* 3 vols. (Paris: PUF, 1972), vol. II, and Eduard Dolléans, *Histoire du mouvement ouvrier,* 3 vols. (Paris: Armand Colin, 1936–53), vol. II, pp. 16–17.

17. Cited in Jean Bron, *Histoire du mouvement ouvrier français*, 3 vols. (Paris: Ed. ouvrières, 1970), vol. II, p. 43.

18. Jay Gould claimed: "I can hire half of the working class to kill the other half," cited in Marianne Debouzy, *Le Capitalisme sauvage aux Etats-Unis, 1860–1900* (Paris: Seuil, 1970), p. 149.

19. Bernard Edelman, *La Législation de la classe ouvrière* (Paris: Bourgois, 1978), p. 33.

20. P. Leroy-Beaulieu, *Traité d'économie politique*, cited in B. Mottez, *Système des salaires et Politique patronale* (Paris: CNRS, 1966), p. 122.

21. P. Leroy-Beaulieu, *La question ouvrière au XIXe siècle*, cited in ibid., p. 121.

22. Taylor, *Principles of Scientific Management*, pp. 23–24.

23. Cited in Mottez, *Système des salaires*, p. 125.

24. Taylor, *Principles of Scientific Management*, pp. 117–18.

25. Ibid., p. 43.

26. Nikolai Bukharin, *L'Economie mondiale et l'Impérialisme, 1915–1917* (Paris: Anthropos, 1969), p. 22.

27. L. Hannah, cited in *The Cambridge Economic History of Europe* (New York and Cambridge: Cambridge University Press, 1965), vol. VII, p. 207.

28. Cited in Bukharin, *L'Economie mondiale*, p. 58.

29. Cited in ibid., p. 59.

30. Lenin, *Imperialism, the Highest Stage of Capitalism* (New York: International Publishers, n.d.), p. 63.

31. Frédéric Mauro, *Histoire de l'économie mondiale* (Paris: Sirey, 1971), p. 212.

32. In France, business banks participated in the industrial development (Bank of Paris and the Netherlands, French Bank for Trade and Industry), and Schneider got hold of the Parisian Union Bank when it was created. But the large deposit banks do not belie the wisdom of Henry Germain, director of Crédit Lyonnais: "Industrial companies, even the most carefully administered, carry risks incompatible with the security indispensable in the investments of a deposit bank." Cited in M. Reberioux, *La République radicale?* (Paris: Ed. Seuil, 1975), p. 120.

33. Lenin, *Imperialism*, p. 121.

34. Rudolf Hilferding, *Finance Capital*, ed. T. Bottomore (London: Routledge & Kegan Paul, 1981), p. 301.

35. Ibid., p. 235.

36. Ibid., p. 326.

37. Bukharin, *L'Economie mondiale*, p. 105.

38. J. Marczewski, *Cahiers de L'ISEA*, no. 163 (July 1963), p. cxi.

39. Phyllis Deane and William A. Cole, *British Economic Growth* (New York and Cambridge: Cambridge University Press, 1969), pp. 216, 225.

40. T. J. Markovitch, *Cahiers de L'ISEA*, no. 179 (November 1966).

41. See Herbert Feis, *Europe, the World's Banker, 1870–1914* (1930; New York: Kelley, 1961).

42. A. G. Kenwood and A. L. Lougheed, *The Growth of the International Economy* (London: George Allen & Unwin, 1971), p. 41.

43. Ibid., p. 42.

44. Bukharin, *L'Economie mondiale*, p. 40.

45. Cecil Rhodes, cited by Lenin, *Imperialism*, p. 72.

46. P. Leroy-Beaulieu, *De la colonisation chez les peuples modernes* (Paris: Guillaumin, 1891), pp. 839, 841.

47. Ibid., author's emphasis. But Leroy-Beaulieu insists in a note: "Colonization is one of the ways of preventing a quick decline in interest, by opening new uses for capital, and this is not the least of its advantages, although no other writer had mentioned it before."

48. See especially Claude Julien, *America's Empire* (New York: Pantheon, 1971).
49. Hobson, *Imperialism* (New York: James Pott, 1902), cited by Lenin, *Imperialism*, p. 84.
50. Hilferding. *Finance Capital*, p. 336.
51. Otto Bauer, *Neue Zeit* 24 (1913), p. 873, cited in P.-P. Rey, *Les Alliances de classes* (Paris: Maspero, 1973).
52. Curiously, by using the concept this way, this approach rejoins the position defended by Schumpeter in 1919: "Contribution à une sociologie des impérialismes," in *Imperialisme et classes sociales* (Paris, Minuit 1972), pp. 39–153.

CHAPTER 5

1. Charles de Gaulle, *Le Fil de l'épée* (Paris: Berger-Levrault, 1954), pp. 54, 90.
2. Cited in Eduard Dolléans, *Histoire du mouvement ouvrier*, 3 vols. (Paris: Armand Colin, 1936–53), vol. II, p. 192.
3. Ibid., p. 195.
4. Cited in Jean Bron, *Histoire du mouvement ouvier français*, 3 vols. (Paris: Ed. ouvrières, 1970), vol. II, p. 146.
5. Confédération Générale du Travail pamphlet, 1913, reproduced in *Histoire économique et sociale de la France*, 6 vols. (Paris: PUF, 1976–80), vol. IV, p. 528.
6. Cited in Dolléans, *Histoire du mouvement ouvrier*, vol. III, p. 264.
7. See P. Fridenson, *Histoire des Usines Renault* (Paris: Ed. Seuil, 1972), p. 76.
8. Because of their mobilization within the home country, the proportion is slightly lower for industry workers (8.8 percent) or transport workers (8.1 percent) than for farmers (10 percent) or liberal professions (10.7 percent). Alfred Sauvy, *Histoire économique de la France entre les deux guerres*, 3 vols. (Paris: Fayard, 1965–72), vol. I, p. 442.
9. Attempts to resolve the international debt problem included the Conferences of Paris and London in 1921, the Conference of Genoa in 1922, the occupation of the Ruhr by the French and the Belgians, and Anglo-American accords on allied debts (1923); the Dawes Commission in 1923; the Dawes Plan in 1924; the Mellon–Beranger and Churchill–Caillaux accords in 1926; the Young Commission in 1928 and the Young Plan in 1929; and so on until the Hoover moratorium in 1931 and the Conference of Lausanne.
10. J. M. Keynes, *Monetary Reform* (1924; New York: St. Martin's, 1972), p. 187.
11. On this point, see Johan Akerman, *Structures et Cycles économiques*, 2 vols. (Paris: PUF, 1957), vol. 2, p. 509.
12. Charles P. Kindleberger, *The World Depression 1929–1939* (Berkeley: University of California Press, 1973), p. 292.
13. An example of the latter approach is John K. Galbraith, *The Great Crash 1929* (Boston: Houghton Mifflin, 1972).
14. L. Robbins, *The Great Depression, 1929–1934* (New York: Macmillan, 1934), p. 11.
15. W. G. Harding, cited in Claude Julien, *America's Empire* (New York: Pantheon, 1971), p. 173.
16. In 1914 the largest U.S. banks had twenty-six branch offices outside the United States; in 1918, these numbered sixty-one, of which thirty-one were in Latin America and twenty-six in Europe (see Olivier Pastré, *La Stratégie internationale des groupes financiers américains* [Paris: Economica, 1979], p. 169).
17. J. Niosi, *La Bourgeoisie canadienne* (Montreal: Boréal Express, 1980), p. 59.
18. H. U. Faulkner, *American Economic History* (New York: Harper & Row, 1960),

p. 607. To this corresponds a tremendous concentration of private property: the richest 1 percent of the population owned 61.5 percent of the shares in 1922, 69 percent in 1939, 76 percent in 1953 (Jean-Marie Chevalier, *La structure financière de l'industrie américaine* (Paris: Cujas, 1970), p. 29, citing K. J. Lampman, *Review of Economics and Statistics*, November 1979.

19. Faulkner, *American Economic History*, p. 613.

20. Akerman, *Structures et Cycles*, vol. 2, p. 484.

21. See J. H. Lorenzi, O. Pastré, and J. Toledano, *La Crise du XXᵉ siècle* (Paris: Economica, 1980).

22. Henry Ford, *My Life and Work* (New York, 1922), p. 87.

23. H. Beynon, *Working for Ford* (Harmondsworth: Penguin, 1973), p. 19.

24. Keith Sward, *The Legend of Henry Ford* (New York: Atheneum, 1948), p. 49.

25. Allan Nevins, *Ford: The Times, the Man, the Company* (New York: Scribners, 1954), p. 518.

26. Ford, *My Life and Work*, p. 147.

27. Ibid., p. 124. Elsewhere he states: "By underpaying the men, we will produce a generation of both physically and morally underfed and underdeveloped children; we will be left with a generation of physically and morally feeble workers who, for this very reason, will prove ineffective once they enter industry. In the end, it will be industry that pays the price." Cited in Benjamin Coriat, *L'Atelier et le Chronomètre* (Paris: Bourgois, 1978), p. 101.

28. All cited in Galbraith, *The Great Crash*, pp. 76, 150.

29. Cited by Julien, *America's Empire*, p. 206.

30. Cited in John K. Galbraith, *The Age of Uncertainty* (Boston: Houghton Mifflin, 1977), p. 213.

31. About the crisis, see the statistical series published in Robbins, *The Great Depression*, p. 235, and the previously cited works of Faulkner, Dobb, and Julien.

32. See especially A. M. Schlesinger, *The Age of Roosevelt*, 3 vols. (Boston: Houghton Mifflin, 1957–60).

33. See Louis R. Franck, *L'expérience Roosevelt et le milieu social américain* (Paris: Alcan, 1937), and Mario Einaudi, *The Roosevelt Revolution* (New York: Harcourt Brace, 1959).

34. *The Public Papers and Addresses of Franklin D. Roosevelt* (1937) (New York: Macmillan, 1941), pp. 209–11. In his second inaugural address, January 20, 1937, Roosevelt said, "I see one-third of a nation ill-housed, ill-clad, ill-nourished," a phrase he echoed often in his efforts to pass minimum wages and hours legislation.

35. The number of union workers went from 3 million in 1933 to 4.7 million in 1936, 8.2 million in 1939, and 13.5 million in 1943.

36. John M. Keynes, "The Economic Consequences of Mr. Churchill" (1925), in *Essays in Persuasion* (New York: Harcourt, Brace, 1932), pp. 244, 259.

37. Ibid., p. 259.

38. Werner Sombart, *Der Moderne Kapitalismus* (Munich, 1928).

39. A. C. Pigou, *The Theory of Unemployment* (London: Frank Cass, 1968), p. 252.

40. Robbins, *The Great Depression*. p. 186.

41. John M. Keynes, *General Theory of Employment, Interest & Money* (London: Macmillan, 1973), p. 279.

42. Distribution, by regions, of British foreign investments (in millions of dollars):

	1914	1938
Europe	1,050	1,750
United States	4,250	2,750
Canada	2,800	2,700
Latin America	3,700	4,900

Oceania 2,200	3,350
Asia 3,550	5,250
Africa 2,450	2,150
World total 20,000	22,850

Source: Peter Mathias, *The First Industrial Nation* (New York: Scribners, 1974), p. 469.

43. Samir Amin, *Accumulation on a World Scale* (New York: Monthly Review Press, 1974), p. 71.

44. Cited in C. Coquery-Vidrovitch, ed., *Connaissance du Tiers-Monde* (Paris: 10/18, 1978), p. 231.

45. See Philippe Bernard, *La Fin d'un monde: 1914–1929* (Paris: Seuil, 1975), and Michel Beaud, P. Danjou, and J. David, *Une multinationale française: Pechiney Ugine Kuhlmann* (Paris: Ed. Seuil, 1975).

46. See the article by T. J. Markovitch in *Cahiers de l'ISEA*, no. 179 (November 1966).

47. Ibid; J.-J. Carré, P. Dubois, E. Malinvaud, *La croissance française* (Paris: Ed. Seuil, 1972); Alfred Sauvy, *Histoire économique de la France entre les deux guerres*, 3 vols. (Paris: Fayard, 1965–72), vol. I; Cepremap, "Approches de l'inflation: l'exemple français," 1977, mimeo.

48. Louis Lengrand, *Mineur du Nord* (Paris: Seuil, 1974), and Daniel Bertaux, *Destins personnels et structure de classe* (Paris: PUF, 1977).

49. Fridenson, *Histoire des Usines Renault*, and Michel Freyssenet, *La Division capitaliste du travail* (Paris: Savelli, 1977), p. 45.

50. Sauvy, *Histoire économique*, vol. I; "Croissance sectorielle et accumulation en longue période," *Statistiques et Etudes financières* 40; R. Boyer, "La crise actuelle: Une mise en perspective historique," Cepremap, mimeo.

51. Sauvy, *Histoire économique*, vol. II.

52. J. Lhomme, "Le pouvoir d'achat de l'ouvrier français," *Le mouvement social* (April–June 1968); Sauvy, *Historie économique*, vol. III. In periods of deflation the workers' buying power progresses through a stronger resistance to the reduction of nominal wages.

53. Cited by Nicos Poulantzas, *Fascism and Dictatorship* (London: NLB, 1974), pp. 190–91.

54. Hitler, *Mein Kampf*, trans. Raynal and Hitchcock (New York, 1940), p. 737.

55. Cited in D. Guérin, *Fascism: Big Business* (New York: Pathfinder, 1973), p. 79.

56. That is, the strata of civil servants, clerks, and wage earners in offices and various administrations.

57. Cited in *Histoire générale des civilisations*, 7 vols. (Paris, PUF, 1953–56), vol. VII, p. 193.

58. Cited by Guérin, *Fascism*, p. 67.

59. Cited by J.-J. Chevallier, *Les grandes œuvres politiques, de Machiavel à nos jours* (Paris: Armand Colin, 1949), p. 369.

60. Poulantzas, *Fascism and Dictatorship*, pp. 189–90, 287, 260–61, 342.

61. Terms of exchange of industrial Europe (including nine countries: Great Britain, Germany, France, Italy, Belgium, Luxembourg, Holland, Sweden, Switzerland) were as follows: the ratio of export to import prices, on the base 1913 =100, rose from 96 in 1920 to 109 in 1929, 138 in 1933, and fell to 124 in 1937 (C. P. Kindleberger, "Industrial Europe's Terms of Trade on Current Account, 1870–1953," *The Economic Journal*, March 1955).

62. In France the share of public expenditures in the gross domestic product went from 11 percent in 1872 to 33 percent in 1920; it fell to 27 percent in 1932, but

climbed back up to 41 percent in 1947 and 49 percent in 1953. Cepremap, "L'Evolution des dépenses publiques en France (1872–1971)," mimeo.

63. In the United States, the percentage of employees in the active population went from 10 percent in 1910 to 14 percent in 1920 and 17 percent in 1940. L. G. Reynolds, *Labor Economics and Labor Relations* (New York: Prentice Hall, 1949), p. 27.

64. See M. Beaud, *Socialism in the Crucible of History* (Atlantic Highlands, N.J.: Humanities Press, 1993 [1981]), chapters 4, 5, 6, and 7. Not considering the Soviet Union to have realized socialism, until 1985 we analyzed the Soviet economy as "State collectivist," and, since that date, as "Statist."

CHAPTER 6

1. Studs Terkel, *Working* (New York: Pantheon, 1972), pp. 221, 225.
2. Ibid., pp. 235, 239.
3. Ibid., pp. 259, 257, 258.
4. Ibid., pp. 2, 3.
5. Cepremap, "Approches de l'inflation: l'exemple français," 1977, mimeo, p. 106; J. H. Lorenzi, O. Pastré, and J. Toledano, *La Crise du XXe siècle* (Paris: Economica, 1980), p. 205. *Economie prospective internationale* 2 (April 1980); "La spécificité du modèle allemand," *Statistiques et Etudes financières*, 1980, p. 9.
6. Colin Clark's work (*The Conditions of Economic Progress*, 1940, 2nd ed. 1951) was popularized in France by Jean Fourastié, *Le Grand Espoir du XXe siècle* (Paris: PUF, 1980); John Kenneth Galbraith, *The Affluent Society* (Boston: Houghton Mifflin, 1959); Ludwig Erhard, *Prosperity Through Competition* (New York: Praeger, 1958).
7. R. F. Harrod had opened the way in 1939 in the *Economic Journal* with "An Essay in Dynamic Theory," then in 1948, *Toward a Dynamic Economy*; William Fellner, *Trends and Cycles in Economic Activity* (New York: Holt Rinehart, 1956); E. D. Domar, *Essays in the Theory of Economic Growth* (New York and London: Oxford University Press, 1957); N. Kaldor, "A Model of Economic Growth," *Economic Journal* (December 1957). The neoclassical perspective was articulated by R. M. Solow in articles in *The Quarterly Journal of Economics*, 1957, and *Growth Theory: an Exposition*, 1970.
8. W. A. Lewis, *The Theory of Economic Growth* (London: Allen & Unwin, 1955); W. W. Rostow, *The Process of Economic Growth* (New York: Norton, 1953), and *The Stages of Economic Growth* (New York: Cambridge University Press, 1960).
9. See, for example, *Newsweek, November 4, 1968*.
10. Sources and indicators used include: Loiseau, Mazier, and Winter, cited in R. Boyer and J. Mistral, *Accumulation, Inflation, Crises* (Paris: PUF, 1978), p. 241 (gross excess of exploitation/gross capital stocks at the beginning of a period); Andre Gunder Frank (gross profit rates); *Economie prospective internationale* (January 1980), pp. 78–79 (gross marginal rates of the manufacturing sector); *Economie prospective internationale* 2 (April 1980), pp. 74, 76 (profitability before taxation of fixed capital; non-financial companies); Cepremap, "Approches de l'inflation: l'exemple français," 1977, mimeo, p. 364 (gross economic profitability).
11. Terkel, *Working*, p. 265. See also André Gorz, ed., *The Division of Labor* (Atlantic Highlands, N.J.: Humanities Press, 1976).
12. See Bernard Rosier, *Croissance et Crises capitalistes* (Paris: PUF, 1975); Jean-Marie Chevalier, *La Pauvreté aux Etats-Unis* (Paris: PUF, 1971); Maurice Parodi,

L'Economie et la Société française de 1945 à 1970 (Paris: Armand Colin, 1971).

13. Charles A. Michalet, *Le Capitalisme mondial* (Paris: PUF, 1976); Christian Palloix, *L'Internationalisation du capital* (Paris: Maspero, 1973).

14. See Chevalier, *La Pauvreté*; Pierre Dockes, *L'Internationale du capital* (Paris: PUF, 1975); P. Allard, M. Beaud, B. Bellon, A. M. Lévy, S. Liénart, *Dictionnaire des groupes industriels et financiers en France* (Paris: Ed. Seuil, 1978); B. Bellon, *Le Pouvoir financier et l'Industrie en France* (Paris: Ed. Seuil, 1980).

15. "La spécificité du modèle allemand," *Statistiques et Etudes financières*, 1980.

16. We can compile the following table (in millions of dollars):

	Total	Factors affecting U.S. external balance
U.S. investments abroad:	115	
capital investments originating in the U.S.	(42)	(−42)
reinvested profits or local loans	(73)	
Revenues from foreign investments:	90	
repatriated to U.S.	(63)	(+63)
reinvested locally	(27)	
Monies from sale of licenses	15	(+15)
Total revenue from foreign holdings		(+36)

Sources: M. Beaud, B. Bellon, P. François, *Lire le Capitalisme* (Paris: Anthropos, 1976), p. 176; C. Goux, in *Critique de de l'éonomie politique*, no. 2, and *Le Monde diplomatique*, March 1973.

17. Cited in Harry Magdoff, *The Age of Imperialism* (New York: Monthly Review Press, 1969), p. 104.

18. Cited in ibid., pp. 104–05.

19. Beaud et al., *Lire le Capitalisme*; Jean-Marie Chevalier, *Le Nouvel Enjeu pétrolier* (Paris: Calmann-Lévy, 1973). See also Samir Amin, *Accumulation on a World Scale* (New York: Monthly Review Press, 1974); Samir Amin, A. Faire, M. Hussein, and G. Massiah, *La Crise de l'impérialisme* (Paris: Ed. Minuit, 1975); Y. Fitt, A. Fahri, J.-P. Vigier, *La Crise de l'impérialisme et la Troisième Guerre mondiale* (Paris: Maspero, 1976).

20. While dollars in circulation in the United States (notes and bank deposits) rose from $220 billion in 1970 to $360 billion in 1979, dollar assets in banks outside the United States rose from $100 billion in 1970 to $660 billion in 1979. One must add to these figures the more than $200 billion in marks, Swiss francs, etc., deposited outside their countries.

21. Michel Beaud, *Le Socialisme à l'épreuve de l'histoire* (Paris: Seuil, 1980).

22. The state-collectivist countries in 1960 absorbed only 3 percent, and in 1977 only 4 percent, of the commodity exports of the developed capitalist countries as a whole. But the developed capitalist countries in 1976 absorbed 14 percent of the exports of manufactured goods of the state-collectivist countries (World Bank, *Report on World Development*, 1979, pp. 163, 165). And the indebtedness of the socialist bloc toward the capitalist countries reached $78 billion in 1980.

23. Andre Gunder Frank, *Capitalism and Underdevelopment in Latin America* (New York: Monthly Review Press, 1962) and *Lumpenbourgeoisie; Lumpendevelopment* (New York: Monthly Review Press, 1972); Samir Amin, *Unequal Development* (New York: Monthly Review Press, 1976) and *Accumulation on a World Scale*.

24. Relative weight of "gross excesses of exploitation" by percentage of the mass of wage payments:

	U.S.	BRITAIN	FRANCE	W. GERMANY	JAPAN
1960	37.0	36.2	71.0	66.9	100.3
1965	40.0	33.2	61.2	53.6	79.5
1972	30.2	30.6	56.9	43.8	73.0
1978	28.2	24.8	41.3	40.5	49.9

25. In 1979 seventeen industrial and energy groups realized profits declared to be greater than $1 billion: eleven oil groups, with Royal Dutch Shell ($6.7 billion) and Exxon ($4.3 billion) leading; six industrial groups: ATT ($5.7 billion), tele-communications; IBM ($3.0 billion), computers; General Motors ($2.9 billion) and Ford ($1.2 billion), automobiles; General Electric ($1.4 billion), electrical construction; Kodak ($1 billion), photography. Of the eleven oil groups, seven are North American, as are all six of the industrial groups (*Le Monde*, July 19, 1980).

26. Terkel, *Working*, p. 261.

27. J. W. Forrester, a professor at MIT, cited by D. Pignon and J. Querzola, in *Critique de la division du travail* (Paris: Ed. Seuil, 1973), p. 158.

28. See Kostos Vergopoulos, *Le Capitalisme difforme* (Paris: Anthropos, 1974), for the working of distorted capitalism.

29. Cited in Magdoff, *The Age of Imperialism*, p. 117.

30. Figures from *Survey of Current Business*, in Serge Latouche, *Critique de l'impérialisme* (Paris: Anthropos, 1979), p. 209.

31. Report of the International Labour Office, Geneva, 1979. A recent report of the U. N. working group on slavery has particularly denounced the trade in children in Thailand, and the exploitation of 500,000 children in Italy *(Le Monde*, August 12 and 13, 1980).

32. From Samir Amin, *Class and Nation, Historically and in the Current Crisis* (New York: Monthly Review Press, 1980), p. 151. S. Rubak (*La Classe ouvrière est en expansion permanente* [Paris: Spartacus, 1972]) had established concurring figures for the whole of the world (in millions of workers):

	c. 1950	c. 1960
Europe (without the USSR)	54.2	69.5
North America	23.1	24.2
South America	10.5	12.3
Africa	2.0	2.0
Asia	29.6	47.0
USSR	30.6	32.0
TOTAL	150.0	187.0

33. See the notion of "protonations" advanced by Jean Ziegler, in *Main basse sur l'Afrique* (Paris: Seuil, 1978).

34. Without speaking of the wealth of the emirs or the oil princes, one could mention the fortunes accumulated by the former shah of Iran and his family and by the clans or families in power in South America.

35. World Bank, *World Development Report 1979*, p. 188.

36. See Jean Ziegler, *Une Suisse au-dessus de tout soupçon* (Paris: Seuil, 1976).

37. According to L. Gérardin, the percentage of the active U.S. population employed in agriculture fell from 45 percent in 1870 to 2 percent in 1980; the percentage employed in industry strictly speaking rose from 17 percent in 1860 to around 35–40 percent from 1914 to 1950, and then fell again to 23 percent in 1980; the percentage employed in "material services" rose irregularly from 17 percent in

1860 to 28 percent in 1980; the percentage employed in information trades rose from 5 percent in 1870 to 47 percent in 1980 (*Le Monde*, June 6, 1979).

38. In 1978 West Germany, France, and Sweden designated around 3.3 percent of their GNP to military expenditures, while for other countries the figures were Britain, 4.7 percent; United States, 5 percent; China, 10 percent; USSR, 11–14 percent; Saudi Arabia, 15 percent (J. Isnard and M. Tatu, in *Le Monde*, February 19, 1980 and P. Lefournier, in *L'Expansion*, March 21, 1980).

39. P. Fabre, in *L'Economiste du Tiers Monde*, December 1979, and P. Lefournier, in *L'Expansion*, March 21 1980.

40. M. K. Tolba, cited in *Le Monde*, June 8–9, 1980.

41. Report of the World Food Council, presented to UNESCO (*Le Monde*, July 18, 1980).

42. See Beaud, *Le Socialisme*.

CHAPTER 7

1. The text of the first edition of this book, made up of the six preceding chapters, was written in 1979–80. The magnitude and the power of current changes have necessitated a seventh chapter. A first version of this chapter appeared in the Seuil Points edition in 1990, a second version in the Dutch and Japanese editions in 1994, and a third for the present edition, written in 1999. The evolution of the title—"The center of the changes" in 1990; "A historical turning point?" in 1994; and "An accelerating transformation of the contemporary world" in 1999—reflects both the continuity and the deepening of my reflection. The changes in my approach were evident in my article in *Le Monde Diplomatique* (October 1994), "Le Basculement du Monde," my book *Le Basculement du monde. De la Terre, des hommes et du capitalisme* (1997), the preparation, with Olivier Dollfus and other colleagues, of the GEMDEV collective work on globalization (1993–98), and the preparation of my paper "Capitalism, social logics and transformative dynamics" for the International Meeting on "Evolution and Transformation of Economic Systems: Comparative Approaches to Capitalism and Socialism" (CEMI-EHESS and GERME-Paris 7, June, 19–20 1998).

2. I wish to thank historians Robert Bonnaud and Jean Chesneaux, geographer Olivier Dollfus, economists Michel Fouquin, Gérard Kebabdjian, Alain de Tolédo, and Merdhad Vahabi, who read initial versions of this chapter, and who helped me with their comments. I wish to thank also Calliope Beaud, who read and commented on several versions of the text.

3. A-cracy: inability of government to carry out effective action at the level demanded by the problems we are facing.

4. See the three works published by Robert Bonnaud in 1992: *Les Alternances du progrès. Une histoire sans préférences* (Paris: Kimé, 1992); *Les Tournants du XXe siècle. Progrès et régressions* (Paris: L'Harmattan, 1992); and *Y a-t-il des Tournants historiques mondiaux?* (Paris: Kimé, 1992). We commend his erudition and ambition.

5. See M. Beaud, *Le Basculement du monde. De la Terre, des hommes et du capitalisme* (Paris: La Découverte, 1997).

6. See the present work, p. 140, and M. Beaud, *L'Economie mondiale dans les années 80* (Paris: La Découverte, 1989), pp. 282f.

7. Ibid., pp. 286–87.

8. It should be noted, however, that official unemployment rates are strongly skewed by the data collection policies of each nation. If, in addition to those people

counted as formally "unemployed," one adds in the number of long-term and discouraged workers not counted in the official statistics, the rate of unemployment at the end of 1993 rises from 5.5 percent to 8 percent in the U.S. and from 2 percent to 9 percent in Japan. The apparent difference between these two countries and the European countries known for high unemployment is thus severely reduced (*AMEX Bank Review*, cited in *Washington Economic Reports*, no. 74, February 9, 1994).

9. For 1980 and 1990, the respective shares are: U.S.: 25.1 percent and 23.7 percent; Japan: 15.3 percent and 19.1 percent; Germany: 15.9 percent and 14.6 percent; Great Britain: 11.2 percent and 9.2 percent; France: 7.9 percent and 7.8 percent (*Economie et Industrie*, Lettre de la Compagnie Saint-Gobain, no. 73, March 1994, p. 6).

10. J.L. Hervey, "The Internationalization of Uncle Sam," *Economic Perspectives*, Federal Reserve Bank of Chicago, May–June 1986, pp. 3f.

11. D. de Laubier, "Une décennie d'expansion des investissements directs," *Economie Internationale*, no. 56, 4ème trim. 1993, p. 14.

12. See Beaud, *L'Economie mondiale dans les années 80.*

13. UNCTAD, *Trade and Development Report 1986* (New York: United Nations, 1986), p. 33. It was thus "against the current" that the French socialist government launched their attempt, in May–June 1981, at a Keynesian social and economic revitalization. The timing of the government's plans within an unfavorable international climate contributed in part to the Left's failure. See M. Beaud, *La Politique économique de la gauche* (Paris: Syros, 1983 [vol. I] and 1985 [vol. II]).

14. UNCTAD, *Trade and Development Report 1986* (New York: United Nations, 1986), p. 155.

15. World Bank, *World Development Report 1986*, Washington, 1986, p. 173.

16. Between 1987 and 1989 the deficit was around 150 billion dollars each year, and then rose to between 200 and 300 billion dollars per year between 1990 and 1993. For the period as a whole the deficit represented approximately 3 to 5 percent of the GNP (*Economic Report of the President 1985*, Washington, 1985, pp. 316–18; and *Washington Economic Reports*, no. 74, February, 9 1994, p. 5).

17. C. Goldfinger, *La Géofinance* (Paris: Seuil, 1986), p. 396; and Beaud, *L'Economie mondiale dans les années 80*, pp. 118f.

18. From 1980 to 1984 the exchange rate of the dollar against the currencies of the industrialized nations rose by 58 percent (*Economic Report of the President 1985*, Washington, 1985, p. 351).

19. World Bank, *World Development Report 1986*, p. 19.

20. M. Dehove and J. Mathis, "Les grands traits de l'évolution du SMI de 1974 à 1984," *Etudes de l'IRES*, January 1986.

21. See part 4 of this section.

22. World Bank, *World Development Report 1986*, p. 39.

23. United Nations Development Program (UNDP), *Rapport mondial sur le développement humain 1992* (Economica, 1992), p. 54.

24. World Bank, *World Development Report 1986*, pp. 230–31.

25. M. Lhériteau, *Le Fonds monétaire international et les pays du tiers monde* (Paris: PUF, 1986); and P. Jacquemot and M. Raffinot, *Accumulation et développement* (Paris: L'Harmattan, 1985), chap. 9.

26. UNCTAD, *Trade and Development Report 1986* (New York: United Nations, 1986), pp. 162–63.

27. Within this fascinating game of global "yo-yo," any one point of view creates its own opposite effects. For example, a fall in the dollar signifies, among other effects, a rise in the yen relative to the dollar: Japanese businesses will earn less

or lose ... and will then increase their own foreign investments. See Beaud, *L'Economie mondiale dans les années 80*, pp. 138f.

28. Dominique Gallois, *Le Monde*, December 2, 1993.

29. Eric Fottorino, *Le Monde*, May 6, 1986.

30. See M. Beaud and G. Dostaler, *La Pensée économique depuis Keynes. Historique et dictionnaire des principaux auteurs* (Paris: Seuil, [1993] 1996).

31. Thus, for the 1989 to 1996 period, the Economic Commission of the United Nations "found no significant difference between the average rate of growth in western Europe and in the United States" (cited in *Le Monde*, March 18, 1998).

32. In November 1997, the national currency lost 58 percent of its value in Thailand, 53 percent in Indonesia, 33 percent in the Philippines, 32.8 percent in Malaysia, 14.3 percent in South Korea, 12.3 percent in Singapore, and 12.1 percent in Taiwan (*Fortune*, November 24, 1997, pp. 32–33).

33. In 1998 the GDP fell in value, relative to 1997, by more than 15 percent in Indonesia, 8 percent in Thailand, 7 percent in Malaysia, and nearly 6 percent in South Korea and Hong Kong (*Fortune*, September 7, 1997, p. 30; and *Far Eastern Economic Review*, June 10, 1999, p. 12).

34. By the end of 1997 Japan had lent 120 billion dollars to Asian nations in economic difficulty. These loans were a burden on its banking system, which was already weighed down by doubtful or uncollectable loans. At the same time Japan held 320 billion dollars' worth of U.S. Treasury Securities, while the foreign debt of the U.S. had reached record levels.

35. This proportion reached a 30-year low in October 1997, and remained low throughout 1998 (*Fortune*, November 24, 1997, p. 28; and September 28, 1998, p. 44). These figures indicate that the yield on the capitalized value of the Standard and Poor 500 fell to less than 5 percent.

36. R. Boyer, "Les mots et les réalités," in *Mondialisation. Au-delà des mythes* (Paris: La Découverte, 1997), pp. 13–56.

37. K. Ohmae, *La Triade. Emergence d'une stratégie mondiale de l'entreprise* (Paris: Flammarion, 1985).

38. O. Dollfus, *L'Espace-Monde* (Paris: Economica, 1994), pp. 22f.

39. The sum devoted to these six kinds of markets—futures on rates, futures on currencies, futures on stock market levels, options on rates, options on currencies, and options on stock market levels—rose from approximately 650 billion dollars at the beginning of 1987, to more than 12 trillion dollars at the end of 1997 (*Lettre de Conjoncture de la BNP*, February 1999, p. 2).

40. Exchanges on the monetary, financial, and stock markets, which in Keynes' time represented twice the value of commodities exchanged, today account for many times—several score, in fact, and growing rapidly—the value of commodities exchanged. Another indication of this transition is that the proportion between the overall value of currency purchase and sales, compared to the overall value of world trade of commodities, increased from 6 in 1979 to 20 in 1986, to 57 in 1995, and will very likely reach 100 in the years following 2000. See Beaud, *Le Basculement du monde*, p. 123.

41. *Le Monde*, December 30, 1998, p. 12.

42. *Fortune*, March 1, 1999, p. 18.

43. Beaud, *L'Economie mondiale dans les années 80*, p. 292. See also pp. 122, 290.

44. The deficit was forecast to worsen in 1999 (*Lettre de Conjoncture de la BNP*, April 1999, p. 8).

45. Beaud, *L'Economie mondiale dans les années 80*, p. 290; and *Lettre de Conjoncture de la BNP*, May 1999, p. 2.

46. *Lettre de Conjoncture de la BNP*, April 1999, p. 8.

47. See Beaud, *Le Basculement du monde.*
48. C. Stoffaes, *Fins de mondes* (Paris: Odile Jacob, 1987); F. Fukuyama, *The End of History and the Last Man* (New York: Free Press, 1992); B. Badie and M. Smouts, *Le Retournement du monde. Sociologie de la scène internationale* (Paris: FNSP, 1992 and 1995); J. Carfantan, *Le Grand désordre du monde* (Paris: Seuil, 1993); M. Beaud, "Le Basculement du monde," *Le Monde diplomatique,* October 1994, pp. 16–17; M. Touraine, *Le Bouleversement du monde. Géopolitique du XXI° siècle* (Paris: Seuil, 1995); and Beaud, *Le Basculement du monde.*
49. See the present work, Chapter 6.
50. Francis Fukuyama, "La fin de l'histoire dix ans après," *Le Monde,* June 17, 1999, p. 1.
51. Beaud, *Le Basculement du monde,* p. 234.
52. The net foreign trade balance was positive for the U.S. at the beginning of the 1980s, but had become negative by 1987. The net foreign debt, to call it by its name, reached 620 billion dollars (8 percent of gross domestic product) in 1995, and 1.55 trillion dollars (17.8 percent of gross domestic product) in 1998. Extension of the current trend would lead to a net foreign debt of 3.65 trillion dollars (36 percent of gross domestic product) in 2003. See Beaud, *L'Economie mondiale dans les années 80,* pp. 290–91, as well as the *Lettre de Conjoncture de la BNP,* May 1999, p. 2.
53. See Beaud, *L'Economie mondiale dans les années 80,* p. 59; "The Fortune Global 500," 1996; and World Bank, *World Development Report 1995,* Washington, 1995.
54. "The Fortune Global 500," 1996.
55. This figure lies in between the working population of France (26 million) and that of Germany (42 million) (World Bank, *World Development Report 1995,* p. 231).
56. See "The Fortune Global 500," 1996; and World Bank, *World Development Report 1995.*
57. "The Fortune Global 500," 1996, p. 72.
58. World Bank, *World Development Report 1995,* p. 182.
59. B. Madeuf, "Du paradoxe à l'auto-organisation," *Cahier du GEMDEV,* no. 5, November 1985, p. 51.
60. Exports by the primary corporation, plus sales by foreign subsidiaries within countries where they are located, plus subsidiary exports to foreign countries. On the economic domain created by multinationals and their subsidiaries, see Beaud, *L'Economie mondiale dans les années 80,* pp. 67f., 74f.
61. UNCTAD, *World Investment Report 1993* (New York: United Nations, 1993).
62. In 1984, among the 200 leading multinational corporations, 51.5 percent were based in the United States, 18.5 percent were Japanese, and 18.5 percent were European (F. Clairmonte and J. Cavanagh, "Le club des deux cents," *Le Monde Diplomatique,* December 1985). In 1987, among the largest 100 multinational corporations, 40 were based in the U.S., 14 were Japanese, and 37 were European (*Fortune,* April 25, 1988 and August 1, 1988). Ten years later the respective figures showed 32 of these corporations based in the U.S., 26 in Japan, and 39 in Europe (*Fortune,* August 3, 1998).
63. In 1991, Research and Development spending per inhabitant (in 1987 dollars) represented $218 in the rich countries, $108 in the NICs of Asia, $29 in the Russian Federation, $6 in the middle-income countries (Russia excluded), and $1 in the poor countries (China excluded) (Communauté Européene 1994, cited in World Bank, *World Development Report 1999,* Washington, 1999, p. 2).
64. Bonnaud, *Les Tournants du XX° siècle. Progrès et régressions.*
65. Ibid., p. 83.

66. F. Braudel, *Civilisation matérielle, économie et capitalisme. XVe–XVIIIe siècles* (Paris: Armand Colin, 1979), makes this distinction more clearly than does K. Polanyi, *The Great Transformation* (Boston: Beacon, 1944).

67. Polanyi remarks that, until the end of feudalism, the social systems of Western Europe "were organized according to principles either of reciprocity, redistribution, domestic administration, or a combination of all three of these." K. Polanyi, *The Great Transformation*; *La Grande transformation*, p. 85.

68. Ibid.

69. Ibid., p. 21.

70. We are thinking especially of Gary Becker. See Beaud and Dostaler, *La Pensée économique depuis Keynes*, pp. 137f.

71. See M. Beaud, *Le Socialisme à l'épreuve de l'histoire* (Paris: Seuil, [1982] 1985).

72. See Beaud, *L'Economie mondiale dans les années 80*.

73. See Beaud, *Le Basculement du monde*, pp. 200f.

74. See M. Beaud, C. Beaud, and L. Bougerra, eds., *L'Etat de l'environnement dans le monde* (Paris: La Découverte, 1993).

75. World Commission on Environment and Development 1987, 1988.

76. See M. Beaud, C. Beaud, and L. Bougerra, eds., *L'Etat de l'environnement dans le monde*, Part One: "Man and the Planet."

77. See Beaud, "Face à la croissance mortifère, quel développement durable?," *Revue Tiers-Monde*, vol. 35, January–March 1994, pp. 131–49; and Beaud, *Le Basculement du monde*.

78. See W. Krelle, ed., *The Future of the World Economy* (Berlin: Springer Verlag, 1989), p. 4; Jean-Noël Biraben, "Essai sur l'évolution du nombre des hommes," *Population*, no. 1, 1979, pp. 22–23; J. Vallin in M. Beaud, C. Beaud, and L. Bougerra, eds., *L'Etat de l'environnement dans le monde*, p. 300; and World Bank, *World Development Report 1992*, Washington, 1992, p. 28. The projection for the year 2050 made by Lester Brown suggests an upper figure of a little more than 11 billion and a lower figure of slightly fewer than 8 billion (L. Brown, G. Gardner, and B. Halweil, *Beyond Malthus: Sixteen Dimensions of the Population Problem* [Washington, D.C.: Worldwatch Institute, 1998], p. 71). These numbers represent a population increase, within the first half of the twenty-first century, of slightly fewer than 2 billion to somewhat more than 5 billion people. Within the second half of the twentieth century, the population gain was 3.6 billion.

79. Krelle, ed., *The Future of the World Economy*; A. Maddison, *L'économie mondiale 1820–1992. Analyses et statistiques* (Paris: Centre de développement de l'OCDE, 1995); and M. Beaud, *Le Basculement du monde*.

80. Bouda Etemad, "Structure géographique et par produits de la production mondiale d'énergie aux 19e et 20e siècles. Un survol statistique," *Revue de l'énergie*, October 1992, p. 695.

81. J. Houghton, G. Jenkins, and J. Ephraums, *Climate Change. The IPCC Scientific Assessment* (Cambridge: Cambridge University Press, 1990).

82. P. Bourrelier and R. Diethrich, *Le Mobile et la Planète, ou l'enjeu des ressources naturelles* (Paris: Economica, 1990), p. 58.

83. C. Clark, *The National Income* (London: Macmillan, 1932); and C. Clark, *The Conditions of Economic Progress* (London: Macmillan, 1940).

84. A. Maddison, *Dynamic Forces in Capitalist Development. A Long-Run Comparative View* (London: Oxford University Press, 1991), pp. 248–49.

85. U.S. Labor Statistics Bureau, and the OECD, in *The Economist*, February 20, 1993, p. 63.

86. INSEE, from *Le Monde*, 18 May 1993; and World Bank, *World Development Report 1999*, p. 234.

87. Patrick Artus, "La croissance française est-elle durable?" *Le Monde*, March 23, 1999; and *Lettre de conjoncture* of the BNP, April 1999.
88. World Bank, *World Development Report 1999*, pp. 234–35.
89. J. Singelmann, *From Agriculture to Services* (Beverly Hills: Sage, 1978); and P. Petit, *La Croissance tertiare* (Paris: Economica, 1998).
90. Maddison, *Dynamic Forces in Capitalist Development. A Long-Run Comparative View*, pp. 248–49.
91. World Bank, *World Development Report 1999*, pp. 234–35.
92. See P. Petit, *La Croissance tertiare* (Paris: Economica, 1998), pp. 69f.
93. A. Touraine, *La Société post-industrielle. Naissance d'une société* (Paris: Denoël, 1969); J. Gershuny, *After Industrial Society. The Emerging Self-Service Economy* (London: Macmillan, 1978); F. Block, *Postindustrial Possibilities* (Berkeley: University of California Press, 1990).
94. Gershuny, *After Industrial Society*.
95. Stoffaes, *Fins de mondes*.
96. V. Fuchs, *The Service Economy* (New York: NBER, 1968); and J. Delaunay and J. Gadrey, *Les Enjeux de la société de service* (Paris: FNSP, 1987).
97. D. Liston and N. Reeves, *The Invisible Economy* (London: Pitman, 1988).
98. C. Goldfinger, *L'Utile et le futile. L'économie de l'immatériel* (Paris: Odile Jacob, 1994).
99. F. Machlup, *The Production and Distribution of Knowledge in the US* (Princeton: Princeton University Press, 1962); and M. Porat, *The Information Economy* (Palo Alto: Stanford University Press, 1976).
100. F. Machlup, *Knowledge: Its Creation, Distribution and Economic Significance* (Princeton: Princeton University Press, 3 vols, 1980–84); P. Drucker, *Post-Capitalist Society* (New York: HarperBusiness, 1993).
101. Drucker, *Post-Capitalist Society*.
102. The word "technoscience" is already in use (J. Prades, ed., *La Technoscience. Les fractures du discours* (Paris: L'Harmattan, 1992), but the adjective "technoscientistic" is not. "Technoscientific" would be false, while "technoscientologic" would be more exact, but would encounter the notorious connotations and reputation of Scientology.
103. R. Richta, *La Civilisation au carrefour* ([Prague, 1968]; Paris: Anthropos, 1974).
104. On the importance of technique and technology in analyzing contemporary reality, beyond the works of Ellul, Brzezinski, and Rosnay, see the immense economic literature which includes Dosi, Landau, Mowery, Nelson, Rosenberg, Winter....
105. This phenomenon was very clearly seen and described by Lucien Karpik in a 1972 article.
106. See A. Gras, *Grandeur et dépendence. Sociologie des macro-systèmes techniques* (Paris: PUF, 1993).
107. For example, in health care new systems are being developed which digitalize information and which can be connected to new kinds of networks: tele-maintenance (of apparatus and software), tele-diagnosis (of the patient), and soon tele-intervention by specialized teams (on the patient).
108. For medical equipment, only 7 companies, and for large computers, 10 companies, account for 90 percent of world production. For public transport, 4 companies account for 70 percent of the world market. For computer services, 8 companies represent 54 percent of the world market (F. Chesnais, *La Mondialisation du capital* [Paris: Syros, 1994], pp. 73, 74, 149, 169).
109. Serge Airaudi, *Le Monde*, April 5, 1994.
110. A lower overall estimate is found in the *Lettre de Conjoncture* of the BNP (April

1999, p. 6): with more than 200 billion dollars spent on research and development in 1997, the U.S. represents about half of worldwide R&D spending.

111. The figures in the table agree with those of the BNP's *Lettre de Conjoncture* (April 1999, p. 6), where R&D is estimated to represent 2.6 percent of GNP in the U.S., 2.3 percent in France, 1.7 percent in Great Britain, and 1.1 percent in Italy.

112. *Lettre de Conjoncture* of the BNP (April 1999, p. 6).

113. Karl Marx, *Oeuvres—Economie* (Paris: La Pléiade, 1963 [1848]), vol. I, p. 163.

114. This statement does not imply that the transformations brought about by capitalism cause the elementary logics of power, possession, and subsistence to disappear.

115. It is, however, quite legitimate to describe the mode of production of this or that level of capitalism (manufacturing capitalism, first or second industrial capitalism, postindustrial capitalism).

116. For capitalism, from its beginnings, joins into the social, political, and ideological dimensions. As discussed earlier, Max Weber and Fernand Braudel both made this point, each in his own way.

117. J. Schumpeter, *Capitalism, Socialism and Democracy*, pp. 116–17. The italics and capitals are Schumpeter's He speaks shortly after (p. 117) of "the perpetual whirlwind of creative destruction," which in his view invalidates the "hypothesis of a perpetual calm" supported by numerous economists.

118. Beaud, *Le Basculement du monde*.

119. H. Jonas, *Le Principe responsabilité* (Frankfurt am Main, [1979]; Paris: Cerf, 1990), p. 14.

120. Ibid., p. 13.

121. Ibid., p. 15.

INDEX